Elizabeth Wurtzel is the author of the best-selling books, *Prozac Nation* and *Bitch*. She graduated from Harvard College, where she received the 1986 *Rolling Stone* College Journalism award for essay writing. She was the popular-music critic for *The New Yorker* and *New York* magazine. Her articles have also appeared in *Mademoiselle*, *Mirabella*, *Seventeen* and *The Oxford American*. She lives in New York City.

Also by Elizabeth Wurtzel

Bitch

Prozac Nation

MORE,

NOW,

AGAIN

A Memoir

ELIZABETH WURTZEL

Virago

A *Virago* Book

First published in Great Britain by
Virago Press 2002

A CIP catalogue record for this book
is available from the British Library

ISBN 1 86049 918 X

Printed and bound in Great Britain by
Clays Ltd, St Ives plc

Virago
An imprint of
Time Warner Books UK
Brettenham House
Lancaster Place
London WC2E 7EN

www.virago.co.uk

for Bruce Springsteen

Too late came I to love you, O your Beauty both so ancient and so fresh. Yet too late came I to love you. And behold, you were within me, and I out of myself, where I made search for you.

SAINT AUGUSTINE
Confessions

There are no seasons in Florida. People say that about other places, they say that about southern California, but I've lived through some freezing nights in Los Angeles. I've snuck around people's homes there and turned the thermostat up to eighty degrees because I've been so cold, especially in the canyons. But here in Florida the ground is flat, the terrain is absolute, it is always warm, it is always bright. The Christmas lights strung on the houses along the highway look ridiculous. Today there was a tornado in Miami. They showed the twister in the skyscrapers on the evening news. No one was hurt.

The only way I can tell the passage of time is how long I can go between pills. Five minutes, maybe. It used to be longer, fifteen minutes, a half hour. But that was months ago. Or maybe weeks. Time passes slowly, or too fast, or it makes no difference.

I crush up my pills and snort them like dust. They are my sugar. They are the sweetness in the days that have none. They drip through me like tupelo honey. Then they are gone. Then I need more. I always need more.

For all of my life I have needed more.

My pills are methylphenidate hydrochloride, brand name Ritalin, but I will take Dexedrine or any other kind of prescription amphetamine that I can get. I used to swallow them, ten milligrams at a time, every four hours, no more than three times a day, as directed by my physician. Then I took more, and more often. Then one day I cut one in half, trying to extend the supply, and some powder crumbled off of my uneven slice. I could feel my face light up: I might as well have been Columbus, discovering America while looking for India. I snorted it up, as if it were cocaine, and something different happened in my brain, a scratchy rush.

Since then, I've been crushing them up like that on purpose. I inhale forty pills a day.

That's how I spend my days: I smash up powder and make it go away.

Right now I live in an efficiency behind the Galleria mall, off Sunrise Boulevard in Fort Lauderdale. This is like some cosmic joke; this whole setup is like a picture on a poster that says THIS IS YOUR BRAIN ON DRUGS. If you knew me, if you saw me in my apartment in Greenwich Village, you would never believe this. No one believes this. Like most stories that involve large quantities of drugs, this one is shaped by incongruous details. I'm a New Yorker, I am not equipped to live anywhere else, I do not have a driver's license, I cannot safely get behind the wheel of an automobile, and here I am in a place without sidewalks.

I live near the mall so I can get whatever I need on foot.

This is not the first place I've lived down here. There was also my mother's condominium on the Intracoastal, which was white and beautiful, with hard western sunlight in the afternoons. There was the Schubert Motel, owned by French Canadians, with a broken air conditioner, so the cuts I hacked onto my legs festered from the humidity. When I went to the emergency room, I told them it was from shaving with a dull razor, which I think they might have believed. The residents on their thirty-six-hour shifts had such a soft innocence. Then there was the Riverside Hotel, on Las Olas Boulevard, with red velvet wallpaper and twenty-four-hour room service.

This apartment comes furnished. I have a Murphy bed and a kitchen table, and one of those desks that is part of the same wall unit as the bed. I have local phone service and an answering machine. I don't have a calling card so I can't return long distance calls, which is why I don't. The entrance is off a catwalk. Down the hall are two call girls, and next door on the other side are two gay flight attendants who work for a charter airline used by hockey teams. Downstairs is a paralegal with a cat who isn't very friendly.

I know how I got here, I know how I found this apartment, I remember the ad in the *Sun-Sentinel*, and still I can tell you: I don't know how I got here.

My life, in all its apparent disorder, has always been so carefully planned, always just as it was meant to be. In my college recommendation, my high school English teacher said that he could see me growing up and writing for *The New Yorker*. So I graduated from college and started writing for *The New*

Yorker. I have always had the gift of making it all look like some big lucky accident, like whoops, here I landed, gee whiz, what do you know. But it's all been so deliberate. I am exactly who you thought I would be. I am the least surprising person you will ever meet.

But not this. This is really an accident.

Every addict tells the same stories about where drugs took her. Mostly it's about where you spent the night, blackouts: I woke up in Brazil, I woke up on a bench in Golden Gate Park, I woke up in a holding cell, I woke up in Mykonos, I woke up in Buckingham Palace, I woke up in my own vomit. In the movies, those stories involve sharp and arch displays of wealth or degrading degrees of filth: In *Scarface,* this schnook from Cuba finds himself in a postmodern house on the Biscayne Bay, all lacquered surfaces, with Michelle Pfeiffer all blond in the background, giving him a hard time. In *Jesus' Son,* everything is tawdry and all the furniture is plaid and shredded: junkies in the Holiday Inn, in the Midwest, in the mid-seventies. In real life, the scion of a family whose name is a corporation traded on the stock exchange is living in a men's shelter, or a kid from the Dominican Republic is smoking crack in a Park Avenue duplex that has a Frank Stella hanging on the wall.

So I guess I am just like everyone else, another fish-out-of-water, or human-being-in-water. But there are no extremes of poverty or wealth to speak of. There are strip malls and a housing complex with a swimming pool that no one ever uses. I sit at a raw bar and eat oysters, or I make copies late at night at Kinko's, and when there is a Clinique bonus, I buy a new lipstick at Burdines.

Everyone here is transient or retired, or sometimes there are college students visiting during school break. No one here has a last name. This is surely the most anonymous place I could ever be. If I tried to tell my neighbors about my life in New York or my work or my friends, they would not care. If it's not of immediate use to them, if it's not about borrowing detergent or a ride to the supermarket, they don't hear it. They are the nicest people, but it's all about the next five minutes.

And by now, my whole life is about the next five minutes.

There are no human beings in this story. Not really. That's my favorite thing about my pills: they are my only relationship. The only thing I care about is where more will come from. That is all I need to worry about. Otherwise I might not exist. I am in a place where there is no difference between May and December, and the only time that matters is the minutes between pills when all I think about is my next line.

When nothing else happens all day, when all there is to show for it is some work I've done or an okay movie I've seen, when it's been nothing special, they are my treat.

They used to be a treat. Late at night, they were something to look forward to. I could tell myself: I can still get high. I would tell myself: This is the sugar in my bowl.

But now it's my life. Pills are my everything.

At the end of the day, other people ask themselves: Is this all there is?

I don't want to wait for the answer. I'm not stupid. I don't wait to see if today will be better than yesterday, because I already know.

And these pills are deep inside of me.

What person could ever get this close? Who would want to?

And I swear to you, and I don't care how this sounds, I think it's love. If you don't understand, you don't know what love is.

REVELATION

One

NUMBERS

I take one one one cause you left me and
two two two for my family and
3 3 3 for my heartache and
4 4 4 for my headaches and
5 5 5 for my lonely and
6 6 6 for my sorrow and
7 7 for no tomorrow and
8 8 I forget what 8 was for and
9 9 9 for a lost god and
10 10 10 10 for everything
everything everything everything

GORDON GANO
"Kiss Off"

The first time I took Ritalin I had been clean for four months. It was pre-scribed because I had trouble focusing. It would take me two hours to write one sentence; I would change outfits six times before I even managed to brush my teeth; I would return one phone call three times. I would linger for a half hour over whether to have Darjeeling or Earl Grey; then the water would need to be boiled again, then the confusion over what kind of tea to have again. Then twenty minutes in the shower before I could figure out which shampoo to use; then indecision over whether to take the A train or the number 1 local. Hours would go by before I could get started on my day, by which time it was already nightfall.

Plus, I was tired all the time, my old reliable antidepressants were not work-ing so well, the whole regimen needed a boost. The Ritalin really helped.

The first time I smoked pot I was in high school, I think at a Neil Young concert. I don't remember it well, because I did not inhale, not for lack of trying. The first time I got stoned I was a freshman in college. One bong hit filled up my lungs like a three-alarm fire, and I could not think straight for at least a day or two. The first time I did coke was also my first year in college, in Noah Kellogg's bathroom, and I necked with a guy named Aristotle, because it seemed like the thing to do. The first time I took Ecstasy it was 1985, it was still legal, it was the first time I had tried anything at all psychedelic. I got scared like a teething infant who does not know what's happening to her, only that it hurts, only that there is no way to communicate this pain except to scream and cry, until Ruby and Jordana hugged me tight, we snuggled on the top bunk bed, and they told me they loved me. The first time I took psilocybin mushrooms was with Ruby. We sat on the edge of the Adams House swimming pool and had a very bad trip, and our friend Paul, who was supposed to be babysitting us, gave us an antidrug lecture that made us feel worse. We swore we would never speak to him again, but then we did anyway. The first time I dropped acid, which was also the last time, I was a freshman in college. It was with a guy whose name was Marshall, I think, he was a painter about to graduate and take a job in advertising, and we went to Walden Pond, swallowed some LSD blotter paper, watched the sunset and the grass grow and the water ripple, and we laughed a lot. The first time I snorted crystal meth, which was also the last time, I was in London in 1995, after my first book was published there. A famous writer gave some to me in the bathroom of a restaurant, and I was awake for the next three days. The food was terrible.

The first time I did heroin was on my twenty-seventh birthday, in my bathroom in the three-thousand-square-foot loft where I rented a room for $750 a month, which is a big bargain in New York City. A Columbia graduate student I had a crush on gave it to me; we kissed on the white tiled floor. Over his shoulder I could see us in the full-length mirror, one of my hands draped on the nape of his neck, another touching his back, and I asked him for more. I kept asking him for more and more. He said a few snorts is enough, but I kept asking for more.

The first time, the first time, the first time: It never gets better than that.

The first book I had published was *Prozac Nation*, in 1994, and after that I got addicted to drugs. The first book I wrote was an illustrated guide to pet care, specifically parakeets, when I was six years old. The first play I wrote I was in third grade, it was based on Edgar Allan Poe's "The Murders in the Rue Morgue," and we performed it at the talent show. The first time I took trigonometry I was in eighth grade, but I had to take it again in high school because it was a requirement. I didn't mind because I loved plotting the sine and cosine and tangent curves on the lime-green graph paper I bought at the stationery store. The first time I had sex I was nineteen years old, late in this day and age, in Washington, D.C., under a hidden patch of cherry blossom trees in the National Zoo, after my boyfriend told me that if I were an animal, I'd be a Geoffroy's cat, which was a rare and beautiful creature. That was the first time I'd ever been fed a line, the kind boys give you, and I liked it even if I didn't believe it.

The first time I qualified at an AA meeting, it was at the Perry Street Group, in 1996, a week after I'd counted ninety days clean. The first time I went to rehab, I thought I'd be there for five days at the most, but then I stayed for four months. The first time I did drugs after I left that serene place in Connecticut was the day I got home.

The first time I learned to drive I was twenty-one years old, it was on the one-way streets and rotaries and against all the jaywalking college students in Cambridge, Massachusetts. But I never took my road test, slept through the alarm on the day I had an appointment, and never bothered to make another one. The first time I got arrested for shoplifting I was twenty-nine years old. I was charged with petty theft because the Robert Lee Morris bracelet I tried to steal was on sale for $299, and the item has to cost over $300 to be grand larceny: it was a misdemeanor instead of a felony, which was lucky. The first time I went to the emergency room I was four years old. I had tripped over a fallen bus pole on Central Park West and smashed my head against my grandfather's gold Impala, all because I was so excited that I was going to get to sit in the front seat for, yes, the very first time. I got six stitches at Mount Sinai.

When you do drugs, you don't count first times because they recede so fast. You count grams and eightballs and ounces and lines, you count how much cash you've got before you have to go to the ATM and get some more. You remember what streets the dealers hang out on. You know that it's Avenue D for dope and East Twelfth for cocaine, and then you get beeper numbers and cell phone numbers, which change all the time because of fear of getting caught, but you remember those too. You try to keep track of which friends you can use in front of, who has the best glass coffee tables for cutting lines, and you remember which ones you have to hide it from, when you have to sneak. You remember which public bathrooms are the best for getting loaded, which ones have nonporous ceramic tiles, and which ones only have toilet bowl lids. You remember that at fancy restaurants, like the Gramercy Tavern and Le Bernardin, the bathrooms have these nice full-length wooden doors, the privacy is so complete, and you can snort up lines with great gusto without anyone else in the ladies' room hearing you at all. You learn that at certain small places, dim sum joints in Chinatown or Caffè Raffaella in Greenwich Village or Serendipity 3 near Bloomingdale's, the unisex bathrooms only hold one person at a time, so no one ever knows what you're doing in there, even though you walk out to long disgruntled lines of people waiting to use it. And here's a good tip: At the Oyster Bar in Grand Central, in the bright pink bathroom stalls, there are flat aluminum armrests over the toilet paper dispensers, which are perfect for chopping up lines of cocaine. You give the attendants a few bucks, and they act as if nothing is strange at all.

When you do drugs, you have to count and remember so many things. I am told that when drunks get hauled into detox wards at terrible public hospitals like Bellevue in New York, the first thing the nurse will ask is what day it is, what year it is. And drunks, who are much more forgetful and addled than junkies and cokeheads usually are, will often say it's Wednesday when it's Saturday, they might miss the month and the season entirely, and lots of times they cannot remember their birthday or how old they are even. They get stopped by the police on the shoulders of four-lane highways or on the sides of little roads or on the avenues and streets of New York City, and they can't walk a straight line, and they think four fingers are three or five. My ex-boyfriend, a recalcitrant recidivist drunk if there ever was one, cannot remember where he lives when he's too far gone. He once sent me a dozen long-stemmed red roses on January 14, because he did not realize that Valentine's Day was actually a month away. But he can always recite pi to thirty-two places, and he always remembers my phone number so he can call me in the middle of the night and tell me he doesn't know where he is, he's been eighty-sixed at some bar, he can't find his way home.

When you do drugs, you count like a chemist: The numbers are wild, the formulas are easy. Then, when you try to get clean, you start to count like a pharmacist: How many hours between doses? How much or how little do you need to maintain? Then, when you finally give it up completely, you count like Noah in his dinky, seafaring ark full of pairs of every animal in God's creation: You count days. You wait for the rain to stop, for the sky to clear, for life to ever seem normal again. And then eventually it does. Then you start to count how many cups of black coffee you need just to get through every day, how many cigarettes you smoke. You know the address of every Starbucks in a mile radius, which is easy because there are so many, and you know the names of every restaurant where they allow you to smoke, which is easy because there are so few.

If you have ever had a problem with drugs and alcohol, you might as well accept spending the rest of your life overwhelmed by numbers. When I was in college, I majored in literature, and I had so much trouble remembering what century the Brontës were in—eighteenth or nineteenth or who cares?—and I have no idea what was Elizabethan drama and when Shakespeare suddenly became Jacobean, when the Middle Ages stopped and when the Renaissance began. But I will never forget 10 October 1998. I will never forget the last time I used.

Every recovered addict I have ever met knows his sobriety date and knows how many years he has been straight. Nine years, ten years, twenty-two years, on it goes. At an AA meeting in a hospital on Las Olas Boulevard in Fort Lauderdale, I met an eighty-year-old man, a World War II veteran who could not remember Pearl Harbor Day even though he was stationed in Hawaii at the time. But he remembers the last time he drank, over forty-four years ago. He remembers the end of the whole mess so well, all the Jamesons, the botched job he did on some assignment as a civil engineer, when he couldn't hide it anymore, when a bridge full of cars would collapse into Lake Erie because of his mistake. Every addict can remember when enough was finally enough, when something had to give, when he spent a grubby night in the county jail for drunk and disorderly conduct, when he lost an arm because he did not notice the gangrene on his hand for too many weeks, when he ended up paralyzed from the waist down in a car accident, when her nose bled for too many hours, when she woke on a pile of puddle and leaves under a tunnel, with her pants pulled down to her knees and blood between her legs: When they knew that the last shot really was the end of it all.

You never forget when it finally stopped.

Even if I remember the first time perfectly, I don't remember the beginning at all. I mean: the beginning of addiction. It's hard to say when it becomes a problem; it sneaks up on you like a sun shower.

You don't understand what I mean? So just try to think about the weather. The first day of winter is December 21. That's what the stargazers and meteorologists have told us since the beginning of the solar calendar. But what does that really mean to you? The first cold day was probably some time in October, and it was already consistently below freezing temperature since sometime after Thanksgiving, so what good is the date really? The solstice and the equinox show up reliably when they are supposed to, year in and year out, but the temperature does its own thing: There is an early spring or an Indian summer or autumn barely seems to happen at all. And it's like that with drugs: Even if you keep a record in your Filofax and you know the first time you did this or that, and then the second and the third and the ninth and the ninetieth, it is still difficult—no, impossible—to say when it went from casual use to a bad habit to a problem to abuse to addiction.

And the indicators are not clear at all: I once used heroin every day for a few weeks; then I stopped and didn't do it again for months, which means that I was not physically addicted. Right? On the other hand, for a while I only did cocaine once a week at most, and yet I can tell you that it was a huge problem. The simplest definition of addiction is when you want to stop doing something and can't. With heroin I could always stop any time, and with cocaine I always wanted to know when the next time would be. I might have waited ten days or more for that next time, but I was always planning for it, orchestrating it in my head, anticipating the next time.

Years before I became an addict, I would go to parties, to literary gatherings and collegial hangouts in New York, and once in a while there was cocaine around, people slipping into bathrooms in twos and threes, and like that. Not often, just sometimes. But when there was, I would love it up, snort it like crazy, outdo everyone else. That's what marks the difference: most people will do a few lines and move on. Addicts, or potential ones, will make it a complete activity.

All I ever wanted was to be good. And it's all turned out so bad.

Two

BYE-BYE LIFE

I'm in love with a dream I had as a kid
I wait up the street until you show
That dream it came true
But you never do
No you never did
As far as I know

PAUL WESTERBERG
"As Far as I Know"

Florida is glorious. I arrive on Halloween, in 1996, and it is so sunny that the world feels like a blank of light, nothing but whiteness. My mother's apartment is completely white—the tiles on the floor, the walls, the Formica kitchen, the faux-marble bathroom, everything is just stark—and life feels simple and shiny. My whole life has been erased by the sun. Whatever is going on in New York is gone, bleached out. All that's left is me.

I don't need drugs, I don't need friends—for all I care the phone can be disconnected. I don't want to see it, I don't want to hear it, I don't want to know about it. I'm through with everything. Bye-bye life.

In New York, I am always scared of disappearing, afraid I'm missing out on something, worried that if I don't go to some party or dinner I will miss some great opportunity, scared that my friends will forget I exist if I don't keep in regular touch—life is all frenzy, all frantic. But here I don't care. I have no object constancy, I have the ostrich's ability to believe that if I'm not there, neither is anything else.

It used to be easier to manage life. I lived in a huge apartment in the Flatiron district and everyone came by and hung out there, all my friends, a bunch of listless bohemians lounging about and drinking tea and beer and carrot juice, and sometimes smoking pot. I didn't have to go anywhere to see any-body, because everyone came to me, I was the barmaid at the neighborhood pub, I was the happy hostess. But all that's gone now. My friend Jason and I had been roommates in this grand apartment because it belonged to a psy-chotherapist who lived in New Jersey and liked to rent out rooms so that the place would not be empty. For $750, I lived with her Steinway grand, her an-tique rocking horses and gumball machines, her shabby chic furniture that she brought from her parents' house in New Orleans, her Persian rugs and Tiffany lamps. We walked on solid wood floors, and I roamed through rooms with southern and eastern exposures and huge industrial windows that let the sun shine in all the time.

But it's not like that anymore. Everybody is all grown up. I'm twenty-nine, everyone I know is hovering around thirty, no one's life is settled in any con-ventional sense, but the feeling seems to be that it's time to try. Jason and I are not roommates any longer, we both got our own apartments after the owner sold her grand pied à terre and we were left homeless. Then Jason started dat-ing Lydia, my agent, then he moved in with her, other friends of mine tried to move in with somebody else or else they moved somewhere else. No one I know has especially succeeded at this business of life, but no one has failed quite the way I have.

Among my pals, I am the only drug addict. They may not be married, their apartments may look like Nagasaki in a walk-in closet, but I alone am a junkie. Samantha moved to San Francisco after her four-year live-in relationship fell apart, she is now a partner at a large corporate law firm and director of their Sil-icon Valley office. She is not so happy, but she is starting over, and she's never even smoked pot. Everyone I know has withdrawn in one fashion or another, and so have I. Here in Florida, I will stay clean, because instead of using drugs to hide, I will just plain old hide. I've gone all the way. I have dropped out of life.

I love it. I am not making this up. This is my idea of heaven. I've got a TV and a VCR, I've got fifty-one channels of cable, I've got a view of the Intra-coastal, I can laugh at the pathos of human existence all day long because it does not matter anymore. I'm gone. I will never go on another date again. I will be all mind, no body, because I have dropped out.

I owe Doubleday a book, I will be honorable about completing it, but be-yond that, it's over between me and the world. Things have not gone very well between us. Fare thee well, my dark star.

People think I do drugs because I'm self-destructive. But, if anything, I am averting suicide. I don't much like my life, but for some dumb reason, I want to be alive, because sooner or later, I figure it will work out. I should and could be in New York, taking steps toward making it work, but I've been trying that for years, and it's no longer feasible. I can't do it anymore. I give up. I surrender. The only thing keeping me from killing myself is drugs—and the fact that I can still run away.

I can remember that when I was about ten, I started to think that it would be so fun to be around for the new millennium, I couldn't wait to see the year 2000. I figured out that I would be thirty-three by then, and I had a definite idea of what that meant. I took it for granted that I would be married with kids, that by then I'd have made partner in some law firm, or I'd have tenure at some tweedy university, or I'd be mayor or congresswoman and thinking about my bid for the presidency. Or, more likely, I'd be some kind of artist, a painter or writer, but my husband would be a more conventional type, maybe he'd be the law partner or professor or elected official, and I would be his glamorous and unpredictable wife. We would have little adorable daughters or bratty, athletic sons. We would be lovely.

But, in truth, I don't think I ever thought this through in such a detailed manner. I didn't have to: It was all taken for granted. It was all so obvious. You didn't wonder about how life would turn out, because you just sort of knew. There was a way things were meant to be, and by the year 2000, they would be that way. Of course. Of course they would.

I have been seeing Dr. Singer for about a year now. She is an addiction specialist, and she used to run a substance abuse program at a major teaching hospital. I had been seeing a psychologist for a couple of years, and going to Dr. Singer, who is an MD, just for medication. But once I started showing up to therapy sessions alternately high on heroin or wired on cocaine, the psychologist refused to treat me until I cleaned up. So I started seeing Dr. Singer for complete sessions, three times a week, because I thought, given her area of expertise, she could help me stop using. And it worked for a while. Under her tutelage I went to AA and cleaned up.

That lasted about four months, all through the summer of 1996. It lasts until my friend Oona, who is my sobriety buddy at AA, calls me to say she has a bundle of dope, and what should we do about this.

I'll be right over, I say. Four months is enough.

I walk out the door with the glee of one who knows that help is on the way.

I am a woman whose husband has been released from a POW camp in Saigon, and I am going to JFK to greet him after six years of no loving, of just waiting for him to come on home. That's how strong my love is for heroin. If you have not been married to a Vietnam veteran, you don't know how it feels to be me.

I get into a cab on Carmine Street, where I live, get out on Twenty-third Street, where Oona lives, and I go into her apartment for the first time ever. It is a tiny studio, with two cats and a TV and not much else. A wretched rusty shag carpet and a ratty futon. I don't know where she is keeping the dope stashed, and all I can say is, Let's do it.

So we do.

Oona is taking time off from Barnard, we have almost the same clean date and we would often go to a lunchtime meeting together, and then to the movies. There was an American New Wave series at the Film Forum, and we sat through all of them, all those afternoon double features, crowded with people playing hooky. We sat through *Medium Cool* and *Panic in Needle Park*, and we spent a lot of time missing drugs together.

That's the problem with AA. It's kind of like prison: It may rehabilitate some people, but many others just learn to be better criminals. Oona and I were great sobriety buddies, but we were even better drug buddies. We did dope and rented movies for at least a couple of weeks. I fell off a folding chair and bruised my whole right side and didn't even notice. And then enough was enough.

So today I walk into Dr. Singer's office with a heroin hangover, a headache like hell, vomiting, shaking, jonesing. I cannot bear to admit to her that it's come to this. I've been doing so well. But I missed therapy the whole time I was locked up with Oona, and there's no getting around what's going on here.

"What do you want to do?" Dr. Singer asks.

"What do you mean?"

"Are you ready to stop using or is this binge going to go on for a while?" She is so calm. She should be yelling at me, saying *Bad girl!*, saying, *You fucked up!* But Dr. Singer is so well trained in the nature of addiction. She knows calm detachment is the only way it works.

"No, I've had enough," I say, because I have. I want to get back to where I was just a few weeks ago.

Dr. Singer nods, says that that's good, says we can take steps to make this work. She pulls out her prescription pad and puts me on ReVia, generically known as naltrexone, an opiate blocker. I take it every day, like I'm supposed to. I agree to go to a therapy group for addicts that meets Wednesdays on the Upper East Side. So long as I never have to go to a Twelve Step meeting again, I will be fine.

Meanwhile, Oona starts doing crack. She calls me from Bellevue one day, where she has been taken by the cops for a psychotic episode all the way east on Twenty-third Street. Other crackheads move into her apartment with her and steal her stereo and halogen lamps. Her mother comes to New York to fetch her cats, Asta and Benji, because she loves animals and doesn't want them to be killed by an exploding glass pipe or worse. Soon Oona's parents will cut her off, soon she'll be turning tricks on the West Side Highway for money to get high. We won't speak again for a year or two. We will lose each other to the damage done.

And me, I think about using and I think about it some more, and I talk to Dr. Singer about it, and she tries to rearrange my antidepressant combination so that the medication will be more effective, and finally she throws some Ritalin into the mix.

By the time I first took Ritalin, I was completely clean. And though a triplicate form is required to fill a prescription for Ritalin, my previous troubles with drug abuse were not a deterrent to my receiving what is thought to be a mild energizer and mood elevator for medical reasons. In fact, my psychiatrist thought that taking Ritalin would curb my interest in doing other drugs, and she certainly got that right. This form of safe speed would be a good way to give me the stimulation I needed without putting my health and life at risk.

And it worked. It definitely worked.

Here is how heroin — how all drugs — makes me feel: Quite simply, it makes me feel okay to be me. Here is how I feel not on drugs: I hate me. If anyone has ever been in love with me for real, I don't know about it. All I can remember is good-byes. Sometimes someone will be standing in front of me, and already I feel him walking away. It's only a matter of time, so what's the point? I have no sense of presence, mine or anyone else's. But on drugs, I could feel that moment, I could be something besides nostalgic for the things that haven't even happened yet. I could live here now.

Maybe I did it once a week, maybe it's a few lines here and there just to get through dinner with my mom or synagogue on Yom Kippur. At any rate, it was an erratic habit for me. I didn't shoot it up, I only sniffed. Since none of my friends do drugs, save for smoking the occasional joint, I mostly used alone and I always used too much. I could sit on my couch — the filthy, beat-up orange one I'd been dragging from place to place since college — for hours and days at a time, floating away on heroin. Heroin and that stupid couch were meant for each other. Reclining in the charmingly musty attic apartment that I lived in, just watching the world go by — which is to say, watching absolutely nothing happen at all — was a full-time activity.

I didn't miss anybody. I didn't wonder if there was a party somewhere that I wasn't invited to. I didn't care that I wasn't in love, that I'd never been in love, that nobody would ever love me because it's too damn difficult. I didn't try to co-ordinate plans with six people at once, everyone arguing about whether to see Clueless *or* Stealing Beauty *or the director's cut of* Blade Runner *or should we just rent something? It's the stupid stuff. It's the maintenance of life, the little things, what to cook for dinner, should I order Chinese or Italian, why haven't I picked up my laundry after six days and can I wear the socks with the holes in them or should I just hand-wash the dirty ones? It's returning the call to my grandmother, which I'm never going to have five minutes to do because the guilt takes everything out of me. It's the books that are not on the shelves in alphabet-ical order so I can never find my copy of* Villette *or* Valley of the Dolls *or what-ever I'm looking for, it's the photographs that need frames, it's the posters that aren't on the walls because I never seem to have a hammer and a nail in the same place at the same time. It's being a grown-up, which I never figured out how to do, and scrubbing the tub, and remembering to eat and shampoo my hair. It's the basics: I can write a whole book, but I cannot handle the basics.*

After a month on Ritalin, after feeling much better, I decide to go to Florida to work on my second book, and ignore how unbearable and confusing life is when I'm not getting high. I have come to Florida to hide from drugs, and from life.

I loll about. I read a lot, in the guise of doing research, but in truth, I really do need to read these books. Maybe not all of them, maybe not from cover to cover, but it is a time-honored tradition for writers to procrastinate by doing more background work than they need to. Before I got here, I logged long hours at the Jewish Theological Seminary, making Xeroxes of books on Sam-son and Delilah, David and Bathsheba, Joseph and Potiphar's wife—all the great Biblical villainesses and their ways. I am reading them, not just in En-glish but in Hebrew and Aramaic, which makes me feel that my mind has not gone slack from all the drugs. I also have a researcher, whom I pay $25 an hour to because she is in graduate school and I am not, who sends me old articles from *Rolling Stone* about groupies, about Janis Joplin, about good girls gone bad. There are *Playboy* spreads of Rita Jenrette, Roxanne Pulitzer, and other naughty wives.

I watch a lot of TV. I discover *ER*, and I love the *Mary Tyler Moore* reruns on Nick at Nite—just as they used to be on, two in a row, at 2 A.M. on the NBC affiliate in New York City when I was in grade school. In the middle of the af-ternoon, *La Dolce Vita* and *Compulsion* show on Bravo, so I drag the TV table out to the terrace so I can get sun and cinema at the same time. I also have a cheeky love of snafus, of human folly, so nothing cheers me more than watching the bridge across the Intracoastal go up every time a boat comes by, not just schooners and cruise ships, but even dinky little sailboats with only one passenger and an antenna too high to pass under the trestle. I love how four lanes of traffic are held up for twenty minutes because one human being, leisurely lounging on his yacht for one, needs to get by. It amazes me that no one else seems to notice that these priorities are completely backward. In New York, no one would put up with this. I wonder if people in Florida are stupider, or just more patient, or if there is even a difference.

Sometimes I walk across the canals to Las Olas Boulevard, a thoroughfare that is either charming or "charming," though I tend to think of it as the former. There are stores that sell knickknacks and tchotchkes for too much money, elephant figurines made of jade, vases with molded cherubs and children made of Czech glass, brushed aluminum bottles, amber jewelry, lavender-scented candles in crystal holders, mason jars of colorful marbles, stash boxes made of wood with gothic motifs. I buy everything. Almost every shop on Las Olas seems to serve multiple purposes—there are souvenirs at the ice cream parlor and toys at the music shop and shampoo at the hardware store. At the bait and tackle dealer, I buy a sleeveless shift, silk with bright flowers in purple and canary yellow and rosy red. At the Lilly Pulitzer boutique I get a flowered sundress. I purchase some green ceramic tables for the living room—a break from the white—and lots of pewter picture frames and coasters in the shapes of playing cards, with diamonds and spades and clubs cut out of them. I get a mobile made of wire and silverware that produces beautiful chime sounds in the breeze and needs to be polished all the time because of the oxidizing ocean air. I order in food—Chinese and pizza and turkey club heroes—and sometimes I even cook chicken cutlets or grill fish from the overpriced Hyde Park Market. I figure out how to brew coffee in the Melitta machine, and I learn to use all the spices and olive oils and balsamic vinaigrettes in my mother's amply stocked rack. I set up a home, as I have never been able to do in New York.

And often I wake up in the morning feeling very happy.

There is a Motorola cordless phone that is small and meant to look like a mobile one, but the reception that's on this cute thing is terrible. People call sometimes, and I say I can barely hear them through the static, so that cuts the conversation short. It is my mother's voice on the answering machine, so people tend to be reluctant to leave messages. I tell my editor and my agent that I am hard at work, which is kind of true since I am taking copious notes as I read, and the calm of it all just amazes me. Why can't I do this in New York? I know it's hard in the winter with the cold and dark, but even in the summer

I can't get comfortable in my own home, I can't shut out the voices in my head that beckon and demand that I do more, run more, pursue more, always search for more. Down here I just don't care.

I take taxis to the mall, and I go to the Borders there and drink coffee on the deck and watch the water taxis float by. I special-order books I need and I befriend the clerks. I have no CD player, no tape deck, nothing to listen to music on, and find that I love the quiet, though I still keep buying new releases because I am convinced I will be going back to New York any week now. An editorial assistant who works at Scribner's, a recent Yale graduate, is house-sitting for me, taking care of my cat, which is a pretty good deal for her since she gets to stay in Greenwich Village rent free. I've got it set up so I can stay here indefinitely, and I just wonder how long it will take before this becomes as lonely and drab as New York. Sooner or later, everything becomes just life, sooner or later the bloom turns brown, and I have to run some more, but I am hoping this will last a while, at least long enough for me to get some work done and stay clean.

I have relatives in Florida—I mean, who doesn't? My aunt Zena and uncle Bill live in Inverrary, due west of here, and play a lot of golf. They are my rich relatives, they lived in a big house in Hewlett Harbor, one of those wealthy enclaves on the south shore of Long Island, before retiring down here twenty years ago. Their apartment is all glass, there is a little bulbous mirror on the terrace door because the pane is so clean that you might not see it, you might walk through it and get slashed to ribbons. They also have some nice art—marble sculptures, a Picasso drawing, paintings they bought in New York, a portrait of my uncle swinging his golf club on the green. He is a big John Grisham fan, so I get him free books from Doubleday, even though he's already bought them all at Wal-Mart, because I know it excites him to get freebies, I know it makes him feel important and, by extension, that I am important.

My mom and I were always the poor city relations, living in state-subsidized housing in Manhattan. I went to private school on scholarship, and you'd think that all my Long Island cousins and aunts and uncles would have thought we were worldly and sophisticated, but all they ever noticed is that my mother never remarried and, now, that I am closing in on thirty and have still not managed to get to the altar myself. They can't understand why a pretty, educated girl like me can't nab a man, like my only value is in my marriageability, and since I appear to be perfectly desirable, they just figure I'm an artist and I'm strange.

"Tell me, Lizzie," my uncle says to me every time I walk into their house for Friday night dinner. "Why aren't you married?"

"Uncle Bill, tell me, why aren't you thin?" That usually puts the conversation to rest.

Unlike anyone else in my family, Uncle Bill has actually read my books and is proud of me. I really do love him, and I love spending time with him and Aunt Zena while I am staying in Fort Lauderdale. They look after me, but not really. Still, they give me a sense that someone down here cares, which I like. I like family. I wish I had more of one.

Bill and Zena's son Lewis also lives nearby, in Plantation. He is an immigration lawyer, he met his wife, who is Chinese and fifteen years his junior, when she was a teenager translating for her parents as he helped them get citizenship. They started dating when she got out of college. She converted to Judaism, they got married on a boat, now they've got two girls born less than a year apart, with that interesting mix of Asian and Jewish genes that has made them both boringly obedient. They clear the table without being asked to, they get good grades without being pushed, but I can't stand that they are eleven and twelve and still such goody-goodies. They sing in the Hebrew school choir. They are hall monitors.

"Why don't you listen to Marilyn Manson?" I ask. "When I was your age I listened to the Sex Pistols and Patti Smith. I gave my friend's older brother blow jobs. I snuck out of the house in high-heeled shoes and tight Sasson jeans. Don't you ever want to misbehave? Just a little bit?" I encourage them to throw their bikes down the stairs and talk back to their parents.

They don't answer me. They just go back to reading *The Baby-sitters Club* books and watching the Cartoon Network, and generally disappointing me with their lack of subversive curiosity. Then again, they are happy and I am not.

Sometimes Lewis and I drive into Miami to see Heat games. Sometimes I'll hang out with him alone and talk about my drug use, remind him how I used to visit him in his house in Coconut Grove when he was still young, when he was a complete vegetarian, when he ate casaba melon and meditated for over an hour a day, and I would try to spook him out of his trance. I think he misses those days. He walks around not quite sure how he ended up driving a Jaguar and living in a gated community, going to synagogue every Saturday, giving money to charity, being a citizen in good standing. He has a wife who is a nurse and getting her Ph.D. in some kind of health care program, and two daughters who are perfectly behaved. He misses his old life, but he looks at me, my lonesome sorrow, and I can tell he's glad that things have worked out this way.

One odd day, I am about to take my daily dose of Zoloft, one ten-milligram yellow pill, and it occurs to me that maybe I can crush it up and snort it. I miss snorting things. I miss the ritual. I miss the burst in my brain. I get a knife and cut it in half on the scored line, then I put it between two spoons to crush it up, like I would do with cocaine that is not powdery enough. It flattens and gets sticky, as if I were pressing down on a wax candle. There is no way I can snort this thing, it is just a white and yellow mush.

I look around the house for other pills. Advil is in caplets, Aleve is coated like Advil, Tylenol is in gels, there is no Bayer aspirin, the vitamins are in capsules or this brown health food store form that just turns to a muddiness when you smash it. Nothing works. I am just going to have to take all my pills orally, like most people do.

For some reason, I don't think to try crushing the Ritalin.

RESEARCH

Three

THIS IS WHAT
MY LIFE IS LIKE

And you may tell yourself:
My God! What have I done?

DAVID BYRNE
"Once in a Lifetime"

I still have phone sessions with Dr. Singer a couple of times a week, based on the theory that I will be here only briefly, so we should not break the continuity. Also, I am on medication, so she needs to keep up with me, make sure the combination is working well—especially the Ritalin since it is so new to me. She believes I am doing well. I believe I am doing well. We both know that it's easy for me to be happy here in Florida, on vacation from life, so we keep up the therapy so that when I come back, I will be able to bring the good cheer with me.

One day I am talking to Dr. Singer, and I tell her that I wish the Ritalin didn't hit so hard, that I could take it more gradually. Or maybe I complain that it does not last long enough, that I can actually feel it wearing off. I say that I wish I could take five milligrams eight times a day instead of ten milligrams four. She asks if the pills are scored, and I say no. Too bad, she says, because if they were, you could split them in half. There is a time-release formula we might be able to try once I get back to New York. It has a slightly different effect, and the Ritalin seems to be working well for me, so she is reluctant to switch.

Dr. Singer suggests that I try cutting the pills in half with a sharp knife.

My mother has one of those newfangled ovens where the burners are under the surface, coils of orange light up when you turn them on, and it's hard to believe that they actually get really hot. I don't take this range seriously until I turn on one of the flames one day, touch it with my thumb, and get a black burn that looks like I rubbed charcoal. After that I just avoid the oven altogether. The top is completely black and shiny, it would be great for cutting up lines of coke.

Not that I would want to.

One evening I get out a steak knife and cut a Ritalin pill in half. This is harder to do than I might have guessed, and it just splits into little pieces, crumbles like a biscuit, with powdery flakes all over the place.

Eureka!

Why had I not thought of this sooner? I swallow a couple of the chunks with water like I normally would, and the rest I chop up into even finer bits. I press on them with the knife and break them down until they're a white powder. I slash on the little granules until they are as soft as confectioner's sugar, and bend my head over and try to sniff the powder into my nose. I realize that it's not going to work without some kind of conduit, so I rush around the apartment searching for my wallet. I can't seem to find it anywhere. I look on the desk and under the bed and on top of the television, until I realize it was on the kitchen counter all along. I am so desperate to find a twenty-dollar bill that I panic looking for one.

I snort up the Ritalin. It scratches and burns my nostrils a little bit, but it's not too bad. And then I feel a tiny rush in my brain. It's nothing too intense, just a little burst, but it feels so nice. So nice. So nice to be putting stuff into my nose again.

I decide that from now on, when I take my Ritalin doses, I will cut the pills in half, or quarters, or pieces, or whatever it comes out to. Part of it I will ingest orally, and the other part I will chop into powder and take in nasally. I can't imagine there is anything wrong with doing that. It's the same thing, after all, the same amount of medication, just an alternate method of absorption, surely that's not a problem. In fact, if anything, it will help me to stay clean, because I will get to have the ritual of doing cocaine and heroin without actually doing them. I have solved all my problems! I am a goddess! I am a genius!

But I don't mention this new nasal dosing to Dr. Singer. I know it would sound weird to her. Of course, there's nothing wrong with what I'm doing, but there's no way to explain it to anybody else.

I enjoy snorting up the Ritalin so much that after a couple of days I figure—what the hell?—I'll just take all of it that way. Why bother to swallow any of it? There's no reason it can't get into my system just as well through my nose.

The only problem is that it hits very hard when I sniff it up, it goes right to my brain, so there's no chance for it to absorb into my bloodstream gradually. The exact problem I was complaining about in the first place—that the Ritalin doesn't last long enough, that I feel the drop-off an hour before I am supposed to take my next dose—happens much more quickly when I snort it. So I try to snort half a pill at a time; I try to maintain at least two hours between lines.

I try.

And then after a few days, I give up on trying. I take a whole pill every couple of hours. I figure that means I am taking eight a day instead of four, which isn't great, but how bad could it be? Plenty of people are on much more than forty milligrams of Ritalin a day, and even the eighty that I have upped it to is not too bad. There are six-year-olds who are given Ritalin for attention deficit hyperactivity disorder (ADHD), and some of them take more than a hundred milligrams a day. If a kid in first grade can handle it, why shouldn't I be able to?

I am so thrilled to have discovered this new use for Ritalin. I am taking it completely legitimately, it has been prescribed for me by Dr. Singer, so there is no possible harm I can do to myself. According to all the literature, Ritalin is not addictive. If it were, they would not be giving it out to patients who are still in elementary school, still in their cavity-prone years. I have finally found a way to stay happily clean. Amazing. Just amazing.

After a few days—not even a few weeks, the escalation occurs very quickly—I have lost track of how much Ritalin I am taking. My guess is that it's ten pills a day, but maybe it's fifteen. As long as I have enough of it, I don't see any good reason to keep count. I figure that if I run out early for some reason, I can always get Dr. Singer to write me a new prescription. Sometimes I run out of Zoloft before I am supposed to, maybe I lose a couple of pills in transit or something, and it's never a problem to get a renewal sooner than expected. I am sure Ritalin is no different.

In the meantime, I am suddenly happy and upbeat all the time. I have a new energy that is delirious, vertiginous. I work out in the little gym downstairs in my mother's building at two in the morning. I can stay on the rickety old stationary bicycle, the kind that has an egg timer and a rolling odometer and rusty spokes on the wheels—the kind they tend to have in retirement communities, although my mother's building is mostly young people—for forty-five minutes at a time. Then I do some weight work on this all-in-one machine, with all its bars and pulleys and keys to load up on the cams. I do arm presses and leg curls, I develop beautiful muscles, I do this every night without exception. Sometimes I'll turn on the sauna before I start my workout, and I'll go sit in it for a few minutes afterward. My heart races.

Once I'm done with my physical fitness routine, I go back upstairs and watch TV, or sometimes I write. Did I mention that I have started writing? It has been completely splendid. Instead of just sitting around and reading books about Jean Harris and Amy Fisher and Bess Myerson, I am now actually taking my research and getting started on my book. I almost can't help myself. Sometimes I don't mean to be writing, it's the last thing I feel like doing, *Imitation of Life* is on AMC and I really want to watch it, but I find myself writing anyway. This has never happened to me before. It is always such a struggle to sit down and focus, and after just a little while in front of the computer, I need to get up and walk around, make some more coffee, water the plants, clean the bathroom—I will mop the floors with a sponge, on my hands and knees, if it means I can avoid writing.

But I would surely have ended up writing about it. I'd deliver a treatise on ceramic tiles. That's the nightmare of my life: I hate writing, but I can't help myself. It's just what I do; it is what I love to do. If that makes any sense. And now, with Ritalin, I don't mind it at all. I have so much to say, and I just can't keep myself from saying it. Sometimes I will sit in front of my little PowerBook for thirty-six hours straight. I will forget to eat, forget to sleep, forget to do everything except go downstairs for my workout, because I am so enthralled with what's on the page. The whole process is completely different for me, because I get to see a whole argument from start to finish without surcease. Normally, even when I'm on a roll, I produce a certain number of pages a day, and that's enough. I have to continue with the same idea the next day, so the thoughts are broken up, reconsidered, and reconstituted. But now I understand the reason why medical residents are kept on twenty-four-hour shifts: economics aside, it allows them to follow a case all the way through, to watch a patient convalesce or deteriorate over a period of time, to witness symptoms develop or dissolve over a full day. And that's what it's like now writing on Ritalin: I see a concept from inception to completion, I never let go of an idea until it is fully examined. I write to fruition, I am fertile and prolix.

My editor is extremely pleased. It's been at least a year since she signed up this book. She has had no indication that I was making progress at all—I kept saying that I was putting it off until I could go to Florida or somewhere and clear my head to write. I would go into her office for these long, languorous meetings where we'd put together outlines and write out ideas on piles of yellow legal pads. And I would keep telling her I'm working on it, it's all in my brain, it's all there, it's just a matter of executing it, which is no big deal. I have stalled her with this excuse and that, I have claimed drug addiction and boy problems—at least I am honest—and now I am at long last delivering. Her faith was not without merit. She is relieved.

"You're like Rumpelstiltskin," Betsy says to me, and I don't have the nerve to admit that I cannot remember who that fairy-tale character is, or what he did. "You are spinning out gold. This writing is much better than anything you've done before." My first book was, after all, just me prattling on and on about my problems; now I am composing essays, examining other lives, thinking about the whole wide world.

I decide to mention to Betsy that I'm on Ritalin, that I believe it is helping me to think more clearly and fluidly, that it's been really good for the work. And she says she is glad to hear it. She's heard so many mixed stories about people's experiences with Ritalin, and she's happy to see that it seems to be helping me so much.

Ritalin *über alles.*

I realize I have run out of Ritalin about two weeks sooner than I am supposed to. I can't figure out how this has happened because, even though I know it's not true, I still believe that I am only taking four pills a day. Okay, maybe a few extra here and there, but if I am already out, I must be taking at least double the amount. I have no sense of how it has multiplied. Granted, occasionally I will chop up two at a time because the more powder I have, the more fun it is. But I don't see how it has gotten to the point where I have a couple of weeks before I get a new prescription and I'm already out.

I assume that perhaps the pharmacist miscounted, maybe he did not give me quite as many pills as he was supposed to. Although I normally fill all my prescriptions at Duane Reade or some other chain, since I've been down in Florida, I've been getting my Ritalin from some elegant little drugstore on the Upper East Side in New York. Because Dr. Singer can prescribe controlled substances only in New York State—though the *Physicians' Desk Reference* only refers to Ritalin's potential for "psychologic dependence" in passing, it is classified by the DEA as a Schedule II drug, the category reserved for legal substances with the highest abuse potential—I have to get the pills sent to me from home. A discount drugstore would never be able to manage that. They might do it with a straightforward prescription, something that is not quite so regulated, but with Ritalin it is just too much trouble.

So a friend of mine picks up the triplicate form from Dr. Singer's office, brings it up to the pharmacist, and she sends it by Federal Express down to me. This is not a hassle at all. This seems to be the kind of clannish neighborhood shop where they are used to having a clientele that winters in Palm Beach or Palm Springs, so they are pretty well set up to be jetting off pills to distant locales. The store does not accept my insurance, so every bottle costs about $150, which means that the clerks are much nicer to me.

So I call the pharmacy and tell them they must have sent me fewer pills than they were supposed to. I don't make this call until it's been a day or two that I have gone without Ritalin because I am trying to push myself to the limit of what is possible for me to handle. After all, if I don't need Ritalin for a couple of days—even if all I do during this reprieve is sleep—I can be sure that I am not dependent on these pills, which of course, I'm not, because they are not addictive anyway. Because I am genuinely certain that the druggist really has shorted me on pills, my voice has a credible tone, there is no reason for the person on the other end of the phone to doubt me.

The pharmacist apologizes and sends me sixty more. Since it is his mistake, I don't even have to pay for them.

One day I am in Fedco, which sounds like it ought to belong to a larger conglomerate, but it is in fact its own entity. This tiny drugstore is stuck in the parking lot between the Galleria mall and Borders. It is open only erratically, and it cannot possibly compete with the Eckerd across the street. I started to think it must be a retirement project for some rich eccentric. Since it is privately owned, Fedco has a lot of odd merchandise I couldn't find at a big chain—the black Magno soap that I like, ponytail barrettes with rhinestone Scotties and poodles glued onto them, Dr. Brown's cream soda, and Kneipp foam bath with juniper, which someone in AA told me to soak in to relieve the ache of heroin withdrawal.

Hidden in a corner near the pharmacy, buried in a shelf of herbs and vitamins, I find a combination pill slicer and crusher. It is an odd contraption: In one compartment there is a slot to hold a pill, and you can press the straight edge down onto it to cut it in half; on the other side is a dome-like thing—it kind of looks like a thick dildo—that screws into a receptacle where you can place pills so that they get crushed up.

This is a wonderful apparatus for me, since it means I can put a whole bunch of Ritalin in it, crush it into powder all at once, and just spill it out throughout the day and cut it into lines. That means that I can measure out, say, eight pills first thing in the morning, and decide that's all I'm going to use all day, that's the limit. This will allow me to keep track of my usage, and it will also mean that I don't have to spend so much time and effort turning the pills into powder. I can't imagine what purpose this crusher serves for anyone who is not snorting up drugs—although it is later explained to me that some elderly people cannot swallow a whole pill, that they mix it in with orange juice and ingest their medication that way. Well, whatever. All I know is that I love this little thing, I can carry it in my bag anywhere I go, I no longer need to find appropriately smooth and shiny and dark surfaces for cutting up lines.

After a few days, I start snorting the Ritalin right out of the cup in the crusher, not even bothering to mete it out into smaller segments. Once again, this means that at first I used the thing to pace myself, to set limits, but after a while I just keep adding in more pills as I run out of powder during the day. Sometimes, to try to conserve my doses and get maximum use of each pill, I will scrape out the bottom of the cup with a pen knife, I will try to make sure I use up every last bit of available powder. This kind of reminds me of those days of doing cocaine, when I would get to the bottom of the vial long before I was ready to stop. And I would use knives, straws, coffee mixers, stickpins, or needles to try to scrape the last bits from the inside of the cap, from the bottom of the barrel. Eventually, I would just put water into the vial, shake it up and drink it, hoping to get some small, scrawny high. Then I would wait for the little bottle to dry out and for the water to evaporate, and I would scrape the condensation out of the bottom. I would snort white residue.

Not that Ritalin is anything like cocaine.

I become a friendlier, warmer version of myself. Morose me is gone. My crabby carping, my running out of the room crying and demanding that everyone run after me—and then yelling at them when they don't, when they act like this is just one of my turns coming on—all of that's gone. I am a pleasant pleasure. I am fun. I am animated and outgoing whenever I am around other people—which is not terribly often—but they tend to assume that I am happy and healthy, that I am loving life. Which I kind of am. My relatives are all charmed. I often see them for Friday night dinners, or sometimes Wandy and Lewis and their two daughters—Jasmine and Jade—will come over to the apartment and spend the afternoon at the beach or walking along Las Olas. I am the new, unknown cousin, and they enjoy getting to know me, and vice versa.

I show them the pile of books and papers that I use for research. The girls are particularly intrigued by the *Playboy* magazines that I have around for a section I am writing about women who have used their bodies to express their sexual power. I am constructing some sort of argument about how posing nude is no longer a form of women's subjugation and objectification—that when people like Sharon Stone and Pamela Anderson and Cindy Crawford do it, it is actually a career move. I try to explain this to my two young cousins—of course I love explaining anything because I love to talk because I just can't seem to shut up ever—and they kind of look at me askance, and we leave it at that.

I go to Wandy and Lewis's house for Thanksgiving. I am supposed to be back in New York by now, but clearly I am not ready to leave anytime soon. Almost everyone at their house in Plantation is Chinese, it's mostly Wandy's relatives. Aunt Zena and Uncle Bill are in Dallas with their daughter, and besides a few husbands and wives, Lewis and I are pretty much the only completely Caucasian people on the premises. I am wearing the brightly colored silk sundress that I bought at the fishing store on Las Olas, and I look gaily Floridian, blonde and blissful.

This is like no Thanksgiving I have ever experienced. There is turkey, of course, but also fried rice and dumplings and egg rolls and spare ribs. The high-MSG Chinese takeout we eat every night in New York, right out of the containers with plastic knives and forks, is nothing like this. Wandy has a Japanese cousin by marriage who has brought sushi, yellowfin and eel and all the fish I love. Of course, other than as scenery, none of this much matters to me because I have no interest in food. I have only been in Florida for a few weeks, less than a month, but Ritalin has already become my life. I just keep running into the bathroom to snort more lines between monologues that I deliver to anyone who will listen. True to the stereotype, all these Asian people are taciturn as all hell. Their command of English is not all that good, so they make a perfect audience for my spiels about political wives and teenage prostitutes, or whatever subject I happen to be writing about that week. Actually, I should say subjects, because my mind has become strangely diffuse, I am all over the place, I am possessed by six different things at once. Under normal circumstances, I would seem like some kind of dilettante, but I am so deeply involved with every different thing that I am deeply involved with that I am more multiply obsessed than anything else. I am disturbed by dabbling.

There are enough bathrooms in the house that no one seems to mind my extended stays every time I duck inside to snort my lines. At some point either Jade or Jasmine asks me why I spend so much time in the bathroom, why I keep running in, and I just mutter something about my stomach problems. This is not entirely untrue: all the Ritalin in my system, without much food to buttress it, has made me feel nauseated and cramped all the time. I often find myself cutting up lines and making more conventional use of the bathroom at the same time.

After a fit of productivity that went on for some weeks, I am now fatigued with thinking. The Ritalin manufactures fascination with so many different ideas that it is impossible for me to sit and concentrate on any one thing. My writing is all over the place. I get a lot done, but it is all disjointed—the beginning of one section, the end of another chapter, but nothing progresses all the way through anymore. Episodes of deep focus are scattered throughout my scatterbrained excess.

I am amped up on Ritalin. I can't feel very much at all, but I just kind of know that I cannot go back to New York just yet. Even if the writing is starting to go badly, at least it is still going at all. In New York I would be stymied by city life. I have been telling whichever friends I still talk to—and only occasionally at that—that I will be home by the new year. I make some halfhearted noises about parties and plans for New Year's Eve. I even talk about having to find something to do that does not involve drugs, that I cannot be exposed to cocaine or even to any of the more benign fancy plants because I have managed to stay clean for a few months, and I want to keep it up.

My mother will be coming down for the winter sometime after Christmas, and there is no room in the apartment for both of us. If there were twenty bedrooms and thirty bathrooms, there would still not be enough room for both of us in a single dwelling. But we agree that we'll find a seasonal rental for me. I talk to my house sitter about staying on at my New York apartment a few more months, and she is delighted to have more time in her rent-free existence.

The consensus among my relatives is that I am thriving in Florida. Ritalin has made me popular. Life is easy.

This is what my life is like: I get *The New York Times* on Saturday night, and watch *Saturday Night Live* as I work on the puzzle. This is heaven.

* * *

By the end of December, I am short on Ritalin again. I still can't quite make sense of this because I still do not think I am taking all that much of it.

I tell Dr. Singer that I am running low. I tell her that I think the friend who has been dropping off my Ritalin prescriptions for me might be stealing some of my pills. One time my friend mailed them to me herself, instead of having them sent directly from the pharmacy, so maybe she took a bunch of them. I am finally recognizing that Ritalin is simply an amphetamine, and if you were a speed freak, you might actually do the drug recreationally. Dr. Singer and I discuss this hypothetically. I ask her what kind of deranged person would take Ritalin for nonmedical purposes—it's okay and all, but you might as well just get cocaine or crystal meth if you want to get buzzed. And Dr. Singer says something about Ritalin's being legal, that many people who are uncomfortable with street drugs would have no problem abusing prescribed pills. I laugh as she tells me this—*how ridiculous can people be?* We both laugh a little. How lucky I am that my problems are with cocaine and heroin, and not Ritalin, which seems to be having a salubrious effect on my psyche.

We laugh, and Dr. Singer agrees to write me a new prescription a couple of weeks early. Even though Ritalin is not a drug you can just call in to the pharmacy, Dr. Singer has been dealing with this particular drugstore for a long time, so they will mail out the pills so long as she promises to send them the form. They trust her to get it to them, so they don't need it before they send me my supply. Dr. Singer has some discussion with the pharmacist about how the friend who once picked some Ritalin up for me might be stealing some of the pills, so the druggist agrees that he will always Federal Express the bottle to me directly.

Trouble is, now that I've used my best excuses—that the pharmacist miscounted, that my friend pilfered my pills—I will no longer be able to come up with reasons to get extra prescriptions. And 120 pills a month is not going to cover it. I will have to find a new way. I will have to get more.

Four

FEDERAL EXPRESS

I need a fix 'cause I'm falling down

JOHN LENNON

"Happiness Is a Warm Gun"

My mom calls my new apartment the treehouse, because it's on the second floor of a two-story dwelling, it's bright and lofty, and there actually are trees with orange and red flowers brushing up and caressing the windows. These flowers have no scent, and if you pick them and put them in water, they die within twelve hours, which seems symbolic of something or other, I'm not sure what. But it is a cheerful place, a bit like a roadside motel. It definitely has a transient feel, but still there's nothing depressing about it. Maybe the gray wall-to-wall carpet is a little drab and impersonal. The plates are plastic, the utensils have scratched-up handles, it's all quite utilitarian. But the best part is the glass eat-in kitchen table and the glass coffee table parked between the couch and the TV. These will be useful.

If I order in all my food and have the Federal Express guy come and pick up my finished pages to send to Betsy, I will never have to leave the house again.

The phone only has local service, and I don't have a calling card. This is fine by me, except that I am going to have to make some long-distance calls for drugs. No getting around that. I go to the 7-Eleven and buy one of those time cards. I have a choice between one with a manatee on it or another with a marlin on it, because this is Florida. I've been out of Ritalin for a couple of days, the options seem absolutely baffling, so I just get both.

I call Max that night. I call him looking for cocaine.

Max and I go way back, I even spent a month at his parents' condominium in Boca Raton writing my first book. So I figure that I can call and ask a favor, no need for formalities, no need to apologize for being out of touch—the bond is understood, tacit and constant.

But perhaps not. Max seems to want me to go through the motions of acting like I care. Yuck. I'm too tired and jonesing to manage it. I've been antisocial for so long that I don't quite know how to make conversation. I am actually awkward, I've lost all my glib grace, I don't know how to talk to my friends anymore. I try to act really casual, I try to make conversation like I've been missing him for the last few months, like I've been meaning to pick up the phone for a while now, but after a few minutes I just break down.

"Max, can you get me some blow?" I ask, all natural. Max and I have done coke together plenty of times over the years, I did heroin with him once because he wanted to try it, I feel like this is a reasonable request. He is a musician, he makes a fortune writing advertising jingles for television, I know he is connected. He's a complete pothead, he smokes every day. How difficult can it be to find coke?

"Elizabeth, I haven't done that in ages," he says, like I ought to know. "Where have you been? Where are you? You're in Florida. That's the easiest place on earth to get cocaine. What do you need me for?"

"I don't know where to go here." I sigh. "Don't laugh, but I actually looked up 'cocaine' on the Internet, thinking I could find a source somehow, like I could read some code on some dealer's Web site and get in touch and order it that way." He laughs at this. "All I found was informational stuff from the DEA and the National Institute on Drug Abuse. Maybe I'm using the wrong search engine, but everything I found was about how to *stop* doing coke, not how to get started."

I can tell he's perplexed. "I don't hear from you in months, and *this* is why you call me."

I can't just admit that's true, but it is. Human beings are objects to me, ways of getting what I need. That's all they are. Dogs are in it for the food, but they also need to love and be loved, they like to be scratched behind their ears and massaged on the napes of their necks—and when you cry, they'll look at you quizzically and lick your lips and cheeks and eyebrows. But me, I'm more like a goldfish: pour the powder in the tank, and let me swim and blow bubbles. "Look, it's no big deal. I mean I don't need it or anything," I say, back to trying to sound really cool. "You know, I cleaned up last summer, I've been clean ever since, I'm working really hard, I'm out of touch with everybody, and I just thought it might be fun to do again. You know, just a little treat."

Max insists that we have a conversation. He doesn't say so, but he's not just going to do me a favor and hang up. This will cost me: I am going to have to listen to his romantic problems, news about this or that producer he works with, complaints about the plumbing in his apartment. And I force myself to be cordial, but I almost can't do it. Without Ritalin for a couple of days, I'm all nervous, I'm ready to scratch the walls. It's strange because I should, if anything, feel relaxed: the buzz from Ritalin is wiry and tense, but I am going crazy from the lack.

Max is chatty, and it's unbearable, but I have to bear it. Finally, he tells me his friend Cornelius, a jazz musician, can probably score him some coke. It might take a couple of days.

I can't say *I don't have a couple of days*, I can't let anyone know it's come to this, this is supposed to be no big deal, just for fun, but finally I can't help it. "Look, Max, I really need it," I say. "Okay? I'm on a terrible deadline, I'm really not getting enough done, I've got to be awake for a few days so I can turn in a few chapters, so I really need this fast. Can you please, please, please, *please* call Cornelius right now, and call me back? I'm really begging you for this favor. If you get me an eightball, I'll pay for it and you can keep some for yourself. But I need it quick. I need it."

I start to cry. Max asks what's wrong, and I'm afraid he's going to say something about how he shouldn't do this, he'd be enabling me.

"Oh God, Max," I sniffle. "I'm having a really hard time here. Don't tell anybody, don't tell Kathlyn or anyone, but I'm lonely and I'm scared and I'm under so much pressure to produce. I'm really falling apart here. I miss you. I miss everybody. But I'm scared to come back. There's too much to do, and life was going so badly. I love you. I really do. I can't figure out what to do with myself. But right now, I can't worry about that because I've got to write. Please just find me some blow and we can talk about it later."

I can't believe I am actually being honest. Sometimes my tears are a rhetorical device, sometimes I am just being manipulative. But I mean what I am saying to Max. I am falling apart and I am scared, and I know somehow that I need drugs to get through. I can't quite use the words *dependent* or *addicted*, because it's just Ritalin, that's all. But I know something isn't right. And it feels good to cry to Max. It's a relief. The truth is a relief.

decide I better wait until the next morning to call Max again. I am up all night in a panic. I try to read. I can't even focus on *Vogue*, I can't even focus on *Mademoiselle*. I watch TV. *The Seventh Seal* is on, and I certainly can't focus on that. I watch MSNBC, reruns of Brian Williams, reruns of *Hardball*, finally Imus at 6 A.M. When will it be late enough in the morning to call Max? Does it matter? I'm awake—why shouldn't he be?

I wait until after nine. I call and get his voice mail. I call again. And again. I leave him seven messages before I lose count. I don't want him to know it's an emergency; I don't want him to think I have a drug problem. If I don't have one—and I don't think I do—then I don't want him to worry; if, for some reason, I do have one, then I *really* don't want him to worry. Then I figure that if I haven't called looking for coke before now, there's no way that he can possibly think I'm an addict. If I were, I'd have bothered him months ago. At worst, he'll think I'm panicking because of work. That's okay—it's good to panic over work, means I'm industrious, means I'm doing what I should be. I call again. I leave more messages.

Why doesn't he have a mobile phone? No one I know does, but why can't he?

I leave more messages.

I go for a walk. I lie down. I wish I could sleep. I can't sleep. I watch more MSNBC.

I can't figure out why I am not tired. Without Ritalin I should be passed out, sleeping the sleep of the dead. That's how it used to be. But not anymore. Is this the panic of not knowing when I will get some again, or is this just some new symptom? Am I doing so much that some paradoxical effect is occurring? I wish I could ask Dr. Singer about this, but I can't. I wish I didn't feel this way.

Finally, sometime in the afternoon, I call Max again. He answers. Thank God. He had left Cornelius a bunch of messages, and they finally spoke. Cornelius can get him an eightball by sometime that night.

"Do you think it will be before ten o'clock?"

"Probably not. Why?"

"I think you can get things to the Federal Express office on Spring Street by ten and still get it out to me for the next morning."

"Elizabeth! Jesus! What's happening to you?" He is silent for a moment. Maybe he's annoyed. Max is never annoyed with me. I don't want him to be annoyed because then maybe he won't do this for me. I have to be nice. I have to be careful. "Look, Cornelius has a gig at the Cedar tonight. I'm going to go by, we'll hook up with his dealer, I'll get it out to you tomorrow morning."

Tomorrow morning? That means it won't arrive for—I do the math in my head, the only thing I can think clearly about is when drugs will arrive—maybe forty-two more hours. What will I do until then?

"Is that the best you can do?" I think I am talking calmly, but I am probably not.

"Elizabeth," he says, then takes a deep breath. "Look, I've done all I can. But I'm worried. I'm actually thinking about coming down there. I talked to Jason. We're both worried about you, and we were thinking that maybe we should come see—"

"Don't do that." Shit, now I sound crazy, I may even be shouting, I don't know what the modulations of my voice are. I go get a glass of water. I don't think I've had a drink for hours. Maybe that's the problem; maybe I'm dehydrated. Except, if I were, I think I would be fainting. I don't think I'd be unable to sit still. "Max, really, I'm fine." I gulp some water. "I'm just on deadline and I'm nervous. That's all. You don't need to come down here. My mom's here. My relatives are here. There are plenty of people looking after me."

"I just think that—"

"Don't think." Sip more water. "I'll be back in New York in a month, and I'll be great. I'll be all done with my book and I'll be relaxed. We'll go see some shows at the Blue Note. We'll go see Beat Rodeo on Monday night at Ludlow. It will be just like it was. I'm fine. Just a little panicked."

"Okay, but—"

"I'm fine."

I tell him to put a fake name and address on the sender's information of the Federal Express label. I suggest that if there is anyone he really hates to put that person's name and address on it so if it gets intercepted, he'll get that person in trouble. For the first time in this conversation, Max actually laughs. *See?* I want to say. *See? I still have my sense of humor. I'm still the same old Lizzie. I'm fine.*

I tell Max, really and truly, not to worry about getting caught, that actually cocaine has no odor, and if he just puts it in one of their small envelopes, it will never occur to anyone that there's contraband in it. If they are trying to stop drug traffic, it would be the big packages that they would go for. Little people like us are not worth arresting.

"Look, Max," I finally say. "I really do appreciate this. I'll put a check in the mail when you tell me what the whole thing costs. Pay Federal Express with a money order. They won't take cash, but we can't use a check or a credit card, just to be safe. Okay?"

"All right, Elizabeth. But if you don't come back to New York soon, I am going to come down there. I'm worried that—"

"Don't be worried. I'm fine."

Okay, that's good. Coke is on the way. I am breathing heavily, like a dog panting on a hot day. Maybe Ritalin is turning me into some kind of canine. I've heard about drugs that have really strange side effects. I should probably look all these questions up on the Internet, but I am too exhausted. And, actually, I kind of don't want to know.

I relax knowing that I will be able to get high again soon. I never think of it as *getting high*. I still think I am just taking my medicine, but there is no getting around it anymore: I am getting high. After I get off the phone with Max, lassitude takes over my body. I feel like I can finally go to sleep. I have not bothered to fold the Murphy bed back into the wall, I have not brushed my teeth or washed my face in quite some time—I'm not sure if it's hours or days—and I certainly have not eaten. But suddenly I am just wasted. I take off all my clothes. The afternoon sun from the west beats in through the window. I like the light, I never close the shades, I never worry about anyone looking in, I never feel modest, and I don't care about other people anyway. I squish up into a little ball under the blanket, the air conditioner is on high and I am freezing, and I fall asleep for the next twenty hours.

I wake up calm. I don't really know what day or time it is. I'm even a little confused on the month, it feels like July all the time here, and the disoriented sensation does not feel so good.

I do not feel so good.

But it's a little bit nice to not be waking up to cutting lines. It will be a nice break, just so long as I know it's only a break. Being on Ritalin all the time is wearisome. Maybe for the first time in a few months it's starting to become apparent that this is time out of mind, that I thought I was on a vacation from life, but really this is just a different version of life. I am actually perfectly alive, and this is what my life has become: I write, I snort Ritalin, I sleep.

I look at my watch to figure out what day it is, but there's only the number, the date of the month, but not the month itself. I know it's either February or March, and anyway, what's the difference?

I call my mom and ask if she wants to have dinner. We can go to Fuddruckers for a burger, or Il Mulino for pasta. Without Ritalin, I actually do feel like eating something besides the Cocoa Krispies and Froot Loops and Apple Jacks and Frosted Flakes that I've been subsisting on. I'm not even bothering with takeout food anymore. It's just sugar cereal and sips of water and cups of tea. Sometimes, if I've run out of milk, I just have the cereal plain, out of the box with my fingers, until I can get it together to run out for another container.

I keep thinking that it will be nice to see my mother when I am not on drugs—it will be nice to see anybody when I am straight. And then I remember that I feel trapped in the car with my mother when I don't have any Ritalin to do, that I always have to load up on it when I know she will be coming by to pick me up to go food shopping or visit my cousins or whatever. My mother makes me feel suffocated. She always has, at least since high school. I miss her desperately when I have not seen her for a while, and then, as soon as she is anywhere near me, I feel like I am choking, I have an experience of my throat constricting. It is a mild version of a panic attack. She demands this, she wants to know that, I am her only child, she has never remarried, and she smothers me with her love and need. She always has so much to tell me about how her investments in the NASDAQ are doing, she wants to know what I think about the new tile for the backsplash in the kitchen, whether she should move to Florida permanently and give up her apartment in New York—or would I want to move into it?

As if I could ever move back into the place I grew up in, the bedroom where I slashed cuts onto my arms and legs, where I lay on the floor with padded headphones on my ears listening to Bruce Springsteen and sobbing—as if I could ever return to the site of my adolescent crack-up. And that is why I feel smothered by my mother: because we are close, because we talk to each other so much, and yet she understands me so little that she actually imagines I might want to live in the apartment I grew up in. My mom is wonderful: she helped me find the little treehouse I live in now, she cooks pumpkin soup and brings it over to me, she lends me her printer because I don't have one down here, she is a supreme mother in all the practical ways—but she fundamentally does not get me. I am almost thirty years old, and I still have to take my nose ring out when I see her, I still have to wear long enough sleeves to cover the tattoo on my arm, I still have to pretend I have turned into the grown-up she wishes I were—and not the drug-addicted, unmarried, childless writer-of-books-she-doesn't-read that I am. I am the person that my mother is closest with in the world—and vice versa, I sometimes think—and she does not know me, or want to know me, at all.

This is a horrible thing. Drugs are a relief from that.

And drugs are a relief from the way I feel about everyone else abandoning me, all my friends meeting for a drink at the Corner Bistro and forgetting to call and invite me along, everyone going away to upstate New York for the weekend and forgetting to ask me to join them, everybody I know heading to our old roommate's wedding in the south of France except for me, all my boyfriends who stick around for a few months and then decide enough is enough.

I mean, I can see that I am not seeing clearly. No one I know manages to elicit as much adoration and attention from her friends as I do. I know that no one is disappearing, my friends always remember to include me—that they tried to call and see if I wanted to meet up, that I was not home at the time. I can see that I imagine all kinds of rejection that never happens. I can see that I beg and plead for love that is freely offered because I somehow believe that if I don't ask for it, everyone will forget about me: I will be a little kid sent off to sleep-away camp whose parents forget to meet her at the bus when she comes back in August. Or else I think people are nice to me only to be nice to me, that they feel sorry for me because I am such a loser—as if anyone could possibly be that generous.

I am clearly nuts. Max and Jason are threatening to come down here and fetch me if I don't come home soon—and I feel abandoned!

I can see that I only feel that way because, compared to my mom, who won't leave me alone, no one else can ever get close enough.

I am cursed with this. Cursed with a personality that feels too much or too little, and never the right thing. So now I am taking drugs, never to feel again.

*O*kay, *so I admit that I am crazy, but I am onto something: The cohesion is gone. Most of my twenties were a college hangover. People watch the show* Friends *and complain that it is inaccurate—people that young and broke don't really live in grand SoHo lofts, do they? And still they watch it. They think they are tuning in to some kind of fantasy about single people in New York City, but in my experience it is pretty accurate. My friends and I always lived in great big apartments. Henry and Ryan had a whole brownstone in Greenwich Village to themselves because they rented it from a travel writer who would only occasionally stop by on brief reprieves from her excursions to the Caribbean and the Amazon. Or sometimes her screwy daughter from Bennington would show up on school vacations. Jason and I had that magical loft that we leased from the loony therapist in New Jersey. My buddy David lived in a huge apartment on the Lower East Side—granted, it had no windows and he shared it with a couple of junkies, but still. Daisy had a rent-controlled apartment with her sister and two friends in the Westbeth artists' community. And a bunch of us lived in a co-op on Lexington Avenue, with a doorman and a marble lobby, when we first got out of college. If you have good contacts—or you know how to read the* Village Voice *classified ads with a bit of perspicacity and persistence, you can live large for cheap.*

And we all used to have relatively undemanding jobs. I worked on my New Yorker *column—wrote it and turned it in and edited it—for three days a month, with the other twenty-eight available for lounging and hanging out. But now our careers have gotten serious, with corner offices and assistants and the authority to make decisions that matter, and downtime is scarce. Now that we all have money, we live alone in these wretched studio apartments that cost two thousand dollars a month. We are all still single—which makes us a statistical anomaly if you believe the U.S. Census—but we hardly ever see each other. We are all out looking for love, mostly in bad places. Sunday brunch once a week, or dinner out once in a fortnight, is not a lot of time to keep up with close friends. I never had a real family, and I have spent the rest of my life looking for one. I liked living communally, and I don't like the way that's just not happening any longer. I don't like growing up.*

I think of the opening scene of Wim Wenders' 1987 film Wings of Desire, *when the angel lands on Earth and peers into all the different windows in Berlin buildings, and at all the solitary lives that go on in each apartment. All these people living as close together as neighbors in urban centers do, with women crying and men yelling, and everybody so all alone. Here are all these people, in such close physical proximity, each one of them desperate and in need of an angel to save his heart or her soul from this desolation, and yet none of them can know or help each other. None of them can reach through the walls to touch anyone else's loneliness, and so the angel watches all of them through the glass panes of their lives, and he is horrified by the alienation he sees.*

So I am glad that Max and Jason want to come down here and make sure I am all right and take me back home with them. But I've got a question to ask: What happens when we get back there? Are you going to take me in and be with me and make me feel surrounded with love again?

But I don't have to ask. I already know. And I am full of hate.

The cocaine arrives at 10 A.M. Federal Express gets it to me just under the wire of what they consider, in their slogan, the world on time. I open the cardboard envelope, and there in a Glad baggie sealed with tape is what should be an eightball of cocaine. Some of it has spilled out, so I bring the envelope over to the coffee table, turn it upside down, and hit it so that some white powder pours out. Then I rip the thing open so that it's like a manila folder, and scrape it thoroughly with my MasterCard so that every little bit of powder is pulled out of the crevices in the porous paper. I am about to throw it out, but I decide to save it so I can eke out some more if it comes to that, which it will.

Max, who claims to no longer be interested in coke, is clearly enthusiastic enough about the stuff to have kept a fair share for himself. Damn him! Or rather, let him. He's been good enough to get the stuff for me; I should be more grateful and forgiving. I should be.

I cut up lines from the spillage, and snort it up. I don't do my usual coke ritual of pushing the powder around artfully, making segments fat and thin, long and short, doing creative drug geometry, the sacrament of whiteness. I just move it into bits and sniff it up. I get the rush, the syrupy saccharine sensation, but it's not the same as it once was. If only it were always as good as the first time. With cocaine you only get one shot of deliciousness, and after that it's all just chasing the dragon, hoping that somewhere between the baby laxative and lidocaine and inositol that it's cut with, there is still that great grand blow to the brain. I feel the freeze in my nose that drips down to my throat and tongue, and it's not the best, but still, I feel myself smiling.

I call Max to thank him, and I am happy enough that I don't mention that there is more cocaine missing than I ever consented to.

I want to be careful with it, make it last a week. That's my plan. But with cocaine, the laws of conservation and caution get defenestrated fast. The cocaine disappears fast. That's what it does. The joke is: What do you do on cocaine? More cocaine.

Within two days it is gone, I am on the phone with Max asking him to find more, and he just tells me to get my butt down to Miami and cop myself. He will not be party to my party, or my dissolution, or whatever it is that is going on down here.

I try to think of a new reason for Dr. Singer to prescribe me some Ritalin sooner than she is supposed to. I try. And I'm stumped. Addicts will do anything for drugs, will find a way always, will land in an SST on any corner of the globe, and will somehow unearth cocaine or heroin or whatever they need among the Aborigines in the outback or the Pygmy people on the dark continent or among the holy lamas of Tibet. But I'm stumped.

There's got to be a better way. There must be some unscrupulous degenerate who will help me out.

And then I remember Ray.

Five

SUPPLY AND DEMAND

From each according to his ability, to each according to his needs.

KARL MARX
Critique of the Gotha Program

Last I spoke to Ray, he was an art director at a huge ad agency that's part of the kind of global conglomerate that also makes processed cheese and hairdryers. It should not be too hard to find him. He was one of Ruby's high school boyfriends, he was a bass player in some cool Dischord Records DC-punk band, and she flipped for him. I figure if I fail to find him through the switchboard, I can always get his number through her.

Shit. Yet another person I have not spoken to for too long, whom I will have to apologize to for being out of touch for too long, and as far as I know, Ruby is working for the World Bank in Odessa. I suppose I can find her through *their* switchboard. I'd have to find a good excuse for needing to reach Ray badly enough to track her down in Ukraine to get his number. *Oy vey.* I guess I could just tell her I'm on deadline and need some speed, which she knows he has, and she would probably find that reasonable enough. After all, I made her miserable first wedding just barely bearable by getting her and all the bridesmaids fucked up on whatever coke I had back then. Now that she has divorced her husband and is engaged to someone else, she probably would not mind doing me a favor.

And then it hits me: I can just call information and get Ray's number like a normal person would. All that scheming, and it turns out to be no problem. He's listed.

Ray is happy to hear from me. Long time no see is what he says. He starts to tell me about his new band, it's called Down Boy or something having to do with dogs, and he's been writing great songs. He wants to send me a tape. I say that's fine. A waste of time, but fine.

For the life of me I do not understand why musicians want me to listen to their demos. I don't write about music anymore. Even when I did, it was only about big, huge bands. Occasionally I would mention a newly signed act that I wanted to give some attention to, but that was never what my New Yorker column was about. It was meant to explain phenomena, not create them.

Still, I tell him to send me his tape. But I want him to send me some Ritalin too. It's no secret that, for his own perverse reasons, Ray has had three different psychiatrists convinced he has ADHD and prescribing medication for it, mainly because he thinks it's funny to see how gullible doctors are. I appreciate his sense of humor. It is sick and strange, but at this point I too would like to have this kind of psychopharmacological grift going on. It occurs to me that maybe I should try to find a therapist in Florida to write me Ritalin prescriptions. I could probably pull it off. But I am starting to think that I am too apparently sickly at this point to get any decent doctor to do anything with me other than send me to the hospital. I've lost twenty pounds in the last few months. I look gaunt and drawn, or at least I do to myself. Plus the amount of effort it would take to be in therapy is almost not worth it. I don't want to talk; I just want drugs. Even the weekly contact I keep with Dr. Singer—and frequently I just forget to bother to call her, claiming a lack of long-distance service—is more than I can stand.

So I tell Ray the same thing I told Max. I am on deadline, I need to finish my book in a month, I need to stay awake constantly, and I want to buy his Ritalin off of him. He also has some Dexedrine, he tells me. Which would I prefer?

And I want to say, Both. I want to say, Send me everything you've got. But once again, I cannot sound desperate, or he'll know that that's exactly what I am, and even if he is kind of a creep, I don't think Ray wants to get involved with my addiction. I have to keep giving him the impression that this is an emergency measure, nothing more.

Then he asks me how much I want. He wants me to give him two dollars a pill. It's not really a profit-making scheme, but without insurance, that's about what it costs, with a little bit of extra money for his trouble.

Once again, I want to tell him to send me everything he's got. But I don't dare. "One bottle should do it," I say. And he tells me he'll send it through the office's DHL account. There'll be no charge for postage and handling.

So I'm back to doing the math. Ray has three prescriptions, two for Ritalin, one for Dexedrine. If I contrive a way to get his whole supply—he says he likes to use them occasionally, but he's been taking St. John's wort for his depression and finds that's just as good—that means I'll have 360 a month from him. Then there's my 120 pills, so it all adds up to 480. That comes out to sixteen a day, and I'm not keeping track, but I have a feeling that won't be enough. On the other hand, if I figure on, say, ten days a month when I do nothing but sleep—and that's about right—then I end up with twenty-four pills a day. That should probably do it.

But maybe not. I don't know anymore.

I could fill in the empty days with cocaine or crystal meth or some other street drug, but unless I find a connection down here, that's not going to work. I've been told that you can crush up No-Doz and snort it, and I've been told that if you empty a capsule of Dexatrim, that can give you a buzz. I've even heard that if you open up a Contac and know which color granule is the speedy stuff—I forget if it's the red or the yellow—and separate it out, you can have some fun with that. I feel like a junkie figuring that Robitussin will keep him from going through withdrawal. It's no substitute for heroin, but it will save you from delirium tremens in a pinch.

And inspiration comes from an unlikely source. I am reading *Allure* on the afternoon that I've spoken to Ray, and, realizing I have two more days until I get the pills from him, I'm not feeling terribly sanguine. Lo and behold, there is an article about nutritional supplements, about health-food store products that are supposed to help with beauty and energy. The reporter mentions something called Escalation, which contains ephedra, among other things. Apparently this natural substance is stimulating enough to have been banned by the International Olympic Committee. *Banned!* My eyes light up, I think I see stars. *Anything* that has been banned by *anyone* must be something I'd like. The writer says that when she took Escalation, it made her so agitated and speedy that she could not stop washing her dishes for two hours. Okay, so she's a civilian, she doesn't know what it is to get really wired, but this will probably do *something* for me.

I run over to Wild Oats, the health food emporium that is just across Sunrise Boulevard, maybe a block away as the crow flies. I find Escalation and buy it, along with some leafy salad vegetables—kind of the way you buy *Time* magazine along with *Penthouse* so no one suspects you are just a pervert—and some arnica cream for these strange sores I am starting to get all over my body from scratching too much. And then I run home.

I try, at first, to empty the Escalation capsules out—the powder inside is white, which I think is a good sign. But it all just turns to mush when I try to separate it into lines. Clearly this is not going to be snortable. Then I remember about the elderly people who use pill crushers so that they can take their medication with orange juice since they can't swallow anything too big, and I decide to dissolve the capsule contents in some grapefruit juice, which I just happen to have. I drink it down. I don't exactly get a tickly thrill. I certainly don't have any great desire to wash dishes. But it does something.

Something. Not much. But I can use it when there's nothing else. That's good. That's very good.

A couple of days after my supply arrives from Ray, it's time for me to get my regular, legitimate Ritalin prescription. I decide it is time to start counting pills. It's time to calculate the damage.

I have this little notebook, it's maybe one by two inches, that Dr. Singer suggested I buy when I was still in New York, to keep track of my moods. I was supposed to write down numbers, in the range of +5 to –5, every few hours, so we could plot my emotions and make a graph out of them after a month or so, and figure out just how bad things were. Or how good they were. I did this exercise for a few days before I got bored with it, and figured if I was at the point in life where I was assigning numbers to my feelings from hour to hour, I might just as well run away to Florida, because life had gotten this ridiculous.

I decide to use this little notebook, which is really quite cute—it is bound in leather and has tiny blue pages that are thin and soft—to keep track of when I take my pills, and how many. The idea is that four is the acceptable amount, and for every pill I take on a given day that is over that amount, I will assign a negative integer, so it will be –1, –2, –3, and so on.

The first day I try to do this, I get all the way up to –34. After that, I figure, why bother? This is out of hand. I know it is. Still, I know that Ritalin is not supposed to be addictive, so I don't figure this is really a problem—I decide it is simply odd behavior. Extremely odd behavior. But as soon as I decide I've had enough of this, I'll just stop. I'll be able to stop. Eventually I will tire of this routine as I tire of everything else, and it will be over.

In the meantime, I better make sure I have enough to keep up with what appears to be a habit of forty pills a day. Or at least thirty-five. I call Ray and tell him I want some more Ritalin and Dexedrine. I tell him I'm not working quickly enough, this no-sleep routine may be going on for a while. I remember that he once told me that *Prozac Nation* was an important cultural document—those were his exact words. So obviously he thinks my work matters, that I am the producer of *important cultural documents*. Surely he will want to support this effort. Surely he will be a willing party to my con.

And sure enough, "How much do you need?" he asks, and I sense he isn't going to judge me.

"Just send me everything you've got. Okay?"

And indeed, it is okay. God bless other people's irritating high school boyfriends.

I am reading *Vanity Fair;* it is the Hollywood issue. This activity actually passes for research, because there is an article in it by a woman who, when she was a teenager, knew the thirteen-year-old girl who slept with Roman Polanski.

Since I am writing about troubled teenage girls, and Polanski's affairs with much younger women has come up many times in this particular chapter, this magazine memoir is germane to my work. In the first paragraph, the author establishes she fell in with a fast crowd in Hollywood, that she had been up to no good long before she met this girl or Roman, long before she'd encountered Roman in some decadent hot tub. "I'd already been sent away for treatment for Ritalin addiction," she writes.

Ritalin addiction? *Excuse me?*

Ah, so. Maybe this happens to people. Here I am, thinking that everything is fine—well, not fine, but you know what I mean—because I am abusing a drug that's basically for six-year-olds. What I am doing with my chopping and snorting is, I figure, at worst embarrassing, and at best helpful to my work. Yes, I know there is something troubling about my behavior, I have a feeling that I am basically gobbling crank with my nose. But the idea that this could happen to *other* people, the possibility that I am not the first person to come up with this activity, that I am not the only one to have invented the wheel, has never occurred to me. Never. The prospect of kids in high school doing the same thing, as long ago as the early seventies, no less, that this is a recognized form of drug abuse, that this is nothing new and may even be common—well, this is definitely news to me. Even when I have wondered how I will ever stop, I could not imagine walking into an NA meeting and talking about addiction to Ritalin. Everyone would laugh! It's just too weird and smarmy, too pathetic. So uncool.

Ritalin is too tender and childish to rate as an addictive substance.

But I guess it is. I guess it must be. I am a Ritalin addict.

Hello, my name is Elizabeth, and I am a Ritalin addict. Probably a cokehead too, while we're on the subject.

All right, so, we've established what I am. We've given it a name. And, according to this article, people have been known to check into hospitals to get help for it.

Of course, I cannot even think about that right now. I have a book to write. I need to do that. But when it's done, maybe next month—I can last that long—I am going to get professional help. I will fess up to Dr. Singer and I will go into treatment.

Oh yes, I will. Just because I am not going to tell her about it right away, just because I am still going to get more pills from Ray, just because I am going to continue with my forty-a-day habit does not mean I am in denial. I am fine. I am truly fine. I just don't have time to stop this right now.

One night in Florida I walked through a parking lot on the way home from a movie, I looked up at the stars all out like a planetarium, I smelled gardenias and Mexican food, I thought about getting back to my apartment and getting high, and I said to myself, This is a dream. I told myself, Someday I will look back on this time as the golden age.

I am happy and free. There are no unreturned phone calls because I don't talk to anybody anymore. There is no rejection because I don't try. I write like crazy. Nothing gets to me. Drugs work. When they work, they work.

I first started to use cocaine because of the phone. It was always the phone. Let's say I liked some guy. It was the middle of the day, he was at work, and I'd call. He'd say, I'm in a meeting, honey—he'd call me honey because he liked me too—and he'd say, I'll call you in five. Five would turn to ten and then twenty more minutes, and I'd be a wreck. Lots of people get nervous waiting for the phone to ring, wondering if she'll call, or if he is still interested after our first date—that's just human. But me, I can't handle the twenty minutes it takes for someone who I know likes me to call back. I am so fucking empty. So I call friends. I ask will he call. They reassure me: it's all a lot of anxiety. Obviously I am not fit to date. I'm in my late twenties, and I don't have the emotional resilience to do what it takes to get into a relationship.

So things fall apart before they start, and I'm always alone. So I date more than one person at once so that the fear of it not working with one is mitigated by the fear that it won't work with another and so on, and I do drugs to mitigate the fear of the whole thing. I do cocaine to get through the twenty minutes of waiting for a returned call. If I don't, I cry like a baby until it rings. I'm ridiculous.

This is how you become an addict. You have no inner resources, you drive people crazy with all your neediness, years go by, you don't grow up, people lose patience, and all that's left is whatever gets you through. Lots of people will go out on a binge if they get fired or if their girlfriend leaves, but not me. That stuff, I can handle. For me, it's the broken shoelaces that have got me hooked. That's what the Matt Dillon character says in Drugstore Cowboy—*he's saying it's the small, stupid shit that makes him use. It's the stuff that most people can handle that makes addicts get high. We get high over nothing.*

And in Florida, there's nothing to get high over, I have no life, I have eliminated the cause, and I've still got the solution.

You want to know why I didn't check myself in as soon as I read that article in Vanity Fair? *Do you really need to ask?*

Most addicts are not even aware that they have a problem until long after they've been dragged into treatment, until they've had an intervention session with their family and friends, until they've been fired and gone bankrupt and all that. But I knew I had a problem of some sort, I knew I needed to get help, and once I'd finished reading that article, I even made a mental note to look into my options. Maybe I was only halfway through. Maybe I even made that decision after reading that first paragraph. As soon as the idea was put into my head, I never resisted it.

And yet, I did. There is a special kind of denial that is completely postmodern, something that only awareness of addiction—whether it's via public service campaigns or from seeing Betty Ford interviewed by Larry King—can produce: the nondenial denial. It used to be that you'd actually say that you weren't a drunk, sometimes you had a few too many, but nothing outlandish. Nowadays you can't get away with that; knowledge of the nature of dependency is too pervasive. So you start to have people like me, people who say, I am an addict and I like it, try and stop me.

Six

YOUR FRIENDS AND NEIGHBORS

Kathy I'm lost, I said
Though I knew she was sleeping
I'm empty and aching and I don't know why

PAUL SIMON
"America"

I knock on Wendie's door one morning before she goes to work, and ask if I can borrow her cat for the day. Wendie lives in an identical apartment in the same building. So far our only contact has been the time my mother left her car idling in front of Wendie's parking space, so she came up to ask my mom to move it out of the way. I can't say she was hostile or even especially annoyed, but she treated it like one of the many inconveniences that adds to the unbearableness of daily life. I notice, when I watch Wendie walk out her door to run errands, that there is a yarmulke-sized spot on the back of her head that looks shorn, there is only peach fuzz there. I know that it is trichotillomania, that she tears out her own tresses, that something is wrong with her, with her bitter face.

But she says sure about the cat, a runty little all-white female called Spot, which is a cleverly ironic name—I like that, it means Wendie has some moxie, some simpatico sensibility—and I carry the thing up to my apartment. I explain that I have a cat back in New York, where I really live, where my real life is, which I will be returning to any week now, or any month. I miss my cat terribly. He is this huge, ridiculous tabby who only has eyes for me. When I went to the pound to adopt a kitten, I really wanted a girl, partly because I think of all cats as girls, mostly because I had a bunch of names picked out that wouldn't work for a male animal. But Zap, as I called him temporarily and then permanently when I couldn't come up with anything better, jumped out of his cage, pushed himself in front of the whole litter, clung to my hair, got tangled in it, and could not be pulled out.

"You may not want him, but he sure does want you," the attendant said to me with a smile. "I think he's yours." So I took him. I meant to get a second one, one of the shy she-kittens who did not have the instinct for survival that Zap clearly had, but my roommate at the time was allergic, so even one was too much.

Zap grew to be eighteen pounds, and he is the happiest, mellowest, portliest creature I have ever encountered. He's sweet and loving toward me, even after we've moved so many times, even after he's been left alone with strangers while I've run away as I always do. For some reason, he's turned out well. I did something right with him. I'm neurotic and undependable, and it has had no effect on his personality. He's always happy to see me when I come home. If I step on his foot because he is walking underfoot because he follows me everywhere, he doesn't hiss and pout and stay away from me for a while like most cats do. He just forgets about it, because he loves me too much to afford to be angry. In this, he is like me. I guess I should say he *needs* me too much to stay angry; he is a house cat, and I am his whole world.

Zap is the only animate creature I miss here in Florida. Unfortunately, Spot is bashful and even a little mean, and having her at the house for the day is nothing great. She doesn't sit on my lap while I write and snort lines. What's the point?

I bring Spot back down to Wendie when I see her car pull up at six that night. I see that she has a VCR. I am the only person I know who doesn't have one, not even at home in New York—I barely have a TV at all. I just have a small white one that is bulbous like an iMac, which my mom passed down to me one year, so I'd have some way to see important news events, like the O. J. Simpson verdict. It only gets reception for Channel 4 in New York, which is NBC, so sometimes I watch Leno and Conan, but otherwise I live in a DMZ, a de-mediafied zone. It's not, by the way, a matter of principle: I am just too disorganized to go to P.C. Richard or The Wiz to buy one, I have no idea how easy it is to call Time Warner and order cable, I have no sense that the simple things in life really are simple. Also, the only credit card I have has a thousand-dollar limit, so I'd have to do the whole transaction with cash, which I never seem to have enough of on me at any given time, and I only recently learned that televisions tend to cost less than a thousand dollars.

By the way, I don't have a wallet full of credit cards, even in an age when sophomores in college have eight-thousand-dollar spending limits on their

gold and platinum plastic, because no financial institution will have me. I de-
faulted on my student loans, I neglected to pay my taxes for a year or two, and
I have a TRW rating that would put me far below those of most South American debtor nations. If Argentina were a person, she'd be me. It's not that I am
trying to cheat the government or the bank—or anyone else for that matter—
but for an entire year I didn't open my mail and didn't pay bills. I didn't know
I was in trouble until my assets were frozen, which I figured out when I
couldn't get money out of my bank account one night at an ATM. I'd been
sent notices by the IRS and the student loan people repeatedly, but I never saw
them in the heap of stepped-on, crushed-up letters and packages on the corner of my bedroom floor, among the envelopes with glassine windows that
were dirtied by my shoe prints after I ceased to even try to walk around them.
Of course, I certainly wouldn't have opened them if I'd seen the things, because anything that has a return address from the Treasury Department cannot be good news, and I was too strung out to handle bad tidings. Finally some
guy from the IRS started ringing my buzzer and harassing me—they actually
do that, you know, it's not just in the movies—but all that did was frighten me
more. Like most heroin abusers, which I was at the time, I didn't deal with
anything I could avoid, I didn't deal with most things I couldn't avoid, so nothing ever got done until it became an emergency. I am 911 girl. Since then I
have turned everything over to a CPA, who, for a percentage of my income,
pays my bills and gives me an allowance because I am too irresponsible to
manage it myself. He co-signed for the one credit card that I have.

That pile of unopened mail, which pretty much covers all of 1995 and
some of 1996, still sits in a garbage bag waiting to be unsealed. Perhaps this is
apocryphal, but I've been told that Napoleon did not read his correspondence
until three weeks after it arrived, because he believed that any urgent matters
would be cleared up by themselves during that time, and anything else could
wait. I would like to say that I was that philosophical about ignoring my mail,
but like the lack of TV, it's all disorganization and fear of what I might find out.
It's like a whole life in paper envelopes that I can hide from. But I guess even
Napoleon had his Waterloo, so maybe he wasn't so clever.

Here in Florida I have the television on constantly, I love it, I can't write
without the background hum of CNN or a matinee broadcast of A Face in
the Crowd. I can't imagine how I ever lived without it. Maybe I'll do something about it when I go back home someday. At any rate, I tell Wendie to
knock on my door if she wants to rent a movie sometime. Amazingly, she has
never seen a Woody Allen flick, she's never heard of Frank Capra or Billy
Wilder, she knows nothing of Five Easy Pieces or Nashville, so she is a captive

audience for my film erudition, such as it is. She becomes a new person I can lecture about the philistinism of America in general, and Blockbuster in particular. When we go to the video store one day and they don't have *Sweet Smell of Success*, I hit the ceiling, I become irate at the poor clerk and ask to speak to a manager, I can't believe they don't have one of the best movies ever for rent.

Blockbuster is based in Fort Lauderdale, and I decide I should call their public relations department and, as a member of the press corps, ask why they are so ridiculous, why they don't treat America's film history more respectfully. Why do they have so many crappy movies that I would not go see in a theater six months prior? Don't they understand that if I wouldn't leave the house to see it, I certainly would not want to sully my own apartment with such crap? And the poor woman in the PR office doesn't know what to say. She tells me something about public demand, and I tell her something about *creating* public demand, about encouraging people to see good stuff instead of shit; I say build it and they will come. We end it all with her sending me a letter explaining that there is a well-stocked classics section at every Blockbuster branch, and she adds a box of videotapes that includes *Psycho* and *The Birds* and *Vertigo*—and *Sweet Smell of Success*, besides. My main thought is that they didn't even send any *obscure* Hitchcock—*Shadow of a Doubt* or *Marnie*, say—but I guess they are trying, though this solves nothing. *I've* already seen these movies—it is the ignorant masses I'm worried about.

I spend several days just snorting lines and thinking about the ignorant masses. I send a check to the American Film Institute's project to preserve old movies, to make new prints of film stock that is wearing out. I decide I should really support the archive of greatness. I harangue my mother, my relatives, and Wendie about the evils of cultural ignorance, and they kind of listen, but I can tell I exhaust their patience.

Is this an early sign of mental degeneration? "One of the symptoms of an approaching nervous breakdown is the belief that one's work is terribly important," Bertrand Russell once said. Since I write about movies, I suppose this fury constitutes work.

Meanwhile, all the same, Wendie and I become fast friends. It's kind of like Rhoda and Mary. In New York, no one knows their neighbors, no one befriends them, so I think this is pretty neat. I guess I do need someone to talk to who is actually nearby. I cut up lines of Ritalin on Wendie's coffee table with *Double Indemnity* playing on the twenty-four-inch TV set, and she does not question what I am doing. I explain that it's medication, and this is just how I like to take it, and she doesn't pursue it. The girl tears her own hair out—

though she never mentions it to me—so she can hardly fault me for what I do. She thinks it's funny, a little bit. One day I try to make her snort some up with me, but she demurs, and we don't discuss it further.

On weekends sometimes we drive to Town Center or Mizner Park in Boca Raton. We go shopping at Bloomingdale's and Saks, and have brunch at the Cheesecake Factory. I order omelettes and frozen peach drinks with no liquor, because it is only very gentle food that my stomach can tolerate. I indoctrinate Wendie with knowledge of albums she really should buy—the first Violent Femmes record is essential, and I can't believe she has *no* Bob Dylan—and I recommend books I think she would like. I tell her she is *so* lucky to never have read *The Executioner's Song* or *In Cold Blood*, because that means that she has something amazing to look forward to—and then I realize that everything I love involves murder. Wendie is a paralegal at a law office in Miami, and she is planning to go to night school to become an attorney; the firm will pay for it. She comes from a small town about two hours from Cleveland, and she is as interested in culture as anybody when you put it in front of her. But like everyone else in Florida, she doesn't seek it on her own. It is useful for her to learn all the things I teach her, and I suppose my condescension gives me some kind of opportunity to feel superior to somebody, which is nice for me because I feel so low.

But there's more: I actually like Wendie. She is an odd girl and seems to have only a couple of friends, whom she hardly sees. She's hiding, just like me. She should be living in Miami, where young people frolic in their communal swimming pools and housing complexes, where the News Café is open all night, and there is fun stuff to do. But Wendie isn't much interested in indulging in the life of a single gal in the Sun Belt. She broke up with some guy a couple of years ago, they'd lived together for a long time, they'd met back in Ohio and came down here together. Ever since, she doesn't date, doesn't go to parties, doesn't do much of anything but sit in her apartment—and now she sits in her apartment with me. In some ways though, I admire her life. If only I could not mind sequestering myself in my apartment alone in New York with no plans on a Saturday night. Maybe if I got a TV and VCR, that would work. Maybe that's my problem. I need to domesticate my life. I decide when I get back to New York, I will set up my little aerie in such a way that I never need to leave.

My friends do start to wonder where I am, why they don't hear from me. On the rare occasions that I pick up the phone while someone is droning on my answering machine—going on about being concerned and am I okay—I just say it's nothing, I am working hard, I'm fine. Or sometimes I'll try: You know how I am, out of sight, out of mind. It will be back to normal when I get back to New York, which should be next month. We'll hang out. We'll have lunch.

Kathlyn stops in Florida to see me on her way home from doing due diligence on a rental car company in Belo Horizonte, a city in Brazil. She has to switch planes in Miami, or so she says, so she figures she should check up on me. Kathlyn is my best friend. She has thought I have a problem with drugs for a long time, has refused to share a summer house with me (she tells me later) because she does not want cocaine in her midst, but I tell her I am doing fine now. I am in Florida, I am writing my book, I am carefree, and I am clean.

Well, okay, I am snorting my Ritalin prescription, and maybe I am taking a little too much, but I think this is, comparatively speaking, a triumph.

We sit at my kitchen table, this modest work of glass, and talk. I tell her it is time for my medication, that I hope she does not mind if I snort it. She can hardly object in my own home, so I cut up lines and inhale them with a twenty-dollar bill that has been rolled up, coated with snot and sticky white powder, for quite some time.

She looks horrified, but I tell her this is just an alternative method of transmission, it's a prescription, it's fine.

"Well, whatever you say," she says, like whatever I say is nuts.

Kathlyn is probably my favorite person in the world. She is a venture capitalist who speaks Spanish and Portuguese, so she works a lot in South America. She is obscenely smart, the only person I know who understands how the commodities market works, and can explain it so that I understand. Barron's quotes her all the time. She grew up in Reseda, California, the same godforsaken place that Erin Brockovich comes from. She has been working since she was fifteen, she once had a job at Kmart; and she once had a job at a concession in a mall that sold things—candles, sachets—that smelled like peaches.

Kathlyn is what most people mean when they talk about a fiery redhead: She is half Irish and half Ecuadoran, with serious tits and ass, and you definitely do not want to have a fight or disagreement with her, because you won't get off the hook easily. But for someone so outspoken, she is also painfully shy. She does not like many people, keeps to herself, has only a few friends. She does not—she cannot—suffer fools. So she would not be my friend if she did not adore me, and I think she is fast becoming disgusted and sad. I love her to death, I hate how she is disappointed in me, I feel terrible that the only reason I returned her most recent phone call was because she threatened to visit.

"When are you coming home?" she asks.

"Next month, I think," I lie. But I am not really lying, because I still believe I will come home soon. I know, but don't quite know, that I am in Florida hiding, and that I prefer it that way. I know, but I don't know, quite a lot.

Kathlyn spends the night at my apartment instead of returning to the Breakers in Palm Beach, which would certainly be much nicer for her. She says she doesn't want to leave me here. She says it over and over again. She says I can get on a plane with her, that my mother can pack up my stuff and send it up to me, that she thinks I should just get out of here now. It's been too long; she doesn't want to lose me.

She doesn't want to lose me.

This is the theme of our evening.

Sometime after midnight, we both lie against the backboard of the bed, trying to read ourselves to sleep under the halogen lights built into the frame. Kathlyn's got some new translation of *The Brothers Karamazov* that she's been trudging through for the last year, I've been stuck on page 15 of *Middlemarch* for the last month, and I consider this scene and realize we are both such goofballs.

"You know, I've got the new *Vogue*. It's right next to the bed if you're interested," I say.

She picks it up and flips through it, she reports that ladylike clothes will be an important look this spring, I start doing the *Times* puzzle like I do every day, and then I break down.

"Look, I know I have a problem." I pause. "After my book is finished, I'm going to get serious help with the drugs. I'll check in somewhere or something. I know I need help. I'm not kidding myself."

"When is this going to happen?"

"Soon." I'm not lying. I really do believe it will be soon. *Soon* doesn't mean the same thing to me that it does to most people, of course, because I'm on speed and I'm in a place without seasons. I don't even know what month it is.

"Okay," Kathlyn says. "Promise?"

"Promise."

But it's back to the same old thing. It's back to: *then what?* Then what happens when I get back? Okay, we've established that *then what* is probably some kind of hospital. So I check myself in, I clean up, and then we're back to *then what* again. Because I really don't think I have a drug problem—I think I have a *life* problem. There are people who are born to be addicts. They have their first sip of beer at eleven, and they know they've found their answer. But I didn't get addicted until relatively late in life, until I'd been in treatment for depression, until love disappointed me, until the publication of my book failed to do for me whatever it is I wanted it to do for me. Save me, I guess. I've been looking for salvation my whole life.

Kathlyn lies sleeping in the bed next to me, all her worries just make her somnolent. She is so cute when she sleeps. It's such a contrast to her toughness, her tightness when she's awake. And I can't interrupt her calm, but I want to wake her and say that I'm lost, I'm scared, and I can't give up drugs or leave Florida because of the *then what* problem. If I had an answer for that, I'd get on a plane with her right now. But I'm on strike from life. Until conditions improve, I will sit in my emptiness, fill myself with drugs, and wait for word about negotiations, because I can't negotiate for myself anymore.

Fix it. That's what I wish someone would do. Fix life, and I will live again.

Seven

THE KILLER INSIDE ME

No matter how bad things are, they can always get worse.

ERNEST LEHMAN
Executive Suite

become obsessed with Timothy McVeigh. When he bombed the Murrah
Federal Building in Oklahoma City in 1995, I barely noticed, except to be impressed that some highway patrolmen caught him so easily after he was pulled
over because he'd forgotten to replace his license plates after he'd left the
crime scene. But I've never been much interested in terrorism. It seems like
someone else's problem. Which I guess is why everyone else is all hyped up
about this debacle: it occurred on American soil, it was committed by an
American, it is our problem after all.

If I did not spend so much time watching Court TV, I'm sure I would not
even notice that McVeigh is on trial in the spring of 1997. But the television is
on all the time, I write at my little fold-out desk, my powdered-up pills and
straw-rolled dollar bills to my left, the remote control to my right, my mug of
tea wherever there is room, piles of paper on the floor next to me, my whole
life contained within a three-foot radius of space.

McVeigh's trial in the federal courthouse in Denver is not broadcast, but I
don't care. Night after night I watch the summaries on Court TV, the post-
mortems with his attorneys, with victims' parents and grandparents and first
cousins and next-door neighbors and fourth-grade teachers, with legal analysis
on MSNBC, with guests on *Rivera Live!*, with discussions on CNN. My God,
with cable TV you could spend twenty-four hours a day watching earlier
broadcasts run and rerun over and over again! What a boon for a speed freak!
I know that the eight o'clock shows are repeated at eleven, the nine o'clock

shows come on again at midnight. Larry King twice in three hours! If I miss a single detail, I can always catch it again. The best legal reporter is by far and away Dan Abrams of Court TV (and later onto bigger and better things at NBC), and I watch his dispatches with great interest. At one point I even call him, hoping to discuss the situation, and he returns the message.

Apparently, he is familiar with my first book. Who knew?

And then there is the Internet! Transcripts from the trial on government sites, articles from the daily *Denver Post* and the weekly *Rocky Mountain News*, and even the sound of Tim's voice on-line from an interview conducted with *Time* magazine. I've only just signed up with America Online, my account is unlimited, I hardly use the phone anyway, so I almost never bother to log off. Eventually, it is all Timothy, all the time.

But it is the muddle of it all that interests me. At the same time Tim is awaiting judgment, the JonBenet Ramsey case is stumping investigators in nearby Boulder and the Denver police are accused of racial harassment after they, for no apparent reason, stop and search some innocent black man driving along the highway. And then on April 2, an Air Force A-10 jet crashes into the Rocky Mountains in what is deemed an "unpremeditated" suicide during a training run. This occurs near Denver, the same week that six other military planes crash at other sites all over the world, prompting Dr. Sheila Widnal, the secretary of the Air Force, to make some speech about how these things happen, it's just one of those unfortunate coincidences that so many accidents have occurred in such a brief period.

Of course, I love the disaster of it all. I watch the cable news channels constantly for more information about all the stupid things going wrong all at once, and plot a trip to Denver in my mind, an excursion I am too disorganized to actually organize, but one I cream over. I would love to go to the Mile High City. I would love to be in a place where everything is going bad and my insides could match the outside. But it isn't going to happen. Instead, locked up in my little treehouse, I laugh and laugh at the pitiful state of mankind, I laugh at all these people trying to make sense of the world while I am here safe, snorting speed, knowing it's impossible. Everyone is so serious and grave and sententious except for me. Is no one else in on the joke?

And the victims of Timothy McVeigh start to really irritate me, and not for no reason. Their bid for significance, their demands for closure, their need to describe the goodness and innocence of the dead, their insistence on filling airtime with their compulsion for attention—they don't seem to understand that they are irrelevant. Insofar as justice can and will be done for these people—and really, there is no justice when there are 168 dead—it is not about personality. For all we know, every single victim was a curmudgeonly creep, a drunk who beat his children, a kleptomaniac, a sex fiend who likes leather and runs up huge pay-per-view bills on the Spice channel. But it makes no difference. The focus on the nineteen children killed similarly infuriates me: I know that they are completely innocent, but no more so than the man who went into the building that day to get his Social Security card. I feel it is an automatic response to be outraged that four-year-olds were killed, but if you deconstruct that reflex, surely you realize that adults are a much greater loss, more costly to their *own* children. I feel that the gut-guidance of everyone's reaction to this tragedy gives me a reason to do drugs. It is one more complaint I've got about the world.

Our sympathy is already so firmly and fastidiously with the dead and the mourners that every time yet another one of them is interviewed by Katie Couric on the *Today* show, the only risk they take is in alienating us. They have nothing to gain—they've got all the public support they could possibly need or want—so I cannot understand why they persist.

For me, this becomes the apotheosis of the evil of media culture. It used to be that crime victims might shyly respond to a few reporters badgering them as they left an indictment hearing. They would look away, wanting privacy and feeling that eerie shame that you feel when you've been harmed for all the world to see; they would cower and ask to be left alone. Loudmouthed attorneys dealt with the newspaper columnists, spokesmen for the police department made their case on the eleven o'clock news. The victims were shell-shocked, expected to work out their hurt with friends and family and priests and counselors. I cannot fathom what makes these people think that a public discussion of their trauma will resolve it, will heal it in any way. It gives me the creeps.

And, if anything, it compels my interest in Timothy McVeigh. The victims are a dispersion of ordinary voices of pain, and I have been hearing about pain all my life. McVeigh is silent, McVeigh says nothing, McVeigh makes me curious. I am bored with the whole rest of the bunch of them. They iterate and reiterate, while he says nothing.

Everyone is for the death penalty. None of my friends, but most people, and in Florida I am among most people. Wendie is for it, the two flight attendants next door are, the two call girls who live down the catwalk are too. They've never even thought of the *possibility* that it is wrong. It is obvious to them that this is the thing to do.

This makes me huffy. It does anyway—I am a death-penalty abolitionist; I feel that in a hundred years, state-mandated killing will seem as obviously wrong as slavery does to us today. But amped up on Ritalin, my arguments get amplified as well. I am full of hate. I hate that so many people cannot make the cognitive leap that they must to recognize this evil, to understand that to have an orderly approach to killing a man—a menu for his last meal, a schedule of visitors in his last twenty-four hours, an allowance of one interview two days before—is infinitely sicker than the impulsive, insane nature of most murders. I'd rather they just handed a bunch of M-16s to the victims' families and friends and have them wreak havoc and revenge on the criminal—at least that would be natural, at least that would be *human*. Not humane, but human. The idea that a man in his holding cell on death row is put on suicide watch—heaven forbid he takes his own life and denies the executioners the opportunity to do it and punish him properly—defines the sickness of the whole business to me. "You may stand them up on the trap door of the scaffold, and choke them to death," Clarence Darrow argued at the trial of Leopold and Loeb, "but that act will be infinitely more cold-blooded, whether justified or not, than any act these boys have committed or can commit." I quote Darrow obsessively—he seems to have been the last attorney to talk a judge or jury out of imposing death on murderers.

In fact, I loll around reading Darrow's writings all the time. In my manic, mechanical focus under the influence, I cannot seem to stop myself from sitting on the floor with an anthology of the lawyer's essays and speeches, CNN or Court TV flashing and buzzing in the background, my legs folded underneath my thighs, my face pressed close to the pages, my shoulders rounded and hunched over, as if I am trying to curl my body around the brilliant rhetoric and take it all inside of me. I cannot separate myself from this book for long enough to get up for a glass of water or do anything besides snort the lines I've got cut up on the back of a copy of *Vanity Fair* I've got lying next to me. I don't change clothes or brush my teeth or bathe for days at a time. I scribble notes in the margins, I underline relevant passages—and eventually I realize that page after page is covered with purple and red and blue ink, that almost every word is underscored in bright colors. There are more of my markings in the book than there is text itself. My hands have imprints all over them; they are like the sponge you use to ink up a stamp. I rub my face, and I have color marks on my cheeks and forehead. I look like a child learning to finger-paint.

I memorize all these anti-death-penalty polemics because I have many people I must yell at, I have many people who need to be convinced that this policy is bad. I will go door to door all over Florida, I will be a Jehovah's Witness and vacuum cleaner salesman for this cause. Pensacola and the Panhandle are not safe. Watch out, Disney World! Be careful, Palm Beach! I am coming at you, and I will not leave until you agree to blow up every gas chamber and explode every electric chair! Certainly, my next-door neighbors will not be allowed to get away with not changing their minds about the death penalty. By the time I'm done with them, they will be agitating for penal reform; they will be petitioning to end the prison system as we know it.

I go downstairs to talk to Wendie, I go down the catwalk to harangue the flight attendants, and I explain why the death penalty is bad: No other Western democracy has it; when we kill criminals, we are on the level of Iraq and Iran. They say they don't want taxpayer money to be used to house murderers. I explain that the death penalty is more costly, that due process and appeals all add up to lots of money, and we want all these things to happen because we don't want anyone put to death wrongly. There is no evidence that it acts as any kind of deterrent; crazy people who murder usually aren't thinking about the consequences anyway. Also, there is the racial bias; almost everyone on death row is black or Hispanic and, above all, poor—there are no rich people among them. And, of course, what if one of the executees is innocent? That happens—a lot. DNA evidence has gotten many a man released from death row, and for many more it is already too late. Not that I care that much about all that—it's just a winning public argument, one that everyone can appreciate.

But those points are extraneous for me: I am much more interested in the moral implications. We already know that killers are bad people, but by using the death penalty, we become bad too. They've already done wrong, but the glee we get on our faces as we shout *burn, baby, burn* makes us ugly, makes us vengeful and sad, turns us into pathetic people. The opportunity to be merciful is one of the most beautiful rights that we have, the possibility that we can be better than the worst things that happen to us, that we can take the horror and use it as a way to become nobler—why should we pass up this chance? The death penalty forces decent people like me to be concerned about the fate of terrible people who have committed horrible acts. If we lock the door and throw the criminals away, they are forgotten, lost in the system. When they go on death row, they become a cause. Attention gets focused on them that could rightly be put to good use, to caring about the righteous instead of the sinful.

"Listen to me!" I yell. "I am appealing to you on behalf of very bad people! The death penalty is making me crazy!"

Okay, so maybe the drugs are making me crazy. But I perish that thought, while my neighbors look at me quizzically. "Why not just throw them all in with the lions in a public arena? Why not have gladiators? Why not let us all get in on this revenge in the guise of justice? Why not force them to suffer like their victims did? Lethal injection is far too kind!" Where am I going with this? Oh yes, I remember. *"Why not let us all have a good time?"* I scream.

And I go on. For hours maybe. To me, I explain, trying to be calm and reasonable, you are wrong to kill even the worst offender, even the confessed baby killer from El Paso or the triple murderer and rapist in Tucson should not die by the hand of the state—long live John Wayne Gacy and Ted Bundy and Jeffrey Dahmer and Aileen Wuornos. Even O. J. Simpson, who should almost be put to death for being such a gross idiot, only deserves life without parole. And without contact with the press.

I don't like being in this position. I don't like having to speak on behalf of saving the lives of people who hardly deserve to live. But I have no choice. I must do this, because no one else will. I don't like worrying about Tim McVeigh. And lately, it is almost all I do.

I start to follow the progress of the *Mir*, the Russian space station that is lost in space and falling apart. I check the Web site every day, to see what's up. Doors keep breaking, walls keep breaking, they lose contact with ground control. It seems to be the Edsel of rocket ships, or space shuttles, or whatever mode of transport it is. The mess has been going on since 1986. There are communication difficulties, fires and toxic fumes, and one fine day, while two *Mir* cosmonauts are floating outside the station, they find a bag of trash wedged in the docking port. In February 1997, I keep close watch on the situation as two cosmonauts battle a fire after an oxygen-generating canister bursts into flames during a routine ignition. They wear gas masks, because even their emergency escape capsule is filled with smoke. Then, in June, a cargo ship crashes into the *Mir*, the worst collision ever in space. The impact creates a hissing air leak, which the cosmonauts miraculously locate and seal off before losing too much oxygen. Of course, not long after the *Mir* went up into space in 1986, the Soviet Union collapsed, which doesn't help matters and becomes the all-purpose excuse for everything that goes wrong.

American physicists and astronauts go up to help out, but they end up getting in trouble themselves. The whole thing reminds me of cult stories I used to hear about in the seventies, when everyone knew someone who had joined up with the Moonies. Whenever friends and relatives went to the compounds and encampments to rescue their loved ones from the fakirs and gurus and charlatans who had taken them in, the rescuers would end up joining up themselves. It was a vacuum of spiritual malaise and brainwashing from which people with the best intentions could not escape.

That's how the *Mir* seems to be. People go to help out, and end up in a muck. I love following the calamity of it all, because I feel that the *Mir* and I are in it together. We are both falling apart, and yet somehow, neither of us is completely destroyed. We keep at it, indefatigable and persistent in our insistence that we just go on. If the *Mir* can make it, so can I.

Late at night, I try to figure out Tim McVeigh, and I try to figure out why I care.

Was Tim McVeigh not the worst-case scenario of a child of divorce gone wrong? The main reason for his turning into what he had become was depression. He had been in the army, a decorated soldier in the Gulf War — a pointless exercise in violence, a waste of a war. But Tim believed in it all. He had tried to become a Green Beret in the Special Forces unit at Fort Bragg, but he'd failed. His body was tired from the war, he had blisters on his feet from shoes that weren't broken in, and soon he ended up back in Pendleton, New York, unemployed and aimless. He was rejected for a job with the U.S. Marshals Service. He hooked up with antigovernment activists when no one else would have him, and he had no one else.

He got dumb jobs, he worked as a security guard, he drove an armored truck, he had crushes that didn't work out, he fucked an older woman who lost interest in him, he wrote insane letters to his local newspaper, isolation and disappointment turned him into a right-wing crank. One day he showed up at his grandfather's house barefoot and wearing only sweatpants in the middle of winter, ran inside and cried, contemplated suicide, decided against it, and then he looked for an alternative. He got into guns and bought four acres of land so he'd have a place to shoot. He drifted through Decker, Michigan, and Kingman, Arizona, and Herington, Kansas, and Waco, Texas. He baited guards at the installation called Area 51 in Roswell, New Mexico, the place where UFOs were supposed to have landed. He went to gun shows in Phoenix and Las Vegas and Shreveport. He even went to one in Fort Lauderdale, at the Broward Center, a multipurpose venue where you could also go see a run by the touring company of *Cats* when there were no conventions in town. He collected flare launchers and ammonium nitrate and assault weapons and automatic guns. When he stole fifty-pound crates of Tovex gelatin from a warehouse, he looked at the dates and grabbed the freshest ones, kind of the way I buy cartons of milk at the 7-Eleven for the Cocoa Krispies I am now living on.

Really, what's the difference between him and me, other than that I am a menace only to myself? Is it so much stranger to drive a Spectra around the country preaching Second Amendment patriotism than to lock yourself in a room in Fort Lauderdale and feed your head with drugs? Look, I know I have an expensive education and financial security, but that's just my good fortune. Everyone who is interested in Timothy McVeigh is interested in him for the same reason that I am: he's a nice, simple suburban kid gone very bad, rotten and murderous. Tom Brokaw describes him as "home-grown, an all-American boy." We all wonder what the variable was, the mutation that sent him off that way when he could have ended up pretty average, an employee of a mechanical plant or on an assembly line like his dad. To begin with, he is boringly normal—and then this.

So I start to feel sorry for him. You see, I feel his pain. I find all these victims and their sundry human attachments small and insignificant annoyances, petty idiots who do not understand the way the legal process works. Of course, I accept that Tim needs to be tried and punished. But I feel for him. I'm in love with Ritalin, and I feel for Tim McVeigh, and I worry about the *Mir*, and that is my life right now.

I start to drive people crazy with the death penalty. I alienate entire rooms of people, even if they agree with me, because I just yell. I ruin Friday night dinner with my relatives all the time, not just because they believe in the death penalty, but because they refuse to accept Tim McVeigh's essential humanity. I scream about the fact that if, for some odd reason, he actually were innocent, we would never know because it is not possible for him to get a fair trial. The courtroom is so biased by the tragedy of the victims that everyone seems to have forgotten that the onus is on the prosecution to prove that McVeigh did it—and not to prove that a really bad thing happened in Oklahoma City. I feel justice has been compromised all over the place, it drives me nuts, and I drive everyone else nuts haranguing them about it.

I can tell what they are thinking: Haven't you got better things to worry about it? Frankly, I want to say, I don't. So there. The government is taking lives as a matter of procedure, and I will not sit by silently and let this happen. I will not bring children into a world where I have to explain that we kill to prove killing is wrong! I rant and rave.

After a while, I start to sound as crazy as Timothy McVeigh once sounded when discussing how the government was eroding the rights of gun owners. I have turned into someone like him.

One day, I rail at people about legal procedure—about the fact that the *state* prosecutes a criminal, that the victims have to stop thinking that this is *their* case when it is, in fact, a matter of the law. The next day, I am back on the case about the horror of the death penalty. I yell on the telephone at anyone who will listen, which soon becomes no one. For the first time in months, I am contacting old friends, and it is only to scream about the injustices perpetrated against Timothy McVeigh. I do not understand why they want to talk about other things, to ask me how my writing is going or if I am enjoying the sun, when terrible things are going on all over the world. I scream: *Why are you asking me about my life when the whole universe is a mess and we have to live in it? Why why why?*

They all say the same thing. They all say: You need to get some help.

Eight

BEEN CAUGHT STEALING

Everybody has his reasons.

JEAN RENOIR
The Rules of the Game

I walk into Saks Fifth Avenue in the Galleria one afternoon and wander around. I am looking for something, I am always looking for something. Makeup, jewelry, bubble bath, a pair of spiky red heels that I will never wear, certainly not here in Fort Lauderdale.

But truly, I am looking for something to steal, for no reason other than that I feel like stealing something. It happens that, as always, I am high, but that's no excuse, because I am a compulsive thief. I've been stealing stuff for years now. It's the kind of thing that teenagers do, but I do not need to be an adolescent to behave like one. I'm kind of late in life on everything: most people who become addicts seem to do it when they are still in high school or college, and most people who become kleptomaniacs seem to get started about the same time, but I've waited until my mid-twenties to get going on all these juvenile habits. I don't know what makes me do it, but I can't seem to stop myself.

It started out with small items, lipstick and mascara at drugstore chains. Then one day I was at Macy's trying to buy a silver bracelet with the seven deadly sins engraved into it. I was standing in my winter coat for at least a half hour, waiting for a clerk to let me buy this way overpriced item, and I was getting hot and nauseated and yawning in that way that you do when you are overbundled indoors. I had already loosened my scarf and pulled off my hat, I felt faint and shaky, and finally I just said fuck it, stuffed the thing into one of my capacious pockets, and walked out the door. Since then it's been Gucci sunglasses from Bloomingdale's, a silver butterfly anklet from Burdines, any number of tester lipsticks from any number of Estée Lauder counters—mostly because I feel like it, but partly because in the crowds of department stores, it's easier to steal things than buy them. I will never take anything from a privately owned store—I have scruples, really I do. But these messes of emporia owned by Federated and other huge conglomerates that don't care enough about their employees to pay them decently and don't regard their customers highly enough to make sure there is an adequate sales staff to serve them—as far as I'm concerned, they are asking for me to become a thief.

This is not the case here in Saks. It is a small branch, almost a boutique, it is quiet, and there are plenty of people to assist me. There's no need for Saks or Neiman Marcus or any of the high-end stores to be particularly big here in Fort Lauderdale, because this is not a fancy town. It's not that people don't have money—there are glorious, gorgeous houses along the Intracoastal, and there are luxurious high-rises all over the beach—but there's no need for anything especially nice here. People walk around in bathing suits and Gap jeans, and that's about it. An Izod shirt would be considered dressy. So Saks is damn near empty. In fact, roaming around the jewelry department at the front of the store, I might just have the place to myself.

Now, please understand, I am a practiced thief. I am really good at what I do, and I don't take big risks. I'm not dying to be caught; I'm not doing this as some kind of cry for help, which is how psychologists explain my kind of behavior. I do this because I feel like it. One of the rules of a good kleptomaniac is that you always buy some item other than the one you're stealing—preferably something more expensive—so that if you get caught, you can say it's a mistake, you meant to purchase it, something went wrong. But for some reason today, I'm just not thinking clearly. I haven't slept for days, I just handed in a long chapter, I should probably take a nap, but I'm too damn wired to sleep. This seems like a good alternative.

I try on a new lipstick formula at the Clinique counter, and I almost get furious when the salesclerk asks if I want to make an appointment for a makeover. They always do that. I wonder if it works. If I came to buy a lipstick, that's what I'm here for. If I wanted something else, I'd ask. And I hate that whenever I *do* buy a lipstick, they ask if I am interested in a lip liner. Once again, if I wanted one, I'd ask. This mesmerizes me. I only wear lipstick and mascara, I am clearly one of those people who just isn't interested, so I can't believe they waste their time badgering me about other things I might buy. Plus, I hate being so thoroughly underestimated. I'm educated! I know my own mind! Goddamn it, *if I want something, I will ask for it.*

The woman behind the counter at Clinique annoys me so much by asking me about a makeover that I decide not to buy the lipstick either. In fact, I kind of want to kill her. Everything that is bothering me about everyone in the whole wide world is directed at this poor person who works for minimum wage and is just doing her job.

What is happening to me?

I wander over to the jewelry department, and decide I want to buy something with turquoise stones. Buy it—not steal it. I look under the glass cases, I study pieces from Lagos and Stephen Dweck and Carolee, but none of it is what I want. It's all old and fuddy-duddy, too ornate—why would you want a turquoise pendant encrusted with rhinestones? Once again I am infuriated because in the whole selection, several counters' worth, nothing there is right for me. What about *me?* When the buyer went out and chose all these things, why was she not thinking of someone like me? Maybe I am the only person in Fort Lauderdale—maybe in all of Broward County—who is even sort of like me, but that does not mean I should be overlooked.

I am once again full of resentment, the same kind I get when I am in Borders and trying to find *Crime and Punishment,* and the clerk suggests that I look in the true crime section. Why can't bookstores have a knowledgeable staff? Why can't they hire college students majoring in English who at least know *something* about literature? Is that too much to ask? I am not walking around Borders looking for some obscure novel by some Egyptian man who just won the Nobel Prize—I am simply trying to find a classic that everyone should have read by the time they graduate high school.

This pisses me off. It starts with the problems at Borders, extends to my annoyance at Blockbuster, and then before you know it I am driving myself crazy about the whole American public education system. If you ask most people what their highest priorities are during an election season, the polls will always say that education comes first. But then when you ask anyone what a good education entails—and I have tried this out on Wandy and Lewis, neither of whom is stupid, both of whom have graduate degrees—they have no idea what they mean. I ask them to define a well-educated person, and they are stumped. Do you have to know geometry? Do you need to have read *Beowulf?* Is it important to know about the Tet offensive? *What do you mean?* What is considered a basic level of knowledge?

One night last week, on the local news, I saw something about a town that was burning inappropriate books—the usual suspects, the nigger-loving *Huckleberry Finn,* the rebellious *Catcher in the Rye*—and I wondered what these people *wanted* their children to read. And when they were interviewed, they all talked about the importance of a good education, but somehow F. Scott Fitzgerald and Ernest Hemingway and John Milton and Ralph Ellison and Pearl Buck—a missionary in China, no less—were all off their lists of acceptable reading material. They were idiots, their children were probably idiots, this whole country is going to hell, and still they are all pleading for better public schools, even though, really and truly, they don't want them.

Here I am, I am well educated, and none of these people want their children to grow up to be like me, which is why I am entitled to steal jewelry from Saks. If you see my logic.

So I continue to stroll around the store in a huff. Then I notice that on one of the counters is a little basket of sale items. Among the pile of coral-bead brooches and clasp earrings with satin flowers, there is a Robert Lee Morris bracelet. It is a triple strand of silver, not one of his nicest pieces, not one of the bulky silver rings with bulbous shapes that are Morris' signature, but it is pretty. I will wear it. I wouldn't buy it, it's nothing I am dying for, but I'd like it for free. The price is marked at $299, down from $598. I have sticker shock. How dare anyone ask anyone else to pay that much for so little?

I feel myself fading, and know I have to get out of Saks, get to a rest room, and snort up some more Ritalin. I've got a bottle in my bag, my pill crusher is in there too, and the bathroom isn't far away. I've spent enough time roaming around the store and trying things on like a real customer would. I wear the bracelet on my wrist, and walk out the opened doors into the mall.

Home free.

And then behind me, I hear a man yelling, "Excuse me, ma'am. Excuse me." And I know I should just run, I know I cannot say that I meant to buy it because it's not like I've purchased anything else, I know this is not going to be good, but I stop and turn around to talk to him anyway.

By the time the policeman arrives, I am no longer denying anything. Actually, I have been a cooperative ewe from the moment the security guard first stopped me. Why fight it? It's clear that the jig is up, that I am starting to show. The security camera has taped me, the evidence is there. I'm sitting in an office in the basement of Saks with some man whose job it is to nab people like me. He tells me that they will only press charges for the sale price, since less than $300 is petty theft, a misdemeanor, as opposed to grand larceny, which is a felony. I thank him.

I'm sure one of the reasons the man was watching me as I wandered through Saks—and as soon as he came after me, I realized he'd been following me around the whole time—is that I am starting to look suspicious. I am starting to look like a person who might steal something from your nice store. My conception of myself is as someone at least reasonably poised, well dressed in that rich hippie way I've been cultivating since college, a stylish person who buys stylish things. I want to be Jane Birkin. But this is no longer true. I look like I've not slept in days, my hair is filthy, matted to my head, and I am skinny in the gaunt way that, frankly, only drug addicts are.

It's not that there aren't plenty of thin and disheveled people walking around perfectly sane and sober. But my jeans have slid all the way down on my hips. My T-shirt is covered with coffee and tea stains because I am always spilling things on myself, and I can't get it together to do the laundry. But most telling, it is at least seventy degrees outside, this is Florida in May, and I've got a black suede jacket on because I am freezing all the time, the way only bony people ever are. I don't look well; my degeneration is obvious. For a while, only friends who know me would be able to tell that I just don't look like my-self any longer. But at this point, even strangers can see that I am pale, that my eyes are droopy and, at the same time, wide open and a bit astonished, because I am always a little shocked from so much speed.

I look like a criminal. A hoodlum, maybe. Master thief, my ass.

The policeman cuffs me behind my back, and I start to cry.

"I'm not going to resist arrest," I say. "There's really no need to do this. Can't I just walk with you to the car?"

"This is standard procedure, ma'am," he says. And as we walk into the park-ing lot, he sees me sniffling, and he maybe feels a little sorry for me. "Look, this is no big deal. I promise. This isn't much worse than getting a parking ticket. There's a $250 fine, and if you can pay it, you can go right home. I just have to take you to the station and book you. That's the way we do it."

I start to cry really loudly. I start to wail. I am really scared. I've been so numb for so long—numb or ranting and angry—and now I feel so helpless. If you are a white middle-class girl, the worst thing that can happen to you— deadly diseases aside—is to get arrested. It's just not in my experience of the world. When I used to cop on the street, I was always scared of being narced, and even worse, I started to be scared of the police whenever I saw them, on the subway or walking around in broad daylight, or just buying coffee and donuts at the deli near my apartment. This made me so sad, because I think of myself as part of the straight world—the cops are supposed to be on my side; they are supposed to be protecting me from muggers and rapists and anyone else who might harm me. Once I started carrying illicit substances in my pockets all the time, the police became the enemy. I was not the innocent white girl whose virtue they were meant to guard. I was suddenly a scofflaw, and they were *the man*.

The police officer radios a car to come pick me up. He requests a female cop because I am a woman, and they need to be careful. I could claim that he was inappropriate with me and sue them. That's what the guy explains to me while we are standing there. I calm down a bit, stop crying, and realize this is an absurd position to be in: this man who has arrested me and is the source of my pain is trying to comfort me.

"Do you think we can stop at an ATM on the way to the station?" I ask. I'm not kidding. "I can get some cash, so I could just get out of there right away."

He smiles. "Sorry, but we don't take detainees to run errands."

"Will they let me bail myself out with a credit card?" Once again, I completely mean it.

"Doesn't work that way."

"A check?"

"Uh-uh."

"So what happens to people who don't have anyone to come bail them out?"

"You spend the night in jail, and get hauled before the judge at the county court house first thing in the morning," he says. "You make a deal with him, and given that you're not a violent offender, and this is only a misdemeanor, I'm sure he'll let you go home."

The police car comes by. It is a four-wheel drive, kind of silly for a vehicle to transport criminals. In New York, police cars are always beaten up and utilitarian. Here in Fort Lauderdale, they look luxurious.

"Okay, ma'am, get in the backseat," the woman officer says. "Don't cry. This is no big deal. Really."

She has long red hair pulled back into a braid. She is pretty and Irish and tells me her name is Sarah. You would think that I would be calm by now—this whole procedure has been relatively gentle. But my hands are still cuffed behind my back, they are still going to lock me in a cell, and I am still going to be strip-searched and fingerprinted the way anyone else would be. I keep on bawling. All my bravado with copping dope on Avenue D, and I am basically a wuss.

At the Broward County Jail, they take away all my belongings—all my clothes and jewelry, my pocketbook and everything in it. When they fingerprint me—they do all ten fingers, and I wonder if my toes won't be next—and have me stand straight-on and in silhoutte for the mug shot, I am crying on and on. By this time I am no longer with the nice uniformed police officers; the people at the station are clerks, and they are nasty.

"For God's sake, stop crying," the woman who searches me says. "Come on. You're a big girl."

This makes me cry some more, so she yells out to one of the other clerks something about having a real baby on her hands. All the clerks are black, I am white, and I can tell that racism is at work in reverse here.

Thank God they don't do a cavity search. I surrender my necklace and ankle bracelet and earrings no problem, but I explain that there is no way I can get my navel ring out. "When I got it pierced, it was locked in," I explain, still crying. "You need some kind of tool to open it up."

"That's fine." She's starting to be nicer to me now that I am wearing an orange jailbird outfit. I think I look more defenseless.

Once I get to my cell, they slam the door, and if my tears have subsided a bit, I am now screaming. Hearing that door slam shut is scary and intimidating, a thunderclap into hell. Because I have lost my freedom completely. I know that's obvious, but it doesn't hit until you've actually been caged. They could decide to leave me here forever; they can do whatever they want with me. There are rules about procedure—I am entitled to complete one phone call, for instance—but really they can do whatever they want. I can't fight back, I can't run away, and if they decide they don't feel like letting me use the phone, what am I going to do? I'm at their mercy.

I have never thought of this before, but I have never been at anyone's mercy in my entire life. For all my complaints about my life, I am completely free.

I call Lewis on the phone they pass me through the bars.

These days, with all the telephone technology, you really may not reach somebody for hours, or even days. If they have an answering machine, you can yell and scream and they'll hear you, but once it gets lost in the voice mail system, it's in cyberspace, you can be completely ignored. It's after eleven, and if they're awake, I'm sure they'll answer the phone. My next option is Wendie. Otherwise, I'm stuck for the night. There is no way I can call Mommy.

"Lewis, I'm at the county jail," I say when he picks up the receiver. "Can you come get me?"

He doesn't ask what I'm in for, and I don't volunteer it. This is just too embarrassing. If I were locked up for possession, it would be a worse crime. I'd be in much more trouble, but at least it would not be humiliating. I mean, *adults* don't shoplift. I have sat at dinner tables and described being fitted for a cervical cap to people I barely know, but this is a secret I will take to my grave. It is truly pathetic.

I am not a cool drug addict. I am pathetic.

"I'll be right there," Lewis says.

"Please don't tell Wandy about this."

"I have to explain why I'm going out at this hour."

I am crying all over again. "My mom can't find out," I sob. "This will break her heart. And not your parents or the girls either."

"I'll be right there, okay?" He sighs. "I won't tell anyone, but let's just get you out of there."

I ask the woman guarding the cell if I can have a magazine to read while I wait. There's one in my bag; maybe someone can bring it to me.

She tells me that prisoners are not allowed to read while they are detained.

"Look, this is America," I say, getting some of my obnoxious spirit back. "I am innocent until proven guilty. I ought to be allowed to have a book in here."

She looks at me like I am nuts, and that ends the conversation. The only other person up here is a woman in the next cell, obviously in for drunk and disorderly conduct, or maybe a DWI. She keeps screaming that she needs to go home and feed her rabbit.

"Listen, I have medication I need to take," I say to the attendant. "I think I am entitled to my medicine."

"Is it a health emergency?"

Is this an emergency? Well, I'm an addict, I'm hooked on a perfectly legal substance, the bottle I am carrying around happens to be one prescribed for me by Dr. Singer, and I am supposed to take it four times a day. Is this an emergency? I'd say so.

"Yes, it is," I say. "It's for my mental health, and if I don't take it, I may go crazy. I may have to be taken to an emergency room for a psychotic episode."

She says she'll call the nurse, see what she has to say about all this.

The alleged nurse is in a white uniform, which gives her the air of having had some medical training, but the hair net on her head and her inebriated state, which I am aware of because the smell of malt liquor is on her breath through the cell bars, make me question her authority.

"I'm on Ritalin," I say. "It's in my bag. I'm due for a dose."

"What's Ritalin?" she asks.

And I can see I'm not going to be able to convince her that I will die without it. I start to cry because it has been hours since I last took any. I have a headache that's so bad. The adrenaline of the arrest kept me going for a while. I didn't notice that I needed any drugs because I was too hysterical. But now it's hitting. I have to say something to get it across.

"It's for a mental illness I have," I try. I start to cry. "It's really serious. This is America. I've not been convicted of anything." I cry and cry and cry. "Please, please, please just bring me my pills." I shrink down into the corner of my cell. What if Lewis never gets here? What if they don't have a record of my arrest and they tell him they have no idea who I am, and I am stuck in this jail forever without my Ritalin?

What is happening to me?

The nurse starts walking away from my cell. "You'll get your pills when you leave," she says.

The attendant asks if I want to talk to the officer in charge of the whole jail. Normally, I would do anything, ask to speak to the supervisor and his supervisor and all the way up to God Himself to get my drugs. But I just can't do it. I just can't.

When they come to tell me my bail has been paid, it's time to leave, I am not as relieved as I thought I would be. I'm too tired to care. There is no bed or cot in the cell, just a bench and a toilet. I have no idea what happens to people who stay here all night.

A police officer leads me to, for lack of a better phrase, the checkout area. I get my clothes and possessions in a plastic bag. "Make sure nothing's missing," he warns. He seems kindly. It almost seems planned that way: The mean people are there when you arrive, you've been reduced to prisoner, and they treat you with total disrespect. But once someone comes to bail you out, you become a citizen once again—you are loved, someone cares enough to pick you up, you must be okay after all.

The man shows me to a dressing room to change. I ask for a cup of water before I get in, and he points in the direction of a cooler with funnel-shaped cups. Once I'm inside, I open the Ritalin bottle, pour about ten into my hands, and gulp them down all at once, the bitter taste of the half-swallowed pills lingering on my tongue. I can feel my eyes light up, I smile. Obviously, the effect hasn't hit yet, it will take a while for the medicine to get absorbed into my bloodstream, but just knowing it's on its way thrills me.

I walk out with the orange jail uniform cradled in my arms. "I know this is going to sound weird," I say, feeling frisky—I've got my Ritalin and all is well. "But can I keep this outfit? I'm willing to pay for it. I'd just like a souvenir of my stay here, since I'm not planning to come back." I say this to emphasize to him that I am a good law-abiding citizen. This has all been some terrible mix-up.

I am ashamed of myself. I want this strange police officer's approval. I want us to be friends. I want us to be on the same side again.

"Let me ask," he says, and picks up the phone.

The answer is a firm no from whoever needs to say yes.

Oh well.

As I walk through the corridor to the parking lot to meet Lewis, I say a cheerful good-bye to all the cops I pass. We're going to be friends now. We're all good, decent people; we're all in it together.

I jump on Lewis and give him a big hug when I see him waiting next to his Jaguar. He has signed the papers to bail me out, so he knows what the charges are, no need to discuss it. He hands me a blue sheet of paper, a receipt I guess. I need to hold it for my court date. Apparently this isn't over yet.

We drive home silently, except for my saying thank you over and over again. He doesn't bring up what happened, and neither do I.

"I'll call you with the number of a defense attorney I know tomorrow," Lewis says as we pull up to my apartment. "You'll have to pay a fine, but that's about it. A night in jail is usually considered punishment enough."

I'll say.

As I get out of the car, I open my mouth to tell him something, to explain, to express something besides gratitude.

"Don't say anything," Lewis says, seeing that I'm at a loss. "We don't have to talk about it. Okay? Just get some sleep."

I swallowed ten Ritalin pills a half hour ago, and when I get upstairs I'm going to cut up some Dexedrine, for variety. They are pretty much the same thing, but the Dexedrine is orange, which is kind of fun. I'm not going to be able to fall asleep anytime soon. Four days awake. That's probably not good.

And as soon as the clock strikes nine, I'm going to call the American Civil Liberties Union and find out what my rights are as a detainee. I'm a card-carrying member—actually, Michael Dukakis notwithstanding, all they give you is a cardboard thing when you join, which I've long since misplaced—and it's times like these that your membership becomes useful. They deprived me of my medicine, they deprived me of reading material at the Broward County Jail. I'm not the litigious sort, but if they have violated my rights as an American citizen, innocent until proven guilty, I will sue their butts off.

I call the lawyer that Lewis recommended, and he doesn't have much to say. He's one of those guys with an office near the courthouse who defends small-time crooks, drunk drivers, and, I guess, people like me. He says the same thing Lewis said—no big deal, I'll have to go before the judge, express some regret, pay a fine, that'll be the end of it. The state of Florida has a one-time-only policy where the record can be sealed on a conviction. Do I think this is the worst crime I will ever commit while I'm down here? I laugh and say I assume so.

Ha ha ha—I'm no felon. I'm a nice Jewish girl. Ha ha ha.

I ask about suing the Broward County Jail for depriving me of my medication, refusing to allow me to read, and generally treating me like a convict when I am still considered innocent in the eyes of the law until my hearing.

"You're joking," he says.

"No, I'm not." I pause. "I'm not doing this for myself, you know. I mean, I'm not going back there. But if they feel that they can treat me that badly, imagine what they do to people who come in there for worse reasons. Even if you are arrested, you're still a human being. I think it's an outrage that I couldn't have my medication. I mean, that's serious. They shouldn't be able to get away with that."

He laughs.

"If you want to save the world, you should do some volunteer work, feed the homeless," he says. "No one has ever filed a lawsuit over missing some pills for a couple of hours and not being allowed to read a magazine."

And he laughs some more. He seems not to understand that I am completely serious. He seems not to understand that I have already looked up the number of the local branch of the ACLU. He seems not to understand.

Wandy calls me the next day to see how I am.

I tell her I'm fine. It's no big deal.

"Elizabeth, you know, I just think that you're on so much medication that maybe you don't know what you're doing sometimes," she suggests. "You probably didn't even know you were walking out of the store with something you didn't buy."

"Yeah, maybe." Why argue with someone who is on your side? She has this gentle voice; she is such a gentle person. I've done nothing to deserve her kindness.

"Maybe you should find out if you aren't taking something that's altering your perception." She's a nurse; she's trying to be helpful. "Maybe you should see a doctor. Your psychiatrist isn't down here, so maybe somebody should make sure that your levels are right."

"Okay, I guess, maybe I should."

She can tell I don't mean it. "Well, look, Lewis and I know you're a really good person, and you wouldn't do anything wrong if something wasn't off with your medication." She hesitates. "I'll do whatever I can to help, if you want me to. We're here, you know. We love you."

Nine

I GOT NASTY HABITS

> What a lay me down this is
> with two pink, two orange,
> two green, two white goodnights.
> Fee-fi-fo-fum—
> Now I'm borrowed.
> Now I'm numb.
>
> ANNE SEXTON
> "The Addict"

Any pill will do. I don't care about the effect anymore, up or down, so long as I'm never just straight. I steal pills from people's medicine chests. Everyone has had a root canal or wisdom tooth extraction at some point, and most people don't finish their prescriptions for Vicodin or Percocet or Tylenol 3, which has codeine in it. My elderly relatives are always having hip replacement operations, or bypasses, and like that, and they too don't finish their Demerol or Dalmane or Dilaudid. They get it as an IV drip in the hospital, and by the time they get home, they've lost interest. I don't understand this, why they leave any pills over. But most people are proudly stoic—they like to take their narcotics for the first day, and then stick to Advil or aspirin thereafter. They go back to work and can't handle the drowsiness from the opiates. This amazes me: I would use minor surgery as an excuse to take off as many days from the office as possible. But it seems that people who are not addicts don't think this way. Don't think like me.

So anytime I'm at someone's house, I steal their pills. The two guys who live next door, the gay couple, are both on Fen-Phen to lose weight, and sometimes they'll give me a few capsules; it's no substitute for Ritalin, but it's a little speedy, like all diet aids. Some people have a few Xanax lying around, because they need them for flying, so I take them, maybe leave a couple in the bottle so they won't notice. But the truth is, they won't notice anyway: I am conscious of every pill I've got, but most people just forget about them completely. If something is missing, they call the doctor and get a new prescription, no problem, when need be. Most people are not like me.

Interesting fact: the pills that are fun to snort are easy to crush. Zoloft and Paxil and lithium are all coated and can't be cut up, but they would be no kick to sniff anyway. I start to think that this is a cabal of the pharmaceutical industry to make us into addicts, because almost all medications that are habit-forming are easy to powder up. I smash the Vicodin and Percocet. I crunch up all the benzodiazepines in my pill crusher. I alternate between amphetamines and opiates and tranquilizers. Some to stay awake, some to go to sleep, what a lay-me-down I live.

My landlord has let me stay on in the apartment for an extra few months beyond March, beyond the season. But in June they find a year-round tenant, so it's time to leave. I'll miss it, I guess. I'll miss my view of the office building that is the corporate headquarters for the Psychic Friends Network, the one Dionne Warwick does television commercials for. It's going out of business anyway, another human snafu, so I guess my daily chuckle would be gone anyway. But I'll miss Wendie downstairs, and the flight attendants and call girls next door, for reasons I don't understand.

Just as well that I will be a little bit farther from the Galleria. If I get anywhere near the entrance to Saks, they are allowed to have me arrested again, and I am so spacy, I might just wander in unaware. God knows I will never steal anything—besides pills from people's vanities and mirrored cabinets—for as long as I live. I have been scared straight. I will pay for every lipstick, every hair band, every gumball, every grain of sand forever more. I will dwell in the House of the Lord for long days.

My mom will be gone for the summer, but her apartment is undergoing renovations for the month—the endless metamorphosis of tiles in the kitchen, tiles in the bathroom, tiles on the living room floor, the woman is keeping Home Depot in business—so I can't go there. Instead I take a room at the Schubert Motel, around the corner from the treehouse, which I have always admired for the big pink neon sign and the blue dolphin in front.

It will cost me $23 a night. It has beige carpets and bad plumbing and a faulty air conditioner: at long last, I will be living like a true junkie. Hallelujah! My room has a rotary dial telephone, so I cannot make calls with my card, and once again there is no long-distance service. And the French Canadian desk attendant has such a poor command of English that he takes messages all wrong, so I am pretty much unreachable. I'm always in my room. No reason I cannot pick up my own phone, but I just don't. Lots of times I'm asleep—the mix of pills means I spend half my life passed out, so why answer? Ah, the addict's life: no one can find me, I've got scented candles lit all the time, lines of powder cut up on the TV set and night table all the time, and since almost all the pills are white, I never know what I'm snorting, never know if I'll end up asleep or awake. All I know is that I will always feel okay because I will never feel much of anything. Hallelujah! Reality is for people who can't handle drugs! Ha ha ha!

My favorite activity is sitting under the incandescent light in the bathroom and tweezing hair out of my legs. I think it is an obsessive-compulsive thing, and I can spend hours trying to make sure that there is not a single hair left on my calves and shins. Ritalin, after all, is an amphetamine, which improves my focus to the point where any activity can become obsessive. People on high doses of stimulants have been known to pluck their eyebrows for hours, to squeeze pimples and tear at imaginary blemishes until their skin is covered with scratches and sores—I like to joke that a speed freak can water a plant for three days straight. When hyperactive children appear to be quieted by Ritalin, it is not, as is mistakenly believed, a paradoxical response. In fact, speed is calming, and creates concentration like all hell. Suddenly, impossibly distractible types can see a task through to completion. This is how I write for hours that turn into days—and this is why I pull at my leg hairs for hours that turn into days.

I can start tweezing at night, not look up for what seems like minutes but is really much longer, and when I finally stop to take a break, the sun is shining. It is not sunrise, or even the morning—it is sometime in the afternoon. I have not stopped for a sip of water, to change the channel on the TV that is on all the time—if I'm watching Nick at Nite, it means that *CatDog* and *Power Puff Girls* and other children's shows will have been playing for hours without my noticing—or to even cut up more lines, because I keep a pile next to me from the time I settle down to do my tweezing. I prepare for this activity as other people would put together a picnic basket or take towels to the beach—this is my recreation.

I still shave, of course, when I bother to shower. But there are always a few strays, so I pull those out first. Plus, within a day of shaving, stubble starts to sprout because everything grows faster in the heat, so it's impossible to keep up with all the little hairs that need to be extracted. I pull and pull and pull. Then I smooth on cortisone cream or bacitracin to keep from getting bumpy infections, but after a while it does not matter. I get rashes anyway. My legs are red and chafed from abuse.

And it is impossible not to cause more damage. If you pull out hair completely, all the way down to the follicle, it grows back subcutaneously and you end up with ingrown hairs. I have to dig under the skin to pull those little pieces out, and sometimes they grow in a coil into long tresses under my epidermal layer, and they'll form cysts and pustules that I squeeze open, pus everywhere. Sometimes it's hard to access a hair that's buried really deep under, so I'll have to dig it out with tweezers. I'll push the metal deeper and deeper inside. I still won't be able to get at the little black thing; it's a tiny piece of dirt. So I will dig and dig and dig some more.

After a while, the whole point is the digging: What else is there under my skin? What will I find inside there? How much blood, how much flesh, how many little cell pieces, bits of pus, cartilage, muscle, layers of skin—what is going on inside there? My goal becomes finding a bone, getting far enough into my leg to touch ossified ivory mass, to massage my own skeleton with my Tweezerman scalpel. I work on this task for hours. Blood spurts everywhere, the white tile on the bathroom floor is covered with stains, blood drips down my legs, there is blood on my hands, blood on the sundress I wear, and I am too busy trying to find a bone to notice. Or maybe I notice, but I don't care. I can't let anything get in the way of my mission.

I have cuts all over my legs, I've had them for months, and I tell people that they are from using a dull razor. Usually I wear long skirts or pants, so they mostly don't show, but if my mom stops by and I'm half dressed, if my skirt blows up on the windy beach, if for some reason my calves show, I just say it's a crime of vanity—of dirty Florida water, a rusty blade, forgetting to put lotion or oil on my legs. It's amazing what people will believe—because the truth would never occur to them. I mean, how could I possibly be lying, since everybody knows that no one sits around for hours tearing hair out of her legs. No one.

There's nothing worse than a sore throat. You swallow Robitussin from the little cup that comes with it, you suck on Luden's and Pine Bros. and then Hall's Mentholyptus when it gets bad enough, you gulp down water and Emergen-C, you swallow echinacea and vitamin C, and still it never seems to hit the right spot. There's always some pain in your neck and your lymph nodes that nothing can reach. And if you do all these things on an empty stomach, you end up nauseated and vomiting, which is horrible also.

Not that it matters, since I don't do any of these things. For a while now I've been taking NyQuil and Benadryl to fall asleep, so when I need any of this stuff for their on-label, appropriate use, they don't help. And I've had a persistent sore throat for months now. Not to mention a runny nose and a sour stomach. That's what happens when you spend your days inhaling pills nasally: You end up with all kinds of sinus problems. Apparently the talc and other inactive ingredients in Ritalin may be even more dangerous than the drug itself as far as your nose and throat are concerned.

All my relatives keep urging me to go to the doctor. They think I am suffering from allergies, that there's something in Florida grass and air that I just can't adapt to. Plus my mother is concerned about my gastrointestinal problems, since I spend so much time in the bathroom. The cuts all over my legs probably need to be attended to also. Wandy worries that the original scabs from my dull razor have been infected by the heat. She hasn't seen the huge sores I've got now, the bloody wrecks with green pus growing over them that don't seem to go away, especially since I keep ripping them open more. Even I am scared by what I see. Even I think a doctor should get a look at them. Everyone suggests I find a general practitioner at the Fort Lauderdale branch of the Cleveland Clinic, so I do. I obviously need some kind of medical attention.

I go to my doctor's appointment wearing new jeans that fit, with a striped tank top in cheerful primary colors. I've showered and put makeup on, I've got flushed cheeks and gold streaks from the sun, so I appear to be pretty healthy. I can still look okay if I want to. Besides, so many people here in Florida are old and haggard, looking bedraggled all the time; as one of the few women at the Cleveland Clinic not wearing a stained housedress and a snood covering my stiff silver hair, I am comparatively fresh-faced, a Breck-girl blonde.

When I get into Dr. Schwartz's office, I complain of chronic stomach and throat troubles, so he gives me a bunch of tests—a blood workup, urine samples sent to the lab. He puts on his stethoscope to check my heartbeat, placing the bell on my back and then on the left side of my chest, listening carefully, as if he were holding a shell to his ear and trying very hard to convince himself that the sound he is hearing really is the sea, that it's not just a mother's myth. I am sure that the rhythm of my heart must be a jarring locomotive rumble or the stiff, slow drip of Chinese water torture—I don't know which one, but it must be all off from the drugs. But when he takes the plugs out of his ears, he says everything sounds fine. When he uses a tongue depressor and flashlight to look deep into my throat, he says that it all looks fine, but he reaches a cotton swab toward my tonsils to take a culture. After hitting my knee to test my reflexes, doing all the usual checkup things, Dr. Schwartz says I look fine; when he gets the test results, he will call. I decide not to show him my legs—I just don't want to talk about it.

And when he calls a couple of days later, Dr. Schwartz says everything is perfectly normal. There are no mysterious enzymes in my blood, no indications of parasites or bacterial infections. All these tests, all to conclude that there's nothing wrong with me, that I simply have irritable bowel syndrome, which is just a way of saying undiagnosable stomach problems, probably caused by stress.

The doctor never ever asks about the drugs, and I don't tell him. That's the thing: I mostly look worn out and tired, but give me a good night's sleep and a decent meal, and I'm fine. I hold up pretty well. "But it's always been my tendency to lie to doctors," writes Denis Johnson in *Jesus' Son*, "as if good health consisted only of the ability to fool them."

Doctors are not hard to fool. If you walk in obviously high, doing the junkie shuffle, they can tell. If you're on crack, swinging and violent, they can figure it out. But coke or speed is only the usual level of human dread raised to the next level. I am already on medication that I have told Dr. Schwartz about, so for all he knows my symptoms may be those of any person with a lot of mental and emotional problems, who has the shakes from nerves. How would this doctor at the Cleveland Clinic, who has never seen me before, be able to figure out that I am not in my natural state of antsy anxiety? I've had sessions with Dr. Singer, who used to run a drug treatment program, where she did not know I was high. If you carry it well, they won't be able to tell. If they don't do a urinalysis, they will have no evidence. They don't suspect. Why would they?

I have an abscess on my leg that I cannot ignore. It is bulbous and green and crusty, it's covered in a bubble of pus, and there is a bruise of deep blue and purple surrounding it, from trauma I guess. I have just read *Gia*, about the model and junkie Gia Carangi—Angelina Jolie wins a Golden Globe for playing her in an HBO movie—and she has an abscess in her hand at the end of her modeling days. Apparently photographers started to call it "that thing." It bled during photo sessions. It was big enough to store her stash in. I have no idea what I might be storing in this thing on my left leg, but I do not want to die of an infection, and I decide I need to do something. I decide this one Friday evening, long after office hours have ended for the day. I could call and make another appointment with Dr. Schwartz, but it seems like I've waited long enough. I feel an emergency coming on, and when I get that sense of urgency, I must do something right away.

I go to the emergency room at the Cleveland Clinic. Unlike in New York, where there would be several people with gunshot wounds at the head of the line, here in Fort Lauderdale, the triage nurse gets a look at the thing on my leg and gets a doctor to see me right away. I explain that I have been shaving with a dull and dirty razor, that my air conditioner is busted, and that this has festered into a sticky, sloppy sore from the humidity. Maybe I admit to picking at it a little bit, worrying the wound, but I cannot explain about the tweezers, about digging to find a hair and then a bone. They might have me committed. At any rate, I do not want psychiatric attention—I just want a doctor to fix it.

Like most emergency rooms, this one is mostly staffed with interns and residents. The doctor studies my leg and says he has never seen anything like this. A razor did this to me? And I explain again that it's not just the razor—it's ignoring it, and then rubbing and scratching at it, and ignoring it some more until it came to this. He basically tells me that this is one for the record. This could make it into a textbook. He wonders if it's some tropical disease. What can have caused this? He explains that he is only recently out of medical school, and this is very interesting to his fresh eyes.

He leaves the examining room for a few minutes, and comes back in with another couple of doctors, also residents. He asks what they think of this suppurating sore. They are similarly amazed. They have never seen anything like this caused just by a razor and some wet heat. They leave and come back with another few doctors. By the time I've left there, my leg has been studied by six interns and one experienced doctor, the one overseeing the whole emergency room. They are mostly just curious, I think. They don't seem to doubt the veracity of what I am telling them is the cause—as ever, why would I lie? I am still a healthy white girl, a little too skinny, but these days that is common. I am well dressed, impeccably made up. I wear my rose perfume. I do tell them the medications I take—I admit to Ritalin, even, because it is in fact a prescribed drug—so they might suspect that I have emotional troubles. But I laugh along with them at their surprise and amazement. I agree it's pretty weird. We're all in on this mystery wound together.

I walk out about an hour later with some topical cream already applied, a prescription for antibiotics, and advice to wash it three times a day with Betadine and keep applying bacitracin ointment. Don't bandage it or keep it covered—just keep it clean. It should be okay, the doctors, all seven of them, assure me. And I believe them, as they have believed me.

First, I did not know how I would explain getting addicted to Ritalin, the drug of choice for first-graders. Then I discovered I was not the only one, that it is surprisingly common. So I figured, all right, I'll come clean with it someday. I can always claim to be a speed freak, which is true enough, and that will cover me.

But this is just so strange. Obsessed with tweezing? *Even ordinary forms of self-mutilation have been exposed as common compulsions, particularly among depressed teenagers. Kids will cut themselves with knives, slash up their arms and legs, injure themselves to relieve other kinds of pain—it is a spiritual release of sorts. In the Middle Ages, physicians would "bleed" hysterics, patients with maladies of the soul; medieval medics understood that bloodletting could be curative, though they thought it was a form of cleansing, a way to release demons from the body. And, in a way, that is what people who cut themselves are doing too.*

I was a cutter when I was young, twelve or thirteen. I would go into a fugue state, fade into a trance, often while hiding away in the girls' locker room in school or alone in my bedroom late at night. And I would pull out the pocket knife attached to my key chain, and start slashing up my legs, slitting shapes—hearts and triangles and rhombi—on the smooth soft skin, the unshaved downy of early pubescence. And it did not hurt at all. It felt good, gentle, pure, pleasant. I am told that cutters have some kind of inner ether, an autoanesthetic or self-analgesic, that makes behavior that would be painful to most people feel sweet to them. The cuts would hurt like hell the next day, but not while I was doing the wounding. The morning after, with my hangover of stabs, I would slather on Neosporin and cut open vitamin E gels and smooth them on to prevent scarring. I would attend to my wounds with the care I should have given to my whole self. And I felt awfully strange about what I was doing. I tried to stop but missed the cold comfort of the cuts too much. I thought it was all quite embarrassing and shameful, but I understood somehow that it made sense.

But not this tweezing. I cannot figure it out. It could be vanity run amok. Cats and some dogs are occasionally plagued by a syndrome called excessive grooming disorder, where they start to clean themselves too much, they lick at their fur until they end up with bald patches. They do this under stress. It is a feline form of obsessive-compulsive disorder (OCD), and sometimes they are treated with Prozac or other selective serotonin reuptake inhibitors (SSRIs). It used to be that all you could do was put a cone that looked like a megaphone around their necks so that they could not turn around and touch their bodies, but now they get psychopharmacology too. So I guess my tweezing makes me kind of like a sick cat.

But I do not know how I will explain this, to Dr. Singer or in rehab or to anybody. I cannot imagine anyone else does this. I know about trichotillomania, I understand that people tear their hair out, and though I find that absolutely repulsive, it seems like an explicable response to stress. After all, we even say, when someone is excessively anxious, that she is tearing her hair out—*it is a com-*

monplace expression, and it must come from somewhere. But tweezing for relief and release? Who would have thought?

Once I get into drug treatment, I will encounter others who have done this. I will meet a woman, a Vicodin addict with a five-year-old son, who would stay up all night, tweezing imaginary hairs from her face. Her husband would be asleep in the bedroom, and she would sit on the floor in her living room, a magnifying mirror on her coffee table, pulling at the fine blonde hairs on her chin and cheeks, on her eyebrows and forehead. When her husband would come out to look for her, to beckon her into bed, she would drop the tweezers, pull the mirror and hide it under the couch, scared to be caught, scared to be found out in this strange habit. She ended up with purple and red dots on her face, broken blood vessels that looked like inverted pimples. She could admit to bottles of Vicodin daily, to stealing a physician's pad to write herself phony prescriptions—she was unabashed about all the things she did to get her drugs. She would even admit to leaving her newborn baby home alone when she went to the liquor store, desperate for a drink, to buy herself a bottle of gin late at night. But the tweezing—it is just too gross, too silly.

I consider telling people that the scars on my legs are track marks, that I shot up dope, that's how I got these blots all over. But eventually, when I get to the drug treatment hospital, I meet so many people with so many approaches to self-mutilation—piercings and body art are the most socially acceptable of them—that I am able to talk about it, at least in private therapy. But it still takes a long time for me to really discuss it in group. It takes many other people admitting to many other odd behaviors before I can even begin to acknowledge my tweezing.

I make more than one trip to the emergency room in the next few months. I get fever blisters, painful lumps, all over my body, so I go to nearby Holy Cross Hospital for treatment—more cream, more antibiotics. After that, when I keep getting more pus on the closing sore that used to be an abscess, I go back to the emergency room at the Cleveland Clinic, but during a different shift, not on Friday night, so I will not have to show the same doctors the same wound. Their mystification was all right that first time, but I cannot go through it again.

And there are plenty more sores on my legs, because the tweezing and pulling and digging do not stop. I cannot control it. I try to. I throw out my tweezers and go to a salon to have my eyebrows done, but within days I am going crazy. One night, in the middle of the night, I do not have my tweezers and they don't have any in the 7-Eleven. So I take a taxi to an Eckerd that is open twenty-four hours a day to get a new set. I cannot stand being deprived of my habit. It's as bad as drugs. I start to think I am really losing my mind.

This is my life: I snort and I tweeze. It could be worse, I suppose. It could be worse.

Every time I need to see a doctor, I try a different emergency room. I have been to every different hospital in Fort Lauderdale and its environs. I don't want anyone to figure out that this is habitual. They will never know that this is anything more than humidity. But I vow to get this thing under control when I get back to New York. I have to find a way to stop this. I don't mind being a drug addict, but I do mind being gross. I cannot possibly have intimate physical contact with anyone right now unless it is very dark. And I do want to have sex again sometime. Any guy who sees my legs will lose his hard-on right away. Any guy who sees my sores will never want to see me again.

Ten

HAPPY BIRTHDAY

I'm near the end, and I just ain't got the time
and I'm wasted, and I can't find my way home

STEVE WINWOOD
"Can't Find My Way Home"

On July 31, I come back to New York for exactly twenty-four hours to celebrate my thirtieth birthday. I get on an early-morning plane, land in LaGuardia, and head to my Greenwich Village garret for the first time since October. I've told my house sitter to clear out for the night, because this is the day of reckoning. I must see what it will be like to be back.

As soon as I walk into the house and climb up the narrow staircase inside my front door, Zap is waiting for me at the top of the steps. Animals are supposed to be angry at you when you've abandoned them for too long. They are supposed to pretend they don't know you, never loved you—they are supposed to punish you for your absence. But not Zap. He leaps on me. I crouch on my knees, and he jumps onto my lap and licks my face, like a small spaniel, not like a cat at all.

I hold him in my arms. "Oh baby, I love you so much," I say, dropping my overnight bag on the floor. I carry him over to the couch. "Mommy misses you so much. I never meant to be away this long. Mommy is in trouble. Mommy misses you so much. I wish you were with me."

I start to cry. He looks at me with incomprehension, because he is a simple cat, and what does he know of my crazy emotions? Dogs can feel more deeply, they are more perceptive: they lick up your tears like delicious food. They sigh and pout on your behalf. But Zap seems to smile that Cheshire smile. He is happy to see me, that's all. He does not care what condition I am in.

I meet Betsy, my editor, for lunch at Balthazar, newly opened and chic, on Spring Street in SoHo. We are rushed, it is crowded, and we barely have a chance to talk. I eat very little of my salmon sandwich. Hunger is one of the five senses—or rather, *taste* would be the more accurate designation—that I have lost to drugs. I run to the bathroom a couple of times to snort lines, careful to wipe off any white crust from my nose, the circles of lava that form around my nostrils, because she cannot know what it's come to.

We take maybe an hour together, just long enough to catch up. I promise Betsy a new pile of pages soon. She tells me she will come down to Fort Lauderdale for a week to work with me at the end of August, so we can just get this thing done. And I am glad to know she cares that much. She just gave birth to her first child in February, and she is in love with the little blonde girl. I know she would not leave her baby for all that time unless she really cared. Betsy is still with me. She does not know about the Ritalin problem—no one does, I don't think—but she knows something is wrong. Something is wrong, and she wants to help.

After lunch, I am up to Dr. Singer's office in Murray Hill. We talk about my imminent return, about hiding from life, about how my only way to cope is to hide.

I have not told her about the Ritalin mess. There is no way I will give Dr. Singer a reason to cut me off, to stop the supply, until I am back in New York and ready to check myself in. I am pretty sanguine in our session, surprisingly happy to see her. Surprisingly happy to be home at all. But twenty-four hours is easy; a bookended period is a pleasure. It is the open ends, the infinite future, that I cannot handle.

I have told Dr. Singer about my legs on the phone. I have told her that isolation, boredom, pressure have driven me to this stabbing and picking and tweezing. I am wearing a long navy blue skirt with daisies, a rayon sheath I bought at Express when I realized I just had to get a few items of clothing that fit. It is a size 2, tiny like me. When clothes are not falling off of me, slipping down my hips and toward my thighs, toward my pubic bone, I don't look quite so gaunt. Maybe none of my friends will notice that I am wasting away. Betsy didn't say anything.

Before I walk out her door, Dr. Singer asks to see the damage done. I walk over to the wing chair where she sits, impassive and serene as ever, and lift up my skirt, hike it up above my knees.

"Well, you definitely have trichotillomania," she says.

"I know. I can't stop myself from doing this."

"Throw out your tweezers," she suggests.

"I tried that," I sigh. "And then I just started poking at myself with a nail scissors, until finally I ran out to the drugstore and bought another tweezers. It's completely addictive."

Shit, I've said the word *addictive*. This may lead her to thoughts I don't want her to have.

"Can you help me to stop?" I ask, and I hear a curve of desperation in my voice. It rises to a squeak as I approach the question mark. "Can you help me get better and learn to live my life here, to live at home?" This sounds like a line in a movie. But real life often does.

"I can. And I will. But I can't do much for you by phone." She looks down at my legs and shakes her head, troubled. "You need to come back here so that we can do some real work. I promise it will be okay. I promise. But you need to come back. You need to stop being afraid and just come home. It will be good."

"I'll be back soon," I say, sure but not sure that I mean it. "Betsy is going to come down to Florida to work with me at the end of the month. I'll finish the book, and I'll be back."

I walk out the door. Another patient shuffles into her office—Dr. Singer does not take breaks between sessions. When I hear talking begin, I go into the bathroom and turn the faucet on so the water covers the noise of my snorting up a few lines of Ritalin. I need some right away, and she just can't know.

I walk over to Fifth Avenue and uptown a ways to visit my friend Ben at his office. He is a movie producer who once tried to option my first book. Somehow it did not work out, but we liked each other pretty well, and stayed in touch. I thought he was handsome, in a bookish Hollywood way. He wore lawyer's glasses and talked about the thesis he wrote on Flaubert, back when he was an undergraduate at Brown. Like most show business people I have encountered, Ben made a big play to let me know that he isn't shallow, that he is an intellectual, that he reads plenty of things that are not scripts. He made such a valiant effort to come across as literary that I did not have the heart to tell him that I could not even get through *Madame Bovary*, and that I never bothered to write a thesis in college. During the couple of years before I went to Florida, we'd had a few three-hour flirtatious lunches at the Four Seasons Hotel and other places where film people tend to linger and wander to each other's tables like it's an old studio commissary. Ben has been married for as long as I've known him, but I think not very happily.

When I first got to Florida, I called him for some research help. I'd hoped he could find me some videotapes of movies that were not yet released and that I needed to see for the book. He dug up the tapes, and after that I phoned him looking for some scripts I heard were circulating—something about the photographer Lee Miller, something else about Janis Joplin, a treatment about the relationship between Sylvia Plath and Anne Sexton—and soon we were chatting all the time. Soon he became the only person I actually spoke to.

When you're in trouble and disgusted and disengaged, sometimes only the comfort of strangers is available. The only confidant you can handle is someone peripheral to your life. That's what has happened with Ben. I can't bear to have a conversation with anyone I am really close with, but I can talk to Ben. It started when he told me about an affair he had for several months with some woman who freelances as a film editor for his production company in Los Angeles. He's only been married for a few years, Ben cannot figure how he ended up doing this, he swears he loves his wife like crazy, and it was just one big mistake. He attributes it to severe migraine headaches, the kind Joan Didion wrote about in one of those arid essays in *The White Album*, which have since been treated. Ben thinks he was sick and anxious and his judgment was warped, and that's all there is to it. It's no reflection on his relationship with his wife, which is just fine.

I, of course, know better and tell him so. I tell Ben that I like to handicap people's marriages—which is not that hard because statistically there is only a 50 percent chance they will work out anyway—and in my opinion his has been miserable all along. He does not like hearing this, but I am so forthright and certain that he can't help listening. We end up talking about it a lot. It seems that this ex-lover has been calling him all the time, making idle threats that might not be idle at all, and Ben is afraid that his wife will find out. My feeling is that he should confess to her anyway. I have pretty firm opinions about this kind of thing: if you have a one-night stand, you are morally obligated *not* to tell your spouse, because it will only hurt her feelings and assuage your guilt. But if you have an affair of any duration, you must fess up, or else the relationship will be tainted by dishonesty, because an extended liaison means something. To me it means that Ben and his wife really do have problems, and they will never work them out—they will never have the chance to make things better—unless they talk about it, seek counseling, take profound steps. By not telling his wife, Ben is leaving open the opportunity to have another clandestine extramarital relationship. If Ben tells his wife, he has to be careful, toe the line, get home for dinner on time every night, check in with her when he's away on business, stay clean. I don't think that's what Ben really wants; I think Ben wants to run around some more.

In fact, I know Ben wants to run around some more.

Ben comes down to the lobby of his office building on Fifty-third Street, and we head for the nearest Starbucks for some afternoon coffee. We talk about the usual things—my book, his marriage. By the time I've gone through several tall cups—I always love that "tall" is the smallest size at Starbucks—of Sumatran blend, it is after six-thirty. I am due at Lydia and Jason's apartment at seven, because they are having a birthday party for me. As usual, I am going to be late, Lydia is going to yell at me, I will have disappointed her and whoever else yet again, I will give her a reason to say I am rude one more time—and I will have yet another excuse to do drugs.

As I try to hail a taxi during the midtown rush hour, Ben realizes he has to be back at work for a conference call with Los Angeles. He's already late. I invite him to come for cocktails and to help celebrate my thirtieth when he's done, but he needs to get home to his wife.

"Why don't you tell her that you've got to go to a friend's birthday party?" I ask. "For that matter, why don't you just invite her along? She works near here, doesn't she?"

"I don't think she'd be interested."

"Oh. Okay."

"And I don't want you to meet her," he adds. "Knowing what you know."

"I see."

A cab finally pulls up to the curb, and I run to grab it before someone else does. Ben follows behind. He opens the door, and as I am about to scoot inside, he pulls me close and kisses me on the lips.

"I'll call you tomorrow, gorgeous," he calls out as the car starts to pull away, into traffic. All I can think is that there is no way I will be anything less than a half hour late. Shit. "Oh, and happy birthday."

God bless Lydia for this party. It is too generous. She's cooked up hors d'oeuvres, little spinach quiches and tuna tartare on focaccia bread, and there are wine and cheese and flowers and flutes of champagne everywhere. I am the last person to arrive. I say hello as quickly as I can, and promise I will greet everyone individually and properly—but first I just have to run into the bathroom for a minute.

By now I am twenty pounds thinner than when I left for Florida, but everyone acts all normal. All my friends are here, I think trying to remind me that life does have a point, and that it would be much sounder and safer if I would just for God's sake come back home. Kathlyn gives me a green tourmaline necklace from Bergdorf Goodman; it comes in a gray velvet drawstring pouch, which I love, which I associate with very special jewelry. Daniel, Kathlyn's boyfriend, has a leather-bound atlas for me, which is exactly what I wanted—I love maps and the hubris of mankind to think that we can delineate the world. Lydia pulls me aside to hand me a white silk scarf from Paris, a silver bullet pillbox from Gucci, and an Elsa Perretti mesh necklace from Tiffany. My friend Jason brings me some long-stemmed white roses, which are gorgeous and ephemeral and useless, since I am leaving in the morning. Max whispers to me that I should just consider the cocaine run he did for me a few months ago my birthday present—for the next few years, as far as he's concerned. Kera gives me a necklace from the Clay Pot, this idiosyncratic store in Park Slope that people seem to go to when they want to find nontraditional wedding bands and engagement rings; it's got a glass pendant with a different shade of purple on each side of the metal setting, and it is sturdy and beautiful. Everything, on this night, is sturdy and beautiful. We go out for pasta at a restaurant in Gramercy Park and talk about the fun we used to have, and the things we will do when I get back to New York.

But it doesn't matter: I spend much of the night hiding in the bathroom, cutting and snorting lines. For some reason, I think no one will notice.

The problem was me. I was it.

That's what I believed. I believed I was the everything.

The largeness of my disaster dragged others—frankly, everyone—down with me. I was certain that entire rooms of people became vertiginously joyous when I was high and having fun, and that anyone who got near me when I was morose and coming down would have to feel my pain as potently as I did. Whether I was high or low, the intensity was so great and the world became so small—no larger than the size of me and my mood of the moment—that it was hard to imagine that anything else was going on. It was hard to believe that there were things happening in the world that were not about me.

On the way to my birthday party, my friend Lily had a car accident in a New York City taxi, nearly had her eye sliced off, and ended up in the hospital and went through several rounds of surgery before she got even sort of better. And never once did I call her to say that I hoped she was okay. But the real problem was not that I shrugged off that accident and failed to call or visit: The problem is that I do not recall this happening at all. In fact, by the time I spoke to Lily again, many months hence, all I could ask was why she had not come to my birthday party. Why had she missed it?

An even bigger problem, I might add, is that this incident is about Lily—it is her story, not mine. And yet I have used it to tell you something about myself. I have used it to tell you that as far as I knew at the time, everything was about me.

On the plane ride home, I understand that I have run out of reasons, that I have now moved on to excuses.

That's the difference between using and abusing: when you use drugs, they are indeed useful; they help you get through. By the time you are abusing, it's just about the drugs; addiction is its own thing. I do drugs because I do drugs—doing drugs makes you want to do more drugs—and that's what makes it an addiction. It feeds on itself, it is a closed system, it has no external logic at all. In that way, it's like true love: at first you fall for the person because of this thing or that. There is a shopping list of reasons—he has an interesting job; he smiles like Tom Cruise; he is dapper like Cary Grant; he can teach you how to drive stick without losing his patience; when he looks at you, it's like the world has stopped. But once you're in love, you can't remember how it got started or why: you are *in love*, you are lost in the person and the relationship, the relationship is its own reason.

And when you break up, once again, you are back to the list. You are looking for someone with that same interesting job, someone who smiles like Tom Cruise, someone with Cary Grant's dash, someone who is calm about teaching you to drive in the Target parking lot, someone who makes the world stop every time he looks at you. And it's ridiculous, because no one else will ever have those exact qualities again. The next person you fall for will have a whole other roster of wonders—he'll have eyes like Paul Newman's, he'll serenade you with his guitar, he'll cook wonderful coq au vin, he'll kiss you and you'll see fireworks, or whatever—and you will realize those individual pieces that make you fall in love with a person don't matter at all. It's the whole thing, it's the entire feeling, it's the big fat love in your heart—that's what does it.

So I could say I love cocaine because it makes me forget that I am waiting for some guy to call me. I can tell you I love speed because it lets me stay awake for days. I could claim that I love heroin because when I'm on it I just don't care about anything at all. And it would be true, it would all be true. But it doesn't matter anymore. I do drugs to do drugs. My loneliness, my self-pity, my romantic failures—those were all excellent reasons to pick up dope in the first place. But they don't matter anymore. The world has gone on without me. Life has gone on without me. Things have changed. For all I know, I could be in New York, hang out with my friends and do good work, and fall in love—and not feel lonely at all. Who knows what my life would be like?

The circumstances that got me started on my addiction no longer exist. I'm doing what I'm doing because I just can't stop.

Eleven

DO NOT DISTURB

Abandon all hope, all ye who enter.

DANTE ALIGHIERI
Inferno

My mother cannot find me for weeks at the Schubert. I'm like Theseus lost in Daedalus's labyrinth. Only the problem isn't that I can't find my way out— it's that no one else can find her way in. When she finally reaches me, from New York, she insists that I move back into her apartment, at least for the time being, because she is worried about what is happening to me at this fleabag. Like everyone else, she knows something is wrong, no idea what. At any rate, I am happy to take her up on it. I miss her place with all its stark whiteness, its view of the Intracoastal, its proximity to normalcy. My God, but I really want to feel a little bit normal again.

Jeffrey, who is married to Wandy's twin sister Wanda (they have another sister, whose name is Wanfa, but who sometimes calls herself Winnie, sometimes Danielle), is doing the renovations on my mom's apartment. There is dust and sawdust everywhere, from uprooted tiles and cement and plaster and drywall. Wherever I cut lines, they are adulterated with all this household debris. You'd think I'd be desensitized—I already have a constant cold—but the powder from the unraveling apartment makes my nostrils tickle and my eyes red, and I can't stand it.

And I really cannot stand Jeffrey. I never know when he'll turn up, so I cannot leave my lines cut up just anywhere. I do anyway. I always forget where they are—kind of the way you carry a mug of coffee with you as you ready yourself for work in the morning, and you soon misplace it, can't remember if it's next to the curling iron in the bathroom or next to the remote control on the night table. With Jeffrey around, this is a problem.

Jeffrey is supposed to call and say he is on his way, but he is family, he's got the key, he's casual about it. He comes in at eight one morning unannounced. I've been up all night, maybe writing, maybe not, and his arrival jars me. It's not even about the drugs; it's about my privacy. Of course, this is my mom's apartment, so in a way I've already surrendered my privacy, and this too annoys me. Everything annoys me. *I just want to be alone with my drugs.* That's all I want. Just leave us alone, let us be happy together. Why can no one just let us be? We are in love, we are a young and misunderstood couple, everyone wants to tear us apart. I mean, no one actually knows about us—we have kept our passion private. And still, they are all trying to keep us separated. The community disapproves; they say it will never work out between us; they say we are young and foolish—they just don't understand. We are Romeo and Juliet! We are star-crossed lovers. No one will let us be.

When Jeffrey walks in, I've got lines cut up on the TV top's smooth black surface, the *Today* show is on, James Taylor is playing "You've Got a Friend" on their outdoor stage as part of their summer concert series, and I am about to snort up some Ritalin. I am so excited. And then I hear the key in the door. Goddamn it! I sniff up what I can. I whiff in deeply and loudly to feel it all the way— snort quality has become almost as significant as drug quality—and sweep up what's left into the palm of my hand, and run into the bathroom. I pick the wrong one to go into. It's the one that's being retiled. It's the one with pieces of Formica all over the floor because the sink is being redone in some version of marble. As I run in, I trip over a faucet fixture that's loose on the floor, waiting to be installed, and I stumble over and land on the cover of the toilet tank, which is on the floor for some reason. Actually, it's on the floor for no reason—it's just that whenever refurbishments are being done, everything ends up all over the place. There is no logic to it, even parts that aren't being worked on get pushed around. There are sponges and VO5 shampoo and a bar of desiccated Ivory soap with cracks like an old lady's forehead strewn about the floor, a bottle of copper polish, an aerosol can of Pledge—stuff everywhere. And I land in the middle of it. Luckily, my palms are sweaty and sticky, the powder adheres to my hands, so I push what's left into a little pile, a chalky knoll, and snort it up before Jeffrey can come into the bathroom to see if I'm all right. When he walks in, my nose is white, the hand I've landed on is gray, and my white T-shirt is black from dirt. When Jeffrey reaches out to help me, I snap.

"I can get up myself!" I scream. "I'm fine!" I don't want to yell at him. He is nice and diffident and Chinese. I hate when I am rude—and I am nasty all the time now. "I'm sorry, Jeffrey," I try. "I don't mean to yell. I'm just— I'll be okay. Please let me just get myself up here."

But he can't leave it alone. His English is not good. He says nothing. He just reaches over to pull me off the floor. "Jeffrey, I'm fine, really," I say, as he grabs my hand. I push myself up with my spare arm, and I feel myself about to cry. Jeffrey cannot see me cry. No one can see me this way. No one.

What is he doing here?! Why is he invading like this?! I hate him. I hate Jeffrey and I want to kill him. I have cuts and bruises all over the fronts of my legs, some skin has ripped off my foot, and there is running, dripping blood. I am in so much pain and I hate Jeffrey. All I can think is how much I hate him.

"Can you please tell Jeffrey to buzz up and announce himself before he comes in?" I ask my mom on the phone later.

"Early in the morning, everyone assumes you're asleep, Lizzie," she says. "Why aren't you asleep?"

"You know, up all night working."

"When is this book ever going to be done? Weren't you going to be finished months ago?"

Jesus, I hate my mom. Of *course* it was supposed to be done long ago. It always takes longer to do everything than you expect at first. Doesn't she understand that *I am an artist?* I'm not like her. I don't have a list of tasks that take four minutes each to accomplish. I don't do them and check them off and move on. I work my own hours, I wait for inspiration, I live my beautiful bohemian existence, and no one can judge me because I am not like everyone else. I don't have to get married. I don't have to have children. I don't have to pay my own bills. I don't have to own a home. I don't have to eat or sleep or see people or answer the phone or make my bed or defrost the refrigerator. Because I am an artist. I am special. I am a goddess. My book will be done when it is. A work of genius takes as long as it takes. The world will wait. It will sit and wait, holding its breath, wondering what the oracle shall decree, and when I am ready, all will be revealed. My people may have to sit, thirsty and exhausted, in the desert for forty years; they may fabricate a golden calf, they may worship false gods, they may die of heat prostration and dehydration; but they will wait for me to come down from the mountain with my tablets of truth. They will wait.

Because I am an artist. The world waits for art.

Okay, so even I don't believe this. But it's a nice try. If I tell myself this for long enough, maybe it will become true.

"I don't know when my book will be done, Mom," I say. "Soon, I guess."

"You need to find somewhere else to stay. You can't be in that apartment. It makes Jeffrey uncomfortable to walk and find you half asleep. He's a modest man. He doesn't like seeing you in just a T-shirt or whatever you wear to bed."

"He said *that*?"

"No." Of course he didn't. My *mom* feels uncomfortable with his finding me in my sleepwear. Jeffrey could not care less. If I want to walk around the apartment naked while Jeffrey frosts spackle onto the walls and floors, that's my problem. I know she's also worried that I am wearing revealing clothes out of the house, spaghetti straps that will show off the tattoo on my back. She's worried that I have my nose stud in and he'll be able to see. He'll see that she raised me badly, that I am her mistake, that she is a failed mother. I am not a good Chinese child who spends her nights doing homework as his kids do.

"Mom, I'm not wearing anything bad," I say. "I'm a good kid. I really am. I hate the way you're always so worried about how I make other people feel, and you're not at all concerned that Jeffrey walks in here unannounced and upsets me. Why don't you care about me? You care about everyone else more than me. You hate me." I start to cry.

"Lizzie, that's ridiculous and you know it."

It's not ridiculous. And I know *that*. "Look, I'll find somewhere else to stay. I'll check into the Riverside. That's a nice place. I'll just go there." I am still crying. "But I hate the way you hate me."

"I don't hate you." She's impatient. She's not even telling me to stop crying. She's not even worried that I'm upset. She just wants me out of her apartment. "Look, you're doing great. I know it's hard to write a book, and you're under a lot of pressure. You'll probably be a lot happier at the Riverside. You can order room service."

Room service *would* be nice. I've been eating the same turkey hero—with extra cheese, no onions, and dollops of vinegar—for three days. I ordered it up a few nights ago from some sandwich place. Miami Sub, I think. It's soggy. Even though I don't like to eat—food is not very important to speed freaks, which is why Dexedrine was once used as a diet pill by Park Avenue quacks—when I do, I'd rather not have sopping, spoiled cold cuts.

"All right, I'll call and see if they have a room."

"No one goes to Fort Lauderdale in August. I'm sure they'll have a room for you."

"Yeah, I know." I've stopped crying.

"Are you okay?"

"Yeah, I'm fine." I really want to tell her, I want to explain I'm an addict and I need help. I want my mommy. Thing is, she is already so disappointed with me. If she finds out I'm on drugs, I'll just prove her right—prove that, as she has always believed, the nose ring and tattoo *are* signs that I'm bad. I *am* bad. I'm not an artist, I'm not a genius—I'm a mess. She's right. "I'm fine, Mom. I've just got to get my work done. I've got to finish and get back home."

The Riverside Hotel is beautiful, old Florida on old Las Olas, a Depression-era yellow structure with a solarium and a backyard on the Intracoastal, chaise longues scattered on the lawn, terra-cotta tiles and ceiling fans in the lobby, lots of Louis Quatorze couches and breakfronts and ornate frippery and froufrou. It's an odd amalgam of Florida bamboo and European elegance, and I guess it all adds up to the ambience of a New Orleans bordello, circa 1898. I make a deal with the manager, and because it is August—and because I will be staying for at least a month—I get a deluxe room for less than a hundred dollars a night. Every day at five, I go down for afternoon tea. I am always just a little too late, and I always get them to dig up what's left of the cucumber and salmon and dill mini sandwiches, or the scones and Devon cream and boysenberry jam. I can never decide if I want sweet or savory. I only eat a few bites, so they have to be just right.

There are also two restaurants—a steakhouse, and an Indonesian-Floridian regional hybrid called Raffles. There is twenty-four-hour room service, so I order up a lot of satay and exotic breakfast fritattas, mostly in the middle of the night. There are spicy fish and chips and gentle coconut rice. The waiters arrive with their trays, leave them on the bureau, see the piles of papers—at least twenty different drafts of every page of my book—marked up with marginalia and color-coded notes to myself on yellow and pink and green Post-its in blue and red and purple ink. They see my lines cut up on top of the TV, and seem not to notice at all. I've got the computer on, the TV on, the lights on—everything's on except me. I am clearly off. I tip the waiters well. I get to know their West Indian names and reggae accents; I make myself at home. I know the desk attendants. I befriend the Bulgarian beauty—an exchange student from Sofia—who is the Raffles hostess, and give her a copy of my first book in her native language. I am not using them, hoping they won't notice my mess—I am just hyped up as all hell, and eager to chat. I no longer have sensible motives for anything. I do what I feel like. I do what I want. I am paying for a hotel room, instead of staying at my mother's, so I can do what I want.

Sometimes I write, sometimes I don't—the only constant is that I mark time. I am just marking time, biding it away, waiting for things to get bad enough that I have no choice, something has to give. Wendie comes by to hang out and have room service; Aunt Zena and Uncle Bill come to have dinner at the crêpe place across the street and admire the tourmaline necklace

Kathlyn gave me; Wandy and Lewis and the girls come over and bring me a cheesecake. I mark time.

On Labor Day weekend, Lydia is in Miami Beach for several days, and she decides to come up on Saturday night, check into the Riverside, and visit. We go see *G.I. Jane*, which has just opened at the movie theater at the Galleria. I am writing about Demi Moore, so I tell myself this is research. Lydia and I both think the movie is decidedly okay. We hang out in my room and polish our toenails in one of probably three dozen shades I've got with me. We muse over mauves and grapes and greens and reds and russets and wines and frosted pinks and Creamsicle oranges. While we pedicure away, my skirt hiked up above my knees as I lean over my toes, Lydia sees all the sores. I'm too tired to hide them anymore, and she asks what's wrong.

"You know, a lot is wrong," I say. What else can I say? "I'm not healthy." I show her the bumps, the red raised spots like mosquito bites, all over my arms. These blemishes are my latest physical symptom—my skin seems to be chafed from some combination of August heat and hot blood. "I need to finish and get home. I'm falling apart here."

"Is there anything I can do?" she asks, helpfully, I think.

"No. Not really. I just need to get home soon." I am hoping this will catch on as a viable rumor with everybody else: that it's all a Florida thing, that once I return to New York it will all be fine.

"Look, just get your work done and come back," Lydia offers. She's smiling warmly—or maybe she's just grinning knowingly. I can't tell which. Is she sympathizing with me, or is she onto me? Maybe it's both. At any rate, Lydia is trying to be supportive, and I know she means it.

I feel this coming from everyone who's close to me: *We'd love to help, but you've got to want it.* "But I could give it all to you now / If only you would ask," Bruce Springsteen sings in "For You," on his first album. It's a song about rushing a girl to the hospital after she's slit her wrists. It's not her first suicide attempt, he's madly in love with her, and everything he does doesn't prevent her from wanting to be dead. Love is not enough—in fact, it's not anything at all. He can't reach her. Just as it is now, for me—nobody can reach me.

But at least I can feel them trying. When I was young and depressed, I never had a sense that anyone cared. That's no longer my complaint. It's just that, indeed, they cannot reach me, because nothing they can do for me will equal the annihilating and totalizing cold comfort that I get from drugs. I used to listen to "For You" on a portable Panasonic tape recorder in seventh grade, while I cut my legs up with a razor blade in the girls' gym locker room. I used to wish *somebody* wanted to give it all to me—I used to ask all the time. Now, with Ritalin, I just wish that they'd leave me alone. That's the main difference between depression and addiction, as far as I can tell: depression is full of need, and addiction fulfills that need.

And right now, I would like to be fulfilled again. Lydia is not going to help me with all her concern, with all her comforting gestures, reaching for my hand, looking me deeply and lovingly straight in the eyes, directly into my dilated pupils. But drugs will help me. That's all I need.

I can't wait for Lydia to get out of my room and go back upstairs to hers so I can cut up some lines and spread them all over, wherever I want. I hate having to hide my habits. Any of my habits. I know I'm showing through. It's tiring to try to cover up anything anymore. I might as well whip out my pill crusher, smash up the Ritalin, cut it up, and snort away. What does it matter anymore?

After she leaves, I go to it, go at it, lines lines lines. And then there is a knock at my door. What now? *Will no one ever leave us alone to do our thing?* I want to be alone with my one true love. If there were a man in here with me, I would hang out the "Do Not Disturb/No Molesta" sign and everyone would go away.

"Elizabeth, Princess Diana is dead," Lydia says when the door is barely ajar. "I just heard on CNN."

She tells me about the car accident in Paris, Dodi and Diana in the tunnel, chased down by the press, the attempts to resuscitate her. It seems unbelievable. She is so alive. How can she be dead? She was just on the cover of *Vanity Fair*, looking happy, looking in love and free. She's been wearing khakis and visiting minefields. She's been doing great.

And it just seems so typical. Drug addicts often get clean, survive the worst, and then die in some strange and unrelated way. Or their bodies, accustomed to the dope that makes their systems go just so, can't cope with the clean. They have heart attacks and seizures from purity. What the drugs could not do for all those years, the detoxification does to them in no time. Or else it's like *The Unbearable Lightness of Being:* Thomasz and Thereza are finally happy and in love and living in the Czech countryside. He stops cheating on her and they dote on the dog Karenin, and then their car crashes. Their Eastern European hunk of junk kills them—an unsteady automobile does what the Russian tanks and years of heartbreak could not do. Life is so tragic. That's what it comes down to—doesn't it?

And I cry about Diana; I mourn. Not because she was a nice lady who sold her dresses at auction for charity, not because she touched AIDS patients, not because she tried to be a good mother even though her life was so strange— not for any of the press release reasons. I cry because she was beautiful, because she had loveliness and charm. I cry because that is enough. A thing of beauty is a gift to the world—you don't need good deeds to make yourself worthy, to make your life meaningful. If you just have the capacity to make people smile, that is plenty. That's not a small thing. That is a gift from God in an ugly world.

It is nice to cry over something or somebody who isn't me. Or aren't all our tears really for ourselves anyway? When we cry with joy at weddings, aren't we really sad that such happiness belongs to someone else? All our emotions, even the generous ones, even empathy, are really just a way of bringing the woes of the world closer to home. It's all one big opportunity to feel, to feel more.

Betsy arrives at the Riverside on a Monday morning and comes right up to my room after checking into hers. She thinks the hotel is funny and tacky. She doesn't love it as I do. This makes me sad.

She sits down on the crushed-velvet four-poster bed—with a mirrored canopy that would have unnerved Narcissus—and tries to decipher the logic of the different shades of Magic Marker and paper. She does this every day, all day, for four days straight. By Thursday, I think she's figured it out. She is supposed to be coaxing me along, trying to drag the last few chapters out of me, standing with a .38 special at my temple and forcing me to finish. But as soon as she sees me, she abandons that plan. I am so obviously so sick.

When she walks in that first Monday, of course I am awake—I am always up these days—I decide to lay it down. "Look," I say. "I snort Ritalin. That's what I do. I snort it all day long. I crush up the pills and inhale them like cocaine. I'm up to about forty a day. I can't stop. I am planning to get help, to check into rehab or something like that, as soon as this book is finished. In the meantime, I can't stop, and I'm not going to." She looks at me impassively. "I don't care what you think about it. So you have a choice. I can sit here and do it in front of you, or I can keep running into the bathroom so you don't have to see. Either way, it's going to happen, so it's just about how bad it's going to make you feel to watch."

She doesn't seem to know what to say. She stares. I think she is going to cry. I think she wants to give me a hug, maybe, but there is an invisible cage, a delicate netting of glass, an ice sculpture surrounding me that no one can walk through. I'm cold. I've frozen into someone who just can't be touched. I dare you to try.

"I don't think you should be thinking about this book right now," she says. "I think you need to get help." It's that simple. No arguments or hysteria or histrionics from her end. Just a mild suggestion. "This can be postponed. You need to take care of yourself."

"Let's just do what we can for the next few days, and see." I am reasonable, so cool, chilly. "I've thought this through, and I really don't think I'll be ready to get help until I'm done with this. So let's just figure out a way to get it finished. Let's be sensible. Let's not fret. Okay? I know this is bad. I'm not kidding myself. But I want the book in the can before I check in. And then I promise I will. The best thing you can do is help me finish. I don't want you to feel guilty or think you're enabling me or anything like that. Let's just be pragmatic. Please. Please don't try to make me do now what I'm going to do eventually anyway."

I'm really afraid she is going to cry. Betsy found me and signed up my first book when she was a young editor. We are so close. I know she is spent. She has just returned to her job from maternity leave to come down here and work with me. It's not fair to put her in this position. I shouldn't have said anything, but what else could I do? She'll figure it out no matter what. It's just too obvious by now. So I am hoping it will make her feel better to know I have a plan, to know I'm going to get help, that I'm not pretending this is okay.

Whenever I talk to anyone I care about, I am always seeking approval. There is always a pleading lilt in my voice that demands love. Even the people I work with, the ones I am supposed to have professional relationships with, all business, get pulled into my need. I can't help it. I want to be adored. I write for love. But I'm not like that right now. I am calm and insistent. I am not asking Betsy to feel anything or any way about me and what I am doing to myself. I just want her to leave me alone. I want everyone to leave me and my drugs alone. For once, the work we have to do is not about our relationship, because we don't have one right now. I am so in love, I can see nothing and no one besides me and Ritalin and anything else I might pump into my body. You're all objects to me now. That's what I want to say to all my friends, my objects. I needed you all so badly, and it was never enough. Nothing you did was ever enough. So now I have found something that sates me. The burden is off of you. You can use me. I will use you. The slippery element between us, the love I am always begging for—that's gone. You should be relieved. I am all mind now. My heart no longer matters. You're safe with me.

"All right," Betsy says. "Let's get busy."

"Good idea," I say. "Very good idea."

That Thursday, I am moving back into my mom's apartment for the rest of my stay in Florida, however long that is. Jeffrey is done; I can have the place to myself. My mother feels sorry for me and tells me to just go back there.

Betsy and I carry my books, my clothes, my notes, my drafts, my computer, all of it. We get it into her rental car, her midsized sedan, probably a Ford Taurus or something like that, and drag it all up to my mom's place.

She is only staying one more day, and we might as well figure out what's left for me to do. We make lists and notes, talk about women in the Bible, political wives, crazy poets, teenage girls from hell. We sort it all out. She is exhausted with trying to tear pages out of my hand, and I keep trying to explain that there is *just one more* revision I need to make. I suffer over every period and comma; I am certain the entire meaning of the whole book might be changed by an aptly placed semicolon.

"Elizabeth, really, it's all here," Betsy says. "Why don't you stop trying to rework it so many times, and just let it go. Let it go and get some help."

I cut lines on the desk at my mother's apartment and snort them up. At first Betsy was insisting I hide when I use; she doesn't want to see. But like everything else, all the other pretenses, the idea that I am going to cover up is gone. It takes too much time for me to keep running into the bathroom and the closet and the other bedroom. The sooner I finish the book, the sooner I'll quit. The less time I spend concocting concealments, the less time it will take until I will do what's right. So I prop my pile of powder beside my computer. I siphon off sections and snort away. It's pretty constant by now. Only a few minutes go by between courses of drugs. I can see—I can feel—Betsy staring at me, sickened, disgusted. I snap.

"Look, you don't know what it's like to be me. Okay?" I think I am raising my voice. I may even be yelling. I can't tell. "What do you know about my life? How do you think it feels? There you are, you're married, you have a baby, you live in a pretty house in Westchester. You've figured it out. You have parents, you have sisters. Whatever else is wrong—you may get depressed; you may fight with your husband sometimes; you may hate your job sometimes. But you don't know how it is to be like me. I've been depressed for so long that I don't remember life before that. Then they gave me drugs to make me better, and they worked for a little while, but they don't anymore. Nothing works. I have so much—you don't know what it's like to have all these things that are supposed to make you happy, and still, and still—" Where am I going with this? "You don't know. And finally, something works. Finally, I find these drugs, and they help. And you're just pissed off because I've found something that works for me, and I don't need you or anybody anymore, and all anyone wants to do is take them away." Actually, no one wants to take them away, because nobody knows about them, but so what? "You don't like the choices I made. That's easy for you. It's so easy for you to judge. Your life is so easy."

Well, I guess she has come down here to work with me. I guess that's a lot.

But it's not enough. Nothing is ever enough. When someone comes up with something that's enough, I'll take it. In the meantime, I have found the answer.

And I have hurt her feelings. She just wants to make sure I am okay, but realizes I cannot really be dealt with. It's sad. She sees she's lost me, that I am that far gone.

"Look, I'm going to get you some groceries so that you have something to eat while you work, and then I'm going to leave you alone." No emotion, no inflection in her voice. She looks at me, but it's not with anger or contempt—it's with pity. I definitely see something like pity on her face. Fuck her. I am fine.

She walks out, and an hour later she is back. Yogurt, cereal, bagels, Lean Cuisine dinners, orange and grapefruit juices in plastic bottles—it's supposed to be fresh-squeezed, but it's not. I hate that. When I was little and we visited Florida, there were grove stands everywhere, you could get fresh-squeezed juice in roadside 7-Elevens. When did that stop? When did everything good go away? The whole world has gone to hell.

"Thank you," I say, as Betsy unloads the bags from the shopping cart she's brought upstairs, and places everything in the refrigerator and freezer and cupboard. "Thank you. I appreciate it."

"I'm glad."

"Please don't go."

"I really think that's what you want."

"I don't."

"I think you do."

"But I love you." I mean it, I think. "Please."

Betsy sighs. "I'm going back to the hotel. I'm tired. I should call home." So she wants to be reminded of her happy life. Fuck her. "I'll come see you in the morning before I leave. My flight is in the afternoon. Okay?"

"Fine."

The next day, before she leaves, Betsy stops by. She strongly suggests that I check myself in. The book can wait. I would not be the first writer to be withdrawn from the catalogue at the last minute. It's happened with some huge authors. It happens, Betsy says. We can reschedule for the next season or the next year. As long as it takes. Get help, she keeps saying. You're going to kill yourself.

And I say I will, and I mean it. But I tell her the book has to be finished first. Which will not be a problem, because it just needs to be revised one more time. Just one more time.

"I'm going to be okay," I say, and walk over and hug her. We are in my mother's living room, piles of paper all over the floors, different drafts and versions of everything, all organized like my mind, which is to say in a way that only makes sense to me.

"I hope so," she says. "I love you, you know."

"Yeah, I know."

I know. But what does it matter? "My supply / of tablets / has got to last for years and years. / I like them more than I like me," Anne Sexton writes in "The Addict." I like my pills more than I like me, more than I like anybody else. That's the only thing I know that matters.

I watch so many movies. I rent a videotape player from Blockbuster and keep taking out more and more miserable films. A *Woman Under the Influence* and *Faces* by John Cassavettes, *The Crossing Guard* and *The Indian Runner* by Sean Penn, *A Place in the Sun* and *The Searchers.* I always have the lights on in the house, in all the rooms. It rains all the time, and there is a contrast between the incandescence and the clouds. I get distracted studying it and keep rewinding to missed scenes. I watch *Apocalypse Now* for what must be the twenty-eighth time, and then I watch *Hearts of Darkness,* the documentary Francis Ford Coppola's wife made about the making of that war epic. What a mess it was, scripts rewritten in trailers while shooting went on outside, Marlon Brando fatter than anyone ever imagined, Martin Sheen's heart attack, Filipino army helicopters flying overhead during shooting, crazy from the heat, a certain disaster.

And then it turns into one of the best movies ever made. Somehow, it comes together. "It was like the Vietnam War," Copolla says, when he introduces it at the Cannes Film Festival. "We had too much money, too much equipment, too much time, and we didn't know what we were doing."

And then, a masterpiece. The end product was nothing like the war.

I take inspiration from *Hearts of Darkness.* Maybe this book will work out too. All this mess, all these people overworked and overwhelmed and crazy from this thing I've been making for far too long, and maybe it will all be worth it. A beautiful book: at the end of all this, beauty. Perhaps it will be like *Rumours,* the Fleetwood Mac album. Christine and John McVie were breaking up, Stevie Nicks and Lindsey Buckingham were breaking up, everybody sleeping with everybody else, Mick Fleetwood all drunk, they are all doing too much coke, and then this gorgeous album. An album I still listen to all the time now, twenty years later. Maybe that's what will happen to this book, all the craziness, everybody coming to the rescue, everybody scared—maybe it will be a work of genius.

Trouble is, you never know. You never know until it's all done. You may end up with *Apocalypse Now,* but you're more likely to end up with *Heaven's Gate.*

Twelve

YOU DON'T KNOW ME

Someone could walk into this room and say your life is on fire

PAUL SIMON

"Crazy Love, Volume 2"

My mom walks into the house one day in October at eight-thirty in the morning, which is reasonable enough, since this is her apartment. She has been driving from the South Carolina border since sometime in the middle of the night, and she's got a whole car to unload, and she is probably expecting me to help.

She finds me sitting on the floor in the den that is my room, watching *Dr. Katz: Professional Therapist*, a cartoon on Comedy Central. Dr. Katz is a psychiatrist, and various neurotic celebrities—Winona Ryder, Sandra Bernhard, Janeane Garofalo, and a lot of comedians I've never heard of—play his patients. They basically do their stand-up routines, which are strangely reminiscent of the kinds of things you say in therapy, which makes me think that if this writing business does not work out, I may have another career option. I love the show. I watch it every Sunday night, and the back-to-back reruns at eight every morning.

Unfortunately, as I am quietly minding my own business, the fire detector suddenly goes off, making that cawing noise that sounds like a nervous seagull calling out for help. I barely notice, because this happens all the time. I always have candles lit, and I hate it if there is wax left over at the end, so I throw matches into the holder to create a new wick, and eventually the mesh of matches turns into a torch, and eventually the glass gets burned and explodes, and drippings of wax splatter everywhere, like a Jackson Pollock painting. I have set two comforters on fire already, so this no longer bothers me.

My mom, on the other hand, is hysterical.

I tell her to just let the candle burn itself out. It will do that anyway. Throwing water at it will only make the flame fly, which will burn the ceiling. I should know; it happens all the time. But she is in a panic. My calm reserve, which I figure should put her at ease, is just making her more hysterical.

"What's wrong with you?" she screams. "You're going to start a fire!" The detector keeps making these horrible noises.

"Don't worry," I say. "Just get your stuff from the car, and we'll have some coffee and watch *Dr. Katz*. You'll love this show. It's very funny."

The various texts I am reading for research—*Samson's Struggle, The Complete Poems of Anne Sexton, In Potiphar's House, The Reproduction of Mothering, The Oresteia* trilogy, *A Vindication of the Rights of Women*—are in high piles against the wall because there are no bookshelves in the house, because my mother doesn't read. There are about eighty books in all. There are papers and printouts of pages strewn all over the floor, and my mom is apoplectic looking at the mess. I actually did a pretty good job of cleaning up in anticipation of her arrival, vacuumed and everything, but my idea of clean and hers diverge widely.

"Lizzie, for God's sake please get up and do something about this!"

I just stay put, staring at the TV, determined that my mom is not going to interrupt my wonderful little life. "Mom, don't worry," I say, looking up at her face, contorted with worry, for long enough to fix a soothing stare at her. "Everything will take care of itself."

"We need to talk," my mother says later in the day, as she wakes me up with a cup of coffee. The coffee is a nice touch. Either she is very happy to see me, or what she has to tell me is so awful that she's compensating in advance.

"I can't live like this," she begins. I roll over onto my side, my face to the wall, hoping she will understand that I am not yet ready to wake up. No dice. "I can't have your mess everywhere. All these books. All this paper."

"It's all in neat piles against the wall," I yawn. "What else can I do? You don't have shelves."

"Can we put these things in boxes and ship them back to New York?"

I pop up, a jack-in-the-box, I spring to life. Send them back to New York? I need them to do my work. "Mom, I'm not done with my book."

"Elizabeth, I don't know how to say this nicely, but—" Long pause. "You will never be done with this book. It never ends. Maybe you should get some other job. Maybe you can't write right now. I don't know what's happening, but you don't seem to be getting anywhere."

Okay, now she's really asked for it.

"How dare you, who have never read a word of my last book, presume to know whether this is working or not?" I am calm, speaking in that understated way that lets people know you are a hair trigger from explosion. "What do you know about my life? What do you know?"

"I know something is wrong."

"Why? Because I'm not afraid of the fire detector?"

Actually, that probably is a pretty good sign that I'm going down. I lie back down again. I can see this conversation is going to take some time.

"Lizzie, something is just wrong." She sighs. "You know how I was so glad you wanted to stay down here. I helped you find an apartment and all." She has this grating Brooklyn accent, and if I don't get some Ritalin inside of me, I may have to stuff my fingers into her mouth and choke her to shut her up. "But it's time for you to go back. It's been a year. This isn't working anymore. I don't know what to do with you. We can't both be in this house. I can't watch you sleep all day and stay up all night. It isn't normal."

"What do you know about normal?" I am no longer speaking in measured tones. "How dare you judge my lifestyle. This works for me. I wrote a bestseller this way—"

"You were not this way when you wrote *Prozac Nation*."

"How do you know?"

"I saw you. You were fine." More sighing. "You are not fine now."

"I'm thirty years old. I'm tired of your judgments. You just don't like me. You never liked me." I am yelling, and I am starting to cry, and I am flat on my back. I curl up into fetal position. I don't know if I am trying to look meek and defensive, or if this is a reflex and I really *am* meek and defensive. I have no natural gestures left. "You hate me! And I hate you too!"

She starts to hyperventilate. Really. Her breathing begins to sound like the fire detector, like a quacking duck. Oh Jesus.

"I don't know what's wrong with you." Now she's starting to cry. "But I can't watch this. Go home. Go see Dr. Singer. Go be with your friends. Some-thing's wrong."

"Oh, what do you know?" She's right, of course. I need to go back. But I'm not going to give this one to her. "You don't know me at all."

At the airport, a couple of weeks later, we both cry. All my boxes have been shipped up by UPS, so it's just me, my computer, and a carry-on bag. I have no strength. I didn't even pack myself up. She did everything. She went into old-fashioned Jewish-mother mode. I lay there, and she took care of everything.

She figures I've slipped back into a bad depression. She asks a lot of questions about my medication. Does it need to be adjusted? Do I need some new pill?

Yeah, sure, I need a new pill. I need a lot of them. Oh, Mommy, if you only knew.

"I have an appointment with Dr. Singer tomorrow," I say, instead of just telling her the truth, which I want to do so badly. But I know it would do no good. She'd be no help. In fact, she'd be the opposite of helpful. What's the word for that? *Hurtful*, I guess. Or *harmful*. My mother has spent all her life wanting so much to be helpful to me, and mostly it just goes the other way. Poor thing. Poor sad thing. She does not deserve me any more than I deserve her. What a mismatch we are.

And we love each other so much.

"Mommy, I'll be fine," I say as I am about to walk through the metal detector. "I'll call you when I get home. God, I have a year's worth of messages to listen to."

"Call me before you do that."

I start to walk away, and I feel my eyes watering up. Here we go again. More tears. Another teary scene between Lynne and Lizzie is about to occur. I run back to her, standing and watching me walk away. She is wearing a pastel T-shirt with shoulder pads. No matter what I do she refuses to see that they look silly. She thinks they balance her out, make her top match her bottom. Instead, they just look dated. And they make her look old, which she's not. So I focus on what she's wearing, the bright overstuffed top. She looks like the Easter bunny. I want to make myself laugh, but I just keep crying.

"I love you, Mommy," I say. "I'm going to be fine. Okay? Will you please believe me? Please."

We hug. She's crying too. "I hope so. I hope so."

I sit next to a young couple on the plane. They are on their way back to New York from the Bahamas. She is French, an Algerian Jew, named Levana. Jacob is a broadcast journalist, and his mother is an actress who had some renown in the seventies, when she tended to be cast in roles that demanded a brainy, delicate beauty. I don't know how this comes up. Maybe he tells me he's from Santa Monica, and I ask if his parents are in show business. At any rate, I am one of the few people on earth who can get excited about his mother, who has mostly been forgotten by time. I tell Jacob that I saw several of her movies as part of a deranged housewife series at the Brattle Theatre in Cambridge. I quote some of her more noteworthy lines, and ask if she can really play the piano, since she was exceptionally good as a musician in one of her films.

"Wow," he smiles. "You really know her career."

"I see a lot of movies," I explain, modestly, I think. I also tell him that I am writing a lot about film in my book, and her performances have come up in a couple of places. I used her as an example of these great actresses from the sixties and seventies who seem to have disappeared—Carrie Snodgress, Katharine Ross, Cristina Raines, Ronee Blakley, the women of the American New Wave. And then I ask, "What's she doing now?"

"Independent movies. And she teaches. She's kind of crazy and difficult." Of course she is. "Hollywood doesn't work for her anymore."

I keep getting up to go to the bathroom and do more Ritalin. I've ground down a lot of pills for the plane, and put the powder in an orange prescription bottle. There are many reasons not to do this. For one, it's easy for it to spill out, those childproof caps are hard to open, but they stay on loosely. And worse, if the security people had decided to search my pocketbook for some reason, they would think it's cocaine, which would be a mess. Thankfully, nothing like that happens.

Jacob and Levana have been dating for only a couple of months, but they just got engaged in Nassau. She is wearing a magnificent ring, a Tiffany-cut diamond from, yes, Tiffany. It looks all wrong on her. She is very hippie-ish, the type who wears silver rings with tigereyes and moonstones and ethnic jewelry that you might buy in a head shop on Eighth Street, but she'll probably grow into it.

"Are you doing coke in the bathroom?" Jacob asks me as I sit down from one of my Ritalin runs. We've known each other about an hour, and I've stood up about five times; I always get the aisle seat on planes. I'd say this was an intimate question, but since the answer is yes, it's okay. If you see what I mean.

"Why?" There has to be a motive.

"Well, we're not holding because we're coming from a foreign country, and they're really strict about drugs on the islands," he says. "You know, they hate that Americans go there just to get high."

"The Bahamas?" It's not like it's Jamaica. "The worst vice there is gambling."

"The whole Caribbean." I can see he is annoyed that I am pursuing this tangent. "So you know, we haven't done any for the last ten days. I was hoping—"

"It isn't coke." Can I possibly explain that it's Ritalin? I haven't tried that on another drug user. Betsy and Kathlyn find it strange enough, but other cokeheads might be truly stumped. On the other hand, they might be fascinated and wonder if they're missing out on something.

"It's speed," I say.

"Crystal meth?"

"No."

"Yeah, you've got white stuff all over your nose. Crystal meth wouldn't stick that way."

He's right. This man knows drugs.

"You know," I say. "I would love to find a way to get some coke back in the city. I mean, for me speed is just a cheap substitute. Are you connected?"

"Sure. Of course."

I smile. "We'll have to hang out."

When we land in Newark, it is pouring. It's October 31, the beginning of the November rains. I miss Florida already.

I pull my black suede fringe jacket on tight, and prepare to freeze. A car is supposed to pick me up. I offer Jacob and Levana a ride into the city. They live in the Village too. On the way home, I find a slip from the ATM in my bag, and Jacob writes down their number and the pager number for his Dominican dealer. We make plans to hang out and do blow together later in the week. Jacob is a television news producer—and his area is the stock market. He puts together a stock market wrap-up report. I can't imagine how he manages. Or maybe the coke helps.

I go straight from the car into my apartment. I don't look around me. It's Halloween, and I don't want to see remnants of the parade in the Village, drag queens dressed like Liza and Barbra, placards that say "Fuck Giuliani!" and demand more money for AIDS research and AIDS care and AIDS medicine. Fuck them all. I've got my own damn problems. Someone dressed as a fairy godmother or an angel walks by as I open the door to my lobby and wishes me a happy Halloween. She touches my head with her magic wand, a long wooden stick with a cardboard star plated in aluminum foil at the tip, and tells me to make a wish.

I *could* wish that my book gets finished soon, I *could* wish that I get clean, or I *could* be fanciful and wish for true love or peace on earth. Instead, I wish to myself that the dealer answers my page. I wish, I wish, I wish.

I'm going to get upstairs. It should not be too much of a shock—it's only been three months. I'll call Mommy, because I said I would. I'll make myself a cup of tea, because I always do. I'll snort up some Ritalin, because I must. And then I'm going to get a hold of José, the coke man. It's too tiring keeping myself supplied with prescriptions. As soon as Dr. Singer sees me, that'll be the end of her complicity.

But that's okay. Cocaine is fine. Just fine.

Somebody once said—and I wish it were I—that the first word in happy is ha and the last word in lonesome is me.

I hate to think that the drugs all come down to loneliness, but that would seem to be the case. They are reliable company. I don't need, much less want, people around when I am using. That often means I have to share my stuff with them, and even more often it means that I have to conceal my use from them. I can't stand people's disapproving eyes. I hate the way they look disgusted. And they do, they always do. I have all these very straight, clean-living friends, which is unusual for addicts, but probably a tribute to my good health. I know that I will get clean because no one around me is aiding and abetting.

But no one around me seems able to touch my loneliness.

Of course, it's not for lack of trying.

When I was in Florida, my ex-boyfriend Jackson came to see me, Kathlyn came to see me, Lydia threw me a birthday party, Betsy came down to work with me, and all my friends kept phoning and looking for me, even after months of unreturned calls and unrequited love on my part. Love is all around, and I know I've got to clean up. I know I cannot forsake this love. I know my friends don't deserve this. I know my life does not merit this.

So I am going to finish writing my book. I am going to check myself in. I am going to do all the things I am supposed to. I'm committed to it—but what will end my loneliness? After I get off the rehab assembly line, after I finish being the recalled model that's gone back to the factory for new parts, who is the owner that is going to claim me?

They can take away my drugs, but I cannot imagine that they will ever be able to take away my loneliness.

Thirteen

IN CASE

I'm Miss World
Somebody kill me
Kill me pills
No one cares, my friends
My friend

I made my bed, I'll lie in it
I made my bed, I'll die in it

COURTNEY LOVE
"Miss World"

How long have I been sleeping? It's dark outside right now, another missed day. But what day? Wednesday? Thursday? Is it already the weekend?

All right, well, let's see. What do I remember? I got some coke the first night I got in, did it until the next evening, which meant that I missed my appointment with Dr. Singer. There was a worried message from her on my answering machine when I came to. Then Ben stopped by, after work, just to say hi on his way home to his wife on the Upper West Side and we ended up necking on my couch. Afterwards we said let's never let that happen again, we don't want to ruin our friendship. But then I kept thinking about when we would do it again. And then I went over to visit Jacob and Levana, my new coke buddies, and we called our dealer—José is now *our* dealer—and got an eightball and stayed up all night doing it. Then sleep.

Now, what day was that? Yesterday? Or this morning? Shit. Does it matter? In Florida it didn't matter because I never needed to be anywhere, but I know there are things I need to do now that I'm back. I just can't remember what any of them are. The phone has been ringing all day. I have the ringer turned off and the volume on the answering machine turned down, but I can hear the beep as it takes messages, I can hear the click as it picks up, and I know something must be going on that I should know about. I'd have to actually stand up and go downstairs to figure out what that might be.

This fucking loft bed! That's what I hate about this apartment: I have to climb up a ladder to sleep at night, like a little kid with a bunk bed. But I'm not a little kid anymore, and it's not fun. It also ruins spontaneity. I used to call my loft the no-doesn't-mean-no bed, because once a guy had actually climbed up into it, it was enough of a pain in the ass that I pretty much had to go through with it — sex, that is — or it would almost be rude not to. But on a more pragmatic level — because, at the moment, no one is up here with me — I should really go downstairs and listen to my messages, see what I've been missing. That's what's funny about checking your messages after several hours, or days — it's like finding out what your life might be like in some parallel universe, what you might have been doing if you had actually been keeping track, if you'd actually been engaged with people during that time, instead of ignoring them. Like: "Hey, it's Jethro, Max and I were just heading to the Old Town for a drink if you want . . ." "Hi Lizzie, it's Lily. I'm going to see *Boogie Nights* at ten on Nineteenth Street if you're interested . . ." "It's Daisy. I'm wondering if you want to have dinner on Thursday . . ." "This is Kathlyn. Just checking in, thought I might come say hello when I leave the office, probably sometime after six . . ."

Well, I guess I should get up and see what I've been ignoring.

My buzzer starts ringing. Goddamn it! Am I expecting somebody? Shouldn't whoever it is call first? Isn't that the polite thing to do here in New York City? This isn't Florida, where people just drop by. Of course, I suppose calling would do no good, because it's not like I'm answering my phone or anything like that, but still. I just want to be left alone here. I've still got some coke, I think, and if not, I'll call José and get more, and anyone else is not welcome.

But the buzzer just keeps going, that loud ranting and raving alarm. Come to think of it, maybe it's the fire detector, although I think whatever candles I lit must have burned out hours — or days — ago. Couldn't say how long it's been.

And the buzzer just keeps at it. Clearly, I'm not getting up to answer it, so whoever it is should just give up, go away.

And then it stops.

But now I hear the sound of footfalls on the staircase. And it sounds like the feet are wearing high heels. I can recognize the noise of stilettos driving into the wood steps like nails; whoever it is should make sure her shoe doesn't get pegged into the staircase permanently. If it's someone coming for me, she would deserve it. Ha ha ha! I still have a sense of humor, see? It's getting nastier, maybe a tad more malevolent, but if you had that sound of the buzzer ringing at you, especially in a completely dark and otherwise still and staid apartment, you would be mean too.

Now I hear banging. And the banging happens to be against my door. Bang bang bang, rap rap rap, knock knock knock. Whoever it is, is hitting pretty hard against that thing, which I happen to know is hollow aluminum. Maybe she— and I know it's a she; I can tell—will just push at it until it opens itself. That would be fine with me. I really don't care who comes in here, to be honest, just so long as I don't have to get up and open the door. I just want to lie here.

The banging noise goes on for a few more minutes until I hear the key turn and the door actually opens. See—I got my wish. I did not have to stand up. I guess one of my neighbors has my key. I'm pretty sure that's true, though it's been about a year since I had reason to think about it. But yes, that's right: the couple who lives right downstairs from me has a spare copy, just in case. I never knew what *in case* might entail, but now I see: I hear Lydia's voice downstairs thanking whoever it is for letting her in, and I hear the key bearer saying something about how he hopes everything is okay, let him know if he can help, and I feel a bit jubilant because at long last, an *in case* has occurred. I've been in this apartment for two years, and finally there is a reason why I dragged my butt down to the corner True Value hardware store and had that key duplicated: it's so that they could come in and find me when I do not want to be found.

"Elizabeth!" Lydia yells from downstairs. She's turned on the overhead lights, which irritate my eyes a little bit, but not that much. "Where are you?"

I see there are a couple of lines cut on the back of a book next to my bed, so I snort them up before I answer. I'm getting good at this—good at the quick sniff, that is. "Lydia?" I yell, like it's perfectly normal for her to be in my apartment, though she has never been here before. "I'm upstairs. In my bed."

I move the book to behind the lamp next to my bed —it's actually just a mattress on the floor of the loft. There is still some coke on it—the book, that is— which I might want to scrape up once Lydia is gone. I stop to look at the title. *Lust and Other Stories* by Susan Minot, a collection of her short fiction. I have several copies of it, both in hardcover and paperback, because I love the title story so much, though the rest I can take or leave. People keep giving it to me. Its cover is shiny and black, a good surface for cutting lines. One of the stories inside is called "Blow."

I hear Lydia clambering up the ladder. I look around to make sure that there is no coke in evidence. I am afraid she will take it away. When did I become her child? Why do I feel like everyone's child—everyone's *delinquent* child? I used to be so good. When did this happen?

"Is something wrong with you?" she asks as her head comes into view, her platinum blond hair leading the way.

"Well, yeah, I'm a little sick, I guess. I've been sleeping off some bug."

"We've been trying to call you for the last two days," she says. What does she mean by *we*? I hear the accusation coming. It's sneaking up, a guerilla attack, but I know it's on its way. I'm not that easy to fool. "We've been leaving you messages. You don't call back. I've always asked you to please, whatever else is going on, just call."

"I was asleep."

"Look, I'm not going to yell at you, because I know you think that I'm treating you like a child." Good for her—she's catching on. "But you were supposed to be at a photo shoot yesterday. We talked about it on Monday, and you said it was fine. What happened?"

"What photo shoot?" I've already done the session for the cover of my book months ago in Miami Beach. That picture has been chosen, so it's all finished with. I have no idea what she's talking about. "Whatever it is, let's just reschedule it. I was sick. I was too sick to move. I haven't been out of bed since—what day is it?"

"Thursday." She is now up in the loft, but she's not sitting down. She's standing, looking peeved—no, *pissed* is the right word—and she knows if she squats down to my level she will lose her authority. I know Lydia. She likes to be in control. "It's Thursday, Elizabeth. And yesterday was Wednesday. Yesterday you were supposed to be at a photo shoot for a Coach ad."

Oh shit. Now I remember. The Coach bag people have been doing this campaign where they use vaguely prominent—as opposed to completely famous—people as models. Kind of like those old Gap ads, the ones where, say, Spike Lee's cinematographer was shown in a T-shirt that he had done up in his own way, maybe cut up the sleeves or doodled something on the front. Now Coach was doing the same thing, and they'd asked me. And God how I'd wanted to. I said yes immediately. It was just maybe a week ago. It worked out really well because I would be back in town in time to do it—and I guess I'd said that yesterday was good for me. Shit.

"All right, Lydia," I say. "I feel like an idiot already, so don't make me feel worse, but tell me what happened."

"Well, you were supposed to be there at nine. At ten, I got to work and there were messages looking for you. So I called you."

"Yesterday morning?" I am asking because I'm stalling. I need to come up with a pretty good explanation for this one. Isn't the flu good enough? I mean, isn't it possible that you could get so sick that you were too passed out to even remember to call and cancel? That happens. Doesn't it? And what if I *had* been in the hospital—what if I'd been hit by a car en route to the studio and ended up in the Saint Vincents emergency room? They would have to forgive me for that, wouldn't they? We could just call them and explain now. "But wait, Lydia, if this happened yesterday morning, why are you only here now?"

"I tried to call."

"Yeah, but you knew this was a really big deal. Why didn't you come here and get me?" Did I really ask that?

But really, it's not all that crazy to expect a human wake-up visit, considering what's at stake. I mean, the *whole rest of my life* is on the line here. Like all the women I know who really ought to know better and pretend that beauty is skin deep and blah blah blah, I really want to be Cindy Crawford. How nice it would be to toss my Macintosh out the third-floor window and spend the rest of my life as a supermodel. I'd chuck it all for the cover of *Harper's Bazaar*. Yes, I am ready for my close-up. I'm ready to sashay down the catwalk. And now, goddamn it, because stupid Lydia wouldn't come to my home and wake me up because of a stupid matter of principle—as if it's *my* responsibility to get myself out of bed in the morning—I am going to have to spend the rest of my life writing!

I should grab this fussy antique lamp that I took from my grandmother's house that is next to my mattress and club Lydia over the head.

"So now it's my fault. Is *that* what you're saying?"

"I had the ringer turned off—"

"That's not the point." Deep, exhausted inhale for emphasis. "The point is, I'm not your baby-sitter. No one in my office is your baby-sitter. We made these arrangements, we talked about them the day before. I spoke to you on Tuesday, and you said everything was fine."

"I did?" I *did*? I must have been high. Yes, of course—I *was* high.

And what does she mean she's *not* my baby-sitter? Of course she is. If I were Naomi Campbell, I'd have a whole entourage. I'd have twenty-two assistants, at least two of them hired to do nothing but apply mascara, so that I wouldn't have to waste precious minutes doing one eye at a time. But now that's never going to happen, and I am going to have to spend the rest of my life looking after myself and worrying about my own eyelashes. Goddamn it!

"Are you *sure* I said I was fine?" I ask, hoping there's been some kind of mistake.

"Yes." Another deep, dismayed breath. "And I said I'd stop by the studio during lunch to see how it was going. I just feel bad because you were so excited." She looks down at me lying on my mattress like I am. "Look, this isn't a big deal for me, but it would have been so fun for you. They were paying you

$5,000, they were giving you another $5,000 worth of Coach products, and the ad would be in magazines and billboards and bus shelters everywhere. You were thrilled. You were so thrilled."

Must she rub it in?

But I do feel kind of bad. Because I can see that Lydia truly isn't angry. I can see she just feels sorry for me. She's on my side, and she does not know what to do to help me. It sucks for her. It sucks for me. This sucks.

"Look, Elizabeth, you've got to level with me about what is going on with you—"

"Wait, can we just talk about the Coach thing for a second? Can you tell them I was sick, really ill, like I had bronchitis or something, that it wasn't my fault, so we can reschedule it?"

"Elizabeth! Damn it! It doesn't work that way." She is tired of standing. She pulls off her coat and actually curls up on the floor. She folds her legs up to her chest and leans on her knees. I've got to give her credit for doing this in an elegant Dolce & Gabbana suit. "There's no way they're rescheduling. It's already cost like twenty thousand dollars in wasted time, in studio space, for the photographer, for everything. They're not going to give it another chance. You're not that important. You're not important at all, actually. It's not like you're Julia Roberts and it's worth it to them to have you in this campaign. It's more of a favor to you than to them."

Ouch. That hurts.

"But, look, if you told them I was severely ill, or that there was a death in the family—"

"I am not going to lie for you."

Why not? Why won't she? Why can't she just do me this one little favor and lie this one little time? Even if she is right, and even if I am wrong, I can't see that an itty-bitty fib—or even a big fat fabrication—is not justified by the enormity of the situation. After all, Christy Turlington is a full-time student at NYU and has mostly retired. The fashion world *needs* me.

"All right, well, then I'll call and explain," I try. "I'll say I'm really sorry, that my appendix burst or something."

"Elizabeth, it's too late." She looks at me and shakes her head. "Just because so many people in your life—including me, I have to say—will drop everything for you, and run down to Florida to work with you and make sure you're okay, does not mean that total strangers are going to do the same thing. They just wasted a lot of money yesterday. They won't take a chance like that again."

"Did you try? Did you try telling them something?" Anything.

She starts to laugh. Thank God, she is looking at me affectionately again.

"You know you're so funny, because you know that of course I did everything I could to stall and delay. You know I would do anything for you. You know it, don't you?"

I smile. I know she's being very generous, and at the same time, I feel like she is acting like my mom.

"So it's really too late?" I ask again.

"It is."

"You're sure?" Because I don't totally trust her—I think she might be trying to punish me, that maybe something can be done, but she doesn't want to do it because she wants me to learn a lesson. Not that I blame her—but if I have to learn a lesson, does it have to be this one? Does it have to be with the Coach bag ad? Because, really, I wanted to do it so badly. It felt like some kind of apotheosis, that it would make me a real celebrity. This would be a whole new thing. Fuck. "I mean, couldn't I just try to call?"

"You really don't trust me, do you?"

Actually, I don't. "Of course I do."

"Because if you listen to your messages from the last few days, you'll hear me calling over and over again, and telling you that if you could just get over there, even though it was late, it would be fine. You'll see I did every-thing."

"All right then." Now I'm sighing. "Now what?"

"I spoke to Kathlyn today." So it's come to this. Lydia is calling Kathlyn to make arrangements on my behalf. They are in cahoots, as if I'm no longer in control of my own faculties. I guess I kind of am not. "She's been trying to call you also. She rang your buzzer last night. We were both really worried. We didn't know what happened. I finally came here now because I thought, I don't know, you could be dead."

"Well, if I were dead, it would be too late, wouldn't it?"

"Stop being clever." She's right. She's being nice and I'm not being fair. "I thought of calling the police, but it seemed like a bad idea. So when I still couldn't find you, I came over myself." I know what she means by *bad idea*. She means I might end up in jail. She knows I'm doing illegal stuff, she doesn't know what exactly, but she knows something is up.

That's a lie: She knows exactly what's up. Everybody knows I'm on drugs. Everybody.

She tells me that Kathlyn would never betray a confidence, but this is a matter of life and death. And I want to say *ix-nay on the yperbole-hay*, but she may have a point. I guess I could probably end up dead from all this. I wouldn't be the first. So she tells me that she knows I have plans to go into treatment when the book is done. She's spoken to Betsy about it. Everyone knows. No need to try to hide it. It's my business what I decide to do about my problems, but she would like me to present her with a plan—when will this happen? When will I be ready to check in, and where will I go? And in the meantime, I need to get myself set up in a way that they can keep track of me, that they don't need to worry about where I am, because it's just too scary. I've committed myself to finishing this book, Lydia points out, and if I'm planning to do that, there's a lot of work to be done—and fast.

"We need to be able to reach you," Lydia says. "Betsy needs to be able to find you, I need to be able to talk to you about work." She rubs her eyes and grimaces. "We need to get you to some place so that we know where you are."

"You do know where I am." Pause. "I'm *home*."

"Where we know you're safe."

"I see what you mean."

Kathlyn and Lydia have called various hotels around town. The only place—the only *decent* place—that has a room available immediately is the Peninsula. It will cost $450 a night.

"All right, whatever," I say, resigned. My drug habit does not cost nearly as much as its appurtenances seem to. Cocaine is costly, but once I get hold of Ray and get his Ritalin from him, it won't be expensive at all. I think I may even prefer Ritalin to cocaine. I might like the effect better. Or maybe not. Or maybe there is not much difference. Perhaps that is the real scandal—a prescription medication that is routinely meted out to children in grade school may well have almost the same effect as cocaine.

Coach hires Katie Roiphe to replace me for its ad campaign. We went to college together, Katie graduated a year after me, and her first book came out a year before mine. I actually like Katie very much, but not her book, which was about date rape hysteria and puritanical feminism, and which I thought was full of sloppy writing and shoddy reasoning. When I talk about her, I use flattery as a dig—I'll say something about how Katie is so smart but it's a shame that her book was so dumb, and like that. I think friends of ours from college believe that I feel competitive with Katie. As if. I mean, *me* competitive? *Moi*? Never!

But this Coach bag thing enwreaths me with envy. Now Katie's picture will be in the pages of *Vogue*, Katie's likeness will be in the window of the Coach flagship store on Fifty-seventh Street. Katie's—not mine! It is small consolation that I was their first choice.

And I know this is ridiculous. For all the dumb things I've done because of drugs, it is this Coach campaign that finally gets to me. Vanity, vanity, all is vanity.

have a nothing-special room at the Peninsula Hotel. It's small and dark, in a corner on the alleyway, in the back of the building. The carpets are gray, the bathroom is marble, the minibar is stocked, the amenities are lovely, but it is a tiny room, the only one available. At $450, I am paying the lowest rate. If I had some kind of corporate deal, if I had done this far enough in advance to have seen what a travel agent could have done for me, I would have gotten a deluxe room for the money. But my life is not like that any longer. There is nothing organized about anything that happens—my life is one long emergency. I call the coke dealer in desperation, and by the time he arrives, I already needed it two hours before. Everything in my life is a *must*—there is no space for desire, for want, for wishes like the ones I could have made when the fairy godmother drew her scepter and granted me grace on Halloween. The only wish I have is for more coke now, more speed now, more pills now. My life is defined by need.

By this time, I have switched from Ritalin to cocaine, because I've spent out my old sources. The night I arrive at the Peninsula, I call Ray to say I am back in town, can he come by and hang out? I tell him I'm at this magnificent hotel, there is a bar on the roof with views of the kaleidoscope of the skyline. I tell him it will be fun, we'll actually talk; it won't be just me calling him to get my supply. We'll catch up We'll talk about rock 'n' roll. He can tell me about the new cool bands, because I've been in Florida for a year, so I am very out of it. I'll give him an update on Ruby, because I've been in touch with her again. She's back from Ukraine and working at the World Bank headquarters in D.C. Her divorce is almost final, and she's getting hitched again soon, to a guy she met in Warsaw, a stringer for *The Washington Post*.

Ray comes over the night after I arrive at the Peninsula. I open the door and welcome him into my room with all the good and gregarious energy I have left. He's got bleached-blond rock 'n' roll hair. I can kind of see what Ruby fell for when they were in high school, but we're thirty years old now, and his idea of a good time is convincing three different psychiatrists that he has emotional problems that he does not have. He is ridiculous, and by association, so am I. Or maybe it's the reverse. Really, who cares? My objective right now is to get his stuff and get him out of here as quickly as I can. In my mind, I ask the angels to please, please, please, let him not take me up on my offer of drinks at the sky bar.

He doesn't. But he does insist on a conversation. Goddamn it! Why can't people just do what I want them to do and be gone? It's a worldwide conspiracy to make me be polite when I don't want to be. When I can't be. Wow! The most strenuous thing I need to do with my day is just pull out a little bit of courtesy, and I hate it.

"What's happened to you?" Ray asks as he sits down on an armchair, while I lean back on the bed. CNN is playing on the TV in the background.

"Well, I'm trying to finish my book, so I'm hiding out here," I say. "I don't think I have much more to do, maybe a few more days—a week or two at the most—so I need some Ritalin to keep me going."

"You've got a problem."

"What do you mean?"

"You think I'm stupid?" he asks. "I see what's going on. I haven't spent time with you in a few years, but I know what you look like. Come on, Elizabeth. You are one of the most vital people I've ever met. Now look at you."

"What do you mean?" I can see this isn't going to work.

"Listen, I'm going to tell you something really nice, because I want you to know this, and then I'm going to band practice." Pause. Pause for the nice thing that he's going to tell me, which I already know is just going to make me feel bad. "When I first met you with Ruby, I was blown away. You were beautiful and you were friendly, and I just loved hanging out with you. Nothing could have been more fun than to just be around you. You were a force. That's why *Prozac Nation* is a great book. It's you. It's the force of you."

Shit. I don't want to hear one more person tell me how great I used to be, and how horrible I am now. I know they think that's a compliment, I know they think they're telling me something about my native character that I ought to be happy about, but it just breaks my heart. What's wrong with me? Even when I was the person I used to be, I was not very happy. If anything, I am happier now, and everyone else is displeased. I can't win.

"Sorry to disappoint you," I say. "But this is the real me, and I'm not doing so well, and I know it. Okay, you're right. I've got a problem. I've got a lot of problems. But I'm going to get help. Really I am. And maybe I'll be the way I used to be, and you can be happy about it, and we can hang out, and you can bask in my motherfucking vitality."

Fuck him. Fuck everybody. This is the real me, and I hate myself. I feel like I am about to get huffy, and I have to quell the urge and be nice enough for the next five minutes so that he'll give me what I want.

"Cool," he says.

"So just let me buy the pills off of you, let me get through this nightmarish process, and then I'll do the right thing. I'll check myself in." Maybe I said too much. *Check myself in* sounds serious. And I can't let Ray think I'm in serious trouble. If he does, that's it for his prescriptions. But what else is he going to do with them anyway? He might as well sell them to me. "Please." I think I'm going to cry. "Ray, please, please, please, don't make me beg."

"Look, I'll give you one bottle, but that's it." Thank God. Bless the angels. "How long will that last you?"

"A while, I guess." About three days.

"All right then." He pulls out a bottle—it's Dexedrine, not Ritalin, but that's fine. I rifle through my bag and find my wallet: $240 for 120 pills. "Look, give me a call if you want to talk."

Yeah, right. As if. I don't want to talk. That's why I've got these pills. They don't want to talk to me, and I don't want to talk to them, and all of us are happy.

I go see Dr. Singer the next day. I've been avoiding it, hoping I could get her to call in a Ritalin prescription before she sees me, before she sees what's going on. She's not an idiot. I can fool her by phone, but in person it's not going to work.

And it doesn't. I walk into her office. I'm shaking because I don't eat anymore. All I take into my body is Ritalin and now cocaine, and it shows. She tells me she'll keep prescribing my antidepressants and my mood stabilizers, but no more Ritalin. I promise her that I will check into the hospital just as soon as my book is done, which will be any day, or any week—or at least any *month*—now. I tell her we should start discussing my options, which treatment center is the right place, because I really have had enough. I want to get better. But until I am ready to go, can she please just keep giving me my Ritalin. I beg her to just give me a maintenance dose of Ritalin until then, that I just need a little bit to get by, that I cannot just stop.

"You can't stop because you're addicted," she says.

"Fine, I'm addicted. I'm not denying it. I'll get help." I try to reason with her. "But until then, I can't stop. If somebody would just tie me down and keep it away from me, I'd be so happy. Believe me, I'm sick of it. My head hurts. My nose is always bloody. It feels like there's not enough room in my brain anymore. I would love to stop. I would love to."

"That's what addiction is," she says, patiently as ever. "That is the simplest definition of addiction: You want to stop, but you can't. You think it's more complicated, but it's not."

"Okay, fine." I am not about to give up. "But right now I am going to die without Ritalin."

She refuses. She says that if I am going to die without it, I need to go to the hospital right away. Once again, I tell her I'll go sometime soon. And then I ask her if she is angry at me for getting addicted to the drugs she prescribed for me in good faith.

"Are *you* angry with *me*?" Dr. Singer asks as a rejoinder. Always a question with a question.

"No, God, not at all."

"Are you sure?"

"Of course not." And I mean it. "You wrote me a prescription for a recommended dose. You didn't know I'd be in Florida for a year. Look, I'm a drug addict, but I still have some sort of faculties for reasoning. I know if I'd been here and you'd seen what was happening to me, you wouldn't have let this go on. I know you wanted me to come back here. I know." I stop to think about what I'm saying. I probably *should* be mad at her. There has to be some element of professional negligence in all this. But that's not what I feel. I feel like I made a choice, or I slipped into a compulsion, or whatever. "Please, please, please don't feel responsible. Please don't. I'll never forgive myself if you do."

I'm sure another therapist could have a field day with my desire to keep Dr. Singer from feeling bad. I guess this might be transference run amok. But I think it's simpler than that. I think there are plenty of people who I wish would feel plenty bad about my addiction. But in the end I know it's my own damn problem. And I'm really worried that Dr. Singer will blame herself for being party to this at all. It breaks my heart. This is no one's fault but mine.

"Listen, as long as I'm here," I say, "I might as well tell you that it's all falling apart. At this point, I'm starting to really fuck up."

"How so?"

I tell her about missing the photography session for Coach. And worse still, I've evidently been replaced by someone who people believe to be my rival.

"It seems stupid that not showing up to have my picture taken would clue me in about how far gone I am when there are so many other signs—you know, hiding in Florida for a year, making a mess of my legs, all that stuff. But, see, I've never missed a professional obligation in my life. I always plow through. And it would have been fun for me. It's not something I wanted to avoid. I just slept through it. I plain old fucked up. And I'm sure there are many more things that I'm going to fuck up. But one of them can't be the book I'm writing. I can't lose that. I can't lose my career. It's all I've got, pretty much. And I'm going to lose it."

Now I am really bawling. I can't talk between the tears. Because really that's it—if I lose my writing, I'm worthless to myself.

"Look, we're going to get you some help," Dr. Singer says, so calm, as if she's telling me we'll find a tailor to hem my pants, as if it's nothing. "You've got to figure out when you'll be ready to check in. You need to be an inpatient at this point. Nothing else is going to work. When you're ready for help, I promise we'll get you there. In the meantime, I've got to tell you that I think you really should just go in for treatment right now. But if you won't do that, we need to figure out when and where. Okay? We'll figure it out. I promise. But you've got to be ready."

Sniffle. "Okay." I see our time is up, and after this whole emotional display, I should just leave it alone, go back to the Peninsula and work until our next appointment. But I can't do that. "Are you sure you won't give me some Ritalin until then? Just a little bit."

"I'm sure."

Fortunately, drug dealers do not have the scruples of friends and psychiatrists. I can buy an eightball of coke a day and have it delivered to my hotel room door, no questions asked. José is just a businessman with a beeper number, and I am an excellent client. So it is all cocaine, all the time.

Fourteen

AND I DIG MY OWN GRAVE

Take your silver spoon
Dig your grave
STEVIE NICKS
"Gold Dust Woman"

Once I move into the hotel, Ben becomes my boyfriend. He comes to visit me, to check the place out, the day after I arrive, and that's it. Here we go.

Maybe Ben is not quite my boyfriend. Who knows? At any rate, he is married. But the Peninsula is convenient for our arrangement, since it is located at Fifty-fifth Street and Fifth Avenue, just two blocks from the Fifty-third Street office where Ben works. Where his wife thinks he is I cannot say, because he is always with me.

Ben doesn't actually do any coke—he just unwittingly facilitates my use. I have stopped eating, have lost all interest in food. So he comes over late in the afternoon with pints of chicken noodle soup from a Korean deli, and force-feeds me. He says that if I just have one spoon of chicken and noodles and carrots—protein and carbohydrates and vegetables, a balanced meal—he'll let me do a few lines of coke without asking me any questions. So I eat a little.

And then we fuck. Over and over again. We fuck and watch tons of pornography. That's what you do on cocaine. I cannot imagine anyone watching porn without coke, and at this point I cannot imagine doing coke without Jenna Jameson and T. T. Boy and Janine and Cheyenne and Ron Jeremy and whatever other pseudonymous adult-film stars there are out there, doing whatever it is that they do on videotapes in the background. Coke and fucking

and porn—with a little bit of writing and a lot of revising in multicolored
ink—is how I spend the late fall of 1997.

I watch porn alone also. With Ben, without Ben, with my fingers on my clit,
or just letting it play in the background while I write. It is embarrassing. It may
even be worse than ripping hairs out of my legs on the scale of embarrassment.
I can't tell anyone about it. I can't even tell Dr. Singer. It's just too gross.

Later, when I get to rehab, I find out this is common. People who do cocaine spend a lot of time watching pornography. There are men who go to Internet smut sites, punch in their credit card numbers on the keyboard, and just
stare at their screens, watching teenage lesbians have sex, watching amateur
videotape loops of suburban couples and college students having sex, of
women being fucked by a horse or a goat or both, of a woman having sex with
248 men in tandem at a race car track, of seven women in an orgy, of two men
and three woman in an orgy, of three women fucking each other's butts with
dildos of various lengths and widths, of six men jacking off while watching a
stripper until their come shoots at her and drips down her legs. If there is any
perversion that you have—even ones that are not so perverse—there is a brand
of pornography that will match it. And coke addicts will run up tabs that are
way past their credit limits, and they'll get new cards to cover it. They'll finally
find free pornography sites. Or they'll just rent tapes and leave it at that. Or
they run up huge bills having phone sex, and they spend a year or two paying
off the phone company.

In hotels, there is Spectravision, so you just press a few buttons on the remote control and get *Debbie Does Dallas 7* or *Where the Boys Aren't 12* or *My
Baby's Got Back* or *Not the Loving Kind.* I do that a lot. At the Peninsula, there
is a VCR in my room, and the concierge has a collection of pornographic
tapes that you can choose from at the front desk. Maybe businessmen passing
through town can go down there and make their requests and not feel stupid,
but I cannot possibly do that. It's different for girls. Ben has a huge collection
of pornography at his office, which he brings over when he comes by. I much
prefer to watch with him. It makes me feel less filthy. Girls are not supposed to
like this stuff. You ask guys, and they'll all admit that they've got a secret stash
of porn tapes somewhere. They'll tell you that their favorite thing is to watch
women give men head, or they're really into anal sex. But girls don't talk about
it. If any of my friends watch this stuff, I don't know about it, and I am certainly
not going to tell them. Like I said, it's too humiliating.

Ben and I don't only stay in my hotel room and watch pornography. I go
with him to a couple of company dinners and cocktail parties. It seems that

around his office, everyone either believes we're really good friends and that is all, or they know we're having an affair and that doesn't bother them. What his colleagues think does not seem to concern Ben, and it certainly does not worry me. I am on so much coke that if it does bug me, I don't know about it. I'm not sure how I would feel if I weren't wired all the time, but I cannot afford to think about it. I've never had an affair with a married man before, and I don't plan to do it ever again, so there is no reason for me to know the protocol. All I know is that I need Ben right now. I need him to get through until I am done with my book and off to get treatment, and I cannot think past that.

We lie in bed exhausted after we've had sex several times in a row, and it's after eleven and he needs to go home. I have this insatiable energy for sex. I would do it another five times if he would or could, the cocaine has made me filthy for fucking. It occurs to me that I ought to find about three more Bens and just have a revolving door of sexmates because I would be happy to do it all the time. I have to write my book, so I have to give most of my day over to that, which is probably the only reason I don't go out looking for more men to fuck.

But I also have feelings for Ben that I think may go beyond drugs and smut. In my way I am in love with him, and he is in love with me too. In some alternate reality, without his wife and without my blow, we could be having a sweet relationship. This isn't all just sickness. But I guess it's defined by sickness and addiction at the moment, so there's no way to look at it as anything but a bad thing. My life right now is all bad things. Ben is a good thing by comparison.

"I love you," he says to me one night, his whole body wrapped around me.

"I love you too," I say.

"I really do."

"I really do too."

And we should just leave it at that. But it's not unqualified love, and we both know it. I'm a sick, sick girl, and he—well, who can say what is wrong with him, why he's cheating on his wife with me. But it doesn't matter. This will be over soon enough. As soon as I check into the hospital, that's the end of this. I love him just for now. I really do—but it's just for today. That's what makes the feeling so pure—I have no expectations of him, I know it's for the moment, and in the context of that safety, I can love him as completely as I am capable of. And maybe it's the same for him.

"I know you really love your wife also," I say to Ben. His chest is to my back, his arms are around my torso, we are both looking in the same direction, and that direction happens to be toward the clock. He needs to leave soon. "And I think the reason I'm in your life is to remind you."

"Remind me of what?"

"That you love her. That as much as you love me—and I believe that you do—what you have with her is important and permanent, and you don't want to lose it. By the time I check myself in, you will know for sure that you do not want to lose her, and you'll be relieved."

This is the coke talking, not me. If I were speaking, I'd be saying, Leave your wife, let's run away, this is true love, don't be a fool. But coked up, I am free to be philosophical, even generous. See? This drug isn't all bad. It lets me mask my worst feelings, my jealousy, my want, my need. That's why I do it. I do it because my desires are impossible, but on coke, I can be simply loving, open.

"I'm not sure what you mean," Ben says.

"Think about it later, or tomorrow, when you're not with me. Think about it and you'll see that you're lucky. I've given you one last hurrah. After this, maybe you'll buy a house and have children. Maybe this will sate whatever need you have to be unfaithful."

"I don't like cheating."

"I know," I answer. "That's my point. Because I think we really are in love, which is why this will help you to realize that it's not worth it. You're going to walk away from me—and you will, I know it. And you'll be so glad that she's still there, that you didn't ruin what I imagine is a really good thing."

"Maybe."

"Look, what do I know? My relationships have universally failed." I pull myself away from him to snort up the lines I've got cut up on the night table. "So maybe I idealize relationships that work. I don't know. I guess I don't understand what makes them work. But I think I have a little bit of insight. Anyway, will you promise me something?"

"Sure."

The coke must be wearing off because I am about to ask Ben for something. When I'm wired, I need nothing. I snort up some more.

"Promise me that you'll stay with me until I check in." I lie down facing him. "I'm committed to doing a reading on December 9." I snort another few lines. "It's a bunch of female writers reading the poetry of male Beat writers. I picked out the poem 'Marriage' by Gregory Corso. So I'm going to do that, and then, as far as I'm concerned, I can go to the hospital the next day. My therapist and I are going to figure out where I should go sometime this week."

"Good."

I'm a little peeved when Ben says *Good.* It makes me think he's eager to get rid of me, when really he is just being supportive. That's my problem in life: I don't understand that every time someone encourages me to do the right thing, it is not necessarily a rejection. It could well be an indication of how much they care. How much Ben cares. But I still feel cold and lonely for a moment, so I sit up again and do some more coke. That's the trick: when I do coke, my emotions are almost reasonable.

"So I just want you to be with me until then," I continue. "After that, I hope you go home to your wife, and that you become a wonderful husband to her and stop having affairs."

"I never meant to have one with you. I think I'm in love with you, and if I weren't, this wouldn't be happening."

"You probably thought that about the last one."

"Jesus, Elizabeth, give yourself a little bit of credit." I guess that's a sweet thing to say.

"I do give myself credit." I lean over and do more coke. "Come on, Ben. Face it. I'm a drug addict and you're married. This doesn't add up to anything very good. I am a sick, sick girl. This whole relationship is facilitated by my cocaine and your troubles with being married, which I hope, for your sake, you just face and deal with."

I think I am being truthful here, and wise.

More lines of coke. My nose hurts and I'm naked, and he's dressed. I feel vulnerable because I have no clothes on, and I feel emboldened because I'm coked up. It's a pleasant combination, actually. "So I'm a bad bet. Your wife is a good bet. You're going to be so glad to have her, and not someone like me. And you'll thank me for helping you realize it."

This conversation is starting to remind me of something out of a Marguerite Duras novel, or some existential French movie. *Hiroshima, Mon Amour*, maybe. I keep thinking that in a minute I will start talking about what happened in Nevers while bombs dropped on Japan. This is the kind of conversation where people say *lover*, instead of boyfriend or girlfriend or person-I'm-fucking, or anything more colloquial. At any rate, I want it to stop. I want him to leave already. It's time.

And then, as I see him about to put on his coat, I don't want him to leave after all. I feel abandoned. "Please don't go," I say. "Let's do it one more time."

"I really need to go." He looks at his watch. Now that he's in his clothes, he's impatient. Lying naked, he'd do or say anything. Standing up, he knows better. "I'll call you tomorrow. Okay?"

"Sure."

He comes over to the bed and kisses me on the lips. Big wet kiss. For a minute I don't feel abandoned. But then he shows himself out. And no matter how much coke I've done—and it's quite a lot—I cannot help that I feel something. I feel something bad. And I start to cry.

When $450 a night at the Peninsula becomes too pricey, I move into another hotel, the Millennium in Times Square, opposite my publisher's offices. The company gets me a corporate rate, and Betsy is happy because I am right across the street. I can run pages over to her office at the end of every day, or she can send her assistant to get them. And everybody is happy.

I go to the workout room in the middle of the night. I write before and after. I sleep sporadically. The dealer comes by daily. Ben visits regularly. The whole routine becomes, well, a routine. I think it's going pretty well, considering. But not completely. I still want to shut everyone out and be alone with my work and my coke and my porn and my married boyfriend, but it's not that simple. When I don't answer my phone for a few days, Kathlyn has security break into my room to make sure I am okay. She explains to the hotel manager that I have an illness—I'm not sure what kind of specifics she gives him—and that it's an emergency. I could be dead.

They knock on my door for a long time. I don't like being bothered so I pretend I'm not there. I have the bolt on, so no one can get in. But after I don't answer for a while, the man outside calls out something about this being security, and says that I have to open the door. I just sit there, pretending not to hear. Finally, they unlock the door with the computerized key and knock the bolt open with a hammer. They find me sitting on the floor in front of the TV—thank God it's just MSNBC—perfectly fine as far as anyone can tell. I've got lines cut up in the bathroom, so they don't see them, and all they can do is apologize and leave me alone again.

Wandy and Lewis and the girls come to New York for Thanksgiving. I decide to try staying in my own apartment for a few days, since my house sitter is going home to the suburbs of Boston and, well, why not? With enough coke, I can probably handle it. The girls want to come over and see where I live, and meet my cat, so it seems like the least I can do is be there. Ben helps me drag all my stuff back home. He pretty much packs everything up for me because I just can't manage anything. I won't be seeing him for four days, and we spend a romantic evening in a taxi, stuck in traffic, trying to get me back to the Village.

By Saturday I can't stand it. There's no way I am getting any work done here. All the coke in the world can't change that in my own apartment, in the site of my life before Florida, I feel like hell. I don't mean that I feel hellish— I actually feel like hell itself, like that Robert Lowell poem where he says, "I myself am hell." I have to get out of here. I have too much work to do to cope with feelings.

I'd been coming in and working at Doubleday's offices on occasion, because the hotel was so close by, and it became convenient. One of the associate publishers is on leave, and in the interest of getting the book done, Betsy
has let me write there sometimes, so that I can hand her pages as quickly as I
can write them and as quickly as my HP portable can print them out. And
right now, it's Saturday night. Almost everyone I know is out of town, home for
the holidays. There is nothing to do but work. I grab my computer and leave
the apartment, and walk out into the evening dark—I hate how it gets so dark
so early this time of year. I miss Florida and its perennial warmth. I take a taxi
up to Doubleday headquarters on Forty-fifth Street and Broadway. Somehow
I convince the security guard that he needs to let me up into the office, that he
needs to give me the passkey to get into the glass doors at reception. I tell him
it is urgent, an emergency. I'm an author, my book is due, my notes are upstairs, and he's got to let me in. Please, please, please. And for some reason,
maybe because I am obviously desperate, he does.

I am settling in here to write my book, and I am not leaving until it happens. That's it. I'm settling in. This is not quite a plan. I don't know what I am
doing. I don't say to myself, This is my new home. But somehow I know that I
will not sleep until I am finished, and I will not finish my book anywhere but
here. The stark office lights, their fluorescent discomfort—this is where I belong. There is a daybed next to a big, huge picture window, so I can nap if I
want to. I can go home to change clothes and shower and feed the cat every
couple of days, but otherwise I have no reason to be anywhere else. There are
coffee and tea in the kitchenette, and in one of the drawers of the desk I find
something that looks like a videocassette case, but it is actually a mirror. It
opens up to a normal mirror on one side and a magnifying mirror on the other.
Whenever I get a new supply of coke—an eightball a day—I pour it into this
mirror case and put it on the floor under the desk in front of my feet. During
working hours, I duck under to snort up my cocaine. It's all in a pile, I am not
even bothering to cut it into lines any longer. Late at night, when no one is
around, I just open it up on the desk beside my computer, and snort away as I
like. I have one mission: Finish the book and check myself in. Nothing else
matters. I am too damn sick to do anything else.

And so it goes. Everything happens very quickly after that. My life becomes
very small: I write, I do coke, I call friends occasionally, and I go back to my
apartment when I need to. Knowing I don't need to be there makes it pleasant
to go home. Sometimes Ben comes over and we go to dinner at Bar Pitti, a
Florentine restaurant around the corner, and then we go back to my place and
fuck. Sometimes I stay there afterwards and sleep, but mostly I just go back to
Doubleday and work. I order up Chinese noodle soup and Texas barbecue

sandwiches that I do not eat, so the cartons of fried rice, with dents in the spots where I've picked at it with my plastic fork, amass on the floor. There are empty Styrofoam cups of coffee and tea everywhere. Piles of books about biblical villainesses and magazines over a decade old—I have the *Rolling Stone* with Madonna's first cover, from 1985—are tossed about, almost as if in deliberate disarray. My editor tells me that the office is starting to look like an installation at the Whitney Museum. The head of publicity comes by to say hello one day, and to get a look at the now-legendary collage I've got going on the floor. She brings the art director in to see, and they decide that they should photograph me lying in my mess, and use it in the press packet.

I quickly become a fixture in the building. The dealers deliver my coke to me in the lobby, and the security guards call me to come down and pick it up. I get to know everyone who works in maintenance at the Bertelsmann compound, and the men on the night shift let me in and out all the time, as though I live here, which I do. Sometimes I go browse in the Virgin Megastore, which is open until 2 A.M., and I buy books and CDs that I will probably never read or listen to. What are the chances I will get through even the first volume of Edward Gibbon's *Decline and Fall of the Roman Empire* in this lifetime? Do I really want the new live Fleetwood Mac album? There is a movie theater in the basement of Virgin, and I see *The Ice Storm* and *The Sweet Hereafter* when I need a break. I snort coke with my coat over my head in the felt chairs, and when I see *Boogie Nights*, I feel like I am getting high in a group because Amber Waves/Julianne Moore and Dirk Diggler/Mark Wahlberg spend the whole movie getting wired too.

One afternoon I go uptown to Barneys on Sixty-first and Madison, and buy myself a Jill Platner bracelet, made of leather strings that connect silver pieces that look like the teeth of a saber-toothed tiger. Afterwards I go to the Paris Theatre next door to the Plaza Hotel to see a rerelease of *Purple Noon*, a French movie from the sixties. I fall asleep in the middle, though I can tell that it is probably as beautiful and important as everyone says. I go visit Kathlyn at her apartment on Jane Street, and I visit Daisy at her place on Fifty-seventh Street, because I still want to have friends when this is all over. Even in my coked-up mess, I keep a few practical matters in mind: Once I am out of rehab, I will need people to eat blueberry pancakes with me for Sunday brunch, to sit with me at Bubby's while I do the crossword puzzle in the magazine section.

None of the people in charge at Doubleday have any idea what to do with me or about me. They don't know how I came to reside in their office, and they can't figure out how they will get me to leave. So they try to act normal. The publisher comes in one day to let me know that the writing and rewriting and revising and re-editing are getting out of hand, the book is probably done already, it's time to stop. He says, "Pencils down," as though I am taking the SATs and time is up. The marketing director sometimes works on Saturdays, so he comes by to see how it's going. There is an editor who seems to always be around, and sometimes we'll order up Chinese food together, which she notices I do not eat. The copy editor is frequently making notations on my manuscript late, and he'll come by with queries about my work in progress; I offer him some coke one night after hours, and he declines but asks to watch me do it since he has never seen that. Brendan, a Doubleday assistant, is a Bennington graduate, so *of course* he always wants to do coke with me when I offer. Sometimes I send him down to the lobby to do a pickup with my dealer when I am in the midst of some deep thought on O.J. and Nicole, and can't be interrupted. I know all the janitors and cleaning women by name. Sometimes they do coke with me. It's like *From the Mixed-up Files of Mrs. Basil E. Frankweiler.* Or Eloise in corporate headquarters. I think I am popular in this building.

One day a bunch of people decide to use my office—*my* office and *my* bedroom—for a meeting. Betsy warns me that I will have to clear out for a couple of hours. I say I will, with much resentment. I decide to take a nap shortly before the appointed time, so a bunch of executives walk into the office and find me passed out on the daybed. I hear them walk in, and I half wake up, but I decide to play dead, because I really am too tired to go anywhere else and sit up. They are so astonished by this person, in grubby jeans slipping down her hips and a dust-dirtied Hanes T-shirt and a thick Shetland sweater draped over her like a blanket, that they just leave and find somewhere else to meet. It is apparent that I have this whole publishing company codependent with me. They should have Al-Anon meetings in the conference room.

For a while, we go on like this. If I did not start having panic attacks, with my throat constricting and my ability to breathe seriously impaired, we probably could go on like this for years. One day one of the assistants hears me heaving in my office. She comes running in scared, ready to administer CPR. Through my heavy suspirations, I explain that this is nothing to worry about, I am just a drug addict having a panic attack, that's all.

Betsy comes in every day, including weekends, to make sure I am not dead, which is ridiculous, since besides that I sometimes can't breathe, I am fine, and I am going to check into the hospital really soon anyway. She starts to cry. She says she is frightened. I tell her I am doing great. As soon as I finish my book, any day now, I will check in.

"What if you kill yourself before then?" Betsy asks, looking truly scared, though I think she is just being dramatic.

"Don't be crazy," I say. "I'm not doing dope. You can't OD on cocaine. I'll be fine. When I'm ready to stop, I will."

"You can have a heart attack," Betsy says. "I feel terrible about this. I feel like I'm letting you harm yourself by letting you work here. I don't sleep well at night. I don't see my kid because I'm here so much. I don't know how to tell you that I am sick to death, and torn up. I am afraid I will have blood on my hands."

"For God's sake, Betsy, just get over it." I don't actually roll my eyeballs, but I do metaphorically. "You're overreacting. I can take care of myself."

She starts to cry, and I don't know what to do.

On a Sunday afternoon, a couple of days before I go to the hospital, I call Rob Bingham. I have just finished reading his collection of short stories, *Pure Slaughter Value*, which Doubleday published recently. Rob is an addict too. He's had periods of being sober—his worst problem is drinking—but as far as I know he is still in pretty deep.

We're friends, not good friends, but he has a literary magazine called *Open City*, and he has huge parties whenever there is a new issue, in his grand loft on White Street in Tribeca. Sometimes really late at night, when only a few people are left, Rob and I have done heroin together on his pool table, or under his pool table, or in the kitchen or the bathroom or the bedroom or any corner or surface. Together we are scary. We can use long past the point when everyone else has passed out or gone home. He has a lot of friends who'll do his drugs with him for fun, and I always think it enables him in some terrible, ugly way. None of my friends use with me. They know it's dangerous to encourage me. No one around Rob, except maybe his poor long-suffering girlfriend, has any scruples or cares. I always say that the decadent people should be kept away from the desperate people.

Rob and I are both desperate. Everyone else around him is just decadent.

When I call him, it is four in the afternoon, and the phone wakes him up.

"I just wanted to tell you that the stories in your book are amazing," I say. "I read a couple of them in *The New Yorker* a while ago, but all of them together are just graceful and disturbing—man, you're good. I think you're the best fiction writer in our age group, you know, among our contemporaries." I am careful to say *fiction*, because I still hope that I've got nonfiction covered.

"Thanks, wow, that's great to hear," he says in a sleepy voice. "That means a lot. I really need to read *Prozac Nation*. I know it's great, and I just never got around to it."

"Don't worry about it," I reply, not at all offended.

We talk for a few minutes about our publisher, about his editor, about the novel he's working on. Short story collections never sell that well, with rare exceptions, like Raymond Carver's stuff. But I bet his novel will do really well. I hope so.

"How's the book going?" I ask. And then I think better of it: You should never ask a writer how his work is coming along. I hate it when people do it to me, and they do it all the time.

"You know, I'm working on it. It should be done soon."

He asks for my phone number so we can get together and hang out sometime. He's got it somewhere, but you know how it is, little pieces of paper scribbled on, or information written on the back page of a book—they all get misplaced in the mess. Then he says he is going back to sleep.

Just two years from now, on Thanksgiving weekend of 1999, Rob will die of an overdose of heroin. He will be found dead in his bathroom by his wife, whom he had married just a few months before. His novel, *Lightning on the Sun*, about a drug deal gone terribly wrong, will be published posthumously. At the end of the book, the main character is killed, assassination style, by some Cambodian guerillas. On the last page, he digs his own grave.

Fifteen

DID SHE JUMP OR DID SHE FALL?

The wise man knows at the commencement of a matter what its
end will be.

Talmud

I am sitting in Dr. Singer's office discussing what to do. The Betty Ford Center
is her first suggestion. All kidding aside, all the jokes about Elizabeth Taylor and
the other celebrities hanging out there, Dr. Singer feels that it's an excellent
rehab that will work well for me. The Hazelden Foundation, in Minnesota, is
boot camp for junkies. It's strict and hard-line and hard-core, and Dr. Singer
thinks it would drive me crazy. Betty Ford is a better fit. I will probably have to
check into a hospital in New York to detoxify first, since I am too sick to get on
a plane as is. But I can go to Betty Ford's twenty-eight-day program, then maybe
go on to a halfway house for a month or two to solidify my sobriety, and then I'll
be spanking new, fresh and clean, a stained shirt laundered in Tide.

But after I call Betty Ford to talk to a counselor there about checking in,
after we go through a discussion of the nature of my addiction and symptoms,
and after we cover all my statistical information, I decide there is no way. Betty
Ford is not going to work.

"The intake person, or whatever you call her, was named Kathleen," I say
to Dr. Singer. "Kath-*leen*. What the fuck can I learn from a person named
Kathleen? She sounds like some sort of sensitive nurse-practitioner type who
grew up somewhere like Gloucester and somehow ended up in southern California. Fuck that."

Dr. Singer has no idea what I mean, I have no idea what I mean, and yet
somehow, what I am saying makes a weird kind of sense. I'm not going to get

anywhere if my attitude is a priori, this is all a joke, some New Age thing, a place where the closest thing anyone there has come to literature is a careful perusal of *Alcoholics Anonymous*, better known as the AA Big Book.

"She just sounded like somebody who read *The Celestine Prophecy*, which is bad enough by itself, and thought it was brilliant, a revelation, something like that." I stop. "And I just cannot take seriously someone named Kathleen." I seem to have forgotten that my best friend's name is Kathlyn. What a difference a couple of vowels makes. "She sounds like a dumb Irish girl, the only girl in a family of nine brothers, all alcoholics. You know, not like me."

Oy vey. With this attitude, I am not going to be able to get help. Of course, without this attitude, I would not need help.

We settle on the drug rehabilitation program at Silver Hill Hospital in New Canaan, Connecticut, a country-clubbish sprawl that famously treats deranged dowagers and literary drunks, but is in fact a psychiatric institution full of people in big trouble. It has a history of taking in precious, artistic types. Truman Capote went there for his periodic bouts of drying out. Photographer Nan Goldin has recently passed through, and over the years there has been an assortment of James Taylor's lesser siblings, a smattering of Kennedys, people like that. Both Tatum O'Neal and Oksana Baiul will check in shortly after I leave, but it is really not a show business retreat. It is solidly Northeast, more preppie and tweedy than anywhere out west. Besides, I am in no condition to get on an airplane.

Also, Silver Hill is a mental hospital, not a rehab. It is staffed with psychiatrists. At a place like Betty Ford, there is a consulting physician who signs off on the prescriptions, but the counselors are in charge. It's not a medical facility. I feel better knowing there are MDs running the place, that it's not all touchy-feely bullshit.

It's not like I am bigoted. I'm the granddaughter of a television repairman and an assembly-line worker at a baby carriage factory. My father was a technician at IBM who did not even wear a suit to work. When I was at Harvard, I always prided myself on my working-class roots, on not being a spoiled preppie. Then, in the publishing industry, I was always happy that I had no connections, that my parents weren't editors and writers, that I did it all myself. My mother is, of course, a snob in the way that only the aspiring middle class can be. When I was in college, and I wore jeans with holes in the knees, my mother would yell at me and say that we had enough money for a new pair of Levi's: Here's twenty-five bucks, don't walk around like that; people will think you come from a bad home. And I'd have to explain that the richest people at school, the old-money kids from manicured homes in southern Connecticut and on the north shore of Massachusetts, were the biggest slobs of all. Walking around like a mess made me look, if anything, wealthy. But she would never get it. She would always get upset. She always thought I looked cheap and tawdry.

On December 9, I do my Beat poetry reading. It is now particularly important to me to prove I can still do what I am supposed to. Lydia comes to see me, and she is glad that I am there and even on time, but she looks at me with a fearful face, like I am ghastly and ghostly. I am wearing a black sheer skirt with a leotard and dark tights and high heels. I am doing my best to be fabulous and fashionable, but Lydia tells me it's not working. My hair is pulled high up into a bun because it is dirty. I have dark roots and streaks of blonde that look like a yellowjacket's back. My face shows completely because none of my greasy hair falls in tendrils and wisps around my cheeks and forehead, and anyone can see the gaunt whiteness of my skin, the way my eyes droop and drop from lack of sleep, the way I obviously appear to be terribly sickly. I have always carried my addiction with aplomb, even my thinness looked lithe for a time, but now that's gone. I look horrible. I look like a junkie or a cokehead or all of the above. I look bad.

The reading is in the basement of the flagship Benetton store, and the incandescent lights push my pallor to the whiteness of Captain Ahab's whale. I read Gregory Corso's poem with a high, hoarse voice. I sound coarser than usual, and I can hear it in my inner ear.

Afterward, I go out for dinner at Café Un Deux Trois in the theater district with Lydia and a couple of writer friends I have not seen since long before I left for Florida, and with Catherine Texier, who participated in the reading with an excerpt from *On the Road*. I try to act normal, and maybe I succeed. I don't know and I don't care. In a week I will be packed up and gone. By the time I see any of these people again, my whole life will be different. I hope.

When I go downstairs to the ladies' room in the cellar, Catherine comes with me. In the stall I take out my mirror full of cocaine and snort some straight out of it without cutting it up. I am sure Catherine has heard me, so when I go to the sink to wash up, I offer her some. I explain that I am an addict, that I am checking in next week, but I'm on my last run and she's welcome to a few lines. I'm sure she has no idea why I am offering her this information — it probably has something to do with the chatty burst of coke after at least an hour's reprieve — but she seems frazzled and vulnerable herself, so I take her into confidence.

Catherine declines my offer. She doesn't look shocked or disapproving, but slightly surprised, like this isn't something that is proffered to her often. And her reaction catches me off guard. I have always assumed that drugs, particularly cocaine, are casually common, a normal party favor, especially among writers, especially in the literary world Catherine has denizened in for so long. Sure, I know I am uncommonly stuck on the stuff, but I don't think of it as just me, my thing. I figure everybody would be excited about the offer of a toot.

But in this underground bathroom anteroom, I realize I am at it alone. Drugs are not everywhere and for everyone. They are nothing like the presumed unassuming glass of house merlot with dinner, and there is no reason for me to think my behavior is just an exaggerated version of normal.

Kathlyn and Lydia confer with Dr. Singer in a conference call, and make the arrangements for me to check into Silver Hill. There is a psychiatrist there whom Dr. Singer has worked with often before—they send each other patients, we shuttle between them—so I don't need to do an intake interview. They discuss the situation and work it out between them, the two professionals. A $10,000 deposit has to be sent to the finance office at Silver Hill before I get there, so Kathlyn puts this on her American Express card and my accountant sends her a check. This all needs to be done as quickly and efficiently as possible. And I become ready to face this future. I agree to check in on December 16. I give myself several days to get what's left of the new book—what's left of it that I can handle—completed.

How did I tell Mommy that I am a drug addict? I just don't remember. Did I mention it in passing during a phone conversation, tell her that all the strange behavior in Florida had to do with Ritalin? Or did I sit her down, go to Au Bon Pain with her in Midtown, and tell her we needed to talk? Was it a formal process? How did it happen?

I don't remember at all.

Maybe someone else told her—I'm pretty sure it was I, but I might be incorrect. It would have been a difficult conversation, I would think. Or maybe not: maybe finally getting an explanation for why my life was as it was could have been a great relief to her. I'm not sure. All I know is that I can't deliver a good scene, one of revelation and sorrow and renewal. I just can't remember. Having to tell her about this—drugs are as low as it gets for her, anything would be better—is so painful that it's gone. It's left my mind. I could ask her, but I don't want to know. It's a memory that does not serve.

A couple of nights before I go to rehab, I go back to my apartment for one last visit. I start to have a panic attack, and I'm certain I will die. After all this, I'm in my last stretch before I give it all up, and now I will die. The heart attack that's been approaching, the one that killed Len Bias when I was a freshman in college—it's finally going to get me. You cannot OD on cocaine the way you can on heroin, but you can have seizures that send you into fits of epilepsy, and it can overwork your hardened soft heart until it explodes, rebels. I am sure this is happening to me now.

Ben puts me into a tepid bath and tells me to relax. It's the drugs. It's a nervous reaction to the cocaine. I am not going to die; it's nothing physical; it is in my head, all in my head.

"You say that like it is supposed to be comforting," I say to him.

"Well, isn't it?"

"Of course not. I mean, it *is* all in my head. My head is what is making me feel like this. My head is why I do coke. My head is the whole problem. And my brain is what controls my breathing, my ability to process information and emotions, and if any of the chemical messages get fucked up—if my head tells my heart to do something wrong—I could end up dead."

"Your head is working fine," he says. "You're making perfect sense. We just need to get you to the hospital is all."

I don't go back to my apartment on that last day. I sit at Doubleday while Betsy's assistant, Brendan, goes down to my place to pick up my suitcase. I'd thrown some stuff together a couple of days before, and it is lying on my floor unfolded and unpacked—but Betsy insists that Brendan can figure it out. She tells me to just sit still and do what I need to, not to worry about logistics. I type away in a deep panic. I've got the mirror of cocaine out on the desk, and I snort it out in the open. I don't mind who sees anymore. Doubleday will be relieved of my drugged-out presence in a matter of hours, our codependency can finally stop, and I just figure, *Who cares?*

Lydia has bought me a Discman and some little speakers so I can listen to CDs while I am at Silver Hill, and I have not yet gathered those together. I give Brendan a list of what to grab: *American Beauty, Highway 61 Revisited, Blood on the Tracks, Blonde on Blonde, Rumours,* all of my Bruce Springsteen, a few Emmylou Harris and Lucinda Williams, some Indigo Girls and Mary-Chapin Carpenter. It is pretty much quiet music, peaceful and disturbing in its way, no Lite FM stuff, but no punk rock either. Well maybe a few loud things, like the Violent Femmes' first album, the Sex Pistols' *Never Mind the Bollocks* and the Replacements' *Let It Be,* so I can listen to "Unsatisfied" over and over again.

Finally, I collect my papers to leave the office. The assortment of books and magazines is still scattered about, but Betsy says she will box them up for me. They will be here to pick up when I get back. It is late in the afternoon. I keep doing cocaine as I pull myself together to check in, and Betsy no longer reacts to it; she's spent. I am supposed to be at Silver Hill for intake at six, but I can see that's not going to happen. My mother is waiting downstairs in her Honda Civic. She's been sitting in an illegal parking spot talking to Lydia for at least an hour while I get it all together. She would usually be furious at me for being so inconsiderate, but today even she is sensitive to how hard this is, and I think it's nice for her to talk to Lydia about how horrifying and horrible this is for her, too.

"I'm scared," I tell Betsy as I pull on my shearling coat, ready to go and feeling freezing. "Um, here's the last of the pages I have done," I say, handing her an uncollated, crinkly, marked-up bunch of papers. "I'll work on more up there."

"I'll figure it out," Betsy says. "Don't worry. The book is all here. You've got to concentrate on getting better."

"I know." I'm so scared.

"Betsy?"

"Yes?"

"What do I do once I get there?"

"Nothing." She pauses, distressed and relieved that I am going, at the same time. "They'll take care of everything. They'll know what to do. Just let them show you. Just let go and stop worrying."

"Promise?" I ask. "I mean, do you promise it will all be okay?"

"I promise."

I didn't see addiction coming. The pills were safe. Even the Physicians' Desk Reference *barely mentions that Ritalin has the potential for "psychologic dependence." And back then I didn't read the PDR. I was careful with heroin, I kept it from becoming a physical problem. I was frightened of being a junkie. I did it only every few days. I kept it under control, I willed it out of danger. You can do that. But I didn't see the Ritalin creeping up. I thought it was a free ride.*

Or maybe not.

Because addiction got me what I needed.

All those years of depression got people to worry about me. But now they're scared. They're really scared. They used to worry that I might get sad enough to kill myself, but no one ever believed I'd really do it, not even me. But now they are scared that I am just going to end up *dead*. They're afraid that they will find me dead. And they mean it. I see the way they look at me. I see fear.

Finally, people take my sorrow seriously.

And really, what is addiction but slow suicide? It's not conscious on my part, but maybe this is killing me. I don't know anymore. I don't want that. But for once I can see that is really on everyone else's mind. Drugs put the fear of God into people the way a bad mood, even one that goes on for a decade, just does not. You can always wake up feeling better; that's always the hope with a depressive. But no one around me harbors that hope any longer. They are petrified. They are disgusted. At long last, my pain is a serious matter.

I've won.

REMEDY

Sixteen

ACUTE CARE

Her bare

Feet seem to be saying:
We have come so far, it is over.

SYLVIA PLATH
"Edge"

It is December 1997, and I am barefoot. When I finally check into Silver Hill Hospital, I walk in barefoot, because I have decided that shoes serve no function.

The ride to rehab is a nightmare. Of course, what else would it be? Everybody does the same thing on their way: Everybody gets high for one last time. People who fly on planes to Minnesota or Arizona or the Betty Ford Center in California sit in the aisle seats, the flight attendant—the waitress in the sky as far as an alcoholic trying to get a drink is concerned—at beck and call, ordering up, one after another, single-serving bottles of Bombay Sapphire Gin and Sutter Home red table wine and Courvoisier V.S.O.P. and Absolut Citron and Stoli Orange and Finlandia Cranberry and Harvey's Bristol Cream and whatever.

The addicts spend long minutes in the lavatories—washrooms, bathrooms, once again whatever—cutting up lines and snorting them. It can be messy. The sinks are conveniently aluminum, but usually wet, which can water down your supply, which is never a good thing, but a particular problem on your last run. (And it's always the last time: people go to rehab eight and nine times, they use while they are there, and yet en route they believe they will never get high again.) Best to put the lid on the commode and cut lines on a black-covered book or magazine, so long as it has a shiny, nonporous surface. The trend toward matte finishes is not a good thing for drug addicts on the go. And junkies on an airplane are in big trouble if they have to cook their dope. Smoke detectors do not prevent just cigarette smoking. And what a mess with the works and whatnot, the belt pulled like a tourniquet on your upper arm, other passengers banging on the doors while you do all this. So heroin addicts who have been shooting up for years, who are skin-popping and searching routinely for veins beneath their fingernails, are reduced to cutting up lines like the rest of us. And when all else fails, the booze cart can always be flagged down as a last-ditch option.

But me, I'm not in a plane or a train or even a taxi. I am being driven by my mother, who has made much fuss about being the one to get me to the hospital. She wants to help, to be a mother. She has no idea that I have a problem with drugs until just before I am ready to check in. She has assumed my erratic behavior is the result of escalating depression. Once she finds out I am an addict, she is frightened, she starts going to synagogue, she wants to know why God has done this. She begs for salvation, she hates herself. She does not know how this has happened. When I say something about *cutting lines,* she does not even know the term, she does not know what I mean, she does not know anything. She is hopeless and despondent. All she can do is drive. Though we are beyond secrets now, it is all in the open, and she knows that much of my life is illegal and immoral and certainly worthy of her disapproval, I still cannot snort coke in front of my mom. I want so badly to ask if she minds, the way you ask a cab driver if you can have a cigarette in the backseat even as you see a sticker that reads "No Smoking Driver Allergic." But I just can't. Whatever shame is left in me will not permit me to roll up a bill and inhale my white lines out of the portable mirror in front of her. She doesn't deserve it.

But it's not so much that I have scruples. It's just that I cannot bring myself to bring it up.

So instead I keep telling her that we need to stop at every passing gas station and rest stop. I run into every dingy bathroom, I get the large keys to every one of those damp, dank toilet closets with dirty water and the smell of air freshener masking the smell of Clorox masking the smell of odor, from every convenience store clerk off the Merritt Parkway, and I snort up my eightball along the way. We stop in White Plains and Greenwich and Darien. But when we arrive at Silver Hill, there is still plenty left. In my entire experience as a drug user and abuser, there has always been never enough, and it seems in perfect keeping with how wrong this all is that I am arriving at rehab with much too much left over.

I decide that this is okay, because they are going to wean me off slowly. They will let me surrender the drugs when I am finally ready. They will let me sit in a corner in some padded room, alone with my beloved white powder. They will let me keep doing it, under medical supervision, until I am just so sick of it, have just truly had enough.

This is not the case.

My mom and I get lost driving around the grounds of Silver Hill, and we both can't stop crying. I walk into the intake room late at night—everything is always late by now—and I don't want to stay. I am leaving. I ask to call a taxi. But the doctor on duty says she can hold me against my will for up to seventy-two hours because I am a danger to myself and others. I am in acute cocaine psychosis. I say I am fine, all reasonable. What is the evidence that I'm not?

"You're barefoot," she says. "It's December and you're barefoot."

And I am frightened, I am so frightened. All the nurses tell me they are my friends, that they will take care of me, but all I feel is them taking it away, taking my cocaine away, and I am on the floor. I can't stop crying, and all I can say is *Mommy, Mommy, help me.* She has already left the building, she is Elvis after a concert, she is off the premises. We have wept through our farewells as if I am never coming back, which in a way I'm not, because the person at the other end of this process is supposed to be a different me. And still, without her anywhere near, I am pleading, *Mommy, Mommy, Mommy, where are you? I need you so bad.* I keep cowering into a corner, jacklighted, saying, *Don't touch me. Don't touch me.* I'm begging them to let me do coke just one last time, watching them take it away, hearing them say anything confiscated will be returned when I leave, but I don't believe them. And I keep saying, *One last time. One last time. Let me go to the bathroom and change my tampon and take a white ride one last time.* And the nurses keep telling me not to be scared, that they love me, as if they mean it, as if it were possible.

"We've just met," I say. "You don't love me," I add, making a perfectly reasonable distinction between what love is and what words of comfort are, words that are not comforting. "And you're not my friends! You all have gray hair. Any friend of mine would dye it."

And finally the psychiatrist on duty, who has been scattered until that moment, in ruffly and fussy clothes with a tangle of unkempt black hair, a look that only mental health professionals can carry off without losing their credibility, says to me: "You will do coke again. Don't worry. Almost everyone who passes through here does it again. This will not be your last time. I can almost promise you that."

And with this vote of confidence, she sticks a needle in my arm, a dose of Thorazine to calm me down, and I am put in a room in the locked ward, put into a deep sleep, the sleep of the dead. I don't wake up again for four days.

think I've slept for all that time, but they wake me to take my vitals and to eat. Blood is drawn from my arms at 6 A.M., my pulse is monitored, and a tourniquet slips tight around my bicep to get my blood pressure. They have to lift my rag doll arms to do the job, and they spoon-feed me. I barely have the jaw power to masticate. I drink a lot of cranberry juice through a straw. That and pineapple juice, straight from the Dole can, seem to be the hospital drinks of choice.

I am in the Acute Care Unit. In a normal hospital it would be called the Intensive Care Unit, but everything here has a different name. A lot of the people in the ACU are here for electroconvulsive therapy (ECT), which is just a nice way of saying shock treatment. Some of them have dissociative disorders, but what that really means is multiple personalities. Drunks are alcoholics, junkies are opiate addicts, the drug treatment unit is called K-House, and the hospital grounds are called the campus. You don't get punished—you receive consequences. Finger painting is art therapy and playing catch is a cohesion experience and chores are confidence builders. You lean back, limber and lax, into the arms of the other patients, and you've landed in the trust fall.

The first night, apparently in my sleep, I stumble out of my room and head for the pay phone. The nurses yell at me that it is too late to make calls, that it can wait until the morning, and more stuff about how they are my friends, how they are on my side, and I just say I need to make one phone call, just one. I know that with a phone card, you just press the pound sign between each call and enter in a new number, so I can make multiple calls and it will only look like one. Ha ha. Even on Thorazine, I am smarter than they are.

I call Mommy, who is not home yet, who is probably sobbing her way down the Merritt Parkway in her forest-green sensible Civic—she is prudent and I am not, forevermore—and tell her I want to leave.

I call Ruby in Washington, D.C., who is also not around, and leave her a message to please come get me out of here. We have not spoken in a while, but a friend in need is a friend indeed, so I figure why not. I call Kathlyn, who tells me she feels terrible, but give it a chance. Before we have time to get into it, one of the nurses drags me away from the phone and back to bed.

I sneak out again a few minutes later. I am in hospital pajamas, a white smock with blue blotchy dots. It ties with a string in the back and I don't wear underwear, so I am rather exposed. In the morning they will give me scrub pants, they promise. I should be in bed now anyway. I am nearly comatose, but my determination to make phone calls matches my willingness to do anything anywhere on earth to get drugs.

I call Samantha in San Francisco, figuring with the time difference she will be awake. I tell her, as I've told everybody, that I must get out of here. She is reasonable, as she has always been, and says it probably feels that way right now, but we all know that this is what I need. Even I know it. I have to at least try a few days. I can always leave then. I tell her that they are holding me against my will, I am under seventy-two-hour lockup. She is an attorney and I am hoping to work up her civil rights ire. But she is a corporate lawyer, and since the people at Silver Hill are not violating any securities statutes, she is not much of an authority.

"Elizabeth, personal liberties is not my area."

"What the hell did they teach you at Yale Law anyway?" I slide down the wall and crouch on my knees. I really am about to pass out. The metal coil phone cord barely reaches. I am stretching my head to be near the receiver. My neck droops, slack, and I am starting to dribble. Is this really time to invoke principles?

"Oh, Elizabeth, please just give this a chance."

"Please make some phone calls and get me out of here," I beg. "You're required to do, what, thirty hours of pro bono work a year." I remember she told me that once when I asked what happened to all her naive notions of justice. "Can't I be one of your cases?"

"Elizabeth! Stop this." She sighs. Everybody who talks to me these days spends a lot of time sighing. "Kathlyn is afraid you're going to die. We've talked about this a lot. I'll come visit you up there when I'm in New York, but you need to be there. Okay? I love you."

"If you say that you're letting them keep me here because you love me, then you don't really love me." I start to cry. "I'm scared they'll never let me leave. Samantha, please."

I cry and cry on the phone. I cry when the nurses pull me away from the phone and say that it is time to go to sleep. My fear of being here is stronger than Thorazine. I should be paralyzed, but instead I am crying and crawling toward the phone. I barely remember where I am, what day it is. I have no notion of the time, but I remember my calling card number perfectly, remember everyone's phone number, etched into some address book in my head. I will call anyone whom I have met or had coffee with in the last five years. Anyone I've sat next to on the subway may hear from me right now. I will call them and beg for rescue.

I will do all these things, but not before morning, all the nurses insist. They know that by then I will be so comfortable, so at ease in my sleepy solitude, so happy to not be hitting the streets and paging people and searching for coke, so relieved to not be lying to doctors to get prescriptions, so glad to not be begging Ray to sell me his Dexedrine and Ritalin, so thrilled to not be living in a hotel and watching pornography and fucking a married man, so ready to just have the whole miserable business of being an addict over with—at least for a little while—that I will never want to leave this place. It is an asylum, and it will be mine.

The first morning, a woman walks into my room after the orderlies have checked my vitals, taken my blood, done whatever it is that they do. They give me a pill to take, thioridazine, brand-name Mellaril, which is another anti-psychotic. They also seem to be giving me my usual medications, whatever antidepressant and mood stabilizer I am on these days. Dr. Singer has given them instructions. The woman who has come in is wearing bright colors. All I can see is something teal, maybe a scarf, something lapis, maybe a coat, but she's a blur.

"I'm Karyn Geller," I hear her say, but her voice seems to be wafting through a heat duct or an elevator shaft. It's somewhere else. "I'm your psychiatrist. I work with Caroline a lot. Caroline Singer, your doctor. She sent you to me."

Why is she talking? I'm asleep. Her voice has entered my dreams, like a minor character trying to chew up the scenery.

"Hello," I manage. I am sleepy and vague, but I want to have good manners. "Nice to meet you, I think."

"Can you get up for therapy?"

This is the woman that Dr. Singer has asked to supervise me? *Can I get up for therapy?* Dr. Geller, I want to say, what does it look like to you?

"I guess not," she says. "All right. Sleep this off. I'll check up on you tomorrow."

When I come to, a few days later, I don't know what I feel. Numb, I guess, but there seem to be more condiments in my mood than that. It's interesting. There are all these ways I thought I'd feel here, and none of them were right. Think of the standard movie scene of a girl waking up in rehab, maybe in *Postcards from the Edge*. I thought I'd feel like, Get me out of here, I'm desperate for drugs. Or I thought I'd feel lonely. I thought I'd feel alienated. I had a certain vision of what it would be like, and none of it is right: I assumed I'd either wake up screaming and crying, in withdrawal and begging for cocaine the way I was that first night. Or I'd be whimpering and crying, asking for comfort in my disorientation.

Truth is, I don't know what I feel. I'm a prism right now. The light is all the hues, but you can see through them. I think about it. I remember ROY G BIV, the grade-school acronym from science class, to help you learn the colors of the rainbow—red, orange, yellow, green, blue, indigo, violet. Maybe I can plug feelings into the letters: so there's regretful or resentful; optimistic or outraged; yucky or yellow, as in cowardly; good or green, as in new; beat or blue, as in sad; insane or idealistic; violent or vile. All of the above.

Maybe I am resisting. Maybe I can't feel anything because it is too scary and unbearable. But I actually think it's simpler than that: I truly don't know what I feel. It's not that I am numb right now—it's more that I have been frosty for so long that I don't know what to make of the thaw, like a confused bear coming out of hibernation after the winter and slipping on the slosh of melted snow, burnt by the sun, astonished by hysterical blindness.

In any group therapy setting—and I've been in a few over the years—they use the "feeling wheel" to help you ascertain your emotions. It always seems so dumb. You get this spinning roulette of primary and secondary colors, as if life were a Vegas gaming table or an episode of *Wheel of Fortune*, but you only get about five choices: There are "angry" and "sad" and "lonely" and "happy" and "calm," or something like that. And I instinctively make fun of the feeling wheel, of this list of fill-in-the-blank suggested emotions, of the sentences they offer like "I feel——when my boss praises me," or "I feel——when my mother yells at me," or "I feel——when I am alone in my room," or "I feel——when my friend calls me." It seems so absurd. Here we are in all our complexity, all the complicated emotions that brought us here, and they are asking us to be so reductive, to be these simple one-word things. It's babyish. In the poem "Family Week at Oracle Ranch," about a stay at a therapeutic center, James Merrill writes: "The connoisseur of feeling throws up his hands: Used to depicting personal anguish / with a full palette—hues, oils, glazes, thinner— / He stares into these withered wells and feels, / Well . . . SAD and ANGRY?" They won't let you say anything but these simple words. Keep it simple.

But now I understand it completely. Because, in truth, I do not know what I feel, lying here. I guess it is sort of relaxing not having to think or worry about anything, not trying to sort out the day's drugs, not needing to shower or forage for food. Ironically, what I liked about cocaine was the way it simplified life, the way it reduced it to sheer need, and to only one need at that. This is the same principle, but it's reduced from one to nothing: I have no needs to concern myself with. Betsy was right: I can let them figure it out for me. I can let them toss me five emotions that are accessible to me. This is a multiple-choice final exam. I'll take whatever suggestions anyone will throw my way, and it's best if they are simple. I need that feeling wheel, because I have no idea what I feel. At all.

A woman walks in the next morning, as I am drinking cranberry juice and wishing I could have something stronger than Sleepytime tea or Ovaltine. Her footfalls are distinctive, heavy and striding, like perfume so strong that it enters the room before the person wearing it. She is a sharp presence in a place where everyone else seems coated in down, the nurses and orderlies so extremely quiet and gentle. The tiptoes of ballerinas in the corps of *Swan Lake* are their model for stepping lightly, leaving the soloists—all the disturbed patients—to squawk and make all the noise.

After she stomps in, she forthrightly says, "Good morning. I see you're awake." She looks at a clipboard where they've written down my pulse and affect, and she pulls out a pen to add some notes herself. What can she possibly have to say? *Patient is awake, not too alert, shows interest in Ocean Spray.* "I'm Karyn Geller. I introduced myself when you first got here. You probably barely remember. I've been checking up on you the last couple of days. Boy, did you need sleep. Cocaine and speed. You probably haven't had a good rest in a long time."

"I guess not."

I am checking her out. She is nothing like Dr. Singer, who is too absurdly beautiful and glamorous for her own good. Dr. Singer has black hair and blue eyes and high cheekbones, and looks like Jaclyn Smith in her *Charlie's Angels* heyday or Lucy Lawless on *Xena Warrior Princess*, only Dr. Singer has a raw intelligence that is a lot more interesting. She is a bit thick-waisted now that she is in her forties and has a couple of kids, but she wears pastel suits and Ferragamo mules in the summer, and she folds her legs up on her chair during sessions, as if to suggest gracious and casual ease. Her office is in the town house where she and her family live, and it all bespeaks the good life, as if to say, Stick with me, kid, and this too could be yours. When I grow up, I want to be Dr. Singer.

I am not sure I will feel the same way about Dr. Geller. She's flamboyant—instead of pastels we've got brights. Her coat is dark, and her sweater is black, but she's got a lot of turquoise and raspberry in her multistrand scarf, and she wears a long gold necklace with an ankh pendant, dangling earrings that swing through her curls, and chunky stone rings on her fingers. Her hair is a tangle of auburn, her lipstick is a heart of magenta, she wears wire-framed glasses, and she is distracted with six other things as we talk. She addresses an envelope, looks at her beeper, which buzzes every few minutes, flips through folders, fills out insurance forms, checks the yellow duplicate sheets on her prescription pad, fingers her rose quartz and turquoise rings, pulls at her jewelry, twirls her hair. And still, I sense that she will hear everything that I say. She won't have that stunning blue-eyed focus that Dr. Singer plants so deep on my face that I have to look away. Dr. Geller is more like me, listening and chatting while doing the crossword puzzle and flipping through *Harper's Bazaar*. I hear everything, but you'd never know it.

Of course, when I do this it annoys everybody enough, but it's far worse if this goes on during a therapy session. I wonder if this is just a disorganized day for Dr. Geller. Something tells me it's not.

I am hoping she won't suggest that I call her Karyn. I like the idea of authority figures making their status clear. It makes me feel safe. I would never survive in a communist state, where we are all comrades and we are all equal. I know in practice that is never how it works, because of course people in packs fall into their own pecking order—there are always the alphas and the betas, right down to the omegas. But still, I would hate the illusion that there are no social strata; I like to know where I and everybody else stands. This may contradict the principles of Alcoholics Anonymous, where there are no leaders or experts, where Tradition Eight insists that the organization should "remain forever nonprofessional" and Tradition Two says that we have "but one ultimate authority—a loving God" and any officers are "but trusted servants." But I have been in elite institutions all my life, I have been indoctrinated with formality, and I will address this woman as Dr. Geller no matter what she prefers. Someone has to be in charge here, and I guess, since I am supine and soft-brained, it is she.

"I am guessing that you aren't ready to have a full therapy session yet," Dr. Geller says. Good guess. "But we need to set up some order to your treatment."

"When do I get out of here?" Might as well get right to the point. "I mean, out of the ACU and into the normal place, whatever that is. I don't want to be locked up forever." And then my defiance breaks. "I'm scared. I'm afraid you won't let me leave here. I mean, I don't want to leave Silver Hill. I thought I would. I thought I'd just get my face and my nose emptied out and then I'd go back to New York and use some more, but I feel restful."

"That's not unusual," Dr. Geller says. "It's nice to get away from all that. People get comfortable pretty quickly. Unless they're heroin addicts, in which case they can't sleep and we end up giving them methadone to get through the first few days because it's too painful. And they want to run out like crazy. We need to put them on seventy-two-hour lockup, or they just go running down the highway to get away. But you've got the opposite problem. You're just exhausted. It must be nice to relax."

"Yes." She's right.

"So what do you want to do about therapy? Caroline thinks you should see me every day." It's jarring for her to call Dr. Singer by her given name. "I think that's probably right."

"How come?"

"Because you're really sick and in trouble." She starts taking notes again. "I know you think it's not so bad. I can tell, I can tell you think you're a mild case, that everyone here is going to be much worse off than you, but you're wrong. Just because you write books or whatever—" I don't like that *whatever*; it's dismissive. "Just because you held it together for pretty long does not mean you're okay. An eightball of coke a day is a lot; forty pills of Ritalin is a lot. People have come in here for much less. People who can't stop taking five or ten pills a day have been through here. You did a number on yourself. You really did. Don't pretend this isn't so bad."

"I'm not."

My nose is running like crazy. That's the only physical reaction I am aware of. I keep grabbing at tissues and dabbing. Dr. Geller notices this too.

"I'm going to tell them to stop giving you tranquilizers so that you can stay awake. It's time. Meanwhile, I'm going to add some nasal steroids to your medication, because you've got holes in your nose, or that's what it looks like to me."

"Good idea." I mean, why not? I hear there is a specialist at Columbia University who does nothing but deal with the noses of recovered addicts, just stemming their sinuses. "When can I join the, what do you call it, normal population? When can I move into K-House?"

"Why don't you go through the activities they've got here tonight for the people who are in this unit? They have group. It'll be good for you."

"Aren't they the real crazies? The shock patients?"

"Actually, they're mostly suicidal teenagers." More notes. "They're nice, sad kids. They've got bandages on their wrists, or they're really skinny from anorexia. Some of them smoke too much pot. That's about it. A pretty preppie bunch, since most of them are from around here. You'll like them. They'll admire you. They've probably all read your book. You'll like the validation." A bunch of teenagers, *oy vey*. They'll all have hippie names like Rainbow and Sunshine, or else the girls will have boys' names like Chandler and Hunter, because that was the craze when the Baby Boomers had their kids in the eighties. Yuck. Or else it's the deep classics and biblical monikers—Emma and Henry, Hannah and Samuel. Or maybe that's my generation's name trend. But anyway, what's in a name—even if it's Montague or Capulet?

I wonder if Dr. Geller would get that reference. I wonder if she knows literature, even basic Shakespeare. I kind of get the feeling she reads books about angels and goddesses, about Buddhism and Vishnu and Kali, and even— heaven help me—*The Celestine Prophecy*. She has a New Age feel to her. Her calling card, which she hands to me, has loopy lilac letters that quote from the gospel of Mark, "With God, all things are possible." I guess even psychiatrists, medical school graduates, who deal a lot with addiction—and in Dr. Geller's case, eating disorders—must adapt to the Twelve Step model. Maybe that's not so bad. I kind of do believe that with God, anything and anyone can be saved—I wish I had faith. Maybe she'll teach me about that. Maybe this is good.

"How do you know that about me?" I ask, meaning that I need validation. I hate to be so transparent. I'm lying here almost mute. There's nothing I've said to indicate that I'm an adulation whore. Not yet, anyway.

"You're an addict. All of you need the same things. You all want attention. You're no different from any of the other people who come through here."

Fuck you!

"Yes, I am."

"Maybe in some ways, but as an addict, you're like everybody else."

I pout.

"Come on, Elizabeth," she says, responding to my sour expression. "I've heard all about you from Caroline. I know you're accomplished. But you can't think about that right now. Just keep the focus on getting better. We'll deal with the rest when you're out of the forest."

"Okay." I'm too tired to be resentful.

"So I'm going to tell the nurse that you need to get out of bed for dinner tonight. No more lying around. And then you'll do group, and then if you have enough energy, we'll move you to K-House in the morning. You put your stuff in boxes, and a couple of porters will take it all over there." Ah yes, it is a country club after all. I don't even need to carry my own things. "So that's it." She wraps her scarf around her neck, looks at her beeper, which is buzzing, and gathers her bag and folders and envelopes and an assortment of loose ends that seem to fall all over the place. "Is there anything you need before I go?"

"Can I ask you something?" She nods. "What should I call you?"

"Dr. Geller," she says. "That's my name."

So she won't want me to be chummy and call her Karyn. There is some decorum after all. Thank God.

Seventeen

KEEP THE FOCUS ON YOU

Well I try my best to be just like I am
But everybody wants me to be just like them

BOB DYLAN
"Maggie's Farm"

K-House is in fact a house, a yellow clapboard with lots of bedrooms, a living room with overstuffed couches and chairs, Persian rugs, colonial wood tables, and a den with a stereo, and a television set with VCR and basic cable. The only indication that it's not just a large cottage for a big family is the fire exits with their blue and red lights, clearly marked for emergencies. The "K" stands for Klingenstein, and you can see why no one would want to say the whole thing. Everyone gets his own room and his own bathroom, and it's all pleasant. The cleaning service comes in to make the beds and scrub the tubs and toilets. It's an easy life. At first, the counselors do bed check every fifteen minutes, but after a couple of days it's down to thirty-minute and then hour-long intervals. They knock first, lest they catch any one in *flagrante* masturbation, so I end up waking up several times a night. The last thing on my mind is sex. Sleep is dreamy and erotic all by itself. I luxuriate in it like a new love.

There are always a registered nurse on duty, a doctor on call, and several counselors around the house. They sit in an office on the main floor with a half-door sealing them off in their swivel chairs and aluminum desks, and they are always easy to find and available to chat. The counselors are all recovered addicts, dispensing wisdom about their days of equestrian therapy at Sierra Tucson, or about first getting drinking privileges at some TC (therapeutic community) back in the early eighties, when the philosophy of recovery was way different—when they believed that just because you were a junkie or a cokehead, that did not mean that you couldn't have the occasional glass of chardonnay; nowadays, total abstinence is the standard.

The members of the medical staff all seem so pristine, as if the closest they've come to doing drugs is inhaling fresh air on a brisk day. In the morning everyone lines up for their meds at a room with a Lucite window that's slid open to hand out pills and water in Dixie cups. We go to a dining hall at Main House for meals—this is the unit for the regular nonaddict mental patients—but you can ask to have food delivered if you have therapy or some other reason to stay in, and the reason can be as simple as "I'm tired." There are granola bars and PowerBars and cold cereal in the pantry, Dannon yogurt and whole milk and V8 and Ocean Spray mixes of cranberry-apple and cranberry-grape in the refrigerator. And there are tons of Ovaltine. That is the staple of K-House. Cold Ovaltine and milk during the day, warm stuff heated in the microwave at night—it provides lots of nutrients and puts you to sleep.

Activity is kept to a minimum. Mostly they leave me alone to read my John Berryman poems and my thousand-page Don DeLillo novel and to listen to Bob Dylan in my room—that voice, it is all that penetrates my dull delirium. They only force me out of bed for group sessions and our nightly Twelve Step meetings, or to go to art therapy, which involves making a lot of drawings and paintings that are supposed to be telling. I use waxy pastels on white construction paper to produce a picture on which I've traced my hands, and put the letters L-O-V-E across one set of knuckles, and H-A-T-E across the other, like Robert Mitchum's perverse preacher in The Night of the Hunter, who uses his fists to speechify about the opposing forces in the world, and which will win out. I don't have an answer just yet, but I'm hoping against hope—that's what I say during the discussion period after we complete our artwork. I beg the instructor to let me weave a basket, so that I can say that I did the thing that everyone imagines is the craft of choice in mental institutions. But the osiers and other materials are not available, so my quest for self-parody is quashed. Instead we stencil T-shirts, and I make one with a bitterly black skull and crossbones and "F.T.W."—fuck the world—underneath, which is the same as the tattoo on my shoulder blade. None of this is terribly taxing, and all of it is kind of fun. All you're supposed to do is rest and recover, get the lead out, get the drugs out, clean up, and calm down.

You can't close the door to your room at K-House during waking hours unless you're changing clothes, which I do several times a day because the weather goes from cold to colder as we progress toward evening, and I go from heavy wool-blend sweaters to weighty cable-knit angoras with lots of fuzz. Or I wear cardigans with T-shirts and wife-beaters that leave my lower abdomen and navel ring exposed, and the counselors often insist that I put more clothes on and cover up better. Also, they want me to wear a bra, which I don't like. You're not supposed to be sexy here in rehab, and I can't stand it. I always want male attention, and I keep my toenails painted even though I never wear anything but thick socks and cowboy boots. I flirt with the male counselors; I flirt with the male patients; I flirt with the male doctors; I flirt with the male volunteers who come in to lead in-house Twelve Step meetings and group discussions. I finally get a citation for "excessively flirtatious behavior" and "stomach-baring attire," which gets posted to Dr. Geller, who laughs and tells me to lay off.

"Humor them," she says. "They're just doing their jobs, and you need to respect the rules, even if it seems silly. This is not a pickup joint. It's a hospital."

Ah, but don't they understand? The whole world is my pickup joint. Take away my drugs, and all that's left for me is men. I know this isn't good, that part of the point of being here is to get over *all* these addictive, destructive tendencies, but I don't know what to do if I am not inspiring some sort of false fascination. When we go to meetings in the auditorium, which are mostly attended by outsiders who live in the area or were once patients at Silver Hill, I check out the guys, see who is cute, plot assignations with no one in particular.

K-House is pretty empty right now. Only the hard cases are at rehab during the holiday season. Most people make it through New Year's and check themselves in as part of their resolutions. The few of us who are here have bandages on our wrists, or else we are skinny and listless and nasal like me. It is only people who are going to die without it who are here now. Not many romantic opportunities in this. A Klonopin addict who thinks she is a poet and lives on the Upper East Side, supported by the considerable trust fund her aging and senile father has given her—which causes all kinds of fights with her young and devious stepmother, or so she says—has the room down the hall, on the female floor, because they keep the sexes sort of separated. A concert promoter from Houston is fun to talk to, but he plans to stick around for only a few days, until Christmas, and then go back to his girlfriend and hope their obsessive relationship including days and nights of cocaine and fucking will somehow not resume. Another guy who works in the music business and lives in L.A. and has a heavy relationship with Vicodin has a room downstairs from mine. He annoys me. He is Jewish and pushy and lies about his close ties to Kiss and Motley Crüe and people like that. Why he would lie about this I don't know. Why he would brag about it is even more mysterious to me, but at any rate he never shuts up. He has a Long Island accent and thinks that because I am a Jewish girl from the Upper West Side, we have something in common. Of course, everyone here thinks they have something in common, we are all addicts, and we are all the same. But that doesn't work with me.

The desire to be seen as superior and singular—and, conversely but similarly, inferior and individual—is a big topic in AA and NA and addiction recovery of all sorts. They even have a term for the syndrome—it is called *terminal uniqueness.* Apparently, it is the big problem, the leading reason that we are all here. We all refuse to be part of the crowd, to walk in the middle of the road in the safety of others. We all think we're special. But the problem is, as I point out to Dr. Singer all the time, I actually *am* special.

Of course, I know that all addicts think that. Whatever they've got to show for themselves, they all believe in some way that they are unique—they think their emotions are special, their inner life is one of a kind. And if they have not achieved much, they believe they are hampered by addiction. Everyone I have ever met at an AA or NA meeting is a genius, despite the evidence or lack thereof. Everyone has artistic talent that was discouraged by their mean, misunderstanding parents. *Everyone* is misunderstood. And they will all point to all the prodigies who were drunks or druggies—Kurt Cobain, Dorothy Parker, Jimi Hendrix, Jackson Pollock, John Belushi, Janis Joplin, Robert Lowell— and they will use this as proof that they too are brilliant, that they are like them. "I have known no man of genius who had not to pay, in some affliction or defect either physical or spiritual, for what the gods had given him," wrote Sir Max Beerbohm in *No. 2. The Pines.* This statement and others like it make those who are defective and afflicted feel better about themselves, which is good as far as it goes.

But too many people misapply it, and this bit of misinformation or disinformation drives me crazy. Just because you feel deeply and indiscriminately does not mean that your feelings are indications of anything other than your flat-out fucked-up life. Just because most or many geniuses seem to be addicts does not mean that most addicts are geniuses. Just because four of the nine Americans who have won the Nobel Prize for literature—Ernest Hemingway, Eugene O'Neill, John Steinbeck, and William Faulkner—were known alcoholics does not mean that if you are a drunk, you are also a writer. The percentages of intelligence and talent among addicts are probably about the same as in the general population—maybe a bit more, possibly a little less. As Oscar Wilde said, "All bad poetry is sincere." The desire—and the great need—to express oneself that you might find among the mentally ill does not mean that very much of their art is worth our reading or listening to or viewing. Just because Anne Sexton became a poet after she wrote as part of her therapy, and just because she was encouraged by her psychiatrist to pursue it professionally, to publish in *The New Yorker*—that does not mean everyone who is plagued by bad moods deserves a Pulitzer Prize.

Aidan checks in over the weekend. At long last, someone who is my handsomely disheveled type. This is his ninth stay at Silver Hill, so he has dispensed with formalities. He has no intake interview; he just makes a couple of phone calls and comes into K-House in his ragamuffin flannels and jeans, with his spare bunch of belongings. He almost looks like a teen runaway in a cartoon. I half expect him to have a bandanna full of necessities tied to the end of a stick slung high over his shoulder, but he's just a junkie seeking refuge. His pupils are pinned, but his eyes are astonished and open, with all the vulnerability and anxiety of a soldier running for cover in an open field with bullets and cannons shooting all over. Aidan's fright and anxiety are sexy, because that's the sick orientation I've got when it comes to men. He spends most of the first day throwing up, in the toilet bowl and elsewhere. He's given methadone and clonidine, and still he paces around, nauseated and exhausted and sleepless all at once.

Given the situation, the last thing he wants is me coming on to him. But who says he has a choice? I think he's hot, and that's all. My ability to appreciate the circumstances of others is not very well refined anyway, and here we are, just a few of us in the winter dark in a swankly shabby house in New Canaan—so let the games begin. I can't win, but I'll still play.

We have some kind of group therapy the evening Aidan arrives, and we all sit around filling out worksheets about what our triggers are, what are the worst things we ever did for drugs, what our reasons are for wanting to quit. I know all the answers to these items, know them only too well. I cannot imagine what the point of scribbling them all down around a circular table in the basement rumpus room might be, but I just go with it. I suppose reiterating the whole mess has its uses. I guess my idea of rehabilitation comes down to being left alone in peace with my books and music for long enough that I lose interest in using, and can reenter sane society as a civilian who doesn't do blow. The notion that there is some necessary therapeutic process in all this does not much interest me. But it's like the toll on the thruway or going to graduate school— you pay the price and fulfill the requirements because it lets you get to where you need to, it allows you to hang out quietly along the way. This is downtime with a price—the monetary one is absurd, something like $15,000 a month— and I guess it's worth it.

I stare at Aidan and make goo-goo eyes at him the whole time. Afterward, I wait to hear him in the kitchen so I can corner him and converse. What a pleasure it is to have a crush on someone! How I've missed the pursuit! He tells me that he used to be in the philosophy department at Columbia. He was working on his Ph.D. in political theory and trying to write a novel besides. He frittered away his fellowship money on the mission of fiction. I figure it will impress him that I am a published author and all. And maybe it would in any other atmosphere, but not here, not now. I keep trying to remind myself that this is not a party, but that's what I want it to be. A dope-free, coke-free, booze-free bash. I'm here to relax and socialize. Anyone else up for a good time?

And this is how I come to be universally disliked at Silver Hill. Everyone here is terribly delicate, including me. We are all undefended, like cars without bumpers or fenders in a world full of road rage—or, more simply, we are addicts deprived of our drugs—and we can only rely on each other to be careful, gentle. That's what I need. But I don't seem to understand it. I do but I don't. My idea of how to get better is to find a similarly addicted boyfriend and for us to go to meetings and therapy and whatnot together. Of course, it is a rule of rehab that there will be no fraternizing. At Hazelden and Betty Ford, they keep men and women separate to avoid the whole mess. But at Silver Hill, the rules are lax—it is in fact the perfect place for someone like me, for someone not quite ready to go whole hog into recovery, but looking for a refuge, looking for a peaceful place for intensive one-on-one treatment where drugs are not an issue. I'm not good at group dynamics—I don't really care about anyone else enough to be. I mean, I care about my friends, I find them fascinating and fun, but that's different: I don't have to listen to them moan and groan as a full-time experience. Their entire essence is not our mutual addiction.

These people at Silver Hill probably won't interest me that much, I don't think.

Except Aidan. We could be friends in another situation. We could talk about Robert Stone and David Foster Wallace and other new writing. At one point I mention this to him.

"It's nice to have you here, nice to have someone to talk to," I say. We are in the late-night brightness of the kitchen. The rest of K-House is always muted, the lamps are dim, their necks craned into sharp angles to face downward, and it's dark outside because of daylight savings time. Most addicts like the barroom atmosphere of shady lighting, but not me. I wish there were halogen torques everywhere.

"There are lots of people here to talk to," he replies. "Look around." Could this be anything besides rejection?

"But we can discuss literature," I explain. "There's more to being here than just reading the Big Book and going to meetings. I think it's important to engage your brain a little bit, at least, in this process. I hate how so many people around here seem dumb and uninterested in, oh, I don't know, culture, I guess." *Culture?* Jesus, that sounds obnoxious. And shallow. "Books, I mean."

"Elizabeth, don't you see that's not what I'm here for?" he asks, impatient, or maybe just sick from withdrawal. "That's not what you're here for either."

"I'm not that sick."

"You wouldn't be here four days before Christmas, even if you are Jewish, if you weren't desperate."

"I'm not a heroin addict like you. I'm okay."

"You think cocaine and speed aren't serious?"

"Not the same." I try to think of the difference. "Heroin's got your body. Cocaine's only got my mind. I get some distance from it, it's fine. It's like a guy who's broken my heart. But your problem is medical."

"You know, you're really stupid if you don't see how serious this is." He stops to think and mix some Ovaltine into milk. "Snorting Ritalin. Sweet Jesus, that's a sickness all its own. Who would even *think* to do that?"

I can't tell if this is an insult, or if Aidan is giving me props. Around rehab, it's a badge of pride to be as extreme as possible, though for some reason I am now arguing on behalf of my relatively salubrious indulgences.

"Well, at least this isn't my ninth time here." Where am I going with this? I *like* this guy. I am supposed to be flirting with him, not fighting. This isn't cutely contentious repartee either. This is not like *His Girl Friday* or Myrna Loy and William Powell, not at all. It's just a couple of drug addicts trying to one-up—or actually, one-*down*—each other. "Look, I'm sorry. I like talking to you, and instead we seem to be arguing. This is coming out all wrong. That happens a lot with me. I get it wrong a lot."

"Well, maybe that's why you're here, and maybe that's why you use," Aidan says. "But try to take it seriously. Try not to think about conversations about *White Noise*. That stuff's not important. You can do all that with your friends when you get out of here. Just keep the focus on yourself."

That's another big expression in recovery—*keep the focus on you.* At the same time, you are also supposed to avoid being selfish, which seems contradictory, though I understand that minding your own business is actually one of the most selfless things you can do around rehab. If it weren't hard to stay in my own head, I would not be nudging Aidan right now. "You don't want to be here nine times like me," he adds, a small concession to friendliness.

No, of course not. But I don't figure on that anyway. I'm safe. So far, in the couple of days Aidan has been here, he's swung from disgusted and resentful to serious and self-righteous, like he just was with me. None of us has any right to lecture anyone else. This is *Lifeboat*, this is the Donner party, this is all about who will live and who will die. For real. I know that sounds like hyperbole, but in the course of my treatment, I will learn that it's really that way. People die from addiction, and the idea is not to be one of them.

On Sunday, a woman in Main House kills herself. She is a doctor, a pediatrician, and just the day before, her husband and two children had come to visit for a family session. She was dark and petite, and beyond that I hardly knew her. Somehow she got through the night, and in the morning, she woke up and hanged herself. I'm guessing it was from her shower curtain rail, because what else could it be? No one gets specific, so I'll never know. Even the rehab rumor mill doesn't come up with any theories.

Sunday afternoon, one of the staff psychiatrists comes by to talk to us, the K-House residents, as a group. The first thing I notice about him is that he is young and handsome. I wonder if he is married, and I see a wedding band on his left hand, so then I wonder if he cheats. This is ridiculous. I've got to get romantic games off the brain. Focus on myself. Focus on my recovery—I have to keep saying this in my head like a mantra. I need to meditate on this idea, sit Indian-style on my bedroom floor or in a semilotus position, some Wyndham Hill music playing in the background, some strawberry incense burning on the windowsill, and while breathing in through my nose and out through my mouth as they say to do in the Transcendental Meditation handbook that I read in some college religion course, I must keep telling myself: Keep the focus on me, keep the focus on me, keep the focus on me, over and over.

After telling us about this woman's suicide, the doctor asks if we have any questions, if any of us wants to share our feelings about this sorry event. No one says anything, because really this does not affect us at all; we hardly knew her. She was in the mental ward, not the addicts' unit. But he won't let it go at that, because he needs to make this into a therapeutic process for all of us.

"No one has anything to express?" the psychiatrist asks.

I feel sorry for him; he is trying so hard. He looks like such a mellow guy. He probably goes hiking in the Connecticut woods on the weekends. This is the last thing he needs. I decide I'd better say something, because it seems like a responsibility. I always take that upon myself—I'm the one who fills in any lulls in the conversation, which people mistake for mindless chattiness, but it is actually a form of insecurity mixed with politeness.

"Well, I'm just wondering, I guess," I try, "how she managed to do this. Not to be insensitive—I'm not looking for gory details. But we're all so carefully watched here, I can't imagine how anyone allowed this to happen."

"I don't know," he answers. And I'm sure that's the truth. She turned the shower on; for fifteen minutes someone looked away; that's all it takes. Murderers of the self are crafty. "But suicides have a special language," writes Anne Sexton in "Wanting to Die," one of my favorite poems. "Like carpenters they want to know *which tools*. / They never ask *why build*." I'm not blaming anybody by asking; I'm just curious. It seems odd. I want to know *which tools*.

"Look," the handsome, winsome psychiatrist says. "This is a hospital. One of the things that happens quite a lot at any hospital is people die. It's not unusual at all."

"What do you mean?" I ask. He's testing my patience now. "People with terminal cancer die in hospitals, ninety-year-olds die in hospitals—that's true enough. But no—young, physically healthy adults don't die in hospitals very much. I mean, I'm sure it happens, but please don't spin it this way. We're drug addicts, not idiots. Don't make it sound like it's okay. You're not trying to avoid a malpractice suit here. You're talking to us. Please be straight. How are any of us supposed to get better if you speak to us like dopes?"

"Fair enough," he says. And the meeting is adjourned.

Niccolo checks in on December 23, and is immediately a pain in the ass. He hits on me in the dining hall, when he is not busy nodding off and drooling. He's got withdrawal going bad, but he can't quite succumb to it. He's still trying to flirt with me, telling me that his family owns the largest bagel bakery on earth, that if I marry him I will be neck deep in Sunday brunch for the rest of my life.

Quite an offer, I think. Quite a romantic proposal. But he mostly just bugs me. This is so inappropriate! We're in rehab! This is not a pickup joint! It is not fair for him to be pushing at me this way.

Now I know how Aidan feels. Niccolo's example is not going to change my behavior, because I'm a girl, and it's different when we throw ourselves at boys—we're not threatening in the same way. But I see that it's unkind. This is not the place.

This is Niccolo's sixth time checking in at Silver Hill. I am starting to see that this is not atypical. The place is homey. There is no strict twenty-eight-day program as there is at Hazelden or Betty Ford. People stay as long as they need to or want to. The lack of formality in the program itself makes the whole hospital rather porous—people run away during treatment, but they are always welcomed back. On the one hand, it is lovely and familial. On the other, this is an instance where tough love would be not a half-bad idea. Some of these people could stand to be sent to an isolated treatment center in the middle of nowhere, far from their families, away from places they can flee to, where the rules are strict and harsh. New Canaan is not a recovery community the way Center City, Minnesota, is; it's a commuter town full of stockbrokers with handsome wives and children at boarding school. It's too easy to leave Silver Hill and settle in with normal life, or move into New York City, and not maintain the kind of sober living that's a full-time pursuit in parts of Arizona or in Orange County in California, which is what the hard cases need. It seems like most junkies go through multiple treatments before they clean up for good. And very few succeed even under the best of circumstances: one in thirty-five is the statistic that keeps getting thrown around. Still, I think many of the patients I come across would have a better chance somewhere tougher, someplace where you can't enter and exit at will.

I get hollered at for letting my belly button play peekaboo above my buttonfly jeans, but Aidan and Niccolo push through the penetrable walls of the hospital with impunity.

On the day of Christmas Eve, Niccolo is a wreck. The night before, we had an in-house AA meeting because so many people who would regularly attend the auditorium meetings are out of town. Niccolo's body was forcedly erect and falling over on the couch like a two-by-four leaning against a wall, but he decided to share at the meeting anyway, to try to participate through his fog and haze and heavy jowls. "I just want to say I'm glad to be here," Niccolo said, his eyelids ajar, just barely, his voice deep and soft. "I listened to the story, and it gave me strength, and I hope to stay straight." That was it.

On December 24, Niccolo asks Aidan where he can score in Norwalk. He wants a connection—he can't bear it anymore. Aidan confides in me about this as we are walking up the lawned hill to K-House. When he shares this news with me, it makes me feel slightly significant to Aidan, like we're in cahoots. But also, some part of me is genuinely concerned. Niccolo looks to be really suffering. "What did you tell him?" I ask.

"That I wouldn't help him, and he should ask for more methadone if he is jonesing that bad."

"Should we do something?" I ask, because I think that maybe we should, I know the rule is that everyone is responsible for his own recovery, that you cannot stop an addict who is determined to use, but still, there must be something we can do. "Maybe we should call Dr. Grubman and let him know that Niccolo is at risk, before the holiday, before everyone disappears." Dr. Grubman is the head of the whole hospital.

"Nah. It's not up to us," Aidan says. "He can take care of himself."

"But shouldn't we do something? Don't we have some sort of responsibility?" I am trying to think of the right thing to say. I want to impress Aidan with my compassion, I want to keep the focus on me like I'm supposed to, and all at once, I want to do what's right. "We can make one phone call, at least tell his counselor."

"I don't want to rat him out."

"If someone's life is in danger, I don't think it's a good time to worry about tattling. He's not going to be punished. He's here, after all. He wants to get better, or he wouldn't be here. They can give him more methadone for his pains."

"I don't know," Aidan says. We are walking outside, approaching K-House and off to our separate rooms. "Don't worry about it."

That night, Niccolo signs himself out of Silver Hill, just walks right out—or actually, he drives away in his Range Rover. No one tries to stop him: he has the right to do what he likes. The only psychiatrist on call is someone who doesn't know him. The nurses on duty are also substitutes, occasional or temporary workers filling in to get time-and-a-half. No extraordinary measures are taken to keep Niccolo on the premises. He has been in and out so much anyway that even if people at the front office did know him, they would be accustomed to his comings and goings. They are unexceptional.

Later that night, more like early in the morning, Niccolo comes back to the hospital. He is high and helpless, he doesn't want to use again, and he wants to check back in. He did some heroin that he managed to scare up in Norwalk, the nearest slum city, and he's had enough. He shot up, and now he's lousy with dope. Letting him return within hours of leaving is pretty much against Silver Hill policy. If he came back sometime later, in a few days or weeks, Niccolo would be checking back in anew. But letting him back after just a few hours puts him pretty much in the category of AWOL, of a scofflaw, someone who is simply breaking the rules since he does not have off-grounds privileges. Just the same, Niccolo is desperate, and he comes straggling back into K-House, back to the room directly below mine, where all his stuff is still parked.

Morning comes, everyone wakes up for Christmas breakfast, such as it is, and Niccolo is still in bed. We figure he's sleeping in, because people do that, and on Christmas there are no rules against much of anything. The holiday spirit around here means that there is no group therapy, no program to attend. Everyone can chill out in their rooms and take the time to relax and reflect. But after a while, one of the counselors goes to check up on Niccolo. He doesn't move. He can't be roused. Finally a nurse is called in, and it becomes clear that Niccolo does not have a pulse. No breath, and his face and hands are turning blue. His lips are purple like Laura Palmer's always were when her corpse was washed up in muddy water on *Twin Peaks*. Finally the medics are called in, and Niccolo's dead body is hauled away. He got some bad stuff and was poisoned overnight, or maybe he just took an overdose of some super-strong skag. He knew what he was doing, knew his own tolerance, so the former is more likely. But really, what difference does it make?

Another group meeting, more talk about our feelings, how this affects us, what harm this does to the Silver Hill community. This time people are crying, Aidan sits on a chair looking stony and subdued, and I sit on the floor in our crooked semicircle and start to cry.

"I thought we should tell someone that he was having a hard time," I sniffle. "But all anyone says is focus on your own recovery, don't worry about how other people are doing. I don't understand this place." Now I am mad. "I don't understand this process. We're supposed to look out for each other. Aren't we? But not too much. Not if it gets in our own way. I don't understand what the point of making recovery a group process is if we are supposed to just focus on our own problems. I don't understand what I am supposed to do here. This all goes counter to my ethics. I'm a shithead, I know it. But I look after my friends as best I can, and they look after me. I wouldn't be here if they didn't. People helped me. People helped me—" I trail off. I'm crying pretty hard. No one else is saying anything. "I'm not blaming Silver Hill policy. I'm blaming myself. I'm blaming myself for trying to do things recovery style, and instead it fails, and I don't understand how this works. I want to be the person I believe I should be, but here I'm told that's wrong. I don't know what to think—"

I stop talking. Aidan gets up to hug me and hold me down on the floor. There is not supposed to be any physical contact between men and women at Silver Hill, but that hardly seems significant right now. None of the counselors who are present try to pull us apart. Maybe their way doesn't work so well. Maybe they are thinking about it.

I call Dr. Geller later in the day. She's Jewish like me, so this is just another day off for her with no meaning. Not that Christmas means much more than evergreens and presents and very bad fruitcake to anyone else, but for us it's not even that much. She knows all about Niccolo, since his brother is a patient of hers. She's been talking to the family all day. She says it's all a mess. If she had been the doctor on call, she'd have insisted they put Niccolo in seventy-two-hour lockup.

"Dr. Geller," I say, talking on the K-House pay phone. "I'm ready to start therapy for real. Not just your coming by to check up on me. Let's have a real appointment tomorrow morning. Okay?"

She's got a busy schedule, but she promises that we'll figure it out. We'll come up with a good treatment plan. We'll figure out the rules. We'll decide how to make my stay here work.

"I want you to sit all the way in the chair with your feet on the ground, and be absolutely present," Dr. Geller says. We are meeting in a house of offices, psychiatrists' outposts and administrative rooms, all very makeshift. Dr. Geller is no longer on staff at Silver Hill. She is on call, and she sees a few patients, but she is mostly in private practice in her house in Greenwich, which I am sure is a lush sanctuary, full of plants and waterfalls and third world art. All therapists' offices I have ever been to are kind of like that—there is a look of calm aura amid the chaotic mind—but I have a feeling hers is particularly that way. She is very New Age. No getting around it. But smart, whip smart. I'm catching on to that too.

"Be here now," Dr. Geller says. "I bought you a cup of coffee at Starbucks. Extra half and half, like you said, so you can feel at home and awake."

"It's 8 A.M." I say. "Don't have wild expectations of me. I can barely sit here and not sleep. If I get too comfortable, I might be lost to the cause."

"Lost to the cause." Her eyebrows raise as if I've said something surprising, insightful. "Is that how you feel?"

"Come on, not this," I say. "Let's not act like every word matters. Let's not look for all my slips, like they reveal something. I majored in comparative literature. I read a ton of Freud and Lacan and Julia Kristeva. I know how to play word games."

"Well, I went to medical school, Miss Smartie," she says. "And I did not read tons of Freud, and I don't know who those other people are. I went to the University of Colorado because I wanted to ski. I was a ballerina in Santa Fe for a year after that. I did not get serious about medicine and about my education until a few years after college. I'm not clever like you. But I know how to make you better. I know what I'm doing. And the first step is for you to stop hiding behind words, behind all the things you know that no one else knows. Because you know a lot. You've seen a lot of movies and read a lot of books, and you know how to write in a way that makes other people feel understood—if that makes sense. I mean that your understanding of yourself makes other people feel understood themselves—and that's all very good. But where has it landed you? It's landed you in a mental hospital. So stop trying to wiggle your way out of facing up to what's going on here."

I've played these games too, I want to tell her. I've had a bunch of therapists who have told me to stop hiding behind words, to get to my feelings, to go for the emotional center and stop skimming the intellectual surface, with all its grace and glibness. This is nothing new to me. But I have to say that Dr. Geller is more direct and jabbing and jarring than any of the other ones. She's laying down the no-bullshit policy right away. That's pretty good, I think.

"I'm going to give you permission to go into town, because I think you need to get out of here. I think walking around is good for you," she says. "So you'll get a day pass. You don't drink, so you probably can't get into much trouble at the bars and liquor stores. You can't drive, so you won't go to Norwalk or Bridgeport to cop, and I don't think that's what you want to do anyway. I think you want to get clean and stay that way. I think you showed up to treat a physical emergency, but you didn't leave right afterward as you could have. So I believe you're here for honest reasons."

"I am."

"I know it." She doesn't want me to interrupt her thought with confirmation of what she knows is true, because she knows it's true and she thinks it's disrespectful for me to treat it like she needs my help on this point. "So I think it's a good idea for you to go wander around the bookstore, buy your books of poetry or whatever you like, and pretend you're smarter than everyone else here, which I hate to say it, but you probably are. And that's not a compliment. I can't remember the last time we had such a dumb population. I looked at the census and it's horrible." These words—*population* and *census*—they mean what they sound like, but it's hospital jargon just the same. "Maybe it will get better after the first of the year. That usually happens. In the meantime, I'm going to give you pretty free rein here, because it's probably what you need. But don't fuck with me."

"Fair enough."

"Listen to what I'm going to say, Elizabeth." Deep breath. "You don't know what everyone is about to say before they say it, so stop thinking that. Even if you do, it's rude, and it doesn't help your case in this world. So listen to me: In session we do honest, serious work. You probably won't get much out of group, but take meetings seriously. No one has ever gotten clean without AA or NA. Don't act like you're better than that. And when you're with me, you have to be honest, you have to face up. Okay?"

She shuffles papers and looks at her beeper, the phone rings and she picks it up, and still she is telling me to be present and face things and hup to it. And, by the way, I *did* know what Dr. Geller was going to say before she said it. I saw the tough-but-tender love speech coming. I'm onto this whole process. But still, it's good to have a therapist who pushes.

And I have to act as if. That's a big recovery term: *act as if*. Act as if you believe you will stay sober. Act as if you like meetings. Act as if you believe in God. Act as if you like getting on your knees and praying each morning and night. Act as if there is a lot of wisdom in the Big Book and the Twelve Steps. Act as if there is a point to making your bed each day, even if you are just going to get back into it that night. Act as if everyone around you is not an idiot, and treat others with respect. They like to say: "You can't think your way into act-ing, but you can act your way into thinking." The idea is that if you do what you are supposed to, your mind might catch up with your body. If I stop acting as if therapy is one big useless joke that I have been in for twenty years only to land in a mental institution at long last, if I act as if this time it's for real and this time it will work, it just might. It just might.

And I have to count on those mights, all of them. They're all I've got right now.

Eighteen

THE THRILL IS GONE

Life as a *commentary* of something else we cannot reach, which is there within the reach of the leap we will not take.

JULIO CORTÁZAR
Hopscotch

The Cottage is like sudden death. It is a dark, bleak vacuum cleaner of human hopelessness. Of course, all of New England at the end of December is pretty gloomy, but not like this, especially since it is basically a gorgeous house, a mansion. Well, not a mansion, but a large and lovely home that young professionals who work in the city but prefer to live outside might rent together.

I have a sunny corner room with lots of windows all to myself. Two exposures. A bathroom with a tub where I can stretch my muscles and bones. There are two beds in the room, and I've been warned that if conditions get crowded, I will end up with a roommate, but Dr. Geller promises that this will never happen. Of course, I need my own room, because I need peace and quiet and a desk for writing. Everybody who lives in the Cottage needs to have a job or be in twenty hours of group program a week, and there is no way I am doing the latter. My job, in theory, is writing, but what I will be writing is anyone's guess.

The Cottage is, by design, a halfway house on Silver Hill's grounds. It is meant to be a place to live for months, or even a year or two, after you get out of formal treatment in K-House. People who have been in rehab in other places can come live here too. It is supposed to be a good place to solidify your sobriety: there is an 11 P.M. curfew; you must be up and out of a made bed by 8 A.M.; you are required to go to a meeting every day; you are with other recovering addicts for support; it is a community. But in practice, the Cottage is an extension of the drug abuse treatment unit at Silver Hill. Most of the people living here don't have jobs, and in fact *are* in twenty hours a week of program at the hospital. But it is cheaper to live here than it is to live in K-House—about $5,000 a month, instead of $15,000—because there is no on-site medical staff, there is only one counselor on duty at a time, and we do our own chores here; no more clean-up service.

Actually, to be perfectly truthful, I should say that we're *supposed* to do our own chores; what actually happens is another matter. We have job rotation, and everyday somebody is supposed to vacuum the living room or take out the garbage or neaten up the kitchen. Almost every day, these things don't get done, and the fact that so-and-so didn't do his share yesterday becomes an excuse for such-and-such to not do it today, because if no one does what he's supposed to do, then why should anyone do what she's supposed to do. About once a week we have community meeting, and we all resolve to do our chores when we're supposed to, and within a day or two, that pretty much goes out the window. Sooner or later, something's got to give. We're all disgusted with the mess, so someone ends up dragging all the trash out because it's too unbearable.

I soon realize that the disorganization about chores, which would seem like just another typical problem with drug addicts, is actually systemic. Because the Cottage does not serve its charter purpose, most things here don't work. In theory—the divide between theory and practice is a constant conundrum at the Cottage—all of us should have leave privileges, all of us should be coming and going all day long from our jobs and other responsibilities, this should be the start of reorientation into workaday life. In fact, it's just a cheaper way to get treatment. People who are too new to sobriety to take care of themselves—much less participate in the upkeep of a household—constitute most of the residents. At one time insurance would have covered a full thirty-day treatment program, but in the age of managed care, that is no longer the case. So institutions like Silver Hill have found makeshift methods of dealing with the disparity between what addicts need and what they can afford. In truth, I should be in K-House for at least a month, but no one does that, so I don't either. People tend to be there just to get through the first and worst week of their stay at Silver Hill, and then it's on to the Cottage.

I move in just after Christmas. I am eager to move along. What I did not count on is the dull thud, the stuckness of the Cottage. K-House has a certain excitement to it. People are suddenly sober, and while that's exhausting and depressing, it is also exhilarating. It's new; it's different; it's a relief. There was one day in K-House when I got into a hot tub on a very cold day, and used this I Coloniali bubble bath that I'd just bought at this overpriced toiletries bou-

tique in town. It smelled of pine and spruce and mint and lavender—a
meadow of aromas. And I lay there in this steamy bath and thought to myself
that this was such a pleasure, such a bountiful luxury—how nice it was to
smell and feel all this warmth, for the heat to touch my skin and bones un-
mediated by any substances I might have previously poured into my body. Afterward, I found myself ecstatically telling one of the counselors that I was in
love with sobriety, that it felt so good to feel again. I was giggling. I even called
Dr. Singer in New York to leave her a message about how well this was working out, that being clean really suited me, that I wish I had known it could be
this rapturous, that I'd have tried it long ago.

But by the time I empty out my boxes of belongings into my bureau and
shelves in the Cottage, the thrill is gone. I am, at heart, still an addict, and for
people like us, the thrill is always gone. It's leaving before it has even arrived.
Every time my dealer dropped off my fix of cocaine, I was already trying to figure out when he would bring more—and this was before I'd even gotten
started on what was there. And pretty soon it becomes a way of life: there are
no moments of joy, because you are always anticipating when the next possible moments of joy might arrive. As soon as tomorrow? As late as next year?
Maybe in a week or two? Not that it matters, because you would not enjoy that
joy either, you'd be too busy wondering where the next fix of fun would come
from. Addiction is, in its essence, an inability to live in the moment.

And at the Cottage, you begin to see the vista of moments. They are amass-
ing ahead forever. You could live here forever. Your stay here is indefinite, and
it feels as if it could be infinite. This is the beginning of forever. And that might
even be okay, after a thirty-day term of proper treatment. That might feel like
a good thing. It might seem like the time has come. But because so many people here are not ready to be here and there are so many different levels of recovery, there is no common purpose.

This is particularly true in the lag time between Christmas and New Year's,
when only the desperate are anywhere near Silver Hill. There are some people who have been at the Cottage for a while, but they are all gone for the holidays, on vacation or at home with their families like normal people.
Personally, I'm happy to be here. I hate this time of year. If I could, I'd check
into the hospital from Christmas to New Year's on an annual basis. Everyone
is out of town, and because I'm Jewish, I'm usually not. And in the history of
mankind, unless you are a prisoner of war, they have yet to come up with a
more horrendous form of torture than New Year's Eve. Everyone is supposed
to have fun, and no one ever does. I've been known to start planning for December 31 on Labor Day weekend, hoping that with four months to figure it
out, I might actually manage to find a way to enjoy it. What a relief it is to be

here at Silver Hill and know that it's just another stupid night in the Cottage. That afternoon, I go into town and rent *Nashville* and *Five Easy Pieces* for the viewing pleasure of the five of us who are here, I buy some osetra caviar and crackers because Why not? And I ready myself for an evening of movies and fish eggs with Aidan and the other inmates.

Believe it or not, it is a lot of fun. It is the first day of 1998, and I have been clean for two weeks.

I promise Dr. Geller that I will go to group therapy for the first couple of weeks that I am at the Cottage because she wants me to mix in with the others. She does not want me to seem aloof and uncaring, even though that's exactly what I am. After that, I can be excused for work detail. Of course, I do not really have a job, but I have to proofread galleys of *Bitch*, there's a bit more writing I need to do to finish up, and Dr. Geller signs off on the idea that this amounts to twenty hours a week of work. She is afraid that I will leave Silver Hill altogether if we don't come up with some alternative to going to their program, and she knows that if that happens, I'll be back to using again.

As promised, after the first of the year, the house begins to fill up. Most of the people do their week at K-House, and then they join us here at Wilton House, which is the proper name of the Cottage, though no one ever uses it. I hate to say it, but the residents are just what you would expect: the heiress, the janitor, the former model, the bored housewife, the fireman, the psychiatric social worker, the Holocaust survivors' daughter, the estate lawyer, the bratty teenager from the Upper East Side, the professor, the preppie, the college student who pays tuition by stripping, the graduate student who has been working construction in Vermont, the former CIA agent who is now a corporate security consultant, and the anesthesiologist from Great Neck who shoots up ether. I am the writer. In terms of fulfilling a stereotype, I could be a photographer or a painter, but I could not be, say, a movie star. That's the one piece of the mix that we're lacking: we have no celebrities.

I have certain favorites. There are a few people I come to really like. Diana is American, but like many young women who have grown up on Park Avenue and in Southampton, she is vaguely British, somewhat French, and totally either Iranian or Lebanese—I can't remember which, but some sort of Christian Arab. Diana, like many young women of the international set, only sort of went to college, and only to some place like Skidmore, some school for debutantes. She has worked as a fashion stylist, but not really—she has no portfolio, nothing to show for whatever it is she did. But she is so warm and friendly, she loans me her cashmere bathrobe for the whole time I am at Silver Hill, and she teaches me about Creed perfume, especially Silver Mountain Water, which is the important fragrance among people she knows.

Diana's best friend at Silver Hill is Lara, who is from Brazil, and once was a supermodel, before Gisele and a bunch of other people made being a super-model from Brazil downright common. Lara has a rented Bronco—it is white, just like O.J.'s, which I make fun of sometimes, and she has no idea what I'm talking about—and every time we go into town, Lara drives through all the traffic lights, since that's what they do in Brazil, because if you stop, you might well end up kidnapped. I am always reminding her that red means halt, but she can't quite get this straight, and after a while I am too scared to get in a car with her, so I just don't.

Lara originally came to Silver Hill after she'd attempted suicide in São Paolo. It was her third attempt. She has two children by two different men, neither of whom she has ever bothered to marry, because supermodels—like teenagers in the inner city—do not seem to like to have kids with husbands. She is now separated from her actual husband, with whom she has no chil-dren. Lara works as a publicist at a fashion company, and she no longer travels as she did when she was modeling, but she knows she is an unfit mother. The two kids are with the father of the second one, but they are sometimes with her parents and sometimes with her brother.

Both Diana and Lara wear gorgeous, fuzzy sweaters and fabulous leather pants every day. They are the kind of girls who look tan without being in the sun and look beautiful without makeup. And, yes, they are both super sweet. You can't help liking them. It's a myth that gorgeous rich girls are snobby and snotty. In my experience, they are usually very nice, because they've had lives of ease and have no reason not to be. It's people like me whom you have to watch out for. Lara starts doing arts and crafts. She starts beading and weaving, and she makes me a bracelet that looks like linked daisies when I tell her those are my favorite flowers.

Mae is another matter. Also hopelessly sweet, but poor and Chinese and from South Jersey. We call her Mae-Mae. She is a student at Columbia, and she makes money as a stripper and dominatrix. She is also a folk singer; she plays her guitar beautifully. Her voice is like Ann Wilson's, from Heart, whom she idolizes. She has a pierced tongue, a pierced nipple, a pierced navel, a pierced nose, a pierced eyebrow, multiply pierced ears, tattoos all over her body. It is sickening to look at her. Which is a shame, because she is actually so beautiful. She explains that her slaves—that's the word for her submissive male clients—like all these body-art affectations, and we leave it at that.

The first week in January, Ben comes up to visit. We had agreed before I checked in that we would see each other one more time once I got to the hospital to—to what? Say a proper good-bye? Try to work things out after all? I have no idea what the point is, but it seems like a good idea.

He takes the afternoon off from work and shows up in a rented red Toyota while I am still at lunch. He is waiting in the Cottage living room when I walk in, reading a script he needs to make notes on, looking as though it is perfectly normal to be sitting in a drug treatment center on a Tuesday afternoon, catching up on his work. He might as well be in some producer's office, waiting to take a meeting, as they say in the film business. Ben is so perfectly at ease that for a minute before I walk over to him, I just stand and watch, take in the view. If I were in his position, every time I heard the door slam or the hinge creak open, I would be looking up to see who walked in; but not Ben. I can't decide if this is exactly the thing I like about him, or if it's precisely the reason I should have nothing more to do with him. Given my temperament—nervous, anxious—this is probably just the kind of guy I belong with; but given my temperament, he is just the kind of person who makes me more nervous and anxious. I feel like I need to do the worrying for both of us.

Finally I walk over to him. He sees me approaching, he drops his script, and he stands up to give me a hug. I am relieved; we are happy to see each other. I want to show him around the house, to take him to my room, but Karl, the counselor in charge of the Cottage, won't let me. Men are not supposed to go into women's rooms.

"What if we were married?" I ask Karl, implying that we are entitled to a conjugal visit.

"Even wives visiting their husbands can't go to their bedrooms," he says with finality. But Karl is kind of a soft touch, so he adds, to make me feel better, "When Richard, you know the fireman, when his family came up this past weekend, I wouldn't even let his five-year-old daughter into his room. It's just the rules."

Karl eyes Ben's wedding ring. This does not help my cause. I tell Karl that we're going into town to visit, we'll be back in a few hours. "I want you back by dinnertime," he says, still looking at Ben's left hand.

"Dr. Geller says that I can stay out until curfew."

"Dr. Geller may run the world, but she does not run the Cottage," Karl says. "Be back by six."

That's fine with Ben, since he has to go home to his wife sometime in the evening anyway. It does not make me happy to hear him say this. I mean, I know it's true, but the less I need to be reminded about having an affair with a married man, the better.

Ben grew up in Westchester, just a few exits south on the Merritt Parkway, so he decides we should take a drive down there. He'll show me his family's home, we'll stop by the ice rink where he played hockey in high school—we'll have innocent fun.

But as soon as we get to Ben's old neighborhood, he gets weird. He starts to slide down in his seat so no one will see him. "Jesus, Ben, it's the middle of the afternoon! Everyone is at work. The roads here are deserted."

"My mom's a housewife."

"It's the middle of January," I retort. "It's thirty degrees outside! She's not going to be walking around taking in the freezing air. You're being ridiculous." God, I hate him for this. "Plus, you're insulting me. Stop treating me like your mistress. You never used to do this! What's happened to you?" I start to cry. Without cocaine, this really hurts. I knew it. I knew it would. I was all cool with him on drugs, but now that I'm clean, I want him to love me for real, or just go away.

I wait for him to say something—anything—but he doesn't.

"Jesus, you are such an idiot!" I scream, because when I get hurt I sometimes yell. I have a catch in my throat, the kind you get from crying too hard. "I mean, you don't even *own* a car. This is *rented*. No one is going to recognize you. No one's even looking for you. This is bullshit. This is your way of pushing me away and making me feel bad and cheap and, and, and—" And what? "And you suck. I used to think you were wonderful, but you suck just like everybody else." More bawling. My face feels hot. The radiator is blowing in my face, and I'm flush with hurt and anger.

"Look, let's just go to the hockey rink," he suggests, and puts his hand on mine to be comforting. To *seem* comforting, I should say. "There will probably be schoolkids there practicing. No one else will be around. We can sit and talk."

"Fuck you." I don't know what else to say. Ben knows he's a shithead—as a rule, any man who cheats on his wife is a shithead—so he can't argue with anything I say, so I might as well be mean.

Once we arrive there, we are silent, except to say stupid things like how blond some boy is, and how the kids get nastier every year, and aren't we so old, and like that. Finally, I can't stand it anymore. "Do you want to fuck in the backseat?" I suggest, desperate to get his attention or approval or something. "I grew up in the city. I never got to do that in high school."

"We can neck," he says. "I don't remember ever actually having sex in a car. That's a myth. Kids do it in the den while their parents are sleeping."

"All right then."

We kiss for a few minutes, but the feeling is gone. Actually, it isn't gone, it's just that it isn't the same. Either he leaves his wife and we live happily ever after, or this just has to stop.

What's happening to me? I never wanted Ben to walk out on Miranda before—as I recall, I counseled against it, very adamantly—and I don't really want him to now. But I want him to *want to*. I want him to love me enough to do it.

"Where should we go now?" I ask. "Maybe you should just drive me back."

"Listen, I think about you all the time, and I miss you a lot," he says. "I have to try to make things work with Miranda, but I want you to know that I really did fall in love with you."

I start to cry again. "You fucking idiot!" I say, all mad and sad and something else—what is it? Where is the feeling wheel when I need it? "You should have thought about all this a long time ago. You should have left me alone."

"I felt like it was an emergency. I felt like somebody needed to take care of you, and it seemed like I was the person." He pauses. "Now it just feels like I was enabling you."

"Look, I'm here. I'm in treatment," I say. I realize I am saying this to comfort him, and I don't know why I feel obligated to do that, but I do. "I told you it would end once I got here, but it's not that easy."

"It's not easy for me either."

"Fuck you!" Back to yelling. "You get to go home to your wife and your happy life, and I'm stuck in rehab."

"I know it seems that way," Ben says, "but I really do miss you, and it's not like I have anyone to talk to about it except you and—"

"And what?" I'm not sure if he is making me angry, or if I'm hoping he'll say something sweet, or both.

"Well, it's just hard." His eyes tear up. He takes off his glasses and rubs underneath them, under the dark circles. "Look, I'm going to think about all this for a while. We were thinking about buying a house. We were talking about having a baby. I'm just going to put all that stuff on hold, and make sure that's what I want. I mean, that *is* what I want, but if I'm still in love with you in a little while, I'm going to have to deal with it."

"Okay, I guess." What else can I say? "But you're going to drop me off at Silver Hill, and we're going to say good-bye, and as far as I'm concerned, that's for good. I won't be your friend. We aren't friends. That's ridiculous. If you decide to leave your wife sometime, you can let me know, but I know that's not going to happen."

"Probably not."

"In the meantime, this is just so sad." I'm crying and he pulls me to his chest and hugs me. "This is so sad. Like everything else in my life, this is so sad."

"I'm sorry," he says. "I'm so sorry."

We drive back to the Cottage in silence. I say good-bye. I will never see him or speak to him again. Not because I don't love him, but because I do.

In our daily morning session, I tell Dr. Geller that I said good-bye to Ben yesterday, that all that is out of my life now, and I'm relieved. It's good. It was the right thing to do. I handled myself gracefully. No scenes. I said good-bye like I was supposed to.

"How do you feel?"

"I told you," I say. "I feel good about it. I'm fine with it. I'm proud of myself for stopping something before it became a mess. I'm proud of myself for doing the right thing."

"Yes, but how do you *feel*?"

"Good," I say. "I said that already."

"You're not dealing with your feelings at all," she says. "This is not Ben you're talking to. It's me. So now tell me the truth."

"I am telling you the truth."

"You're lying. That's why you feel depressed and empty. Because you're afraid to feel. That doesn't mean you need to call him in desperation. But you need to feel it, to not be afraid to feel it. Admit that it hurts."

"I don't want it to hurt."

"That's the point."

"Look, he's married. It was all so—" So what? "It was inappropriate. I pride myself on treating it with some grace, with being a lady about it."

"You're not understanding what I'm saying!" Is she yelling? Dr. Singer never yells. "*This* is why you do drugs. *This* is why you feel terrible. You think it's because you feel everything too much. But it's not. It's that you don't feel things enough. All those times that you panic and get hysterical waiting for some guy, any guy, to call you, it's not because your feelings are exaggerated. It's because you don't feel at all."

"That's crazy." I think I may be about to cry, but I don't. "My feelings are excessive and inappropriate, and too much for anyone to handle. So I do drugs, and it's manageable."

"I don't think that's true. I think if you weren't afraid to feel things, it would be okay. If you were not afraid to hurt when you hurt, it wouldn't be so bad.

But then you push it away, and you end up going crazy and feeling crazy about nothing—about waiting twenty minutes for a call—because you don't allow yourself to just feel what is really there."

"But I hurt when I wait for a call, and I act out *because* I hurt."

"The phone calls, or the lack of them, is not the problem." I want to correct her and say that the appropriate verb is *are*, but I don't. Another distraction from my feelings is what she would tell me. "You have been pushing aside your real feelings for all your life, and they come up at the wrong times. Every time you feel so much pain—so much crazy pain—over these little things, it's because you don't allow yourself to just feel about the things that matter."

I'm silent.

"Look, when your parents split up, when your dad disappeared when you were fourteen, you just went numb, because there was nothing else to do. What could you do? You were a little kid; you couldn't change anything. And now you're a grown-up, and you can change things. You can make decisions about who to be attracted to, who to love, and you make choices that are all wrong just to test yourself. Just to see how much you won't feel."

She's right. I think she's right.

"So you overreact to nothing, but that overreacting is not *feeling*—it's *reacting*. If you just sat there and said to yourself that it hurts and there's nothing you can do, you'd get through it. Instead you drive yourself crazy wishing these things didn't hurt. You feel stupid and bad about yourself for being bothered, and then you drive yourself crazy. The feelings come out in strange ways." She pauses. "*That's* what's inappropriate. Before you even know a guy well enough to be attached to him, you feel deeply, because you are so desperate to feel something, and then you sabotage it. You don't give it a chance to get to the point where real feeling would be appropriate."

"I never get that far."

"Because you are too busy getting worked up about all kinds of things that don't matter so that you don't get to the point where it does."

"That's not my fault."

"Yes, but it is your fault that you're sitting here with me now, and I'm asking you how you feel about Ben, and you're telling me you handled it well, and that's cool. That's not cool! You're in a mental hospital! You're safe! You're with me! You're here so that you can be in a safe place where we can deal with your feelings. And what do you do? You tell me it's all cool. In fact, given what happened with you and Ben, given that you have been drugging yourself for so long and he supported you through it, you should be hurting terribly. *That* would be appropriate. But instead you sit here and lie to me. Stop lying. Stop lying to *yourself*."

I start to cry. I'm scared of her. "What do you want me to do? I'm just doing my best to hold it together."

"Stop trying so hard to hold it together! Just let yourself feel and you'll be amazed to find that the results are not so bad. You talk to your friends, you talk to me, you talk to Dr. Singer, you get through what you need to, and it's fine. You will be fine feeling your feelings." She stops for a second, to think I guess. "You sit here correcting my grammar, you sit around being so smart, being so analytical, anything to avoid your feelings!"

"*I hate my feelings!*" I scream. I may be disturbing all the other patients in all the other offices, but I can't help it. "I hate my feelings, and if you had them, you'd hate them too."

"That's a good start," she says. "Even hating your own feelings is a good beginning. But I'll tell you, that is not what you hate. You hate your anxiety, and all your anxiety comes from trying not to feel. It's a coping mechanism, and it isn't working."

I'm crying. She hands me a Kleenex.

"Look, most people wait by the phone to some extent. That's what courtship is about. But they get through it. They give it a chance. They try to get to know the other person. They take their time. They try not to like someone too much before it's appropriate. They are careful with their feelings, because they need to protect themselves. But you don't do that. You invest yourself in something before it's even right, you act out a whole relationship's worth of emotions before it's even happened, and you don't give yourself a chance to feel when you're supposed to. You think you are feeling something for some particular guy, but he is just giving you the opportunity to feel for your whole damn life, and that's not fair. In the meantime, you *did* get to know Ben. You *did* spend time with him. It was stupid, but you can't just walk away from it and say it was all nothing. That's not fair to you. That's pretending something happened that didn't."

I want to say that she's transposed terms—what she means is, *nothing happened that did.* But once again that would be avoiding things. Then again, even having the thought is avoiding things. I diagram sentences to detach myself from their contents.

"Look, I think your parents did not give you any space to feel about the things that went on between them. You just had to manage everything. You just had to manage all those emotions and keep them from becoming too much because there was no room in all their chaos for a little girl to feel bad. And your mother, who is crazy, has such exaggerated responses to everything you do—she's actually the person you learned how to do that from—that once again, you could not feel what was going on. You were trying to manage her, and to manage your response to her. And that was not fair. Here some terrible things were going on, and you pretended they were no big deal. Even if everyone's parents are getting divorced, it doesn't mean that your parents' divorce doesn't hurt you."

"But it didn't." I'm sniffing. "I was so young I don't remember. And now I'm trying to manage you the way I tried to manage my mother, because you're yelling at me and telling me what I should feel, and it's just as bad."

"Exactly!" She smiles. "Now you're getting it. I'm pushing you into the same corner you've always been pushed into, but now I'm telling you to *please* react. Don't run! I'm jabbing at you, because here you have a time when feeling would be the right thing, just like feeling would have been the right thing when she drove you crazy. Only then you were a little kid. You depended on her, so you had to do the best you could to manage it, but you're not a little kid anymore. You're here in therapy. I'm here to help you. You have nothing to be afraid of. I know you hate the way this sounds—you hate therapy-speak—but you are in a safe place. There are acres of grass and forest here for you to run to. You're safe. So try to feel now. The boyfriend who hurt you when you were fourteen, who you mourned for months—you were doing that because it was safe. You could turn to your mother for help then. She could finally do for you what she should have done all along. But that wasn't about him."

"See, that's what I mean. That *was* about him. He *did* break my heart. And now all these years later you're telling me it's about something else. I agree that being nervous and hysterical about when some guy will call may be a way of avoiding something more hurtful, but it's precisely because it hurts so much to feel more than that, that I avoid it."

I'm talking in circles. I think Dr. Geller may be also. This is too much. She is pushing me too much. Or maybe this is what I need. Maybe Dr. Singer should have been doing this all along. I don't know. I could not have walked around New York City having some kind of feeling festival, that's for sure. I could not very well have doubled over in pain walking along Thirty-fourth Street at three in the afternoon. But here I can. So I should. Trouble is, I'm not using this time right. I'm busy having a crush on Aidan. I'm busy duplicating the life I have in Manhattan, the one where I fall in love with men who are bad for me, instead of using my time wisely. When I was in Florida, I was so excited to be relieved from all that pursuit. But I could not stand the emptiness I felt without it, so I did drugs. Now that I'm here, I'm scared of the feelings I might have if I just used this place correctly, if I just went through rehabilitation, instead of treating this like a vacation. I'm retreating to old habits—looking for love, hanging out, trying to have fun for fear of what might happen if I don't have fun. Here is this place where I can walk around in a troubled state and people will be supportive, but I don't want to do that.

I want to have a crush on Aidan. That's what I want to do. Same as ever.

Why don't I just give myself a break? Wouldn't that be nice? A break would be really nice.

"I know you're right," I say to Dr. Geller. "I see what you mean. I see that I go crazy with anxiety and respond to every little thing, instead of enjoying the big things, but I don't know how to stop that." Again I start to cry. "It's so hard."

"What's so hard?"

"It's so hard to be a human being." I start to laugh, to laugh and cry at the same time. "Isn't that ridiculous? Simple human things are difficult for me. It's pathetic."

"It's not pathetic," she says. "Sweetheart, you were not given a very good set of tools to work with. Like I said, even if everyone on Earth had to survive their parents' divorce, it doesn't make it any less difficult for you. You're entitled to feel as bad as you do about it. And they handled it terribly. They made you choose between them. They were, like I said, so crazy themselves that you had to keep your own feelings in check." She stops to think. "Look, maybe your feelings were pure joy, you were so sick of how the two of them were together. That's possible, you know? But you couldn't have even felt that much. You were just trying to keep it all from falling apart. All your life, you're just trying to keep things from falling apart."

"You're right. I know you're right." I'm bawling like crazy, and she just hands me the whole box of tissues.

"And it's not just that you're afraid of your bad feelings," she says. "You're afraid of good ones too. Because what if things go wrong? Instead of just enjoying, you worry. You just worry. You can't keep an open mind and see what happens, and enjoy it as it goes, because you are just trying to manage all your emotions, good or bad."

"I know." She's very smart. She's onto me. She won't let me get away with my bullshit. It's pretty impressive. I can see why Dr. Singer likes working with Dr. Geller. I wish I could have both of them as my two-person therapy team forever.

"But what can I do to change?" I ask, still sniffling, but the tears subsiding.

"Like I said: *Let yourself feel.*" She looks at her watch. "While you're here, don't waste your time with Aidan. I already told Karl to keep you separated, because I don't want you wasting time with him. Not here."

I see her point, but I *like* wasting time with Aidan. If they keep me away from him, what will I do with myself? Feel my lousy feelings, I suppose.

"I like your ring," she says, seeming to change the subject. This is probably a way to make a transition out of therapy mode and into time-to-stop mode. Over the years I have become very aware of how all the different therapists do that. Some stretch their legs; some fold them up; some inhale deeply; some exhale; some just say that time is up. And some, like Dr. Geller, just shift into a new subject. "It's very beautiful," she continues, and I pull it off to show her. It fits tight around my right ring finger, and I have to lick my knuckle to get it off. Everything is getting a bit tighter, I'm gaining back some weight I lost.

"It's lapis lazuli," I say. The stone is rounded into a cabochon, and is high up on the setting. It's almost vertical. Everybody notices this ring, its royal blue oval jutting out of my finger. It looks like a contraption that Wonder Woman might have used to stun her enemies.

"Do you wear it for good luck?" she asks.

I think about that for a second. "No, no, that's not it." I have so many talismans, so many coins and keepsakes that I carry in my jeans pockets and touch throughout the day for comfort. But that's not how I feel about my jewelry. I wear it because I like it, no other reason.

"So you wear it just because it's beautiful?"

"Yes."

"You enjoy it?"

I nod my head.

"You need more stuff like that," she says. "You need more things you can just enjoy, so you learn how to feel nice, as much as you know how to feel bad. If you just felt your feelings as you go along, instead of trying to invest this or that with stuff you don't feel at all, you'd be surprised how much easier life will be. You can enjoy love while you have it, and mourn it when it's gone, instead of mourning it before it's even happened by crying when someone you don't even know that well doesn't call right away. You should enjoy how much you like someone, and not worry about it. Then you can be miserable when—or if—it doesn't work out. But don't get things out of order."

She looks at her watch again. "Time to stop?" I ask. I like to volunteer my way out so that I don't have to feel rejected when she asks me to leave. See? There I go, managing my feelings again.

"It is." She suggests I go into Greenwich and buy some nice jewelry. "If you can learn to just enjoy these simple things more, maybe it will be easier to enjoy everything else."

Nineteen

CONSEQUENCES

I got a cold mind
To go slipping across that thin line
I'm sick of doing straight time

BRUCE SPRINGSTEEN
"Straight Time"

We don't do much. We sit around a lot. We string beads and chat. We read magazines. The Cottage subscribes to *Sports Illustrated* and *U.S. News & World Report*, which are the two least likely periodicals any drug addict would read—unless of course Spree is choking his coach or Clinton is fucking an intern—since there are no sports fans or newshounds among us. I manage to get everyone to let me watch CNN on the eve of Karla Faye Tucker's execution, which gives me an opportunity to lecture my housemates about the evils of the death penalty. Somehow Dylan, a working-class teenager from Bridgeport who wears low-slung jeans—which I have to explain to him are a hip-hop reference to prison uniforms—convinces us to switch to the Discovery Channel. Addicts love nature shows. They're trippy. We watch a wildebeest getting ripped apart by a tiger because he is the runt of the pack; the others avoid him because he slows the rest of them down. It makes me miserable. In AA, one of the slogans is "Stick with the winners," which means avoid the losers who relapse. The program and the savanna are strangely similar.

No one around here much cares about much of anything. People are always looking things up in the *Physicians' Desk Reference*, which has photographs of different pills and functions as junkie pornography. Lara and Diana and I buy *Vogue* and *Elle* and *Vanity Fair* in town and share them. We also like *The National Enquirer* sometimes. *The New York Times* gets to our doorstep daily, and I leap for the crossword puzzle before anyone else can get to it, but no one else wants it anyway. Mae-Mae plays the guitar. We go out to the local multiplex to see *Titanic* and *Good Will Hunting* and *Wag the Dog*. We rent movies and order in food. There are white square boxes with crust and half-finished slices of pizza on the kitchen counter and the coffee table all the time. People smoke on the porch. We answer the pay phone when it rings, which is all the time. The person whom the call is for never seems to be around. We are supposed to write messages on the chalkboard, but that almost never happens. Marlon, who is nineteen and whose mother runs an auction house in New York City, watches the WWF, so I watch with him.

People go to group in the counseling building from nine to noon, but not always. Someone is always coming down with a cold or some other ailment that Karl can't prove they don't really have, which becomes an excuse to stay in bed all day. I claim to be proofreading my book in my bedroom, but I actually close my door and get back into bed. Karl catches me doing this once—when I don't respond to his knock, he barges in—and after that he insists that I take my tasks into the dining nook, a small room off the kitchen that no one ever uses. Mysteriously, as soon as I start working in there, people decide it's a great place to hang out after all, which gives me an excuse to go hide in my room and sleep. After a while, Karl stops caring. What can he do? This house is overrun with mendacious addicts with only a few days clean. This is not how it's supposed to be, and he kind of throws up his hands in frustration after a while.

This is what we do at the Cottage: We wait to be clean long enough to say that we've been clean long enough. It takes time to get time. Who can say how this system works, or even if it does? This is not exactly rehab-as-boot-camp. It's more like rehab-as-sleepaway-camp. And yet, in some way, I can feel it working. I go to therapy with Dr. Geller every day. I read a lot. I finally finish *Middlemarch*. I go to meetings every night. We eat brunch at the greasy spoon in New Canaan, and we have turkey club sandwiches at the diner after meetings. This is the quiet life. Yes, it is also the easy life—but it is the quiet part that is more important. Not much happens. As the weeks progress, the days get a little longer, the sun shines a little brighter, the grass gets a little greener—and because time is so blank, I notice it pass more acutely. I feel more. Spring is on its way. Soon there will be daffodils and daisies.

By the end of February, I realize I am part of the place. We are a family. I love everyone in their own way just because they are here. I like communal living; it is good for me. Even the obnoxious hotelier from Florabama, Alabama, who is married to a middle-aged German man whom she doesn't have sex with starts to grow on me. I come to appreciate what a struggle it must be to be married to a man named Hans. I even like the luxury-car dealer from New Hope, Pennsylvania, even though he squints his eyes to get a better look at my breasts underneath my T-shirt, and tells me that they are a pretty good pair of 34Bs.

I become close with Kathleen. Yes, her name is *Kathleen.* She is the other counselor in the house. I sit in her office and talk about being scared and lonely, like it's small talk. I complain that the guy who works at OTB is stupid, and I ask if she thinks the scars on my legs are permanent.

I am considered a pain in the ass, and I know it. I get consequences all the time. At first I have to write essays about why it is bad to come in ten minutes after curfew, or why I should not be hugging Dylan, or why it is wrong to walk around common areas in just a towel, even if nothing shows. Finally, one day I tell Karl that I refuse to write any more explanations for my behavior unless he pays me for them.

"The going rate is two dollars a word. If it's Condé Nast, it's more like four," I say. "Of course, if it's *The New York Review of Books,* I think a dime a word is a lot to expect. So what do they pay here at Silver Hill?" I have no idea why I am saying this. For one thing, I'm not really sure what periodicals pay these days, it's been so long since I've done magazine journalism. For another thing, it's just plain old obnoxious and supercilious. But then again, so are all these essays I seem to be generating. "Look, when Aidan does something wrong, you don't punish him by asking him to build some shelves, even though, God knows, we could use them," I say, trying to be reasonable. Aidan has been working as a carpenter for the last month or so.

Karl smiles. "All right, then," he says. "For not sweeping the porch yesterday, I want you to rearrange the pantry with the dishes in it today."

"Karl, that's ridiculous," I respond. "It's full of Styrofoam cups and paper plates. It's perfectly neat. I'd just be moving things from one place to another, for no good reason."

"Then it shouldn't take you very long." He starts to shuffle around some papers on his desk, as if to say, end of discussion. "Now get to it."

One day, as Karl is telling me I have to vacuum the foyer because somebody else took the garbage out for me the night before, I ask why they call them consequences, when we all know what they really are: punishments.

"If they were punishments, we'd make you sit in a corner with a dunce cap on," he says. "These are consequences. The idea is for you to learn that your actions have consequences. It's a life lesson."

"I don't need to come to rehab to learn that," I say. "I mean, I see why we have to make our beds in the morning—that's not arbitrary, that's a good idea. But this is make-work. I know it, I resent it, and the main thing I learn from it is that people sometimes ask you to do stupid shit for no reason."

Karl looks at me, partly perplexed and mostly entertained. He's come to enjoy my rants. He sees them as a symptom of addict arrogance, nothing more. Which is a shame, because I am making a reasonable point.

"And you know what, come to think of it," I continue, "the real lesson I've learned over the years is that there is often no correlation between your behavior and the consequences. I mean, the reason I do drugs is because the world is so capricious and unpredictable. You do nice things, and people are mean in return, or you act like an ogre, and people are incredibly kind in response. Sometimes *a* plus *b* equals *c*, but lots of times it doesn't. Think about it: Down in Florida, I used to feed this stray cat. I'd do it every day. And then just once I tried to scratch her ears, and she bit me. Her teeth broke my skin. Now, that wasn't very nice of her. Still, I kept feeding her because I knew she was frightened, and that's why she did it. But there's a perfect example of behavior not having a logical outcome. There's a perfect example of no good deed goes unpunished. Don't you think?"

"But—"

"I mean, Karl, if you wanted to teach us a lesson about coping with the world, you'd make people who vacuum when they're supposed to vacuum sweep the floors for everybody else, and you'd give me a medal of honor for sitting on my butt and doing nothing. The truth is, consequences are bullshit. This system teaches us nothing."

"You think too much," Karl says.

"Well, at any rate, just enough so that I don't like the doublespeak of words like *consequences* when what you mean is *punishment*," I say. "And thinking is an occupational hazard, besides."

"Well, it's not going to do you any good with your recovery," he says. "Try to keep it simple."

"I *am* trying to keep it simple. That's why I want you to simply say *punishment*." I can't tell if I'm raising my voice or whining. Truth is, I am arguing with Karl for its own sake. I don't really care what they call it, and I don't really mind vacuuming. But I love moot court. "All I'm saying is there are all these built-in contradictions in this process, and if you're a thinking person, you've got to notice them."

"You've been frying your brain for a few years now," Karl says. "Why not give it a rest?" He sighs. "Look, Elizabeth, I see what you're saying, but I don't think you really mean it. This is a game for you. You need to take your recovery more seriously. When you've been clean for five years, you can start challenging authority again, but right now, why don't you just try to be part of the group? Why don't you try to see what the common purpose here is?"

"I know," I say. "But you're asking me to check my brain at the door, and that's not reasonable. I had a pretty good life. I didn't use it right, but that doesn't mean it's all bad. I wish you'd understand that."

"I understand," Karl says. "And the cure is still the same. Try to be a participant, and stop being a critic. You're not doing yourself any good."

All meetings have names, and there is one called "Wave the White Flag," because unconditional surrender is the basic tenet of recovery in general and AA in particular: "We admitted we were powerless—that our lives had become unmanageable" is Step One. "Made a decision to turn over our will and our lives to the care of God" is Step Three. The principle behind all this renunciation of self is quite solid: most people try to trick themselves into quitting in all sorts of desperate ways—I'll only use on the weekends, I'll only drink after ten at night, I'll throw out all my stuff and tell my dealer not to sell me any more—and none of them works. By the time we check ourselves in, we pretty much need to be saying, I give up, nothing works, help me, show me the way, do for me what I cannot do for myself.

But I had a lot of trouble with throwing the whole thing away. I could not renounce my past. I never fell in with a bad crowd—in fact, miracle of miracles, I found my way into a good one. I am the bad crowd. So I could not stand this whole indoctrination thing where you're supposed to make all new friends in NA and AA and recovery. I don't want new friends. And besides all that, I don't feel like my life was all bad before I checked into the hospital. I just don't see why I have to give it all up and commit to recovery-as-life. If one's existence is defined by using drugs, is it better to then have one's existence defined by not doing drugs? Obviously, the former is worse, but I just wanted to go through my paces and get out of there. I did not want to become part of the recovery cult.

And often when I went to group therapy—as I did when I first got to Silver Hill—I ended up saying things like this, and I could, indeed, feel everyone in the room looking at me as if we were in an induction meeting for some religious sect, and that I was just one of those bad people who didn't get it, who would not accept Reverend Moon or David Koresh or Jim Jones as my savior. Once again, I felt like a moral failure because I did not wish to join this cult. So I stopped going to program.

One Sunday night at a Cocaine Anonymous meeting, a Vietnam veteran spoke, and he told his stories of the trenches, of POW camp, of homelessness and unemployment upon his return, of years in the mental word at a VA hospital. He is what they call a "low-bottom" case, this is a guy who had really sunk. After he finished his qualification, I was moved to raise my hand and say that his history, all the warfare and displacement and psychiatric illness—that I was truly amazed and awed by what he was saying, that he is a living miracle. And then I added that my pathetic little life with my luxurious problems that are mostly of my own invention seems so small and silly compared to what he has been through. I didn't quite say that I was not worthy of his woeful life, but that was implied and it is how I felt. I finally said that nothing that has happened to me merits my presence in this room.

I believed that I was giving him a compliment, that I was showing respect for his ordeal and rightly belittling my own. But after the meeting, the Vietnam veteran approached me to reproach me. "You're never going to get better if you think this way," he said. "We're all here as addicts, and our suffering has no rank. My troubles are no worse than yours."

But I could not accept this idea wholeheartedly, because it is simply spurious. There are people who have done heroin for twenty years, and people who have done themselves in with coke after a year. There are degrees of addiction, and of intelligence and accomplishment. When I was dealing with my depression, I always had a bipartite understanding of what was happening to me: I understood that for me, personally, I was in hell; my pain was as acute as anything the planet had yet come up with. Comparing myself to people starving in the Sudan, to Holocaust survivors, to homeless men sleeping on the subway, and to fifth-stage cancer patients—there was no point thinking about all that. Any of those predicaments were obviously and objectively more atrocious than my little mind sickness. But you can only live in your own experience, and for me, my life was the worst.

Still, I hate to lose perspective, hate to think that I'm not onto myself or anyone else. I hate to be a fool, or even just appear to be one.

So I never succumb completely to love, sex, dancing, any pleasurable experience. I quit ballet when I was a teenager because I could never let my body remember the steps. I always thought about the next jeté, the next pas de deux. I could never let my noncerebral physical self just feel it and take over. I always kept my eyeball on the next thing, the potential for hurt. And of course, this is my whole problem in life, it is systemic, it is pandemic—it is my miserable tendency to observe experience rather than inhabit it. I never want to be the one idiot who has actually signed a deal to buy the Brooklyn Bridge.

And, indeed, there is no way to get completely recovered without complete acquiescence. That is the point. The twenty-year junkie and the twenty-month cokehead both need complete capitulation to get better. The cure is the same for all of us, no matter how bad it was. Degrees don't matter when it comes to getting better.

AA is a cult, but it works. It's the only thing that works at first. You can have your critical mind back later, people told me, but for now, I had to surrender. It made sense. But as someone who even kept a distance from everything until drugs caught me off guard—someone whose orgasms were well thought out—I needed to soberly surrender as I had previously complied with getting high. But drugs don't give you a choice; recovery does. You get your brain back, and you need to shut it off.

Heaven help me.

And, in fact, at the end of the day, that is what they told me to do: They told me to ask God for help, for willingness. Heaven, indeed, was the only thing that would, that could, help me.

One Friday evening, Aidan doesn't come back to the Cottage after work. He's been renovating a house in Westport. We're allowed to go out in the evenings, but unless you've made prior arrangements with Karl, you have to check in at the end of the day if you've been at your job since morning. These are house rules.

We all figure that Aidan has got stuck in traffic. I remember that an ex-girlfriend had called to say she'd be in town for the weekend, and maybe Aidan decided to go straight from work to meet her. Maybe he'd tried to call in, but all the lines were busy. The pay phones are always engaged. And Karl and the other counselors are on the phone so much that it is possible that he could not get through on the switchboard either. There must be a good explanation. Aidan is so dependable.

As I am sitting and worrying with everybody else, something hits me: I really do care about the useless bloke after all. To start with, I wanted a playmate, a flirtmate, someone to distract me from me, but over time, I have developed actual feelings for him. One night, not long ago, the only counselor in the Cottage was Edie, who is spacy as anyone who is still high. Aidan came into my room after everyone had turned in, and we started to kiss in the dark. Eventually, I even turned the lights on because I like to see what's happening. I like to look. And we ended up out of our clothes, his jeans and flannel shirt in a heap on my floor, our naked bodies pressed together on this tiny bed that I was certain we were going to fall out of.

We were so nervous; we were so afraid of getting caught. People were sneaking around all the time in the Cottage. I used to call it a hotbed of hot beds. But Aidan and I both had a lot to be afraid of. We'd been here for a while. By that time it was at least ten weeks, and we had invested more in our recovery than most of the people who were passing through for a matter of days. We *needed* to be here. We could *not* get kicked out. And as a result, we stopped our sex play before it really got started. We were naked and lonely and together, but I remember saying to Aidan that this was a mistake.

Somewhere along the way, my recovery had become more important to me than boys. I could not tell you when or how that happened. But it did. Some tectonic plates had shifted, and some tremors had ceased. I was tired of being the way I was. I wanted to get better.

And Aidan and I became friends. And we did talk about Don DeLillo and Denis Johnson, and it was nice. And now this. Just when I am starting to feel like I belong here at Silver Hill, like I am going to recover with or without my brain still intact, Aidan decides to jump bail.

I mean, frankly, if he is out using right now, which seems pretty likely, then we might as well have fucked! I'm not saying that would have been a good idea for me, but it was as much out of respect for him, for his ninth attempt at rehab, that I stopped myself. It was because I had come to believe that we were in this together, that our mutual recovery—and the recovery of all of us people shipwrecked in this halfway house for mental patients—mattered all around. It would break my heart if Aidan, along with Dylan and Marlon and Lara and Diana and Mae-Mae—the core of Cottage people—were to leave and resume a life of abject addiction again. It would truly kill me. I know, I know: keep the focus on you. And I also know: codependency is bad. But fuck it: I care.

The night goes on. It gets later and later. We are all sitting around upset; none of us has actually gone to our Friday night meeting. There is some substitute counselor on duty. She is younger than me, younger than most of us, and when she tells us that we all need to go to sleep or we all need to do this or that, I actually say, *Fuck you!* I actually say, *You don't know Aidan, but none of us is getting into bed until we know he is safe.*

For once, for the first time maybe, I realize that everybody sitting around the common room, worried and fretting, appreciates me and my big, obnoxious mouth. As ever, I might not be the person you want to share a house with, but I am exactly who you want with you in the emergency room, when the triage nurse needs to be convinced that the cut you made on your thumb with a serrated knife while chopping tomatoes—that will maybe need two stitches—is much more important than all the gang members with their fatal gunshot wounds arriving in droves. I'm the one you want with you when someone needs to make it clear that there are things that matter more than the rules.

Finally, it is nearly midnight, and Aidan calls. Aidan tells us that he is in his apartment in Norwalk, that he went by to get the last of his belongings since it is the end of the month and by the last day of February he needs to be out. And he ran into his old connection, and some Rastafarian he used to do dope with, and this and that went down, and now they were all in his apartment getting high, and he doesn't know how to stop. I get on the phone and ask if he wants us to come get him. He says he does, that he's had enough.

I am so relieved.

I tell the poor benighted counselor-in-training that Dylan and Lara and I are going to go get Aidan, and that is that. We get into Lara's Bronco—Dylan drives, he knows the way to Aidan's place, and Lara can't be trusted with red lights. Lara is in her nightgown with a coat pulled over her; I am in sweatpants, a shearling, and clogs with no socks. Clearly the two of us are not the ideal EMTs. But Dylan is so in control, he is my nineteen-year-old hero, and we are on a mission of love.

It is sort of ridiculous: since the day I arrived at Silver Hill, I have been waiting for this kind of adrenaline rush, I have missed the adventure of copping and using. My God, I have missed the adventure of managing to get in and out of Barneys without spending my whole IRA account on some turquoise ring and some faux-fur scarf. I miss the chase. But all the same, as much as there is a thrill to our rescue run, the truth is I just want to get Aidan back where he belongs. I just want to know he is safe with us again. I can't stand the idea of losing him to—to this, to this of all things, to this stupid fucking dope.

I check myself a couple of times: Am I just selfishly sad that I could be losing a guy to be pretty for and play cat-and-mouse with, or am I honestly out here for his welfare? And, for that matter, am I on this nighttime frigid ride because I care or because I want to be involved, I want to be heroic?

But I stop pursuing these questions because, you know what: Who cares? For some reason I care enough about Aidan to do what I can to pull him back, and that's good enough.

Dylan goes into the apartment itself when we get to the building. Lara and I don't trust ourselves to enter into what must be Aidan's opium den—we are both pretty sure there's a good chance that we'll just pick up too. Dylan has no such fear; he's been clean for six months, one of the few Cottage residents who actually belongs there. The view through the passenger window is not a happy one. It is scuzzy. Aidan lives—or lived—in a basement apartment with bars on the windows, which were no doubt high up on his underground wall, which no doubt let in a junkie's notion of decent lighting, which is to say almost none. It is dreary. Lara and I wait in the car, snuggling to keep warm in the backseat, not saying much, just occasional murmurs about how we hope he's okay, we hope he doesn't change his mind about coming back.

"That motherfucking idiot," I whisper.

"I know," she says, with her Brazilian accent. She sounds silly when she curses in English, so all she can say is, "I know."

On the ride back to Silver Hill, Aidan is quiet, occasionally vomiting out the window, with great aplomb I must say. He might even be better at it than I once was. I was always very polite about throwing up on dope: I made sure to use a plastic bag if I was in a car, or to warn the driver to pull over to the shoulder of the road, and I once stuck my head out a subway window, so as not to mess up the car for the other passengers. I was much more considerate on heroin than I have ever known myself to be clean. And Aidan is the same. We don't say anything to him, and when we get back to Silver Hill, we leave him at the ACU for the night.

I walk him to the door, rows of glass panes in front of a vestibule, and rows more before you get into the admitting area, all of them locked. As a nurse comes through with her bracelet of keys to lead Aidan away, I say, "I ought to give you a shot in the head for making me live in this dump."

"What?" He's too bleary to get the joke.

"It's a Tennessee Williams line," I smile. "I think Stella says it to Stanley in *A Streetcar Named Desire*. But I could be wrong. Maybe it isn't even Tennessee Williams, but you get my meaning."

"Not really." He is nodding off on his feet.

I hold his shoulders and shake him a bit. "What I mean is, don't do anything like this ever again. I know it's hard. It's *so* hard. If anyone had ever been kind enough to tell me it was this difficult, I'd still be using. But you know, I once heard somebody say that if you aren't scared, it isn't brave. That's a good line, don't you think?"

Aidan nods—I'm not sure if it's in agreement or exhaustion.

"Look," I try, "if you can't stay clean for yourself, then do it for everyone else. I know that's not what you're supposed to say. But you matter. We were all worried about you. That's not to make you feel guilty. Just loved. You are loved."

"Why, thank you," Aidan says, and he starts to stumble over like a drunk as the nurse leads him away. He's trying to imitate Marlon Brandon as Stanley, I realize. Well, kind of. "I shall return," he says.

By the next day Aidan is back in the Cottage. Karl makes him sign a relapse agreement, a commitment not to use again, subject to expulsion if it is violated. Aidan is provisionally allowed to stay in the Cottage. This is where he belongs.

This is where we belong.

Twenty

DAISIES AND DAFFODILS

Just once I knew what life was for.
In Boston, quite suddenly, I understood;
walked there along the Charles River,
watched the lights copying themselves,
all neoned and strobe-hearted, opening
their mouths as wide as opera singers;
counted the stars, my little campaigners,
my scar daisies, and knew that I walked my love
on the night green side of it and cried
my heart to the eastbound cars and cried
my heart to the westbound cars and took
my truth across a small humped bridge
and hurried my truth, the charm of it, home
and hoarded these constants into morning
only to find them gone.

ANNE SEXTON
"Just Once"

Hank is Irish, and he looks it. He's not black Irish like Bono from U2—dark hair and blue eyes and etched features. Hank is what you'd call a real Mick, kind of the way Annie Hall says her grandmother would call Alvy a real Jew. Hank is the oldest of nine boys, and he grew up in Oak Park, outside of Chicago. The family moved there to get away from the Irish Catholic ghetto, full of screaming children, and every time the boys would fight—which is to say, constantly—his mother would tell them to shut up or people would think they were a bunch of dirty Irish kids. Somehow, Hank is the only one of all his brothers who became an alcoholic. He is a drunk, and unlike everybody else here—and I mean everybody—it's not about drugs at all. Hank just drinks, a real Irish boozer who looks like Dennis the Menace, with a turned-up nose and reddish hair that's gone gray. As time has gone by here, the gray is growing into its original auburn, it's as if the chemicals in alcohol have aged him. Take them away and he's transformed.

I'd have to say that Hank is not good-looking at all. Under normal circumstances, I would not even talk to him; he is such a hopeless nerd. And I'm not sure he would have noticed me either. He wakes up earlier than I do, which means he gets to the *Times* crossword puzzle before I do, which drives me crazy. He tells me we can do it together, and I say that I prefer to do it alone. He accuses me of being a selfish only child, and I can't argue with that, so finally we arrange to have two papers delivered every day. After that, there is no reason for us to ever talk again, so we don't.

Then one night we are all sitting around the living room, and the movie *Contact* is on some cable station. Jodie Foster is an astrophysicist who is searching for intelligent life somewhere in outer space, somewhere out of this world, and there is some technology that she is using that Hank seems to know a lot about. I mean, *a lot.* Now, understand, everybody here at Silver Hill is a rocket scientist in his own mind, so most of the time when I hear anyone going on with their expertise on national security issues in Uzbekistan or Picasso's Blue Period, I mostly smile to myself; and if I hear that someone's made a mistake, I am the first to correct it. And, to be honest, the former Soviet Union and modern art have never really come up here at all anyway; I was just hallucinating about that. I constantly fantasize about moments like the one in *Annie Hall* where Marshall McLuhan steps out from behind a placard at a movie theater line to tell some pretentious academic, "You know nothing of my work." I spend a lot of time at Silver Hill hoping to show people up.

But this is not the case with Hank. He obviously knows from whence he speaks.

"How do you know so much about the space program?" I ask. He is sitting on the La-Z-Boy, and I am on the floor just in front of him. Adlai, this absolutely awful Miss Porter's girl, whom I think Hank might be sleeping with, is sitting on the arm of the chair. She eyes me suspiciously as I talk to him. "I mean," I continue in my line of questioning with Hank, trying to be humorous, "are you or have you ever been an astronaut?"

"When I was in graduate school," he says, "I did a lot of work with NASA. They sponsored a lot of my research."

I decide not to pursue a conversation about the impropriety of the government meddling with academia. It would just be a way to stir up trouble, since in truth I don't think it's necessarily a conflict. In fact, I'm not sure I have an opinion about it at all. I tend to manufacture my positions on most subjects as I go along, to make myself seem well informed, which I only sometimes am. "What was your area?"

"Theoretical math."

"If it was theoretical, what applied use could it have for NASA?"

"It's too hard to explain."

"Try me."

"No, trust me," he says, sounding a little harsh, like there is an edge beneath this seemingly sweet demeanor after all, "you wouldn't understand."

"Okay, okay," I apologize. "Sorry for asking."

"No, it's fine." He pauses. Adlai continues to eye me, as if to say, *Stay away from my man.* I would love to tell her not to worry; he's all hers. Adlai hasn't worn anything besides sweatpants and white turtlenecks since she's been here, and though she is supposed to have checked in for drinking, I always suspect that she is actually just suffering from an anxiety disorder. She's got the nutty look in her eye that I have come to associate with mental patients, not dipso-maniacs. She is clearly disturbed and depressed, two conditions I tend to have a lot of sympathy for, but she's so obnoxious—she's got that cruel preppie girl's sense of entitlement, which is the reason she doesn't want Hank talking to me—that I can only hope that things get worse for her.

"It's just that these things are always surprisingly interesting to me," I say, and I mean it. "When I saw the play *Arcadia*, I remember wishing I could do that kind of math. I actually saw it twice—I'm a big Tom Stoppard fan any-way—but it's a particularly brilliant piece of work besides. If you're a language person, numbers always seem like this beautiful and mysterious world. Do you know what I mean?"

"Yeah, I do, and it's actually infuriating to me," he says. "It's just a mistake that all you literary types make that math and numbers are a metaphor for something else. When in reality, mathematics is only about itself. You can't explain it in other terms. It doesn't have any meaning except within the disci-pline. So you get Martin Amis writing *Time's Arrow*, trying to use physics as a way to explain human motives, and it doesn't work. It's just cheap science. If you know anything about it, you get really mad."

"What about Einstein explaining the theory of relativity by saying that when you're sitting on a bench next to a pretty girl, the time passes faster than if you're sitting next to an ugly, horrible guy?" I ask. "It seems to me that Ein-stein was happy to try to make his theories accessible and comprehensible to ordinary mortals. I'll bet you have an interest in making what you know seem more recondite because you fucked up, and he didn't."

"Maybe so." He smiles. "Einstein had a bit of the showman in him always."

"So what happened? Did you drink your way off the tenure track?"

"Pretty much."

"Congratulations." I hesitate. "Look, I'm sorry if I'm snapping at you, but I really don't appreciate being told what I can or cannot understand. I'm sure I won't really get it, but your a priori presumptions and superiority are offensive."

"Maybe that's because they remind you of your own."

"Touché." I smile. Adlai looks furious.

After that, Hank and I become fast friends. Best friends. Best friends at Silver Hill, anyway. There's no issue about sex or romance because he's not my type. In fact, I'm the opposite of attracted to Hank. Does that mean I'm repulsed? No, not quite. It's just that I don't particularly think of him as a date or a potential date or even a date substitute. I just like talking to him.

Turns out he was an undergraduate at Harvard, then on to Stanford for his Ph.D. After Stanford, he got an assistant professorship at Berkeley, because he did some important research into integers while he was a grad student.

"So did you add a few extra digits to pi?" I joke.

"No. All the interesting work with pi was done last century."

"Before the calculator?"

"No, not that. But once computers could figure it out, it was all just numbers. But any new use for pi was worked out long ago."

"All right. So you took the Pythagorean theorem to new levels."

"No, not that either. That one was pretty much settled with Pythagoras, and that was a long time ago. The architects are the ones who have made the new developments in that area."

"All right. So tell me about the integers."

"You don't give up, do you?"

"No."

"I can't explain it. We'd have to get out a pen and paper, and it would still be impossible."

We are sitting at Gates, a restaurant in New Canaan that seems to employ many Silver Hill alumni. I pull a purple Pilot out of my handbag and push a napkin in his direction. "Try me."

"Let's talk about something else."

"You know, I *took* AP calculus. I know a little about math."

"You know, I *taught* AP calculus. I know a lot about math."

"When did you do that?

"For a year between college and grad school. Brats at New Trier High School."

"Oh yes, the legendary public school in Illinois. The one with its own television studio."

"That's the one." He smiles. "How do you know about that?"

"I know about a lot of things," I say, trying to sound sharp and enigmatic. "But seriously, Jonathan Kozol talks a lot about it in *Savage Inequalities.* Compares it to the high school in East Saint Louis, where they don't even have a single microscope."

"Good. Better topic. Education. You probably know more about that." He tends to speak in staccato one-word sentences, which I eventually realize have the rhythm of simple math equations. Who says numbers are not a metaphor?

"More than you?"

"No." He smiles again. "Nobody knows more than I do about anything. But we can probably have a conversation, at least."

"Fuck you." I throw a napkin at him.

"Sure."

Neither of us is going to group. He's had enough of the whole place. He's been in trouble for using the Internet in his room, and the first night he got to the Cottage he was sent back to K-House because Adlai had beard burn on her face—they were found alone in her room together, so it is clear they were kissing. He's not gotten along with Karl or Kathleen from the get-go, and he's ready to move on. He thinks he should stay in the area, and his aunt and uncle have a house in Weston, which is nearby, so he's going to move in there. They're in Jupiter, Florida, for the winter—the town where the woman who was allegedly raped by William Kennedy lives, I point out—so Hank has the place to himself for a while.

Aidan and Diana have both moved out. They are renting a house together in New Canaan with a couple of other people, and it seems pretty clear that they are romantically involved. Diana adopts a chocolate Labrador retriever, and her life as a girl in recovery in Connecticut is complete. Mae-Mae moves back into her place in Manhattan, which is on Carmine Street, right opposite mine, so we plan to hang out and go to meetings together when I get back. Lara is readying herself to return to São Paolo. My era at the Cottage is coming to an end. By this time the place is overrun with college students who have left before the semester is over to keep from completely failing out. One of them, with dyed magenta hair, has stolen a couple of lipsticks from me, and there is a bad scene when Kathleen confronts her because I won't. I tell Hank that I want to move into his aunt's house with him. He thinks it's not a bad idea.

Once he's settled in Weston, Hank rents a truck because his car—some kind of SUV is my guess, because like most drunks Hank probably needs to be prepared for the possibility of off-road driving—was impounded in Taos, New Mexico. He still needs to pay a fine for a DWI, and in his alcoholic grandiosity Hank is convinced that the New Mexico state police have hung wanted signs with his picture on them in various post offices. Apparently, all he could find at the rental place in Weston was this blue pickup, so that's how he gets around. Hank comes around the Cottage every day to see me, and to go to meetings. He drives me into town to run errands—between the two of us, we always need to pick up prescriptions for Antabuse and antidepressants at CVS—and to buy things I don't need and can't afford, which is pretty much all there is in New Canaan. This drives Adlai crazy. She still has to go to group while Hank and I go to lunch.

I tell her not to worry, that we're just friends. By this time, Hank has long ago lost interest in her, so she's upset anyway, and I don't blame her. But I kind of do, just for being so annoying. She's one of the people here I will never come to like. No one else likes her either. By now, I am pretty tight with everybody—after that night that we fetched Aidan out of ruin in Norwalk, everything changed—but Adlai never fits in. She whines, mostly about Hank, and tries everybody's patience. One day she walks into my room in tears and says what I know she's been thinking all along. I am reading *Fermat's Enigma* on my bed, minding my own business. I'm hoping Hank will engage—or indulge—me in some conversation about Fermat's last theorem, since I'm now pretty up on it. "Stay away from my man!" Adlai screams.

"Jesus, God, Adlai." I am startled, even though I expect this. "There is nothing going on between me and Hank." I pause. "Besides, he's not your man."

Kathleen hears her scream and comes running in. When I first got to the Cottage, Kathleen was really mean to me, or at least that's how I felt. In my endless need to ingratiate myself with *everybody*—and I often just end up alienating them in the process—I would go hang around the counselors' office during Kathleen's shift and talk to her about my troubles. Which were endless. Kathleen is a hardy girl from a hardscrabble background with thick, lined skin and bleached-out hair—just as I imagine anyone with that name to be—so my nonsense doesn't much interest her. In the interest of doing her duty, Kathleen just responds to me with program slogans: Keep the focus on you; one day at a time; let go and let God; and so on. Finally, one day I asked if we could just talk like two humans, and once Kathleen realized I was serious about recovery and in the Cottage to stay for a while, our whole dynamic changed. I eventually figured out that if all you do all day is deal with newly clean addicts—the most manipulative and untrustworthy people under creation—you've got to be defensive. Someone who seems just great one day could show up with a needle in his arm, seeing stars, the next. But once Kathleen and I get past this, I come to simply love her. Just like with Karl. These people, in their way, have saved my life.

So naturally, when she hears Adlai screaming, Kathleen comes running. No matter what, Kathleen is going to be on my side about this one, because we all know that Adlai is fucking loony. By the time Kathleen gets here, Adlai has stomped out and is on the stairway heading to her room. It really should have padded wallpaper. Come to think of it, Adlai should probably be in a higher-security section of the hospital, where they do indeed have cushioned walls. Oh well.

I explain to Kathleen what Adlai was yelling about. "Why are you two fighting over Hank?" she asks. "He's horrible."

"Ah, come on. I know he was probably rude to you, but he's really not so bad," I say. "But Adlai's way off the mark. It's not like he's incredibly handsome or anything, so I'm not sure why she thinks everybody is after him. We really are just friends, and she really is crazy."

But for some reason, feeling sane and generous, I pad up to Adlai's room to make sure she's okay. I know a little bit about romantic jealousy, and I know how painful it is. I feel sorry for Adlai, sorry enough that I tell her I will stay away from Hank if it will make her feel better. I mean it. She's fragile, and he's not that important to me. I think about how I have suffered over men, knowing that they don't want me or that they like some other girl better, or that I am too needy and alienating to them, and I actually see myself in Adlai. I see her obsessive crush on Hank and remember every single time I became infatuated with some guy who wished I would just leave him alone. I remember that a large part of the reason I started doing cocaine long ago was to distract myself while I waited for some man to call me, and I remember that one of the reasons I ran away from Florida was to escape the pursuit of pursuing romance. These episodes—and I don't know if it's right to refer to a constant state of affairs as *episodes*—have been so painful for me that I actually have empathy for Adlai. Awful, annoying Adlai—I hate to think I am doing unto others as I would not want done unto me.

Besides, it's bad karma. Okay—that's the truth. I have been in rehab several months, I am all fresh and clean, and the only reason I might ever again experience the emotions Adlai is having right now is if the gods avenge my unkind behavior to her. If I can allow Hank to upset Adlai—even if I am only contributing indirectly—then that means it's okay for the next guy to upset me. And I'm through with that.

Then I go to Florida one week—the Cottage is a halfway house, after all, and people are allowed to go on vacation after they've been there and stayed clean for a while—and it happens to be the same week that Hank goes to Chicago. He's been coming by the Cottage to try to get me to hang out with him again, and I keep insisting that I won't unless he settles matters with Adlai, because I've got to live with her and he doesn't. But then he offers to drop me off at JFK, since our planes are departing the same day, and I can't say no. We end up talking on the phone all the time between Florida and Chicago. I miss him terribly. It's ridiculous. You'd think we were in love, but of course we're not.

Once I get back to the Cottage, I decide that Adlai can fuck herself. Hank is my friend, and that's it. I encourage him to have an honest talk with her, but either way, I am keeping out of it. It's not my problem.

Hank and I start going on long drives around Connecticut. He shows me Darien and Greenwich and the other towns in Fairfield County. One day he takes me to the mall in Stamford, and I drag him to the MAC store to help me pick out a new lipstick. He likes a pink one called Shrimpton. We go see *Wild Things* one afternoon in Norwalk.

One Saturday night, Hank is supposed to call me after the Silver Hill NA meeting so I can join him for dinner with his aunt and uncle, who are back in town. For some reason I never hear from him, and I feel vaguely rejected, that old ugly trepidation comes back to me—but I tell myself that it's just Hank, don't be silly. Hank is my friend. It's no big deal. The next day we have brunch at Gates, and he says he tried to call but the phone at the Cottage was busy. He thought of just driving by, but with his relatives in tow it was just too complicated. And it is terrible how relieved I am to hear that it was all just miscommunication and misunderstanding, nothing else.

We are just friends. Just friends. I don't even find Hank attractive. Not at all.

By this time I am spending a couple of nights a week in my own apartment in New York, preparing to be back there by April 7, the day my book comes out. I go in to Doubleday for a champagne toast one morning. I'm an hour late. Lydia frets and Betsy looks annoyed, but everyone knows I'm in rehab—how could they not?—so they are forgiving. I spend days in New York, at photo shoots and doing interviews, sometimes in my house or at Bar Pitti, but mostly at the Oyster Bar in Grand Central because it is convenient to the train back to New Canaan.

Sometimes I go to Dr. Geller's house in Greenwich for therapy, instead of seeing her at Silver Hill. She sends me to see Dr. Singer on one of my jaunts into the city, because I have to make the transition. Dr. Geller tells me to go see *Deconstructing Harry*, about a man who gets it all right on the page, but fails at life. She asks if I want to be like that, or would I prefer to get better. Dr.

Geller insists that I do not have to choose between my life and my work, that it's up to me. I look at her dubiously, and just kind of hope she is right.

"Have faith," Dr. Geller says.

"I'm doing the best I can."

One day, Hank asks me to come by his place in Weston. He usually would pick me up, but he's got a pile of shit to do. So he tells me to take a cab. When I get there, I ring the bell and there is no answer. I knock and knock, and get that scared feeling I get when I think someone might be disappearing. Finally, he comes to the door with a towel wrapped around his waist because he's just climbed out of the shower. And it hits me. *Mon Dieu!* He's got a beautiful body. Jesus. I never knew. I could kind of see, could notice the curve of his long legs one day in the sun when he was wearing khakis, but this is different. He's got these lovely big shoulders, and a strong chest, and, well, who would have thought.

We go out for clam chowder in Weston.

I talk to Dr. Geller about this. "I'm afraid I'll have to sleep with him."

"Why?"

"I don't want to. I'm not attracted to him." This has become a mantra already. I sometimes think that for the biographical blurb on the flap of my next book, they will have to write, *"Elizabeth Wurtzel, who is not attracted to Hank Kennedy, lives in New York City."* "I mean, I really don't want to sleep with Hank, but it just seems like the thing to do." Actually, it seems like the thing *not* to do, but whatever. "Things seem headed in that direction. We're together all the time. We adore each other. Actually, I think this is how it's supposed to be. You know, you get to know somebody, see how wonderful he is, and fall for him, instead of the opposite, which is always how it goes."

She doesn't want to say that rehab romances don't work, that we'd be better off as friends. Instead she just tells me that I shouldn't do anything I feel is wrong. Dr. Singer says the same thing, but she knows I will do what I want. I tell her it doesn't really matter because I'm not into him anyway. "Good," she says. "Let's keep it that way."

One day in March, my last month at Silver Hill, I am walking across the campus. It is a very sunny day, and I am hiking up the hill to Main House for lunch, instead of walking on the paved tracks, which are for dorks who can't climb. I used to be one of those dorks, I used to tiptoe along the towpaths, I used to get lost between K-House and the Cottage, but now I am here. This is my life. This is my life *not* on drugs. This is my brain *not* on drugs. And it's not so bad. That's the best I can come up with: It's not so bad.

I'm not in love. My book is kind of a mess. I'm not so sure how well I'm doing, deep down. But this moment feels okay. And I think: I know what life is for. I don't know how it will go, I don't know anything at all, but it feels okay. Going to meetings every day, getting on my knees and praying to whatever is out there every morning and every night, hanging out and talking to the other people in the house, it's had an effect.

So it figures I would meet Hank. I am the healthiest and sanest I have ever been. I am capable of having healthy, sane attractions. But I know this stability is not solid, though it sure does feel that way. That's why they say not to get involved for the first year. It's particularly hard to resist when you feel so fresh and open. You feel capable of love for the first time ever — but that does not mean you should express it. You should hold on to the feeling and let it sink in. If you act on it, there is a good chance it will go away.

And I don't want it to go away. I don't think I have ever felt this free and easy before, ever. Maybe when I was a very little girl, but even then I was nervous and tearful. After my parents' divorce, I was always asking Daddy when he was coming back home to Mommy, I was always feeling my life and myself slipping away, the way squirrels squirm and run away when you chase after them in Central Park. Even when I was four years old, it all felt so slippery, I always had this sense I was falling down, like my knees were always scraped, like my shoes were always scuffed, like I couldn't catch myself and no one else could hold on to me either.

But now I feel fine, safe. Like I can handle whatever comes my way. In a meeting somebody once said that if you've got one foot back in the past and another ahead in the future, you are pissing on the present. And I don't want to do that anymore, and — surprise! surprise! — I'm not doing it right now. Spring is here, and in the little garden at the entrance to Silver Hill, there are daisies and daffodils.

"You know, I didn't even notice you when you first got to the Cottage," I say to Hank one afternoon, in the beginning of April. We are sitting at Gates again, picking at our salads with blue cheese dressing, sipping iced tea, chatting with the waitress who used to be a patient at Silver Hill. "You made no impression. I guess I met you that time you came running by with Adlai, and I told you that you should move in."

"I remember that."

"And then, that was that." I pause. "What did you think about me before we became friends?"

"That you were pretty." He doesn't even have to think about that one.

"That's so sweet."

"And that you were a pain in the ass. I wanted nothing to do with you. The one good thing about you was that you were pretty."

"That's not so bad."

"But I'll give you a compliment," he offers. "I hope you'll like this. Because what I want to tell you is that the fact that you're pretty is your least good quality."

"Really?"

"I know you probably don't like that, because you're a girl."

"And I'm vain."

"But the best thing about you is that you're smart," he says. "Not clever and bitchy smart, the way you are with everyone around the Cottage. You should cut that out. You don't give anyone a chance to know you and find out what a great person you are, that you're very good to talk to. No one will ever find that out if you keep letting all these other things get in the way. You're wasting your intelligence trying to show everyone how intelligent you are, and it just pushes people away. Not everybody wants to get mixed up in all your badinage. You should stop doing that. You're so much better than your own behavior."

"Thank you. I think."

"No, really," he says. "I'm being serious. You're your own worst enemy. You think it's kind of funny that you're high maintenance and difficult, but it's not, and you're not. There's a lot more to you, and if you don't quit with all the other stuff, all the things you do to get attention, no one will ever know." He pauses for a minute. "And you're not serving your own cause."

"Which is?" I'm curious to know what he thinks it is.

"To get by in the world. You do drugs because you feel lousy about yourself. And because you don't like yourself, you're nasty to people, which means you don't get the response you want, which makes you feel bad, and then on it goes like that." He stops again. "Your whole thing is that you want people to like you *anyway*. You want people to like you in spite of yourself, and that's kind of a lot to ask. The people you work with will put up with it, because they're invested in the part of you that is good—which is your intelligence. But it doesn't have to be that way. You can just be cool. Instead of being the difficult girl, you should just be the cool girl."

"I see." I'm a little hurt. This is a compliment, I know, but I'm not sure how I can change the things about me that are irritating. He's right. I know that I do these things, even as they're happening. I don't think it's cute. I think it's me. And everyone should put up with it. It's like I'm testing them, to see if they'll get past this to the real me. I should stop it. "I'll take that under advisement."

"Elizabeth, I'm serious."

"I know." I know, but what can I do? I've been this way for so long. Maybe getting clean will help. It's an opportunity, isn't it? An opportunity to start all over. I'm lucky to have it. But next topic. "So I was amazed that you got into all that trouble that first night because you seemed like such a nerd."

"A complete chump, huh?"

"Yeah, I guess."

"Dr. Grubman knows better." He signals to the waitress for our check. "That night when Kathleen called him to say that she just wanted to send me back to K-House because I was kissing Adlai and whatever else, he just spoke to me and said that he knew if there was trouble, I must have caused it." Dr. Grubman was Hank's therapist when he lived in San Francisco, and he knew him as a hard-core, unrepentant alcoholic. Now Dr. Grubman is the head of Silver Hill, which is why Hank came here in the first place.

"I can't imagine somebody thinking of you as a troublemaker," I say, honestly amazed. "You're just a sweetheart as far as I can tell."

"But I'm a real drunk," he explains. "You don't understand that because your problems are on a continuum—your drugs relate to your depression. But with me, if you take away the alcohol, I'm fine. When I drink, I'm horrible. And I don't know why I drink. I come from a family of drinkers. Two of my father's brothers died of alcoholism. One was a professor at MIT, another at the University of Chicago. They were brilliant men, and one drank until his liver died, and the other drove off a bridge. No one knows if it was an accident or not. But we're all pure alcoholics. We're driven by loving to drink, and I can't have one beer and not have thirty. It's different from how you are."

He tells me about all the awful things he did when he was drunk. For one thing, he screwed up his academic career. In math and physics—the pure sciences—most people do their best work before they turn thirty-five. Their brains need to be too clear and agile to do that kind of intense thinking as they get older. You have to get tenure by your mid-thirties, because after that it's unlikely that you will do the type of research that makes universities want you for life. And by the time his contract was up for renewal at Berkeley, Hank was drunk all the time, and the math department knew a hopeless case when it saw one. He went and worked in Silicon Valley, and made a fortune. He was drunk all the time, but he could do his job wasted; it was that easy for him. The only problem was that they frequently couldn't find him—he'd get fucked up and get on a plane to Australia, or he'd hide in a fishing village in Canada with no phones for two weeks. His assistant spent a lot of time just trying to figure out where he was. But the company never fired him. He was valuable for them, even after two bottles of Macallan scotch in one night.

But Hank was also a mean drunk—or more correctly, he was mean when he wasn't drunk. The weekend he was supposed to be getting married, he was in bed in a hotel room in Nob Hill with a woman other than his fiancée, who was effectively left at the altar. He got so drunk that he ended up walking naked onto a BART train one night, and got arrested. After that, he quit his job, took his money, and bought a house in Taos, New Mexico, because he liked skiing and hiking. He worked in a bookstore for a while, but mostly he just got inebriated and intoxicated every night. Taos is the kind of small town where the cops pick up drunks after last call at the local bars, and make sure they get home safely. So Hank was okay there. But then his car got impounded in December, so he headed home to Oak Park for Christmas. He spent the holiday enjoying the company of several bottles of scotch, and mixed gin and tonics for a bunch of chipmunks in the backyard. Hank sat and talked to them in the snow while the rest of his family sat inside wondering what to do. That night he went walking through Chicago, so drunk that he hanged himself from a fire escape. The police rescued him before he actually managed to kill himself, and he had no ID, so they took him in to Cook County Hospital, where they locked him up for a few days. While he was there, he got near a mirror, broke it, and slit his wrists. He finally told the doctor what his name was and how to find his parents, and that's how he ended up at Silver Hill.

"I can't imagine," I say. "You're so nice. You're so sober. I can't imagine you like that."

"It's true."

"I don't believe you."

"Well, if you're lucky, you'll never have a chance to find out."

"I hope not."

It's my last week at Silver Hill, and it is definitely time to go. Dr. Geller thinks I should come back once my book tour is over, come back to a safe place. She's afraid I need reinforcement for all the progress I've made. This seems crazy to me, I've been here for four months, and most people don't make it through four weeks.

"Just because most people have to go back to their families and jobs, just be-cause they don't have insurance, doesn't mean it's wrong for you to make the most of it if you can afford to," she says. "Back before managed care, when insurance covered it, people would be here for a year or two sometimes."

"You're not suggesting that?"

"No, of course not." I'm not sure she doesn't really think that's what I need. But never mind. "But I am saying that you might want to stick around and give yourself a chance to feel completely better."

She has a point. The sun has come out. I walk around the grounds feeling so alive, loving the green and the blue, and I know what life is for. Why take a chance on losing that? Just because four months should be long enough doesn't mean it is. And who says that it should be anyway? The Cottage is supposed to be a halfway house. It really does function as part of the institution itself, but if I had gone to Hazelden, say, I would probably be in some kind of sober living place in Saint Paul for a year after I left. It takes a long time to get clean, and if you can afford to, it's a good idea to stay in a safe environment for as long as you can. It's not like life has to stop. People who live in halfway and three-quarter houses have to have jobs. But they also have to go to meetings, and they have to live right—and they're safe.

Maybe after all the years of unsafety in my mother's house, it would not be so bad to grow up all over again in a better space now. Maybe I should use the Cottage the way it was meant to be used: as a place to really live until I'm ready to go. Or maybe I should move to Minneapolis, to some place where people really do stay for a year or two, because that's more acceptable in Minnesota, the recovery state, the land of ten thousand lakes, ten million mosquitoes, and untold numbers of junkies. There is particular incentive to stay in Minneapolis because it is a very liberal midwestern city with excellent health care coverage. If you are a recovered addict, you need a lot of doctors' appointments anyway, and if you are HIV positive, this is even more the case. So the public health system ends up taking care of all these at-risk people.

But I am so dying to be a normal girl. I want it so badly that I am going to sabotage this opportunity. I want so much to get out into the world to prove that I *can* get out into the world that I am going to leave here before my time. I want so much to test my ability to have romance that I will try it out before I am ready. I want to take what I know and use it.

Alexander Pope says, "A little learning is a dangerous thing." The amount I've received at Silver Hill is just enough to get me into trouble, and not enough to sustain myself. I will go on my book tour; I will do the things I am supposed to do, once again, just to prove that I can do them. Finally, at long last, a moment when my feelings are okay, when I am learning to express them, but I can't go all the way with it. I think I should be a grown-up and deal. The thing is, as Dr. Geller has pointed out repeatedly, most people had an opportunity to be pure and to feel what they wanted without bounds when they were little kids. Even other children of divorce mostly had a reprieve until they were, say, ten years old, or whenever their parents eventually split up. Those first few years are crucial. If you can just be safe until about age four, there's a good chance that you will be well prepared for the rest of your life.

In *The Drama of the Gifted Child*, Alice Miller refers to a case study of a man who "lived with his single mother in extreme poverty for the first year of his life and who was then taken away from her by the authorities. He was placed in one foster home after another, and in all of them the child was severely mistreated." Nonetheless, the doctor who treated this man at a psychiatric hospital reports that as an adult he healed a great deal more swiftly than many patients whose histories of abuse were far less severe, whose worst problems were those that result from the petty indignities that we all suffer in our garden-variety dysfunctional families. While the attending physician saw this man's miraculous recovery as an act of God, Dr. Miller disagrees. "Was it really God's grace that helped him as an adult, or is the explanation more prosaic?" she asks. "If this man had a mother who, in spite of her poverty, gave him real love, respect, protection, and security in his first year, he would have had a better start in life and then would have been better able to deal with later abuse than would a patient whose integrity was injured from the first day of her life."

Studies have shown that the brain gets hard-wired in those first few years, and by about age four, if you have grown up with pandemonium, your mind can only deal with what is chaotic. It does not know how to react to anything else. In fact, it reacts to everything—to halcyon calm, to the most primordial peace—as if it actually is in turmoil, because that's all it is trained to do. This is like being in *The Manchurian Candidate*. It's like being programmed to act a certain way at the sight of the Queen of Hearts—only I react to the other fifty-one cards in the deck in exactly the same way. Happy things, sad things— I often can't distinguish, and my predominant response to everything is fear.

Brain development has always fascinated me. I remember reading Noam Chomsky's work about a priori language acquisition when I was in college. His point was that after a certain age, if you have not been taught a language, it's too late. They've tried all these "wild child" experiments, with Kasper Hauser and others who were locked in a room alone until after age ten, and none of them could be taught to speak. It was easier teaching Helen Keller how to talk than giving language to these completely sensate human beings who had not been exposed to any stimulus during their developmental years.

And it's like that with emotions too. Your programming happens early, and correcting bad input is almost impossible after a certain point. I mean, computers with bugs can usually be fixed, and if it's a bad enough problem, you need to replace the whole thing. But you can't replace a human being, and you can't supplant your own brain. Who can say if therapy, even with all the good medications, will ever be enough? But given the progress I've made just being here, I ought to consider it worthwhile. I ought to not be embarrassed that I need to correct my pre-Oedipal years of miswiring. Why am I ashamed? Just because so much has gone right for me, I think I ought to cope better. I've been so lucky. There is so much good that it seems ridiculous, pathetic, and spoiled to keep reverting to long-ago events and use them as an excuse.

What I can't quite accept is that getting help is not an excuse. It's the opposite of an excuse—it's an action, a solution. It is taking care, and that's never wrong. Even though it seems as though I ought to not need all this much care, if it's available and I am in a position to access it, why shouldn't I? I nearly killed myself with drugs. I had—and still have—a life-threatening illness. Is any amount of treatment too much to save my own life?

But I can see this is going to be an unfinished project, as ever. Given how deep down drugs have got me—but not nearly as deep down as depression has always had me—I really should take this to the limit. I don't want to waste my thirties the way I wasted my twenties. I should not be afraid. I should not worry that if I take a break from my life for a while, it will disappear. That eventuality is far more likely if I don't get this stuff completely worked out. It is a festering wound. It's cumulative insult. I'll need repeated surgical procedures because I failed to get the right operation in the first place. Or it's like antibiotics: if you don't finish the whole bottle, the bacteria reassert themselves.

But anxiety has still beat out feeling, no matter how much I've learned from Dr. Geller. Even though she's taught me so much about not being nervous about my emotions, to trust them, that sense that I better hup to it has won out. I am going back to New York. I've been away long enough. Time to get on with life, such as it is.

RELAPSE

Twenty-one

MIND PLAYING TRICKS ON ME

The heart opens wide like it's never seen love
Addiction stays on tight like a glove

EMMYLOU HARRIS
"Where Will Be"

Hank drives me home in his rented pickup truck, and we are happy. We are happy and chatty all the way down I-95. We sit in the cab, my belongings are on the flatbed in back, and we are doing seventy-five on the freeway.

We are happy and chatty unloading boxes into my attic apartment in the tilting old house on Carmine Street. We listen to Big Star and Serge Gainsbourg and Bob Dylan on my stereo, and music never sounded so good. "Wish we had / A joint so bad," Alex Chilton sings, and I spin around the apartment and lip-sync. The cat is pleased to have me back, perched on the kitchen counter, watching the proceedings, Cheshire-smiling.

Then the phone rings, the first call since I've walked in, and it's Jacob. I have not spoken to him since before I went to Silver Hill. I'd almost forgotten him and Levana, his fiancée. But here he is on the phone, after all these months.

And I can't help myself, I ask, Are you holding?

A few hours later, we are cutting lines on the little green steamer trunk that passes for a coffee table. I am snorting a few here and there, shyly, as if I've been caught naked. It's okay, I keep telling Hank. This is all just to prove that I still can do this. After all, I'm cured, four months in rehab, clean as Ivory Snow, sitting with white powder that can't hurt me anymore.

I'll just do this tonight, I insist. It's only a test.

Hank smokes a cigarette and watches me and Jacob. At the Cottage, Hank and I were the only people who didn't smoke, and now here he is bumming one of Jacob's Marlboro Mediums. That's the thing about cocaine, he explains. Even if you're not doing it, it makes you want to do other bad things. Hank knows he can't drink, so he keeps lighting up cigarettes.

Jacob has come by after work with an eightball. He can leave the TV studio as soon as he is done with his trading-day report. Jacob keeps saying that he feels terrible. I've just left Silver Hill today, I've been clean four months, and now he's giving me drugs. He knows he shouldn't be doing this.

But I know Jacob is a social user. He needs a partner to do lines with. Levana is back in Paris right now, and without her, I'm his coke buddy. That's just the way it is. I assure him that I'd be doing this with or without him. It's my little experiment. I'd have contacted José myself. Jacob should not feel bad for facilitating what would have happened anyway.

And I mean it. Or I don't mean it. Or I don't know. It's not like I had a plan, not like I said, As soon as I get back to my apartment, I am going to use again. I was not even particularly craving it, or thinking about it at all. But as soon as I heard Jacob's voice, I knew I had to. It made sense. There was no moment of doubt or crisis because I knew it was meant to be. God intended me to do cocaine within hours of leaving Silver Hill. After all, what are the chances that my first phone call at home in months would be from the one person I did coke with before I checked in? I never did drugs with anyone; I was a solitary user. Jacob's call was written on the wind. I can't fight with that.

It gets darker as a couple of hours go by, and duller and sadder, and it's the same as ever: doing coke makes me want to do more coke; there's nothing else to it. It does not make me want to dance or chat or write or make love—it is utterly self-reflexive. Hank makes phone calls to find other friends to hang with. He doesn't want to be here for this. He kind of says, Do what you want, I understand, I'm not judging you, but I've got to go. Finally he leaves, tells me he'll check in later. He calls from a restaurant an hour after, wonders if I want to join him and a few people for steak frites at Les Halles, and I tell him I'm still doing coke with Jacob, call later.

Jacob is with me all night. We never leave my apartment. My nose burns and the muscles in my shins hurt as if I've been on my feet behind an accessories counter at Macy's for a twelve-hour shift, which is weird because I have not stood up at all, except to get water out of the Brita container in the refrigerator. I make a note to myself to change the filter in the morning. Also, I keep loading in new CDs. It's been so long since I've listened to a real stereo and *Highway 61* never sounded so good. I want to listen to *American Beauty*. I explain to Jacob that Jerry Garcia was a cokehead, the Grateful Dead is not just for pot smokers, and he says fine, whatever.

Finally at five in the morning, I announce that I am going to take a bath. I pour some vanilla bubbles into the hot water in the tub, I watch the tawny gel swirl under the faucet, and I climb in. My face glows red from the heat after a few minutes, my nose is running, and I ask Jacob to come in with some more coke. He cuts some lines up on a hand mirror, and sits on the floor, on the bath mat next to me.

"Can I join you?" he asks, meaning inside the tub.

"Don't be ridiculous," I answer, impatient by what a dumb question it is. "It's not like that between us. Besides, you live with Levana."

"I'm not sure she's coming back."

"Sorry to hear that." I snort up some coke and sink into the sweet white bubbles. "Besides, I'm involved with somebody else."

"Really?" Jacob is surprised, and come to think of it, so am I. "Who?"

"Hank."

"The guy who was here before?"

"Yes." I didn't realize this was true until I said it, but in fact, I seem to have fallen in love with Hank against my will. How do these things happen? Shit. "Besides," I continue, "my book party is tomorrow night, or more like tonight, and I need to get some sleep before I go have my hair cut this afternoon. You need to leave."

"If that's what you want."

"Can you throw me a towel?" I wish he'd just go. I wish this had never happened. How am I going to get through this day and this night? I must never do coke again. It was okay just this once, but once is enough. "I'm going to get out of here and get into bed. Okay? Please be out of my apartment before I get out of the bathroom."

"Okay."

I know I am being cold, but I want to kill him. I never want to see Jacob again. But he'll be at my book party. I hope he isn't holding. Or maybe I hope he is. I put an old J. J. Cale album on the turntable before I climb the ladder up to my bed. I love the smell of vinyl; it's so tangible. Of course, right now I can't breathe. I lie down and listen to the lyrics: "She don't lie, she don't lie, she don't lie—cocaine." Of course, that's the biggest lie of all.

It is late at night, after my book party, which was at a loft on Greene Street that belongs to this dandyish millionaire named Henry Buhl. Henry founded something called the SoHo Partnership, an organization that trains homeless people and puts them to work in the community, and Doubleday has donated a bunch of copies of *Bitch*, which I've signed, in exchange for the use of his home, with all its gothic, blood-red velvet furniture and candelabras with artfully dripping wax. I met Henry through Matthew, a guy who used to live in Greenwich Village and then bought a house in New Canaan after he checked out of Silver Hill. It's a fun party. Even I have fun. I am an hour late because it takes me so long to get into this black chiffon dress after I return from the hair salon on the Upper East Side. Betsy comes to my apartment to pick me up. She tries to be patient. She tries not to rush me. She tries to indulge my iridescent eyeliner. I have just gotten out of rehab the day before, and she wants to be careful because I'm fragile.

At the same time, she's got this look on her face like if we don't get out of here in five minutes, I'm going to kill you.

I don't do cocaine at the party. No one does, as far as I know. It's understood that this occasion is in honor of a person who just checked out of a treatment program, and everyone is respectful. Besides, I don't think there's a lot of drug use at social gatherings in New York anyway. It was always just me, off in my corner or hiding in my apartment. I see Jacob for a minute, and pretend that I don't. Kathlyn and Lily and Daisy are all there, all my old friends. Tom Beller and Rob Bingham, two fiction writers whom I last saw at Andie Gregg's miserable wedding, show up for several hours. The guy whom I lost my virginity to is there with his fiancée. Gregory, my ex-boyfriend, is also around, talking Karl Marx with investment bankers. Two different men whom I have had long-standing crushes on ask for my phone number. How they got to my party I don't know, but I'm glad. There are reporters and publishing people and, for whatever reason, Uma Thurman's two younger brothers, whom no one seems to know. If they do anything with their lives besides being Uma Thurman's brothers, no one can say.

And this makes me smile: I am *really* back in New York, I am really in a place where you can meet someone at a party whose only claim in life is that he used to be Sylvia Miles's lover, or he's the son of Ben Vereen, or, I guess, as in *Six Degrees of Separation*, he is the imaginary child of Sidney Poitier, and he'll get everyone walk-on parts in *Cats*. You see, I tell myself, here is the reason to stay clean: because life is so ridiculous, and if you're sober, it's funny; if you're high, it's just depressing.

Or maybe it's the opposite. But I hope not.

Meanwhile, I keep retreating into the bathroom, full of froufrou curtains and exotic toiletries from St. Barth's, to splash my face with icy water, to wake myself up a bit. I'm beat. I wish, I wish, I wish I had not done cocaine last night. Never again. Never ever again.

Hank crashes at my house afterward, after a bunch of us have gone to dinner at some SoHo bistro called Match. He is sleeping on my couch, the horrible orange velvet clunker of would-be furniture. He's six foot three, but we're both too tired to open the foldout bed. It's ridiculous. I'm lying alone on my perched mattress; he's lying alone just below. Neither of us is asleep, we know it would be wrong for us to be in the same bed, but it seems even more wrong for us not to be.

"Hank," I yell from up in the loft. "I'm lonely. Why don't you come up."

"If that's what you want," he calls back. Before I can answer he's up the ladder, and crawling toward me. I'm in a T-shirt, he's in his boxer shorts, and he gets under the covers next to me.

"Let's just go to sleep," I say.

"That's fine." And as if to remind me that it's up to me, "Whatever you want."

I explain all this stuff about how I'll change if we sleep together, I'll become dependent, everything he likes about me will go away. I've been saying my prayers and going to meetings and doing so well. That slip last night was just a slip. It won't happen again. I don't want to lose what I had. I don't want to lose myself. If we get involved, that will go away; all that I've gained will evanesce.

"Hey, slow down," he says. "We don't have to sleep together. We don't have to do anything."

Hearing him say this just makes me want him more. He pulls off my shirt, looks up at me for a second to make sure it's okay, and as he starts licking my breasts, I smile. "Hey, no fair," I say. "Now I'm completely naked, and you're not."

"Be patient."

"Okay."

Hank works his way down my body until he's—God, I wish there were a better way to say it besides *eating me out* or *going down on me*, but you get the idea. I start to giggle, and then—well so much for being just friends.

I appear on *The O'Reilly Factor.* I spend the night before doing coke, because Jacob left some in one of my kitchen drawers on his way out the other morning, with a note that says, "Just in case." I find the little plastic bag of powder while I'm looking for some coffee filters, and since there it is, I figure that it's meant to be.

On no sleep, I can't put sentences together. Bill O'Reilly, who's really not so bad in all his orangy pancake makeup, sees that I'm not making sense, so he moves on to yes or no questions.

"Is Hillary Clinton a bitch?"

"No."

"Monica Lewinsky?"

"No."

"Amy Fisher?"

"No."

"Madonna?"

"No."

"What about Paula Jones?"

"Actually, yes."

"Elizabeth, you wrote a whole book called *Bitch,* and you only consider one of the women I've mentioned who is in your book to be a bitch," he tries. "Does that make any sense?"

"Well, I mean, they are bitchy in the classic sense of the word." Okay, you're doing fine. "But I'm trying to reclaim the term." Stop. Don't even go there. "Basically, they're all just women trying to make their way through the world, doing the best they can. They're not bad people."

"I see."

Things go better on CNN, because it's a segment for *Show Biz Today,* and it involves lots of clips of entertainers who are thought to be bitchy, with just a little narrative from me, and a shot of my book in a pile at Barnes & Noble. The reporter is a sassy, flashy woman, who at first wants to set me up with her brother, a nice Jewish boy who has made a fortune manufacturing barrettes and hair bands. I tell her I've just gotten out of rehab, I tell her about all the Ritalin and cocaine, and by the time I am exiting the studio, she isn't asking for my phone number any longer. Anyway, Hank is my boyfriend, so it doesn't matter. At least, I think he's my boyfriend.

My book tour is, I guess it's fair to say, a mess. I'm always upbeat and enthusiastic about readings, but the interviews are unbearable. The same questions over and over again. Always about my book. I want to talk about anything else, but I guess that's not what I'm supposed to be doing. A reporter in Seattle is from Idaho, so I decide to engage her in a conversation about potatoes, white supremacists, Mormons, the overwhelming growth of Boise as a high-tech company hub. By the time she tries to ask me questions about who is a bitch and who isn't—which isn't what the book is about, I actually have no idea what it *is* in fact about, nor does anybody else, it seems—it's time for the next person. Then there is the radio interview on the sports station in Philadelphia, where the reporter wants lessons on how to be a bitch. "I have no idea," I say. "I wish I knew."

Finally, in Boston, I call José and get him to send me an eightball of coke. I promise to pay him when I get back, and he goes along with this. I give him the Doubleday publicity department's Federal Express number. My drug dealer, you see, trusts me. I spend a whole night in my room in the Charles Hotel doing coke and watching pornography. By morning, I've had no sleep, and I have to do a newspaper interview. The reporter is a recovered addict, so we talk about how great it is to be clean. After she leaves, I run into the bathroom and do some lines.

Then I meet with a guy from the Boston *Phoenix*. He's actually the movie critic, and it's great fun, but I'm too exhausted to enjoy it. We talk about Sue Lyon in *Lolita* and Drew Barrymore in *Poison Ivy* and Joan Crawford in *Mildred Pierce*, and I am just so relieved that we don't have to talk about my book. So relieved that I agree to have dinner with him after my reading at the Harvard Coop that night. I go to an AA meeting in Cambridge in the afternoon, because I've insisted that meetings be worked into my schedule, as if. Afterwards, I do some blow in the bathroom at Starbucks before my reading at the Coop. By the time I am supposed to have dinner with the guy from the *Phoenix*, I'm out of coke, and I can't face it, but I have to. We go to Casablanca, an old Harvard haunt, and sit in the wicker chairs, surrounded by images of Ilsa and Rick, of Bogie and his cigar at the Café Américain, in murals on the pastel walls. I can't stay awake with no coke. I run into the bathroom, get into the corner of a stall, curl up into a ball, and close my eyes for a few minutes, for relief.

In New Haven the next day, I am excited because Hank is going to come meet me at my reading at the Yale Bookstore. I check into the hotel and nap. I wonder if I can cop on the street somewhere, but I don't have enough energy. I call Hank to make arrangements, and he tells me he's got bad news. *Oh shit* is all I can think. No coke and bad news are not a good combination.

"My uncle had a heart attack last night, and it doesn't look good," he says. "My parents are flying in right now, and there's no way I can leave the house, except to pick them up at the airport."

"Well, can't you come spend the night with me here?" I try. "They'll be asleep, and there won't be any reason for you to be there."

"Jesus, Elizabeth, are you hearing what I'm saying?" He sounds disgusted. "My uncle is *dying*. My parents will be coming here to stay. I've been really lousy to them for the last few years, and I've got to be here with them now. Don't you get it?"

"Yes, but—"

"Jesus, you really are selfish!"

"No, I'm not." Yes, I am. "I just want to see you."

"But it can wait."

"I guess."

"Jesus, Elizabeth, what's wrong with you?"

"I don't know."

I call Hank late at night, after my reading, to apologize for not being understanding. I don't want him to know that I'm coming down from a few days of coke, that I'm not in my right mind. I figure I'll just say I'm tense. The first time I call, he seems happy to hear from me, but he's abrupt; he's got to go. So then I call five minutes later to apologize for calling so late. He says it's fine, but don't do it again. But then I call ten minutes later to apologize for calling when all this other stuff is going on.

"Elizabeth, enough!"

"I'm sorry."

"If you're sorry, you'll go to sleep. We'll talk in the morning. Okay? You've really got to get a grip here. Everyone in the house is trying to sleep."

"I know. I'm sorry. I'm sorry I'm so awful."

"You're not awful." He sighs. We're back to people sighing when they talk to me. "You just need to sleep."

I go back to New York for the weekend, but I don't see Hank because he's busy with his parents, with ferrying them back and forth to the hospital in Stamford, and I'm convinced he hates me. And I start to hate myself. The inner resources I developed at Silver Hill, the ones that should make me capable of dealing with a relationship, of not *needing* so much—those skills have all been sacrificed to the relationship I find myself in. Before they had a chance to work, they were taken away. What a mess I've made.

Might as well do drugs. Might as well.

The tour goes on that way. I do coke and do interviews about how great it is to be clean. I get coke FedExed to me here and there. In Los Angeles, I run out of cocaine the night before I am supposed to appear on *Politically Incorrect*. I can't screw that one up. Have to be good on network TV. Have to make pithy points. Have to be alert. Have to keep good comic timing. Back when the show was on Comedy Central and it was taped in New York, I appeared on it about once a month, whenever there was a last-minute cancellation. I was a reliable panelist. A little bit camera shy, but I always had a few funny things to say, especially with Ted Nugent and Barry White, who gave me the opportunity to make some comments about the myth of vaginal orgasm and the horrors of bow hunting. Bill Maher liked me and would pinch my butt whenever I came on. But I can tell this is not going to be me at my best.

A car is picking me up to take me to the studio at four o'clock, and at noon I wake up and decide to call my friend Liam. He's a recovered alcoholic, we've gone to meetings at Perry Street together before, and during some hard times he spent a few weeks sleeping on my couch, back when I lived in the loft on Eighteenth Street.

Amazingly, Liam answers his phone, and he's at my hotel room fifteen minutes later. The door is open, and he walks in, hair drooping in his face, in his usual black blazer and gray T-shirt, the last rumpled man in Los Angeles. He looks like Mickey Rourke in *Barfly*. Years of sobriety, and Liam still has the affect and the style of a classic movie drunk. He finds me wrapped in a blanket on the couch, shaking and my teeth chattering, blood dripping down my nose, my head fallen into my chest, my T-shirt with drops of blood all over it.

"Okay, baby," he says, and walks over to me and lifts me up in a ball. "I'm not going to ask what you've been doing, and you don't need to tell me because I don't want you to lie." He carries me into the bathroom, puts me down on the floor, and turns on the tap in the tub. "Okay, now, we're going to get you into the bath, I'm going to bring you some water from the refrigerator, I'm going to order you up some coffee and toast, because you need to eat even if you don't feel like it, and we're going to get you together for TV."

He pulls me out of the blanket, which is hard because I'm clinging to it. "Just let go," he says, unbending my fingers one at a time because they seem to be stuck. "The water is warm. You'll be fine. Trust me." He gets me out of my shirt and into the bath. Then he hits the phone to order up room service. He reminds me of Harvey Keitel in *Pulp Fiction*, the guy they call in to fix the mess when John Travolta and Samuel Jackson have botched a murder really badly. I'll just let him figure this out, because I have no idea how to get out of this one.

After he's ordered up some version of breakfast, Liam comes back into the bathroom, puts a washcloth under the faucet, and wipes off my face, blots the blood and mucus from under my nose. "I don't know what you did to yourself, but you sure did make a mess," Liam says. "Tomorrow I'll take you to an AA meeting. We'll get you through tonight, and tomorrow you've got to start taking care of yourself."

"I know." I start to cry.

"Don't cry," he says. "This happens to everybody. All addicts screw up sometimes. Okay? Don't feel bad. You're not a bad person. You're just an addict. You're doing the best you can." He pulls a towel off the heated metal rack, pulls me out of the tub, wraps me up, and walks me over to the bed, where I crawl under the covers and lie down in a fetal position.

"I don't know what made you think you could go on a book tour the week after you got out of the hospital," Liam says, shaking his head and pouring sips of coffee into my lips. "Open up, darling. You need to drink this."

"I was in for four months," I say, as Liam taps a napkin on my chin to absorb the dripping coffee. "I thought that was long enough. I thought I'd be healthy and fresh. If anything, I thought it was a *good* time to go on a book tour. I'd be relaxed. I'd be ready."

"God, no." He's bringing some toast over to the bed. "Give yourself a break, kiddo."

"Too late now."

Of course, *Politically Incorrect* does not go well at all. I wear a pretty dress. It's navy and tight and sleeveless and makes me look sleek, so I figure afterward people will be able to say, *Well, at least you looked good.* I sit there silent. I figure I'll just let Al Franken and Gloria Allred have it out; they don't need me to have a perfectly miserable time yelling at each other. And just when I think I'm safe, like a kid who has not done his homework and whom the teacher has managed to ignore until five minutes before the bell rings, Bill Maher tries to engage me with a question about Amy Fisher. I mumble something about how I think Joey Buttafuoco is to blame for everything she did. Bill argues with me about that, and when the camera comes back onto my face, I freeze. I just freeze. Like Jessica Savitch. "Let's go to a commercial," Bill Maher says, "and we'll see if you can form an opinion."

And so it goes. I fall asleep during an interview with a woman from *LA Weekly*, which is a shame because I like her and she is a fan of my work. She ends up writing about how I seemed confused and distracted the whole time until I finally just nodded off at the restaurant table, at a little café next door to Book Soup, where I've just done a reading. The readings all go well. I can always get myself revved up for those because I really enjoy them, but I need to spend the rest of the time sleeping. Alison, the publicist from Doubleday, meets me in Los Angeles, and baby-sits for me through the whole Midwest. I stop doing cocaine the whole time she is with me, and as ever, the readings in Chicago and Milwaukee and Minneapolis are wonderful, but we keep canceling all but the most crucial interviews. Things get better in Seattle and

Portland, but it's all I can do to stay awake and cope. Betsy meets me in San Francisco, my final stop, and we have a fun dinner at Chez Panisse in Berkeley. In fact, we have fun in general. She sits in on all my interviews and makes sure none of them goes on for too long, and with her there, I feel safe.

Once I am back in New York, I still have one last trip to make, to do a reading at Olsson's Books in Washington, D.C., which will be taped for C-SPAN. I bring lots of coke with me, because I've stopped pretending I am going to get through it any other way. And it all goes really well; I am cheerful; I make some good jokes. I have fun. But then about halfway through, I notice that my father, whom I have not seen since 1991, is sitting in the audience, right in front of me. Just when I see him, I feel the cocaine start to wear off, I feel myself needing a few sniffs to get through the next half hour, and I can almost feel my face droop, I can feel my features melt like the Wicked Witch of the West under a dousing of water. I'm sagging. As soon as I've answered the last question, I run back into the office where my coat and handbag have been stored. I lunge into the bathroom and cut up some more lines. I tell the bookstore manager, who is waiting for me to come out and sign books, that my father is there, that I haven't seen him in seven years, and I can't go back out unless he leaves. I don't want to be mean, but it's just unfair for him to try to effect a rapprochement with two hundred people waiting for me to write little notes in their books.

The poor guy, who is after all a bookstore employee and not a social worker, goes out and finds my dad—I tell him he is tall with medium-length brown hair and a beard, that he looks kind of like me—and asks him to please leave, that I cannot deal with a reunion in this place. I find myself sitting and seething with anger: How *dare* he do this? My father is such a romantic, I know he is imagining some beautiful public display where we tell each other that we've missed each other so much, it's been so sad all these years, and like that. He's envisioning a scene out of *Oprah*. He disappeared when I was fourteen and did not get in touch with me for years. Yet he always manages to turn up when he thinks my life is going well—and then he takes a hike when the workaday realities of maintaining a relationship set in.

How *dare* he show up at a reading like this! This is my job, this is my work—why is he so disrespectful?

My father has been addicted to Valium since 1970—he takes twelve times the normal dose every day—and I realize that he's so out of it that he doesn't understand that this is real life, this is not a movie. In movies there are beautiful, crazy scenes of long-lost lovers turning up at unlikely places with shy faces and red roses. But here, today, in Washington, D.C., that's not going to happen. He lives in Vienna, Virginia, which is about a half hour away, and I just want him to go back. I tell the bookstore manager to let him know that I will call him, I will get in touch with him, but not now. Please, please, please, not now.

The man comes back to fetch me after a few minutes. I am slouched in a swivel chair, about to cry, but too coked up to feel anything but anxious and annoyed. "How'd it go?" I ask.

"It was okay," he says. "He seemed sad, but he seemed to understand. He wanted me to tell you that Daddy loves his little one."

His *little one*? Has he forgotten that we have not spoken in years, and affectionate names he used for me when I was four years old are no longer appropriate? Well, whatever. What can I do? I reapply my lipstick, splash some water on my face, and sign over two hundred books for the next couple of hours.

When I get back to my hotel room, I call Betsy crying. I am supposed to do a reading in Madison, Connecticut, the next day, at this wonderful independent bookstore that authors are always willing to make a detour to because it's such a lovely, literary atmosphere. But there's no way I can do it. No way. Betsy says we can cancel it. I get back to New York, climb into my loft bed, and go to sleep. I can't move.

I'm sitting in my apartment waiting for Hank to call. Actually, I'm trying to *not* wait for Hank to call, but I guess we're back to this. Hank is as reliable as anyone. We spend lots of time together, we talk all the time; this is a good thing. But he doesn't understand: Now that we're sleeping together, I need him to check in with me regularly. Every day? Every hour? I'm not sure what exactly *regularly* means. Maybe Hank can devise a mathematical formula, like the one that measures the speed of terminal velocity, to assess how many phone calls it takes to satisfy my notion of *regularly*. It could be an SAT question. Something like, if x = most people and y = Elizabeth, which of the following four equations expresses the difference between normal need and Elizabeth's need? Until someone comes up with an answer, all I know is that I feel desperate all the time. Hank goes to Shelter Island for a couple of days, and I wonder why he doesn't take me with him. I go to Napa Valley for Samantha's wedding, and I wonder why he doesn't want to come with me.

When I was at Silver Hill, he was around all the time. Now where is he? Why does he suddenly have all these things to do?

He doesn't love me anymore. I know it. That's what it is. We were supposed to get healthy together. We were going to go to meetings at Perry Street, and stay clean, and say our prayers, and be good. Instead I sit in my apartment doing blow, wondering where he is.

Then Hank calls, we talk for an hour, he comes into the city to hang out, we go see *Kurt and Courtney*, we go see *Two Girls and a Guy*, we have dinner with Kathlyn and Daniel, we have dinner with Lydia and Jason, we have fun like we used to, and I feel fine.

Then he goes back to Weston, I don't see him for a day or two, I call the dealer, I do coke to pass the time, and I am the same person I was before Silver Hill. Jesus God, I'm the same person I was before I went to *Florida*. Four months at rehab, and nothing has changed.

This is how it is, how it always is with men: It feels good at first, it feels soft and solid, slipping into love, sliding into the sweet thing. But then it's just like falling into a muck. Everything I learned at Silver Hill is gone. I am obsessed with Hank—*Hank! My friend Hank!*—the way I've been with everyone else before him. And I could say something, should say something, should make this stop before it gets any worse, but I'm not going to do that. I can't. I am not good at walking before I have to run. I'm an idiot. I deserve to be a drug addict. I never learn.

I should move back into the Cottage, really I should. And I know it. But that would be admitting defeat. That would prove I'm not fine. And I'm fine, really I am. Tomorrow I will go to a meeting. Tomorrow I won't use. Tomorrow is Day One.

After I admit I've been using, Dr. Singer prescribes ReVia. She has not seen me—I've been on the road—so she has no idea how bad it's been, and I'm not completely forthright. I make some noises about a few slips, and leave it at that. Even though ReVia, an opiate blocker, has no effect on cocaine, it's supposed to relieve cravings of all kinds, so Dr. Singer thinks it might be helpful.

But all it does, after the first dose, is give me a headache. An insane headache. It is Friday night, and I am supposed to meet my friend Toby for a movie. I don't know how I'll manage. I take a handful of Tylenol, swallow it down with some Snapple peach iced tea that is much too sweet, and hope for the best. I call Hank in desperation but he's not around, and that's when I realize I am over the edge. I am supposed to go see him in Weston tomorrow, but we have not made definite plans. I am certain he will disappear before I get there. I won't be able to reach him all day. I will hop on a train anyway, take myself out there, show up at the door, and wait on the front porch until he returns from wherever he's disappeared to. I can endure it. I will bring a pile of

Vogue and *Harper's Bazaar* and *New Yorker* magazines. I will sit there forever if I have to. He cannot disappear on me like this, not Hank. I won't have it.

I sit on my floor with my coarse, pulsing headache and cry. What is happening to me? I call José's beeper, and wait for him to phone back. The phone rings a few minutes later, but when I pick up it's Hank, wanting to figure out when I am going to come out.

My mind is playing tricks on me. Hank is doing everything right. It's *me* that's all wrong.

It's *just* Hank, I remind myself. How is it that even with Hank it's come to this? Even with someone I was friends with first, where we did it all the right way, it still feels lousy. Dr. Singer says this is just what happens with rehab romances, but I am not satisfied with that answer. I want it to be specific. It should be different. We're not just a pair of people who met at rehab—we are *us*, we are *Hank and Elizabeth*, we are individuals.

"Maybe so," Dr. Singer says. "But once again, your experience as an addict is not that much different from anyone else's. You can't think your way out of this one. That you and Hank are so smart does not mean you can overcome the realities of recent sobriety. The reason they warn people about this is long experience. There's no reason for you to be different."

"But it's *me*. It's *Hank*."

"Yes. It's an addict. And a drunk. And we have to stop."

I gather my belongings—the sunglasses on my lap and the case falling out of my pocketbook and the half-eaten glazed donut and the keys that have fallen down the side of the cushion of the chair and the shredded-up meeting schedule that I will never use—and make my way out of her office.

As I grip my hand on the doorknob—and my keys fall on the floor—I turn to Dr. Singer and ask, "Am I going to be okay?"

"You're going to be fine," she says, crossing her arms, looking down at the floor.

"Are you sure?"

"I'm sure."

"Promise?"

"I promise."

There's still more publicity to do in June. By this time I am doing coke almost every day, telling everyone that I'm not, and so it goes. This is almost worse than it was before I went to Silver Hill, because at least then I was honest, at least then it was a group project that everyone close to me could get involved in. But now I just keep denying that there is a problem. I make some television appearances where I am clearly disoriented, and afterwards Lydia always asks if I was wired when I went on the air.

"No, no, definitely not," I answer, calling her from a phone booth so I can get off when my quarter has run out. We don't have to have a long, taxing conversation.

"Don't lie to me," she says. "If you're using, I understand that that's what happens, and we'll just find a way to get you some help. If you're not honest with me, I can't do anything to help you."

"I'm not lying," I insist, impatient. Why doesn't she just leave me alone? And actually, I'm not lying. I snorted coke last night; I haven't actually done any *today*.

"All right," she says, sighing as ever.

The operator comes on to tell me to please deposit ten cents for the next three minutes. "Lydia, I'm out of change," I say, relieved. "Gotta go."

In the beginning of June I go to Holland, where I've always had a good audience. Everything is fine for the first few days, but then a novelist whom I met the first time I went to Amsterdam, to publicize my first book, comes to interview me. I have a huge crush on him, even though he is skinny and wears black eyeliner, and is into this gothic thing that I usually don't like. He's well known in Amsterdam as a brilliant novelist and a hopeless junkie.

"Let's get high," I say, as soon as he walks into my hotel room, which overlooks a canal and is all bright and airy and very un-drug-like.

"Sure," he says, and pulls out a stash of heroin and his works. In the next few hours we go through a bundle of dope—he shoots up, I snort up—and we smoke a whole bunch of crack, and then we go for a walk and visit the Anne Frank house. After that we go back to my hotel. There is more smack and more crack. I change dresses several times because I have brought all these pretty lacy things with me, even though it is too cold to wear them. But all doped up, I feel warm and sensual, so I revel in this silly fashion show.

We finally end up naked in my bed, too high and exhausted to do anything but sleep.

In the morning I can't get out of bed. I vomit on the floor next to the night table, and tell Saskia, the publicist who is handling my schedule, that I must have gotten food poisoning from all the raw oysters we ate in Brussels a couple of days before. Never mind that food poisoning doesn't incubate for that long. I try to get dressed to go to the hotel drawing room to do interviews, but I fall over as I walk out the door.

"We need to get you a doctor," Saskia says. She has that Dutch innocence about her, and I feel terrible failing her like this. Her eyes are hugely blue, her skin is translucent with youth and idealism. She is actually wearing a jumper and a headband, she is straight and studious. We worked together on my first book, and I just don't want her to feel disappointed in me now, especially after the last book went so swimmingly well. A few years back, Saskia was an assistant, but now she is in charge. This is her first big project, and I am going to fuck it up.

"No, I'm fine," I insist, as I lie on the floor in the hallway outside my room, my feet lingering across the threshold. "I'll just get up and get into bed, no big deal." But then I can't stand up, and Saskia has to walk me back into my room, my arm around her shoulder, my feet twisting behind me in a palsyish dance. Saskia sits at the desk and calls the concierge to ask him to send a doctor. She keeps glancing over at me, frightened. I am wearing a long gold silk skirt that I bought in Antwerp a couple of days earlier, with a black leotard. I could almost look elegant, if only vomit did not keep dribbling out of my mouth.

When the doctor arrives, Saskia leaves me alone with him. He is wearing wire-rimmed glasses and a denim work shirt, with a mop-top haircut like something out of *A Hard Day's Night*—a casual Amsterdam physician, laid back like everyone in Holland.

"Have you been doing heroin?" he asks. It's his first question. He has not even opened his medical bag, has not even pulled out his stethoscope. I used to be able to fool doctors so easily.

"No, of course not. I just got out of rehab. I've stopped using."

"We have many drug addicts here in Amsterdam," he says, ignoring my denials. "I treat many. I understand how easy it is to relapse. If you're honest with me, it would be much better. I won't tell anyone at your publisher."

"I think it's just food poisoning," I say. I'm not going to give up this oyster alibi.

"There is a lot of very strong heroin on the streets here, and if you've taken some, you need to tell me." He peels my eyelids back, and sees that my pupils are pinned. "I know you've been taking heroin. Why won't you just admit it?"

"Because I haven't been," I say lazily. I mean to be very tough and severe and certain, but I'm just too sleepy.

"All right, fine." He gives up. The Dutch are too polite to pursue any argument beyond a couple of compulsory back-and-forths. "I'm going to tell the young lady outside to stay here with you. If anything gets worse, I will tell her that you must go to the hospital."

"Sure." I roll away from him and fall asleep as Saskia comes back into the room.

I am supposed to leave the next day, but I'm too sick. The only alternate flight they can arrange will require a stop in Iceland. I don't get on the plane so much as I fall into it. In Reykjavík, I wander in the airport and miss my connection, so I take a taxi into the center of the city and check into a hotel, and spend the next twenty hours asleep. I had thought I'd walk around, take in the hot spring waters, experience the healing properties of lava, but there's just no way. Here I am, nearly at the North Pole, and all I can do is pass out. My luggage has gone to JFK without me, but I have one carry-on bag with my toiletries and jewelry in it. Somehow, I leave it at the hotel when I check out, and I cannot remember the name to call and ask them to send it to me. I lose all the rings and earrings that I've carried with me, including the lapis lazuli cabochon that Dr. Geller found so beautiful. At long last, everything I had at Silver Hill is gone.

By the time Hank leaves on a cross-country trip to Taos on June 25, I am a mess with him. I know he's not coming back. He's bought a new Jeep, since it's easier than getting his car back from the police. That's what I love about him: He is such a drunk, even when he's sober. Only a drunk would buy a whole new car to avoid paying a DWI fine and some overdue speeding tickets.

He decides he will spend the night with me and leave directly from my apartment. He just needs a few weeks' break from his aunt and uncle is all. He'll be back sometime in mid-July, maybe as soon as Independence Day, definitely before my birthday. In the morning we go to Nobody Beats the Wiz on lower Broadway, and Hank buys the kind of Discman that doesn't skip when it bumps around, the kind used by runners. I had offered him mine, the one Lydia bought me for Silver Hill—I don't need it anymore and I'll do anything for Hank—but it isn't sturdy enough for the road. He gets an adapter so the player can be powered by his cigarette lighter, and some little speakers. He's going to drive all the way to Taos, stopping for some fly-fishing with a buddy in Montana. He'll phone every day, at every stop. He'll miss me terribly.

He asks to borrow some of my CDs. I've got more than a thousand, on top of all the vinyl I still play on my wonderful old turntable. He has already told me that I am the only girl he has ever met with excellent music taste, who doesn't just buy what her boyfriend likes, or whatever most chicks do. That's always been my coolest quality as far as most men I've know are concerned, so that's nothing new. Still, anything that makes Hank love me more makes *me* like *me* more. He takes some Emmylou Harris and Lucinda Williams and Mazzy Star and Chris Whitley and Nina Simone. And I make a list of them; I write it on a piece of fax paper, the old-fashioned roller kind where the ink fades within six months. I take down the titles so I know what they are. Deep down I doubt I will ever see him again, and not my CDs either. At least if I have a list I will be able to replace them.

Hank calls the next day from Amherst, Ohio, about which there is not much to say, except that it has a NASCAR track. He had hoped to floor it and be in Michigan by now, but he didn't want any more moving violations on his record. I tell him that I've just returned from the gynecologist's office, that I have a terrible urinary tract infection.

"I feel fine," he says. "I guess I didn't catch it."

"I said I had a UTI, not the clap." I laugh. "Hank, it's not that kind of thing." I am so happy he has called like he said. "It comes from a rupturing in the vaginal walls. You get them from rough sex or frequent sex or sporadic sex—pretty much anything will do it. And once you've had one, you spend the rest of your life getting them. It's a bacterial infection—it doesn't usually affect men."

"Did we have rough sex?" he asks.

"No." I smile. "We had frequent sex episodically, one week on and one week off."

"Oh. I see."

This is what I like about Hank, his absent-minded-professor quality. Over thirty-six years of girlfriends, and he still has never heard of *interstitial cystitis*—the proper word for a bladder infection—which seems ridiculous, since all my friends have had them repeatedly.

"Don't worry about it," I say. "It's just uncomfortable. You take antibiotics and it's cured."

"Okay. Good." He's calling from a miserable motel, and he wants to go to sleep. He wants to get an early start tomorrow. "I'll get in touch from my next outpost."

He calls from Livingston, Montana, and Telluride, Colorado, and every other stop along the way to say he loves me and misses me and can't wait to see me, maybe I should come out and visit. But I know that's not going to happen, and I know he's not coming back. It's all so sweet, but I feel him slipping away. I think about the Replacements song "Sadly Beautiful," and the line "Baby needs a brand new pair of eyes / Because the ones you've got now see only good-byes."

Good-bye, Hank. Farewell, my lovely.

Twenty-two

TERMINAL UNIQUENESS

Early one morning, half past four
Cocaine came knocking on my door
Cocaine, run all around my brain

Hey baby, you better come here quick
This old cocaine is making me sick
Cocaine, run all around my brain

Well I reached into my pocket, grabbed my polk
Note in my pocket says "No more coke!"
Cocaine, run all around my brain

Cocaine's for horses, not for men
They tell me it'll kill me but they won't say when
Cocaine, run all around my brain

Yeah baby, come here quick
This old cocaine's about to make me sick
Cocaine, run all around my brain

"Cocaine Blues" (traditional)

I spend the whole summer doing drugs and waiting for Hank to call. Probably I do some other things, but they don't matter. And I can't tell anyone. I've been in rehab four months and I'm using again. No one will ever understand. So I keep it to myself and avoid everybody.

At least before Silver Hill I asked for help. No one was disappointed in me — they treated me as if I was sick, which I was. But now this is just shameful. There is no way anyone who is not an addict can comprehend that you can spend four months in treatment and then use the day you get out, even though it happens all the time. In fact, my guess is that it happens more often than not, and re-lapse—within a matter of days or weeks—is almost the rule. It seems that after rehab, many people feel a need to test themselves, to prove they can handle it, that they really *are* better—in fact, they are cured. They can use occasionally safely, they can be like most people again. It's ironic, of course, that the way that you prove you are healed is by doing the very thing that damaged you in the first place. I suppose it's not entirely counterintuitive: someone who breaks his leg skiing is likely to hit the slopes as soon as his bones are sufficiently merged and melded so that he can quickly overcome any fear he has of standing on skis. It's like the old adage about getting right back on the horse after you've fallen off.

But what can be said of an idiot who does drugs the first day out? This is what the Big Book and even the average idiot would call insanity.

And it's too insane to explain to any of my civilian friends. The smart thing would be to go to a meeting, where almost everybody in the room has experi-ence with relapse, but I cannot imagine how I will tell anyone—even people in recovery—that I spent four months at Silver Hill and used that first day out. I simply cannot cop to it. Shameless me with my raunchy talk—but I cannot admit that I am just like all the other addicts who fuck up. Maybe it happens to everybody else, but that does not mean it happens to me.

I am terminally unique.

And when I admit that to myself, I understand the major failure in my treat-ment at Silver Hill: I never surrendered completely; I never gave up on my self-conception as one of a kind. And in truth, in order to completely recover, you've got to do that. You just do. Otherwise you will find yourself sitting in a garret in Greenwich Village going through an eightball of cocaine a day after you have sunk sixty thousand dollars into a four-month hospital stay.

I got the crucial lessons from Silver Hill. I learned about going to meetings. I learned to love many people who were quite different from me. I learned that it feels better to be clean than dirty. I learned what life is for. But what I did not learn is that as an addict, I really am as goofy and grotesque as the next person.

I thought I could handle a romantic relationship that started in rehab, be-cause it was Hank and me, and we were *us*, we were *special*. I thought that somehow I could do drugs and still maintain the principles of sobriety: the need for rigorous honesty, the importance of feeling my emotions and not being scared of them, of praying to God and having faith. I saw no reason why I could not do all these good things and do drugs as well. I did not quite get that, by definition, if you are doing drugs, you are hiding from your feelings, you're not having faith in a loving God to see you through, and you are of ne-cessity being dishonest, because, let's face it: every day that I use I tell myself I am not going to, but I do anyway; I certainly lie to everybody else about it. I tell myself I will go to a meeting tomorrow, that Day One starts tomorrow, but this never happens.

At Silver Hill I came to believe that taking drugs was a symptom of my depression, but I never quite understood that it had become a problem itself. I believed I had gotten *addicted* to drugs, but I did not believe that I was an *addict*. Hence, I felt that if I cured the addiction, I could use again. I did not understand that it was the addict herself that needed to be cured. I had come to separate my behavior from my essential self, even though I believe that you are what you do.

I remember learning in the *Nicomachean Ethics* that Aristotle taught that happiness was deeds, not emotions. And I always liked that. I always liked the idea that if you made certain choices and lived a certain way you would be happy—happiness is not a *state*, it's an *activity*. Of course, that is the Twelve Step premise. As they have been telling me since I first got into recovery, *You can't think your way into acting, but you can act your way into thinking.* Somehow, as soon as I got out of Silver Hill, I figured that my feelings were finally straight, and I seem to have forgotten that my solid emotional state needed to be buttressed with good living, day by day. I thought willpower alone could keep me sane. Abandoning all the things I needed to do—praying, going to meetings, and, most of all, not using—turned me into a wreck obsessed with Hank and otherwise doing little else besides drugs to keep from being obsessed with Hank.

I had reverted completely back to type. Congratulations, Miss Wurtzel: you are the same as ever. Your resilience, your ability to bounce back to your old bad habits, is admirable. You are to be commended for your stubborn desire to stay the same. Your uniqueness has made you a common idiot.

By refusing to admit that you are a common idiot, you have become one.

Hank doesn't make it back for the Fourth of July. Hank doesn't make it back for my birthday. Still, every day I wait, like Penelope without a loom. He moves out to a mesa outside of Taos, really settles in, but he still insists it's just for the summer. He calls almost every day, and I am usually snorting lines when he reaches me. Then, as July turns into August, Hank doesn't call every day anymore. Every few days.

Then finally one Monday afternoon, I phone him. A woman answers. "Who is this?" I ask.

"A friend."

"I see." I am about to cry. "Well, is Hank there?"

He picks up another extension. The woman hangs up. "Who was that?" I ask, knowing I should just be cool, but I can't be. I'm losing him. How can this be happening with Hank? He was my best friend. And now this.

"My neighbor. Rachel. I'm driving her to the airport."

"I see." I'm relieved. She's just there to get a ride. But I can't let it go. "Are you sleeping with her?"

"No." He sounds annoyed. "Elizabeth, for God's sake, she's my neighbor. And besides, it's none of your business."

I start to cry. "This hurts. Imagine how this would make me feel."

"Shhh," he says. "Nothing's going on. Rachel's got a flight to make. I'll call you later."

Days go by. I finally hear from him. He tells me to stop worrying, that nothing's changed. We talk about when I might visit. Labor Day weekend maybe. But he might be coming back so soon that what's the point.

It is a Sunday afternoon in mid-August. Hot, the dog days of summer. Dr. Singer is out of town. Most of my friends who have normal jobs are on vacation because nothing much goes on this time of year because everyone else is on vacation too. As far as I am concerned, this is one big conspiracy to drive me crazy. I am all alone in this city, my air conditioner has broken, it needs more freon or something like that, and I am boiling and alone. Hank had said something about my coming to Taos this week, so I never made an effort to plan anything else. But now he's still there, I'm still here, and cocaine is my cold comfort. And I am falling and fading fast, and I know it.

So I page Paco, José's partner, who comes around to the front of my building to pick me up so we can do a deal. I get into the burgundy sedan with its tinted windows, and sit down in the backseat. Next to me is his three-year-old son, playing with his Hooked on Phonics game, so I ask him if he likes to learn. He says yes. I ask him if he wants to go to college, and he does not know what I mean, so there goes that.

The child's mother, who may or may not be Paco's wife, sits in the front seat, so I tell her how cute the kid is. I hand five $20 bills to Paco, and he puts five little plastic bags of coke in my hands, and we drive around the corner a couple of times. I live near Washington Square Park, and there are always tons of cops around trying to catch the petty pot dealers who loiter in the plaza, so we have to be very careful. We have to keep moving so that it does not look like anyone has made a quick stop to make a delivery and dash away. At night, there are lots of stops and starts in this neighborhood, lots of out-of-towners checking out the scene, but on this weekend afternoon with the city half-empty and everyone's actions more conspicuous, we need to take precautions. We have to appear to be on a leisurely drive. Which is why I am going to be in this car with this makeshift nuclear clan for at least a little while.

I chat with the mother in the front seat, and in her deep Dominican accent she tells me about their district in Washington Heights. I talk to the kid a bit more, I ask where he is in school, and I realize that on some other planet, or at least in some other place, this would be a perfectly normal Sunday afternoon outing. We kind of are a family: I need these people and they need me for our mutual survival. Any day now I will be offering to sponsor their citizenship applications and tutoring them for their GED tests. This is the beautiful American way. And it is not happening on some other planet. It is happening right here in my life, and who can say that this is not perfectly normal.

I never get to Taos. I wait for Hank. I wait and wait. Finally I decide to move.

I will find a new apartment where nothing has ever happened and start anew. My lease is up, and I am getting a little too old to live in a place where I have to climb a ladder to get into bed. I am a little too old for a house with a tilted floor, where I have to hold the banister as I walk up the four flights because the stairway is so slanted that I often feel vertigo, as though I am going to fall. The pink rubber ball that the cat plays with always rests on one side of the room because it just rolls that way. My shelves appear to be keeling over. I often refer to this little eighteenth-century building, with all its tragic and triumphant charm, as falling-down house. I have a feeling we are going to topple over any day now. I will die as bricks fall onto my head and crush my skull. I will be sweating because of the faulty air conditioner, and my last thought will be, *Where did the coke disappear to in all this rubble?* My life will flash before me, and it will all be white powder.

Actually, life itself is not unlike that.

I look around at different apartments. August is a horrible time to move in New York, especially in the Village. NYU students are back to school, and everyone is looking for a place to live. I see different things. Something is wrong with all of them. In the Village, it is hard to find anything that is not a walk-up, and unless it's just one or two stories, I've had it with climbing flights of stairs. If it isn't too small, it's too dark. I am determined to find something bright and cheery, something that makes me feel clean. I want prewar but well lighted, which is hard. I finally see a place I love, a duplex with a spiral staircase and skylights and a couple of bedrooms that is very cheap. And then I find out why: It is over Ollie's Noodles, a Chinese restaurant, and the tenant who is moving out, a Columbia Law School student, tells me that she has ten or twenty mice, that it's to the point where she thinks of them as pets because two cats and traps everywhere cannot get rid of them.

There's no way I can live with that.

And then finally I find a place in Tribeca, far below Canal Street, on the south end of Manhattan. It's a newish building, and I don't like the idea of living in a place with no history, no vintage. But the apartment has a western view, I can see the Hudson River, and I overlook an elementary school and the American flag on the roof, which I love. There is a dishwasher in the apartment and a laundry room in the basement, which is a luxury after years of dragging bags of clothes to the Chinese laundromat two blocks away. The bathroom is marble, the floors are wood, and the windows are shapely. They jut out in an oval, so it's not completely charmless. There is access to the roof. Battery Park is nearby.

But the advantage to Tribeca is something else entirely. The FBI field office is a few blocks away, and the central police precinct is even closer—the police horses are always docked nearby. And it is a family neighborhood. The school across the street is the best public school in New York, so many couples with kids want to live in the area. There is also a lot of good loft space, room for lots of children, and it is just above the financial district, so rich Wall Street investment bankers have bought apartments in the converted factories and warehouses. All I ever see are strollers and stay-at-home mommies with their little kids walking toward the park. There is a pretty public garden right opposite my building. Although Tribeca is supposed to be a hip downtown neighborhood, it is really more like the Upper East Side shifted to an area below SoHo. Per square foot, it is more expensive to buy a place in this area than it is on Park Avenue—only Fifth Avenue and Central Park West cost more. My rent is high—too high—but as long as I am not buying, I can afford it. So against everything I believe in, I decide to sign a lease in this bright new place where the doormen are called concierges, and the flowers in the lobby are delivered fresh every day.

It is a good idea. This is a drug-free environment. It will be impossible to get into trouble around here. This building is filled with fifty-year-old white couples with adopted Chinese daughters named Rose and Filipino nannies named Marife.

All I know is that here I will be safe. In my new apartment I will not do drugs.

Right before I am about to move, I have a meeting at Doubleday to sort out what new publicity we will do for *Bitch*, since my tour was such a disaster. There's no way they will let me go on the road again for the paperback, so we need to come up with new plans. It is my idea to have this meeting, with the vice president for media relations, and Betsy and Lydia.

Somehow, I just don't get there. Well, I do, but two hours late. Suzanne, the publicity head, is not mad, because she hasn't had to deal with me enough to be fed up with things like this. But Lydia has gone back to her office before I've arrived, and Betsy is fuming down the hall.

I apologize to her, and I apologize to Lydia, but they are spent. They've been through this too much.

"I know you're doing drugs again," Betsy says.

"No, I'm not," and I explain that I had a stomach virus, that I was throwing up.

"Fine," she says, and doesn't argue.

"I know you're doing drugs again," Lydia says, and she cites all my appearances on MSNBC and CNN to talk about Monica Lewinsky and Hillary Clinton where I was fading in front of the camera, where I needed to be prompted by the interviewer more than once, where my eyes were far away, where I kept dabbing my nose with a Kleenex.

"No, I'm not," I say, and tell her it's just that staying clean is tiring, so I always look dazed. My nose is still healing. But I'm not using. If anything, I'm recovering.

"I know you're lying," she says. "But fine. I can't argue with you any more."

The content of life is not that different; it's the context that changes. I can have conversations with people, I can read my mail, I can feed the fish in the aquarium. I can have unilateral debates about capital punishment for hours. No one disagrees with me, and still I'm fighting, I'm yelling. But sometimes I'm like that anyway. I don't need drugs to be a pain in the ass.

The picture you have of a drug addict, with everything run amok, dirty dishes in the sink, garbage cans overfilled, never emptied, rats and roaches everywhere and no one notices—that picture is not quite right. It's not Frank Sinatra in The Man with the Golden Arm. *It's not all stealing TVs and living in crack houses and shooting galleries. Eventually, at the end, it can be like that. That's when you bottom out. But even then, if you're like me, you can live in a lovely place and have clean blond hair and wear mascara every day. Years can go by where all procedure is the same. Most people will say,* We had no idea she was on drugs. *And it's not because they're stupid. It's because the changes are subtle, the universe is parallel, you speak a little too quickly, your voice is more shrieky, you seem not to be paying attention, you stare too long and too hard at the wall or some detail in the Persian rug. Most people can't tell that's a problem. Most people have their own problems.*

It's the people you are close to, the ones who love you, the ones who have seen your heart, who have touched your soul—to them, it is obvious that something is wrong or missing. Your heart and soul are missing. They feel it. It hurts them. It kills them.

But then when you say, I'm fine, I still go to work, I still eat breakfast. What makes you think there's a problem? *they can't answer. They'll say,* Something is just different. You're not here. I miss the person you used to be. What's happened to you? *But they can't point to any one thing.* You get angry a little too quickly, *they say. And then they say, trying to find a real example:* When I asked if you'd mind throwing this envelope in the mailbox as you walk by it—don't even go half a block out of your way—you act like it's a big nuisance. Like you've got so many better things to do, when you do nothing at all, all day. *Or maybe they notice that whenever you're supposed to meet them, you have an errand to run on the way, you swear it will take five minutes, fifteen tops. But then you are two hours late. You say you got detained because some man on the street had a heart attack and you waited with him for the ambulance, you helped the* EMT *resuscitate him, you were busy being a hero, and no one dares to say that you were waiting for the man on Avenue D, that that's where you really were. They don't say it, because you'll just deny it. And what's the point, because you argue so vehemently, you walk out, you slam doors, you say,* Fuck you. I haven't used in a month, you don't trust me, you don't love me. *And everyone gets exasperated. Then two hours later, you call them. You say,* Don't you love me?

There are tears and there are loss and sorrow, but all the evidence is circumstantial. They can't find your stash. For all they know, you were in the bathroom for twenty minutes with a stomachache. They can't prove their suspicions. Somehow, on drugs you become a brilliant high school debater. You become fixated on winning your point, because all you've got is being right. The idea that there is an emotional context does not matter. The idea that it hurts the people who love you, that it just does, has no effect.

Someone says, I love you, *and you don't care. You ask them. They tell you with frustrated, downcast eyes, but really who cares? It means something, it's a nice thought, you feel it a little bit, but really, how can it compete with the drugs? Nothing can compete.*

Twenty-three

I THREW IT ALL AWAY

I've been waiting my whole life to fuck up like this.

ROBERT STONE
Dog Soldiers

Moving is hell. Mae-Mae comes over to help me pack. Finally she just packs everything up herself because I am helpless in the face of it. I insist on paying her, because she does all the work, this is hardly a friend lending a hand. She insists I don't. I insist I do. We go back and forth about it for a while. I try to estimate her hours, try to figure out a rate, and finally I just write her a check for two hundred dollars and insist she take it, and she is so worn out that she just does.

My mother helps me get the cat and my clothes and a few personal belongings over to my new apartment. Zap sits in the back of the car, by the window on top of the seat, panting and screaming, his tongue drooping and spittle dropping out of his mouth, petrified. Once I get inside the apartment, I hang up my clothes and set up a few rudimentary items, get my computer on my desk, push a table around, put some dishes away in the kitchen cabinet. My mother helps me take the boxes of research material into the storage area I have downstairs, another benefit of this nice full-service building. My shelves get delivered, a new bed arrives to replace the futon I've been sleeping on in the loft, and I put up the antique black wrought-iron headboard that I inherited from my parents' first apartment, which was stowed away in a closet while I lived on Carmine Street.

But I know I cannot empty boxes without using cocaine, so I just don't bother. Mae-Mae says she will come help me unpack. But it's not as convenient as crossing the street and she is spent from having packed me, so we keep making dates for her to come over, and she keeps canceling at the last minute.

So the boxes just sit there, untouched, as if I am planning to leave again some-time soon. I empty my books out onto the living room floor. I need to hammer the shelves into their cases, and there's no way I can do it myself, so all the books stay in piles. The CDs traveled in their towers with duct tape across them, so I don't need to unpack them. My stereo has broken en route, so I just listen to music on the little Discman and speakers that Lydia gave me to take to Silver Hill. Thank God it didn't go to Taos with Hank.

Hank shows up a week after I move in, just before Labor Day weekend. He has job interviews, so he is in the city. He is thinking of working in technology, or at a hedge fund, or maybe crunching numbers as an arbitrageur. He is thinking about a lot of possibilities, but his favorite seems to be returning to Taos and bumming around for another year or so, until the money runs out. The thought of this breaks my heart. Of course, if he wants me to go back there with him, that's another matter. I would love to. Sure, we've only been together for a few months. Sure, we've only been in the same place for less than that, but I'm ready to pack it in and run off with him if he asks. I'm ready to go with him to New Zealand if that's what he wants. Nothing in my life means anything to me any-more besides Hank. It's all gone, and I'm gone on him.

On the day Hank is due, I put on a pretty black and burgundy sundress with lots of little flowers on it and an elegant tight bodice. I apply lipstick and eye-shadow and all kinds of makeup that I never wear, get myself all done up for Hank. I am, deep down, such a girl. Hank arrives at my apartment in a dark businessman's suit, carrying a duffel bag, at four o'clock. He proceeds to un-pack. I flip through a loose-leaf notebook he is carrying around with graphs charting financial cycles for the next thirty years, a phone list that includes Rachel's Taos number along with several others scribbled in, with area codes I'm not familiar with. She seems to live in many places. But what do I care? From the looks of things, Hank seems to think he is moving in here with me, although we have not discussed it.

We don't discuss anything any longer. I don't ask him his plans because they never seem to include me anyway. I know I will just irritate him by asking when he will be back, and I'll start to sound clingy and needy—and even I hate hearing myself that way, so imagine how he feels. Partly, it is so annoying to listen to me in that mode because it is false: I can't control myself, but it's just like what Dr. Geller told me I shouldn't do. It's misapplying my emo-tions—it expresses a need for affirmation, not a need for love. So I just shut up, keep my own counsel, and hope Hank will turn up. Now he has.

At five-thirty, just an hour and a half after his arrival, I leave Hank alone for a couple of hours. I am going up to Smithers, a drug treatment program at Roosevelt Hospital, to attend an introductory meeting for its evening sessions. I have decided to take new steps toward getting clean and staying that way, and Dr. Singer thinks this is the best outpatient program in New York, and maybe anywhere. I explain to Hank that I really need to go to this, I tell myself that I should not drop everything just because he's here, and I run out of my building, run for the number 1 train, and head uptown.

This is the beginning of everything new: Hank is back, I am not going to do coke anymore, the miracle begins today.

But when I walk back into my apartment at eight or so, Hank is gone. All his stuff is gone. He has left the keys with the doorman. There is a note written in a childish scrawl on a paper towel, the ballpoint pen has made slashes with its nib. "Have gone to Connecticut. Will call later." I can hear him saying this, hear him pronouncing the middle "c" in the state's name. I guess this must be some kind of new record: How many couples can say that they lived together for just ninety minutes?

I call his aunt in Weston to see if she's heard from him, but she hasn't. I sit frozen and desperate in my house for hours, call friends crying, ask Kathlyn to come over and stay with me. I am scared to go out again in case he comes back—if he does, there is no way I am letting him out of the house again—and I am afraid to be alone because I already feel so alone. And I know he will not call later. I know I will probably never see him or hear from him again. He is that slippery.

What has happened to him? What has happened to my Hank? The one I used to know would never do this, never disappear like this.

When we met at Silver Hill, he described his behavior as a drunk, what he was like, how he would rage for days, go naked on a train in Chicago, get on a cruise ship to Alaska. I thought he was lying. Because at Silver Hill he was so dependable. He would come by in his pickup truck to take me into town to get my prescriptions filled at CVS, or to have lunch at Gates, or to go for a drive to the beach in Westport. We would plan to see a movie after an AA meeting, and he would get me just as it ended, on time, always when he was supposed to. He did what he said he would do, like most people, I guess. I could always find him. I never wondered.

I call Kathlyn again. She says she won't come over. She has just returned from vacation, and she's unwinding and watching a rerun of *Seinfeld*. I am welcome to come join her.

"I can't leave," I say. "What if he calls?"

"He can call your cell phone, can't he?" she asks.

"He can," I say. "But he probably won't. My guess is he's really not dying to find me, and he'd rather just leave me a message."

"Oh," Kathlyn says, because what else is there to say?

I have just bought a mobile phone. It is a birthday present to myself. But it is really more of a gift to Lydia and everyone who needs to reach me and complains that they can't. I'm always wandering the streets during business hours—that is, when I am not sleeping. I go out for tea at a place in SoHo called, appropriately, T, in the middle of the afternoon. I buy peridot rings and amethyst necklaces and candles that smell like frankincense and marbleized paper stationery and more purple Pilot pens. I go to therapy and sometimes meetings. Entire days go by when the only useful thing I do is contribute to the gross national product. So now I carry around a phone, and anyone can reach me anytime, but I know that Hank won't make use of it. He doesn't have a cell phone, so the only way to leave him a message is on his machine in Taos.

"Do you suppose Hank is drinking?" Kathlyn asks.

"No," I say, without even thinking. "God, no. He's been staying clean and going on hikes and doing all this nature stuff. He's definitely not drinking."

"You sure?"

"Positive." But as soon as I say it, I start to wonder if it's true. After all, everything he's doing would indicate relapse: he's run away—*pulled a geographic*, as they say in recovery—and he's not going to meetings, and he's cutting the people who know him in sobriety out of his life. He's cutting me out of his life, it seems, and I've only known him as a sober person. I may in fact be the only one he's close to who has never seen him drunk.

That's the crucial difference between Hank and me: my personality is not predicated on drugs. For the first twenty-seven years of my life, I did not have much of a relationship with controlled substances at all. I had my phase during my freshman year of college, but that mainly involved Ecstasy, and by sophomore year I had lost interest. Hank started drinking before he was a teenager. His development into an adult was completely shaped by alcohol. For him to be sober is not natural; he would need to re-create his heart and soul in order to accommodate a life without booze, and there is no way he could possibly do that without meetings. Even I, who have nothing but clean-living friends, am not able to stay straight without going to AA and NA. How could Hank, living in almost complete isolation on a mesa in New Mexico, be keeping sober? Maybe that's what's happened to him. Maybe he's drunk. Or at any rate, he is at the very least a *dry* drunk—without actively participating in a sober lifestyle, he has reverted to the habits and traits of an alcoholic, but without the benefit of alcohol itself to cushion his contact with life's slings and arrows. It would almost be better if he were actually drinking, because at least that would provide a coping mechanism. Without liquor, all that Hank can do to get through the day is avoid it all. Which means avoiding me.

If he is not already drinking, Hank probably will be sometime soon. I suppose I should just come to terms with that. And I know that alcohol changes people. I am told by my friends that I am a different person on cocaine, but I don't see it. I can't see myself. Liquor, I know, makes leaps in personality like no other drug: cocaine you're wound up, heroin you're wound down, but alcohol you're just all over the place, streamers flying around a maypole. But I never knew anyone could be this squirrely.

Hank is obviously slip-sliding out of my life. I don't hear from him all night, and when I finally talk to him the next day, he says something about how he had to have dinner with some potential clients or some people he used to work with or something like that—it all sounds terribly dubious, fishy—up in Westchester, in Rye. I mean, since when do you have a business meeting in *Chappaqua?*

"When are you coming back to the city to see me?" I ask.

"I'm not," he says. "I'm getting on a flight to New Mexico later today. I don't want to be here anymore."

"But what about, um, what about—" my voice trails off. "Hank, what about seeing me? Don't you want to spend some time with me?" I have that feeling of tension behind my eyes, the kind I get when I am trying to hold back tears—when I am desperately trying to stay cool. And I know I have to. Any sign of emotion from me is only going to alienate Hank. He can't handle it. I should just give up on him, for Christ's sake.

"No, I don't," he says, all harshness. I feel like plastic wrap being ripped across a serrated edge. It's that sharp and painful. "I want to go back to Taos. I want to get away from here."

"Do you want to stop by on your way to the airport?" I try. After all, I'm on his way to any of the three.

"No, Elizabeth, just forget about it for now." He pauses, and I can hear a little bit of compassion in his voice. "Look, I'll be back in a month or so, and I'll see you then. I'm sorry about this. I just can't be here right now."

"Okay," I say. "I understand." I do, but I don't. I understand he needs to run and hide, and I know one of the things he needs to run and hide from is me. And I know it's nothing personal—and that only makes it worse. If he were doing any of this in response to me—even if he were being incredibly mean—it would almost feel better than knowing that his decisions have absolutely *nothing* to do with me. Whenever somebody says, *It's nothing personal,* I always want to remind him that that's no comfort at all.

Okay, well, I'm not going to start using again over Hank. I'm going to stay straight in spite of him—or maybe because of him. It does not matter which.

So I go to meetings, I do all the right things, I commit to a Wednesday night group at Smithers. I'm going to get with it. It's going to be good.

And then one night, in the interest of healthy living, I decide to try to unpack. It will be easier to stay clean in a clean house. I will set up my shelves, I will buy a couch and a coffee table—I can even do that through a catalogue from Ikea or Pottery Barn without leaving the house—and I will become a citizen of the world. I will belong to the living. I will call Time Warner and have them send over the cable guy. I will buy a dish rack and wash my mugs and plates as I use them. I will go to the Food Emporium and pick up some canned soup and radicchio and other salad greens, I will get some Paul Newman oil-and-vinegar concoction, and I will start eating again.

I pull some sealing tape off a wooden milk crate that I've had for years, since I was little. It is bright orange, painted in acrylic, from back in the days when milk was delivered in bottles to the door, along with cloth diapers. The tape completely covers the whole top of the box, since it's open. Inside are some old notebooks, some research and documents that I referred to when I was writing my first book. I should really just take it down to my storage room, but I'd actually like to use the box itself—it has a lot of colorful character—along with three others that I have just like it, as a TV stand, a place to keep some books and magazines. It is decorative in that artful artless way. So I take out its contents and decide I'll transfer all the stuff into a utilitarian cardboard box. When it is finally empty, I notice something at the bottom, something shiny and small and smooth and glass. I pick it up, and lo and behold, it is an amber vial of cocaine. A bullet. It must be very old. They haven't been bottling cocaine for years. They switched to little bags sometime in 1996, as if the collective subconscious of drug dealers screamed out all at once, "Plastics!" As if it were the man talking to Dustin Hoffman as he floated in the pool in *The Graduate*.

And I know what I should do. I should call someone from recovery, maybe Mae-Mae, or maybe one of the people from the Tribeca meeting who has shoved her phone number, written on the back of an ATM receipt, into my hands as soon as she's learned I am a newcomer. I could do that. Anybody from AA would gladly drop everything to come here and help me flush the contents of this miniature jar down the toilet.

But it's not going to happen.

If this vial has been sitting in this box for the last two or so years—how it got there I cannot imagine, but I do seem to recall some night long ago when I was certain that I was running short—then it's meant to be. God—or Satan, I suppose—wants me to do cocaine. He put this here for a reason. I had no intention of unpacking; there was no reason to ever look in this box. This is kismet, serendipity, happy happenstance. I unscrew the little black cap off the little stained-glass bullet, stick the vial into my nose, and snort up the powder.

After two years, it is still delicious. I spend the rest of the night getting wired. And when I run out, I page Paco for more. When he comes over, he gives me a big hug, tells me he was worried about me after he hadn't heard from me for so long. Tells me he missed me. I give him a copy of *Nación Prozac*—that's the Spanish translation of my book—along with several twenty-dollar bills, and we're back in business.

It all starts to happen all over again. One night I am supposed to go to the premiere of some Kris Kristofferson movie that sounds kind of tedious—something about a military man—but no one ever invites me to these things anymore, people seem to think I've moved to Florida, so I am excited. I am supposed to bring one guest with me, but somehow I've invited Kathlyn and Lily and Mae-Mae and Toby, and all of them seem to want to go. The dinner afterwards is at Lespinasse, a fancy-schmancy French restaurant where there is a six-month wait for reservations, so all of them turn up at the Paris Theatre next door to the Plaza Hotel at seven o'clock, and of course I'm not there. I'm not there because I'm asleep. After being awake for twenty-four hours, I am now on the twenty-four-hour sleep part of the cycle.

Kathlyn calls from her cell phone. I hear her voice yelling to me on my answering machine, so I reluctantly pick up the receiver, just barely awake. I tell her that I'm sick, I've got the flu, oh my God I'm so sorry for not checking in earlier, I've been passed out with a fever, you know how it is. All my friends have found each other, and I tell Kathlyn to just lead them all in and tell the publicist that I'm on my way, and I fall back to sleep. I have no idea what makes me think I am so significant that the people in charge of this premiere are going to let in four of my friends without me, but I just kind of know it will be all right. It always is. Movie publicists tend to be friendly to people who are theoretically invited to some event.

They call a few more times that night. I hear Mae-Mae's voice from a pay phone at the restaurant. I hear Lily phoning up once she's home because she's tired and needs to go to work the next day. And finally Kathlyn calls me from a taxicab to say that she's just had an accident. The driver stopped short, and she was flung into the Lexan divider. She's chipped a tooth, and she's got a shiner on her eye and another bruise on her cheek.

"Jesus," I say, as if I care. "Do you need me to come over and take care of you?"

"No, no, that's okay," she says, sounding calm and frantic all at once. "I'm really okay. Daniel is supposed to come by later. Besides, you've got the flu."

"Yeah, I do. But if you need me, I can pull myself together." Thank God, she doesn't. If she did I'd be obligated. Here we go again. I'm back to being a fucked-up failure. I get back into bed, fall back into the slumber of the dead, the sleep of the guilty. I'll get some more cocaine tomorrow.

Kathlyn comes by to see the apartment after work on Friday. She is supposed to stop at home and change clothes, but she calls from a taxi to say she is on her way, she is coming directly. She works on lower Broadway, in the financial district, which is right near my new place, so it's silly for her to make a detour uptown first. She thinks I'll be happy to see her earlier. She thinks I'm looking forward to company. So I just go along with it, tell her I can't wait.

But this sucks. I have already called my dealer. He too may be on his way. I need my fix. I cannot go without it. When she arrives, I say that I have to go out and buy some laundry detergent. Why not wait until later? she asks. I say that it's important to go before the supermarket closes, that I resent the markup at the convenience store. I figure I can appeal to her sense of pragmatism, that my thrift will win points with her.

And I am right. She says she'll just wait and play with the cat. God, she is easy.

I call Paco again—I knew there was a reason to get this mobile phone—and ask when he will be here. I tell him to meet me at the Food Emporium instead. Shweew, we manage. When I get to my apartment and see Kathlyn again, she is astonished by how much more cheerful and less anxious I am. She thinks I've been clean since Silver Hill, or at least I think she thinks so— and her hope is her denial—so she figures I am just happy. I'm wired, not happy. She's been in her house in Bridgehampton four days a week all summer—she's the boss, she can work wherever she likes as long as she's got her computer and her hookup to Bloomberg—and then she was on a dude ranch in Montana riding horses for two weeks, so we haven't really seen each other much all summer. It's been so long since I have spent time with her or anybody else that she no longer knows what my normal state is.

get clean again. This time it lasts for a couple of weeks. I go to my Wednesday night group at Smithers, where everyone is newly sober and everyone is relapsing all the time, so I am not ashamed to discuss my on-again, off-again relationship with cocaine. I go to meetings every day, mostly at Perry Street, mostly during the day when no one I know is there, and I confess about my relapses, and everyone is supportive as all hell. People there seem to be constantly slipping themselves. I realize there's no reason to hide my own bad habits. So I stay straight. The principle of the program seems to work its magic on me. By sharing with other addicts, I end my isolation and start to feel okay again. It makes sense: it's fall, after all, back to school, time to start again.

Then one night I am alone in my house, preparing for an overseas work trip. I am going to Stockholm to do publicity for the Swedish publication of *Bitch*. Scandinavia is an international hub for depression, and my first book was so big there that I am almost a rock star.

And then it happens again. I pull out my loden-green peacoat because it is already cold in Stockholm. I reach into one of the pockets—it's torn and I end up pushing my hand through the acetate, into the lining of the coat—to throw away any loose papers and credit card receipts that might have been stuffed away there. And amid all the used movie tickets, soft from age and sweaty palms, and among the folded and crumpled-up phone numbers with names I can no longer place, I feel a little plastic bag of cocaine. How did this get here? I seem to recall being with Ben one night last year and having the distinct sense that I was short one bag—could it have been in this half-ripped pocket all this time?

Jesus Christ—do the surprises never end? I am almost ready to call someone for help. This time it starts to seem too ridiculous to indulge one more time.

But then I say to myself: *one more time.* What's one more time? I'll just finish off this little bag. It's not so bad. There isn't that much in it. I can handle a little bit. I've already converted what money I have into kronor, and I am otherwise all tapped out. I'm waiting for a couple of checks to clear, but I have no available cash. I thought about asking Kathlyn or Lily if I could borrow money, but it's too embarrassing. I've done it too often. They both always have the same reaction: You make enough money, so why don't you ever have any? And I always make excuses—I forgot to ask my accountant to make a deposit into my bank and like that—which are basically true. But in reality I am a hellhole of financial mismanagement, for obvious reasons, and I hate having to explain. I have a small balance left on my credit card if I need to buy anything while I'm in Sweden, but that's it. So I won't be able to get any more cocaine anyway. It will be fine. Lydia has already arranged for me to take a car service to Newark with a company that her agency has an account with, since she wants to be sure I get to the airport on time. So I have not even put aside any spare bills for the ride tomorrow. I'm perfectly safe.

And then two hours later I am on the phone with Paco. He tells me I can pay him when I get back.

Here we go again.

It's three in the afternoon, and I call Mae-Mae. I have just phoned the car service, and I was supposed to have called hours ago. They won't have anything available until five, which is when I need to be at the airport. I still have not packed, although I have had my bag out and open, waiting to receive its contents, for some hours now. It seems like so much trouble to get my jeans out of the closet. I am still wearing the same clothes I had on yesterday. I need to shower.

"Mae-Mae, help me," I say with little conviction when she picks up the receiver. "I need to be at the airport by five, I haven't packed yet, I can't get a car to take me, and I have no money. Can you please drive me?" She's got this banged-up old station wagon that used to belong to her parents.

"You can't take a taxi?"

"I have no money. None." How to explain? "You know how when people say they don't have any money, they usually mean they have a few dollars, but they're running low? Well, Mae-Mae, I truly have *no* money. I think I've got a token. But there's no subway that goes to Newark."

"I see."

"Look, Mae-Mae, I've been doing coke all night. All right? That's the truth." I can't lie anymore. "I found some from a long time ago in my coat pocket, and I got started. I thought I'd just do a little, and that's not what ended up happening. You know how it is."

"All right, look, I'll come over and get you. My car is parked uptown, so I can't be there before four."

"Why can't you come now?" I'm whining. "My flight is at six, I need to be there by five." I think for a minute. "Look, maybe we can make it in an hour. All right, just get here as soon as possible."

"Are you still doing coke?" Mae-Mae asks. She hasn't gone to any meetings and somehow she has done no heroin since we left Silver Hill. She was a hard-core junkie. It seems so unfair that it's so easy for her to stay clean.

"I've got a little left," I lie. "Actually, I have a lot left. I got enough for the trip. I know I'm not going to get through the next few days without it."

"All right, look, I'll be there soon."

I take a shower, which doesn't help, and it's really hard for me to manage to get shampoo to my hair or soap to my body. I'm just wasted. I sort of pack. Mae-Mae arrives at four-thirty, I still haven't put my toiletries together, and it's clear that there's no way I'll be at the airport on time. With rush hour traffic in the Holland Tunnel, forget it. Mae-Mae pulls me up off the floor, asks if there's anything I need to take that I haven't got in my bag—do I have enough sweaters?—and I keep doing lines until we finally have to leave.

"Maybe you need to go to meetings," Mae-Mae says as we pull out of her parking space.

"This is just a freak event. I'm fine."

We need to stop and get gas, I need to get some bottled water because I'm dehydrated, but none of these things matters because the bottleneck traffic into the tunnel means that we are stuck on Canal Street for over an hour, waiting to enter. Plus the car has blown a fuse, the windows are open, and when it starts to rain we can't close them. The drops seem to be horizontal, flying into the car like houseflies. I am wet, I am wired, and I am in a 1974 Impala station wagon with wooden panels on the exterior. It's almost seven by the time we get out of the tunnel in New Jersey. Since I've obviously missed my flight, there's just no reason to even bother. I call SAS to see when the next plane to Stockholm leaves, and it's not until tomorrow morning. Fuck it. Mae-Mae gets lost looking for the airport. She is supposed to meet a friend in Hoboken—that's part of the reason she was willing to give me a lift, she figured she'd drop me and go to Hoboken afterward—so I tell her, Fuck it, let's just go there for dinner.

We end up in some dive eating fish-cake sandwiches with too much tartar sauce. Mae-Mae's friend never shows up, and as we sit there something hits me: This is really horrible. This is not just some small mistake. This is a serious mess. I have never missed an airplane in my life, certainly not an international flight, and I am expected in Stockholm in the morning to do a press conference as soon as I arrive. I've already been informed that fifty journalists will be there, and they've done this so I can get several interviews out of the way at once and won't need to work so hard. My Swedish publishers know that I just got clean. They know I have limited energy, so they have done this to make it easier. They even included an NA meeting in my schedule.

Oh well.

That aside, I have been writing a column for *The Guardian* in London every other week, and I have one due this Monday. It's Thursday. I was going to get it written before I left, but there went that. It's already not been going well. I've been getting high or falling low almost every time I've had to hand one of my pieces in; the work has been uniformly haphazard and shoddy, and always late. I am always lying to my editor, poor Georgia, telling her that I can't get on-line to e-mail the thing to her, claiming to have already faxed it, it must not have gone through—and never just admitting I have not bothered to write it at all. I'm going to have to get it done this weekend in Stockholm, with no sleep, interviews to do—what a nightmare. I could call now and ask if we can postpone it a week. Certainly Georgia would understand about this junket, she would certainly rather it be in good condition late than a mess on time—but that would make me feel like a failure. I've got to be stand-up about this. I've got to fulfill my obligations.

I hear myself thinking this. I'm snorting cocaine right out of a bag as Mae-Mae gets lost again looking for Newark, it's already after eight o'clock, I'm about to transport an eightball of cocaine on an international flight—and I am worried about *fulfilling my obligations*?

Somebody should just commit me now. I am no longer competent.

I call my friend Toby on the way to the airport, because he is friends with my Swedish publishers, so I want him to get in touch with them and let them know I will be missing my flight. Toby is an editor about town, and I figure he will like the opportunity to get involved with a potential international mishap—I am hoping this task will bring out his sense of importance. Lucky for me, I cannot make calls outside of North America on my mobile phone, so I have an excuse not to call them myself.

"Am I enabling you?" Toby asks as soon as I make my request.

"No, why?"

"Because you're probably late because you're using." How'd he get so clever?

"No, that's not it at all," I say. "It's just that if you don't take care of this, I'll have to ask Lydia to do it, and you know how angry and crazy she can get."

"So there are no drugs involved?" He's not going to give up on this one.

"No, no—just traffic." It's true. There is terrible traffic. "Please just take care of this for me. I cannot get in touch with Kajsa and Ernst any other way, and after the last few years Lydia is always mad at me for one reason or another, so I don't want to get her involved." Toby and Lydia hate each other. He thinks she's a loony bitch, and she thinks he's a social climber, and both of them kind of have a point. Whenever I am mad at either of them, I complain to the other one because I am sure to get sympathy. Lydia never invited Toby to my thirtieth birthday party, and he has never quite forgiven her for that, so I am hoping I can make use of his animosity. I cannot believe Toby is not going to come through for me now. Goddamn him.

"All right, fine, I'll make the call," he relents. "But promise me that you're not in any kind of trouble."

"Toby, you're a prince!" I say. "Thank you so much. And no, I'm fine, just tense. I'll bring you something fabulous back from Stockholm. I promise." There is nothing fabulous to be found in Stockholm, but whatever.

We arrive at the airport after nine o'clock. Obviously it's too late for the Stockholm flight. Mae-Mae goes to park the car, and I run to the SAS counter, as if by rushing I still might just end up in Stockholm on time after all. The SAS agent tries to find me an alternate route. I can take Aer Lingus and change flights in Dublin. I can take British Airways and change flights in London. I can take Lufthansa and change flights in Frankfurt. I can take Icelandic and change flights in Reykjavík—but I remember what happened the last time I tried that route, so there's no way I'm going to go through that again, although it would give me the opportunity to find the hotel I stayed in and try to retrieve my lost jewelry.

Finally I just say, "Look, just get me to somewhere in the neighborhood. Oslo, Helsinki, Copenhagen—if I just get to the general area, I'm sure I can figure it out." Luckily, there is a midnight flight to Copenhagen, so she books me on that and arranges for me to catch the shuttle to Stockholm.

Mae-Mae makes calls on my cell phone while I make my arrangements with SAS, and as soon as I'm done, I run into the ladies' room to do more cocaine. I've got it all figured out. I take my diaphragm out of my pocketbook—I've at least had the good sense to make plans for transporting contraband—I put several little bags of coke into its cup, and then I insert it into myself and make sure it is firmly in place on my cervix. All done.

Once I'm finished with this procedure, I say good-bye to Mae-Mae and head toward the security check to go to the SAS gate. "I love you," I say as I hug her.

"I love you too," she says. "We'll go to a meeting when you get back."

"Sure," I say, and I kind of mean it. I'm really worn out. I've had enough. I have never made so much effort to hold it all together and see it fall all apart. I've come so close from so far.

From there on, everything happens very quickly. I go to Nathan's Famous to get a hot dog before my flight. This involves walking through the metal detectors once again. This means I risk getting caught with drugs after I've already gotten away with it, but I just don't care. I think it's funny. I chat with the female security guard for a few minutes before I go through. She is admiring my armful of bracelets—rose quartz and turquoise and amethyst and mother-of-pearl and aventurine and crystal, all in a pretty row—and I am especially friendly because I have just done some coke so I've got this new burst of energy. Instead of being suspicious, this lovely young woman—who is after all probably bored by looking for guns and bullets and other weapons of destruction as suitcases and shoulder bags pass through the radar—is glad to have someone to talk to.

At Nathan's I sit at a table with some missionaries on their way to Singapore, I ooh and aah over their little redheaded baby. We discuss being Jewish; I am once again as friendly as can be. By the time I get back to the security check, my new friend is happy to have me to talk to again. I've bought a pile of fashion magazines, and in *Elle* I show her pictures of pretty bracelets and necklaces made of semiprecious stones like the ones I am wearing—all while I stand there with a couple of hundred dollars worth of cocaine between my legs.

I spend the entire flight to Copenhagen lecturing this family of Danish Orthodox Jews about Samson and Delilah. I tell them that I went to religious schools, and they seem baffled that I appear to know so much about Judaism, but I am still eating the nonkosher meal they serve on the flight, which happens to be reindeer. I share my copy of the Wayfarer's Prayer, which I carry in my passport case everywhere, written out in both Hebrew and English, and I feel smug and arrogant that I happen to have it to say and they don't. What would they have done without me? I keep running to the lavatory to coke up, and I have equine energy. I am a racehorse about to take the Triple Crown.

Once I deplane at Copenhagen, I discover that the shuttles to Stockholm have just changed schedules, so all the flights have been delayed for several hours. That's nice, I think. I'll just do some shopping. The duty-free stores in Copenhagen's airport are considered some of the best in the world. This tiny little socialist country is extremely industrious, the producer of many wonderful consumer goods—LEGO, Dansk, Royal Copenhagen, Georg Jensen, Bang & Olufsen. So much for the idea that without capitalism people are slothful, living off the dole, and wasting away. So I go on an insane, manic spree. I take my little trolley and go nuts. The stores do not have the capacity to check credit cards through to the United States, so I can spend far beyond my limit. Gucci bags, Ferragamo sandals, a Georg Jensen silver necklace, a Prada sweater, a Skagen watch for Mommy, LEGO sets for my nonexistent little cousins whom I ought to buy presents for, a Mont Blanc fountain pen for signing books. I also pick up a few bottles of Absolut Vodka, in Citron and Kurrant and Peppar flavors, as gifts for the people in Sweden. This would seem like a rich instance of taking coals to Newcastle, but the value-added tax in Sweden is so high that even alcohol produced in the country is too expensive for the natives—and heaven knows, they love to drink. Since I am going to be almost a full day late, it seems wise to arrive with presents.

I shop until the stores close down. By the time I get to the gate for the Stockholm shuttle, they've canceled the next several flights because the new schedule has screwed everything up. They've added in an extra one late at night, but that won't be until eleven o'clock. I won't get to Stockholm until sometime after midnight.

So much for Scandinavian efficiency.

As I wait to board the plane, I talk to some American tourists from El Paso, because I am chatty as all hell, still all coked up, and to top it off overtired and punchy. We talk about Texas. I tell them I wrote for *The Dallas Morning News* ten years ago, and I show them the Lucchese alligator-skin cowboy boots that I bought in Houston when I was last there. They own some too, and we discuss how they last a lifetime, they are so well made. I recommend a couple of restaurants in Stockholm, inform them that the food is uniformly terrible, to stay away from the whale meat that people seem to eat so much—it is one of the few exotic foods that does not taste like chicken, that simply is disgusting—and I tell them they should visit the islands off the coast, and to buy lots of garnet and amber, because so much is harvested from the Black Sea, and it is extremely beautiful and cheap. Whew. I talk a blue streak.

By the time I get to Stockholm, my publishers are all so glad to see me alive that they cannot be angry. They have been waiting for hours because SAS would not give them information about my new itinerary, since it is against the law to inform anyone about the status of a passenger. I get to the Grand Hotel and blessedly pass out.

Somehow I make it through. I have enough coke for the first couple of days, but for the last few I just have to pull through. It is simply exhausting. Kajsa and Ernst, the two owners of the publishing company, are mostly in London, where they are starting up Boo.com, the Internet fashion retailer that is underwritten with over a hundred million dollars by several American investment bankers. The company will go bust within a year. This will be a front-page story in *The Wall Street Journal* as the paradigm of failing e-tailers, and there is fascination about how all these wise financiers were hoodwinked into investing in this disaster. But for the time being, Kajsa and Ernst are flying high, having big-money fun, and the publishing company has been left in the hands of underlings, all of whom are so sweetly respectful of me that it is heartbreaking to know that I am failing them so. I do my best to be good, to give good readings at bars and nightclubs, to live up to their kindness, and I hate their bewildered, gentle, and concerned faces. I hate the way they worry that I am simply sick and that they are pushing me too hard. I hate myself for no longer being worthy of any of this. I hate myself and I want to die.

They've put an NA meeting into my schedule, but I just tell them there is really no point. I write my column for *The Guardian* at the last minute, and it is atrocious. The Swedes cancel all my interviews for the last day because I can't get out of bed, and I feel too sick to do more coke, even if someone could get some for me. I've had enough. I'm spent. This is awful. I never want to do cocaine ever again for as long as I live.

I am an awful person. These people are sweet. They truly care. Come to think of it, Betsy and Lydia and everyone I work with truly care. But not anymore. No one cares anymore. I just disgust them. I disgust myself.

I should either clean up or kill myself. This is a worthless way to live.

Of course, I do get more cocaine as soon as I get back. There's no way I can handle Lydia yelling at me, all the fallout, straight. In fact, I wonder if there's even a point. I skip my Smithers meeting. I hide in my house ashamed. I have never had Lydia this angry at me before. I have never failed professionally. In fact, Ritalin started out as a way to be a better professional, to be more alert and loving and fun. Drugs are not working anymore.

She tells me that *The Guardian* is canceling my column and that I will probably never be invited back to Sweden again, even though *Bitch* is selling well there, and *Prozac Nation* is still a huge hit.

"Nobody wants to deal with you anymore, Elizabeth," Lydia says. "Nobody cares how talented you are. It's just not worth it. It's not worth it to Georgia at *The Guardian* to always wonder if she is going to get your column, or if there will just be a hole in the paper." She stops. "And you know, you're not even writing very well any longer. Your work is suffering from whatever you're doing to yourself." She stops again, waiting for me to say something, but I just don't. "And how could you miss your flight to Stockholm? *What is wrong with you?*"

"It was the traffic. It was so bad." I am sure if I say anything more she will remind me that I could have taken the car service, that I could have given myself enough time to get to the airport, and that I just didn't. So I change the subject. "Besides, how could I possibly write a decent column on no sleep?"

"You're lying."

"And I can't help it if the fax got lost in cyberspace, or whatever transmits it."

"Stop lying." Again she is waiting for me to say something, to fess up, but I just won't. "I can't work with you like this. Betsy doesn't want to work with you anymore. Doubleday does not want to send you on tour, which is exactly what you're so good at. They feel that not only will you not be able to sell your book—they are actually afraid that you will turn people off to it. No magazines want you to write for them. You are losing everything. Why won't you just be honest with me and let me help you get some help?"

"I've been going to Smithers," I say, knowing it sounds lame.

I had so much, and I threw it all away.

But I can still get high. That's all I've got left.

RECOVERY

Twenty-four

LOVE IS HARD TO STOP

Here's a toast to all that's good
And here's a toast to hate
And here's a toast to toasting
And I'm not boasting
When I say I'm getting straight

LOU REED
"The Last Shot"

I rifle through an old Filofax, two years old, from 1996. I look through the dates in spring and summer, looking for a phone number. Any number. Any number from AA that's not somebody I hung out with back then, because I just can't talk to those people, just can't tell them enough is enough. And I find it. Stone O'Malley. Stone owns some bars, some hip-people bars. He used to be a club kid. Now he's an actor, an actor who owns cool places where fashionable people hang out. He's what people meant back in the fifties when they called some guy a cad. He only dates models. He's full of himself. And still, I know, he is the one to call.

I get his answering machine. It has the number of his mobile phone on it. Without leaving a message, I just punch in the 917 number. I just hope he picks up.

"Stone, my name is Elizabeth Wurtzel," I say before he has even said hello. "I met you at Perry Street a couple of years ago. I don't know if you remember me, but I need help. I need help."

"Okay," he says, and he sounds serious, sententious, like he is really listening.

"I can't stop doing cocaine. I've been doing it for days. I just shot some up.

I've never done that before, and my heart, it won't, it won't stop." What can I say? "I'm waiting for a delivery of more. I'm getting more, and I'm going to keep doing it." I pause, waiting for him to say something, anything, but he doesn't. "I'm not going to stop right now. But I want to. I want this to be the end. My whole face hurts. I'm bleeding. I can't go on. Please help."

He says he's at a wedding, some South African friends. He'll be there for a couple of hours, but then he can meet me. He'll call me when he's ready to leave, I'll come to his apartment on Houston Street, he'll make me some chamomile tea, and we'll just sit there. We'll sit on his couch until I feel okay. He promises that he will sit with me until it's okay. He promises.

"I'm so sorry," I say, not really meaning it. "I'm so sorry to bother you. I don't know who else to talk to. I've already used everyone up."

"It's okay," he says. "We'll get you through this. I'm going to call you really soon. You just stay at home, and I'll call. It's going to be fine. Okay? It's going to be fine."

And for some reason, I just believe him.

I walk to Stone's apartment. It is farther away than I think, or maybe it just feels that way. It's a big beautiful loft in a messed-up old building. The buzzer doesn't work. He has to come downstairs and let me in. I stand with my nose pressed against the vestibule door. It takes so long for him to get there, or maybe it just feels that way.

I've got five dime bags of coke stuffed in my pocket. They are going to be gone by the time I leave Stone. That's the end. That will be the end.

He talks to me a little bit, explains that the dog is his but the cat belongs to some Australian Victoria's Secret model who's in the *Sports Illustrated* swimsuit issue. I have no idea who he is talking about. I wonder why I chose him. And then I remember: I'm safe. I sit on the sofa with him, and for the first time in a long time I am not afraid that this guy is going to touch me, to try to kiss me, to do something he should not. He is a cad, but he takes recovery seriously. Besides, I am not a supermodel, or even just a plain old model. As far as Stone's concerned, I might as well not be female.

"I need to do some coke," I say.

"Do you really have to?"

"Look, you have a choice. I either cut it up on the coffee table in front of you, or I go to the bathroom and hide, but either way, I'm doing it." I've been offering up these options for much too long.

He tells me to use the bathroom.

I should feel bad about this. Recovered addicts still get tempted, even after a few years, maybe even forever, but I just don't care. Drugs: first. Recovery: later. Other people's feelings are running a distant third right now.

We sit on the couch and watch David Letterman, which is surprisingly soothing. Tart midwestern humor is exactly right for me now. Nick Cave is the musical guest. I don't really know his work. I know that lots of cool people love him and that he wrote a novel. I probably should like him. It's just Nick and the piano, his voice is as soothing as everything else about the show, and I just sit and listen. Stone knows that I can't talk right now.

> *I don't believe in an interventionist God*
> *But I know darling that you do*
> *But if I did I would kneel down and ask him*
> *Not to change a thing when it comes to you*
> *Not to change a hair on your head*
> *Leave you as you are*
> *If he had to direct you then direct you into my arms*
> *Into my arms, oh Lord*
> *Into my arms.*

The idea that someone out there ever felt that way about someone else out there seems like a reason to live at the moment. Such a purity and clarity of feeling has to be a gift from God. And I start to mumble to myself, or maybe I'm just talking in my own head, but I beg Whoever or Whatever is out there to maybe, please, someday and some way, reveal to me a little bit of that divine glory. Whatever tiny corner of a shred of paper is left over from someone else's happiness, I'll be happy to have it for my own. I start bargaining with God, making a deal, something about showing me love for the world as is, for myself as is. I'll be good, I promise, I promise I'll be good, just let me know something about the things Nick Cave is singing about.

I've been looking for that feeling everywhere I go. I've been waiting for someone to see all the good in me at every truck stop and intersection along the way. I've been waiting all my life for the moment to arrive when I can just stop. Stop looking. When I can be here now. At the Mustard Seed AA meeting, in midtown Manhattan, there's a sign that promises, "We will love you until you can love yourself."

Well, fuck that.

I know I will never be well until I like myself just as is, which is impossible, which is what the drugs are all about. Or maybe it works both ways. Do I do drugs because I hate myself, or are the drugs making me hate myself? I'll never know unless I stop, and I can't seem to stop. I can remember the end of my time at Silver Hill, remember that moment walking on the grounds on a sunny day, early spring, the New England chill against the bright solar light, and I remember thinking: *I know what life is for. For once I know what life is for. I don't have all the answers, don't know what will happen next, but just at this moment I understand that my life matters, that there are good things ahead. I don't know what they are, but maybe it will be all right.* I felt peace. I understood that corny thing people say: *I am at peace with myself.* And I wanted to think of better words for it, wanted to think of a way to say it that was less trite, more apposite and writerly. And then I remembered: sometimes these simple words that everyone uses are just right, are just good.

God in heaven, if I got to that place, how did I lose it? It's like I was hijacked, mugged, like someone just ran off with all of my stuff. Peace of mind is no better than four years of high school French: if you never have occasion to speak a foreign language ever again, you forget it; if you don't live in Paris or Provence, sooner or later there's nothing left but that certain *je ne sais quoi* and this is what *tout le monde* is saying and, when all else fails, *Parlez-vous anglais?* I forgot to remember that feeling, and now it's gone.

Shit, I can't stand it. I get up and run to the bathroom and snort up a dime bag of cocaine.

It doesn't help.

I spend several hours sitting on Stone's sofa. It is a complete activity. Normally, I think of sitting still as, for lack of a better word, a passivity. But this is the most strenuous form of not moving that I have ever experienced. You could run the Boston Marathon, and you'd still have nothing on me.

Stone brings me chamomile tea, he refreshes my cup repeatedly, he asks how I am doing, he tries to ignore my periodic jaunts to the bathroom. We have tacitly agreed to pretend that I am just drinking too many fluids; that I am cleansing my system. This social compact seems to work for both of us right now.

We talk a little bit, about Perry Street, about why I can't go back there, all the shame I feel. He starts to say something about how you should never feel embarrassed to go back, that the shameful thing is *not* going back if you need to. And I know he is right, but I don't care. I always proceed, I always do what I want, I impose, I do cocaine in front of people that I should't, I am fairly oblivious to how my behavior affects other people, but still, given a situation where it is perfectly acceptable for me to go back, where I will be greeted with welcoming arms, I cannot possibly do it. It would be like saying, *You win.* I cannot concede defeat even though, sitting here with Stone, I am absolutely conceding defeat.

He tells me he prefers Narcotics Anonymous meetings anyway, that there are plenty of people in NA with solid sober time, and it's more intense. He tells me there is a meeting on Saturday night at seven o'clock in the East Village with a lot of people who have long-term clean time, a lot of good strong women. Everyone always points out to me that this or that meeting has "good women," and I know it's because you are supposed to rely on people of your own sex to get you through, to be your sponsors. And still I hate how it sounds. It sounds so forced. Is there anything about Twelve Step meetings I *don't* hate at this point?

But just the same, I am going to meet Stone at NA tomorrow night. I am going to go. I need to start thinking more like an engineer and less like a scientist: I need to think about what works, not about why.

I am up all night, reeling from cocaine. I've done at least an eightball in the last several hours and I don't know how much in the preceding days. I am up all night drinking tea and talking to my cat.

I was away for a year, and I left Zap alone with various house sitters. By all rights he should have forgotten me completely. But no. No one has ever been so happy to see me as he was the day I returned. He jumped on me as I walked through the door and came up the stairs. He ran toward me like a puppy and licked my face. I have had him since 1989, and his love is so simple and pure. He still loves me. It was just like when my dad would show up outside my high school or in front of my apartment building after he had gone missing for a couple of months or years, after I had no idea where he'd been. I should have snapped at him, got mad like he deserved, but instead it was always, *Daddy, Daddy, I've missed you so much. Where have you been?*

You see, none of us has good judgment when it comes to love, and love is hard to stop.

I toss around like a bale of hay on a flatbed truck driving across a bumpy stretch of rural roadway. I can't sleep. I get up and go through the garbage, find the little plastic bag that had my last bit of coke in it, scratch into its corners to see if there's anything, even a few flecks of powder, left in the crevices. Of course not. I want to call the dealer and ask him to bring me some more. Of course I want to. I tell myself this is perfectly normal, withdrawal sucks, but I can get through it.

I think about the time, just a couple of weeks before, when I had paged my dealer and was waiting for him to call back and tell me where to meet him. I sat in my black-flowered sundress, propped up against the headboard of my bed, my arms folded against my chest, holding myself and rocking like an autistic child hiding in a corner, waiting for the call, waiting as a complete activity. *First thing you learn is that you always gotta wait.*

The cat jumped up on my stomach and looked at me like, *You're not going to do that bad stuff again.* He looked at me as if to ask, *Aren't we having enough fun here, just me and you, hanging out?* He looked at me as if he could not believe I was really going to put him through another night of powder cut up on mirrors, windowsills, kitchen counters, photo frames, book jackets, magazine covers with pages torn into ribbons and rolled up like straws—he looked at me as if he would be so sad if we went through another night of nosebleeds and palpitations. He broke my heart.

And for just a second there, I felt a little bit serene. When the phone rang, I let the machine get it. I did not get high that night. And, you know, it wasn't so bad.

I show up at the meeting at eight o'clock, an hour late. Like most NA meetings, and even some AA ones, it is hard to find. There are a church entrance, an anteroom, a chapel, a courtyard, a gate to walk through, a pitch-black night, a candlelit room to search for, a door that's hard to open. It's enough to make you go use again.

I finally get inside. The meeting is called "Second and Second," and although most meetings with that name would be located at Third Avenue and First Street or something like that, because disorganization seems to be no obstacle when it comes to NA, the Church of the Nativity is actually on Second Avenue and Second Street. I see Stone sitting in a bridge chair around the table at the center of the room, many people surrounding it on high stools and on their feet. It's the East Village, so there are plenty of chin studs and eyebrow rings and green hair and blond dreadlocks. But there are also some normal-looking people, mostly perfectly employable types, so I feel all right. Well, as all right as I can feel when I have not used since I fell blessedly asleep sometime in the morning.

I have missed the speaker. I am here for open sharing by show of hands. One of the rules—or rather, *suggestions*—of NA is that you not talk out loud at a meeting if you have used controlled substances in the last twenty-four hours. You are supposed to approach people afterward, ask for help one on one, or just listen and absorb the wisdom. So I stand in the back of the room and pay close attention to everything everybody says. I act as if it matters to me, because, unbelievably enough, it really does. For the first time ever, I think, I will do just about anything to stay clean. I will even listen to other people.

A girl sitting in a chair next to me, a girl with bright blue eyes and one of those pixieish shags like Meg Ryan's, starts asking in a whisper if anyone has an aspirin. She says she's got a premenstrual headache. I have Advil in my jacket pocket. Advil is one of the four major food groups for me right now, so I hand her the whole hundred-caplet bottle. I figure that if I take three or four at a time, who can say if she doesn't want that many too?

She takes just one.

With three minutes left in the meeting, the chairman asks if anyone has a burning desire, if anyone is afraid they will use tonight, or hurt themselves or somebody else. I hesitate. I am not supposed to talk. But then I raise my hand.

"My name is Elizabeth, and I am an addict," I say when he signals me. "I have used in the last twenty-four hours, so I am not supposed to speak, but I just need to say that I am desperate, that I want to stop, I'm scared I won't be able to, and if anyone can help me, please tell me what to do."

I cannot believe that I mean what I say. What happened to my sense of irony and horror? But, once again, I really will do anything. Many women come up to me after we close the meeting with the Serenity Prayer. Maud, the woman I gave the Advil to, says she has fourteen years, and gives me her phone number. Plum, a transvestite or transsexual or something like that, introduces me to her Yorkshire terrier, gives me a hug, and gives me her phone number. Other women bring me meeting schedules, and circle the meetings they think I would like. People offer me pamphlets, NA literature, and I am actually a bit shy when I tell them I've already got all that stuff, recovery is not new to me at all. I know lots of people go to rehab for four months and start using the day they leave, but it still seems idiotic.

But everybody welcomes me like the Prodigal Son, and Stone tells me he is proud that I spoke up. Once again, I cannot decide whether to be moved by his support or disgusted by his condescension, and once again I decide: Whatever works. I've got to stop judging *every little thing*.

It is 10 October 1998, and this is Day One for me. There will not be any more Day Ones. I don't have another Day One in me. This is it.

Twenty-five

I LOOKED AWAY

Now I can't do the talk
Like they talk on my TV screen
I can't do a love song
Not the way it's meant to be
I can't do anything
But I'd do anything for you
I can't do anything except be in love with you

All I do is miss you
And the way we used to be
All I do is keep the beat
And bad company
All I do is kiss you
Through the bars of this rhyme
Because I'd do the stars with you anytime

MARK KNOPFLER
"Romeo and Juliet"

I get pregnant. A week after I get clean, I get pregnant. And I know exactly how it happens. I know it as it is happening and can do nothing to stop it. I know exactly where my diaphragm is. Only two weeks before I had used it to carry contraband onto an international flight, and I know exactly where to find it. But nothing like that is going to happen. Hank is going to fuck me when he wants to, how he wants to. He is not going to let me get out of my bed even to walk into the bathroom. If I do, he may just leave.

He doesn't say that if I get up for birth control he will leave. But I know how easily he disappears. I am scared to look away. You think I am exaggerating, that I should know that you can avert your eyes from someone for a few minutes and he will not be gone, but I don't know that. With Hank, I have no idea what might happen. I have not seen him since early September, after he left my apartment—snuck out—while I was uptown at Smithers for a couple of hours. If you think I am going to let that happen again, you are crazy. You don't know how I feel about Hank: I feel crazy. And I can do nothing to stop it.

We were supposed to meet for dinner earlier. He had called to say he was in town, complete surprise, and we made plans. But instead he met up with some friends. He got drunk all over the city, uptown, downtown, midtown, the Plaza Hotel, a dive called 2A, the Liquor Store Bar near my apartment, Lucky Strike in SoHo, everywhere. He doesn't have a mobile phone. All night I leave messages on his answering machine in New Mexico: I am here now, I am with Lily, I am with Mae-Mae, I am at the movie theater on Nineteenth and Broadway, I am back at home. I have not yet experienced Hank drunk. I do not understand that he goes on what he calls "benders," and anything can happen. He can say anything, he means it all, he means none of it; he has that short-term amnesia that drunks get in a blackout. I have never seen Hank like this, and I will eventually realize I have never seen *anything* like this. He is the drunkest drunk I have ever met.

Nothing prepares me for this. So I just act like it's normal. I leave messages about where I am because I treat it like it's all logistics, the confusion of making plans in New York City on a Friday night, the kind of thing that just happens.

It is sometime after four in the morning when my phone rings. It would be so good if I had a digital clock, if I could give the detail that it is, say, 4:22, since the precision would authenticate my desperation, would make it clear that every minute matters. But this is real life, and in real life all I know is that the phone wakes me up very late. The miracle in this is that I am actually asleep, that I have managed to stop worrying about Hank's whereabouts for long enough to just fall off.

He is drunk, slurring, says he is in a house next to the Holland Tunnel. He is with his friend Jimbo, his favorite drinking buddy. I say I'll come find him. I ask for the address, or even the coordinates, which he can't figure out. All he knows is he is next to the Holland Tunnel, and all I know is that I will find him. This is ridiculous. It would be better if he called me to bail him out from the city jail, the "Tombs" as it is called, because you can get lost underground there for days, drunk and disorderly, or in for soliciting or possession or whatever lame-ass charge they drag you in on, on a Friday night. I am more likely to find him there than in some unspecified New York City apartment, but somehow I just will.

And indeed, I do. There is a house right under the entrance to the tunnel. The door is open, there are motorcycles parked in the living room or whatever you want to call it, and I walk back to the bedroom and find Hank and Jimbo asleep in their clothes—designer suits, as it turns out, Hank had a job interview earlier in the day—on a double bed on the floor. I am in jeans and cowboy boots and a man's oxford shirt. I have even bothered to put on some lipstick and mascara, as if Hank will know the difference, and I drag him out of the bed. It's like pulling someone out of quicksand; he is just drunk deadweight. I walk him stumbling out of this ground-floor apartment.

I seem not to get it: I seem not to understand that this is Drunk Hank, as opposed to Sober Hank, that I am not getting the person I came here for. I don't get it. I have no idea if I will ever get it: I am so stuck in last spring, when he was my best friend and the most wonderful man on earth. So I just keep pulling him across these streets, streets covered with white lines and arrows pointing all different directions, crossroads that are not designed for pedestrians, that are only meant for vehicles entering the tunnel to return home to New Jersey after a drunken night on the town. I pull him all the way back to my house.

We stop at the Korean convenience store down the block for some Orangina—the international drink of choice for drunks and addicts, a bubbly thirst quencher that won't upset your stomach and still tastes yummy—and head toward my lobby. Hank throws the bottle on the sidewalk; all the orange liquid explodes. A couple walking out early in the morning—they're just waking up, heading out to the Hamptons or something—starts to scream that we can't leave all the shards there, that there are dogs and children that might get hurt. But we ignore them. I have only one thing on my mind: I want Hank up in my apartment and back in my life. I have him here in New York, with me, where he belongs, and I will never let him go. If I have to come up with a thousand stories like the woman in *The Arabian Nights*, if I have to entertain him with all of my body, mind, spirit, and soul, I will do it. He is never leaving me again. If I have to stand guard, a vigilant female sentry, and keep him from walking out my front door with a steak knife and a grapefruit spoon, whatever weapons I have at my disposal, that's what I'm going to do. I have never been so determined to cling to something or someone in my whole life, as far as I know.

I really don't want to have sex. I really just want to hold him here and sleep. Actually, I have no idea what I want beyond Hank here with me, but I strip out my clothes to get into bed, because it seems like the thing to do. He loves my body, so it's a good start. I will soon understand that he loves whiskey,

Macallan to be specific, more than anything else, but I figure my physical self might just rate a close second. I write books, I give lectures, I have good friends, I am a good listener and a better talker—I have an entire personality that is not entirely unappealing; but the only part of myself I really believe in, that I really think men care about, is my body.

Sometimes I think that if I just got a job as a stripper or a go-go girl, if I danced in a cage with men throwing twenties at me, let their fingers stuff bills in my red lace garter belt, it would be more honest than all the things I actually do to earn a living: at least I would believe I was doing honorable work that I am capable of. That's where I'm at right now.

So Hank pushes me onto my back, opens his zipper, and fucks me. I am not sure if we even kiss, I am certain there is no foreplay, I have no idea what is in it for me, but here we go. One of the reasons I never bother to put in my diaphragm is that I can't quite assimilate the information before me. I don't quite realize we are actually having sex, it all happens so fast. In fact, it happens again and again, so fast, I lose count at five times. I want him to stop, I want him to let me stand up for a second, I want him to let me catch my breath, I need to go to the bathroom, but I dare not ask. I am scared to move. I am scared to let go of him.

I am crazy. I am extremely crazy. I think if I look away for even a few minutes, Hank will be gone. But I am right. You know what they say: The journey of a thousand miles begins with one step. This is particularly true if you are talking about a drunk. A drunk walks out the door one day, and ends up in New Mexico. In an airport, if he turns right, he is on a plane to New York, if he walks left, he is on a flight to Fargo, and the decision is made by his feet.

The first song on the Derek & the Dominoes album Layla is "I Looked Away." The idea is that you can lose someone so easily, that love is that elusive: "She took my hand / Tried to make me understand / That she would always be there / And I looked away / And she ran away from me today." Just like that. Your head is turned, and she is gone. "Came as a surprise to me / She left me there in misery / Seems like only yesterday / She made a vow she'd never walk away." A vow: people make vows all the time. And then they break them. But, of course, they don't really break them. When you say to someone, I love you, you absolutely mean it at the time, but then things change. Every time a friend of mine breaks up with someone and there's all this hurt, and she'll say that he told me this or he said that or he promised this, the assumption is it was all a lie. And I always have to explain, it was true. It was true at the time. The time passed by.

And I cannot seem to understand that time has passed, that Hank is someone else now. When he went to Taos for two weeks in June, when he promised he would be back no later than my birthday in July, I kind of knew it wasn't true. He broke the continuity. We had a setup, we had a life together, we were in early re-covery together, and everything then is so labile, so plastic, you never know. But I knew: I knew he was gone.

So I have him back that night—October 17 is the exact date—and I am afraid he will walk away if I let him go for just long enough to walk out the door. He is slippery and slimy, a writhing snake, a cat squirming out of your hands as you try to pack him into a carrier case to go to the vet: Hank is no different from any animal scared of being trapped. Like all stupid women, I figure I can trap him for a while between my legs, and I am right. As long as I hold on to him with my body, he is mine to keep. We fuck that night, no birth control, and I am so ad-dled the next day that I don't take a morning-after pill, which I have done before, which I know works.

I am obsessed with Hank. He is all that's in my head; he is all over me, all in-side me. He is long gone, he is on a train back to his aunt and uncle's house in Connecticut, he may not even remember my name, but he is all I can see. I have not managed to trap him, but without even meaning to, he sure has got me.

I've continued to go to a therapy group for addicts every Wednesday night. This is a compromise: Dr. Singer thinks I should go into a full-time day pro-gram, but the thought is unbearable to me. I'm going to meetings every day. I can't see the point. Smithers, the treatment center at Roosevelt Hospital, has a five-day-a-week group, but they've also got some evening groups, so we agree to start there. It is very different from Silver Hill: every patient is a professional; everyone has a serious full-time job. There are an advertising executive, a law-yer, a woman who works in publishing.

There is one guy, a software mogul of some sort, who starts coming to NA meetings with me. I have no idea what his drug of choice is exactly, mostly he seems to smoke too much pot and take too many psilocybin mushrooms. I have a difficult time taking his problems seriously. I know that marijuana is ac-tually more dangerous than people think, that you really can get hooked on it, but I just don't get it; if you can't snort it, swallow it, or shoot it, I have trouble seeing it as real trouble. Unless it's crack, but that's different. He starts calling me all the time, inviting me for dinner after group, and eventually I realize he is interested in me, even though all I do is talk about Hank. That's how it al-ways is—you talk about one guy, and it doesn't scare anyone else off. They fig-ure you just need to be saved from the asshole who is driving you nuts.

Then there is Joey, a federal judge who thinks he is really a jazz saxophon-ist. Joey lives in a tiny apartment in Brooklyn since his wife kicked him out, he has two college-age kids who don't much like him, he is always carrying his in-strument with him to group slung over his shoulder in its case, and he really annoys me. He hires hookers to come to his place and shoot him up with co-caine. He can't stop doing it, he watches pornography constantly, he loves doing girls and drugs all at once. During the day, he wears a robe and presides over trials that mainly involve organized crime, RICO statute violations, stuff like that. Joey is a Bush administration appointee. He starts reading my first book. Then he starts writing me notes asking if we can get together privately and talk, and at group he yells at me and says that he's read my books, he knows that I always have people coming to my rescue, I have no idea what it's like to be old and lonely like him. After he's done being hostile, Joey calls me more and sends me more notes. Eventually I have to tell our group leader that I feel like I'm being stalked. She doesn't know what to do.

The only guy who is not pestering me enough—who isn't turning up at all—is Hank. A couple of weeks after I last saw him, I get an e-mail from him saying something about being safely back in Taos, that his experiments with cocktails in New York did not go very well, hope all is well.

By this time I know I am pregnant. I'm not late yet, but I am sleepy all the time, and I just *feel* pregnant. You know how they say that women always know these things? Well, this is something I just know.

I wait for Hank to call or show up at my door, surprise me somehow.

I become extremely superstitious, which I am anyway, but this is off the charts: If I am good, Hank will come back. I return phone calls promptly. I make my bed every day. I get to meetings on time. I never leave my towel on the floor after I shower. I wash my tea mugs as soon as I put them in the sink. I wash my hands every time I go to the bathroom, even if I am just about to get into the shower. I give spare change, sometimes even dollar bills, to every beg-gar on the street, in the subway. If I owe anyone money, and I always do, I pay it back. I carry a bunch of amulets in my pocket—a turquoise scarab, a worry stone, Bruce Springsteen's guitar pick, my grandfather's silver monogram ring, an angel coin, a heart-shaped stone—and I transfer them from one pair of jeans to another every day, and if I miss one of them, I am sure it is the end. I keep candles lit at all times, especially ones that smell like roses and promise to cast spells of love. I wear the same perfume every day. I never take off the lit-tle ruby and gold chain around my neck. I wish on wishbones and on air-planes flying across the night sky that I pretend are shooting stars. I take everything as a sign from up high: if I order something off a menu and the restaurant is out of it, it is bad luck; if I get tickets to a movie that I'm sure will be sold out, it is good luck. If I am listening to a CD as I am on my way out the door, I will stay until the song ends, but be sure to be gone before the next one begins. If I miss an answer in the crossword puzzle, I'm doomed; on Saturday, the hardest day of the week in *The New York Times*, I spend hours with a dictionary until I fill in every letter. I am scared of the number 13, to the point where I won't go to Lily's apartment, because it is on the fourteenth floor, though it is actually the thirteenth. The building just skipped that unlucky number out of superstition—but they can't fool *me*: I know the truth, and I won't be taken. I say the appropriate blessing before every item of food I eat, sometimes saying the same one more than once to be absolutely certain, which is actually wrong to do since it is taking the Lord's name in vain. I pray on my knees with my hands interlaced on my bed every morning and every night. I am nice to my mother. I call my grandmother on a regular basis. I stay clean.

Above all, I stay clean. If I mix drugs into this problem, I will surely be punished from on high. Or worse: I will make my difficulties here on Earth even more impossible to manage. I have come to believe the NA dictum that there is no problem that drugs can't make worse. Just add to the confusion. Maybe you feel better for a little while, but you wake up to the same mess. I have come to understand this: I have come to understand that everything has a better chance of working out if I just stay clean, not because I will be rewarded by the powers that be, but because I will take better care of myself. For some reason, even if I let myself get pregnant that night, I still believe, in principle, in taking care of myself.

Recovery, in some way, has worked.

The day after my period is late, I take a home pregnancy test. When the result is positive, I schedule an appointment with my gynecologist for the next day, and sure enough. I arrange to have an abortion the next week. I am matter-of-fact about it: This is a problem that needs to be taken care of, and I will. This is not an emotional issue, it is just a physical mishap, and I can handle it. I won't even tell Hank about it. There's no reason for him to know, because I can solve it myself. I have friends. I have been clean for over a month, and if I can do that, I can do anything.

Besides, this is all my fault. It's my fault for not using a diaphragm when I knew I should have. I am not going to get Hank involved at all. I don't want to cause him any bother. He is already drunk and lost in New Mexico. He already has too much on his mind. I have started to get phone calls from him all the time, because he is drunk all the time, and for some reason, I am the one he wants to speak to when he gets like that. I'm his girl. He calls me from Denver and Durango, from Santa Fe and Sedona. He calls from a fly-fishing expedition in Wyoming, from skiing in Idaho. Friends of his from Taos sometimes call me when they can't find him, when they're worried that he's in trouble somewhere. I have no idea how they have my number, but this makes me feel important, special, like they know I am a big part of his life, so if he is lost he might be with me.

I decide this means that everything is still good between me and Hank. Sure, he is drunk all the time, but I don't care about that. We can always get him help, get him back into Silver Hill. As long as he loves me, everything will be all right.

The day I find out I am pregnant, I go to a gallery on the Upper East Side for an exhibit of a first printing of *Ulysses* that James Joyce had made for his dear friends and patrons. These are rare books, the kind of thing I can't stand. I hate when books are pristine objects and not living, used things. Funny thing is, the pages of most of the copies are not even cut open; even the people close to Joyce could not get through his book. I get a chuckle out of that. I hate James Joyce. I hated *Portrait of the Artist as a Young Man*, I hated *Dubliners*, I know he is in the canon, but to me he is pretentious and tedious to read. He is like one of those guys I met in college and avoided. He is an *artiste*. I hate that.

While I am sipping ginger ale and chewing on crudités and looking down at Joyce's text through one of the display cases as if I care, a colleague of Ben's approaches me. Pamela is actually his boss, and I saw her quite a bit when I used to be at his office all the time, just before I went to rehab. It's probably been a year since I last ran into her, and true to my word I have not been at all in touch with Ben, so I am kind of happy to make contact. For all the bitterness I often feel about everyone and everything, I truly hope Ben is happy and doing well. I wish him some kind of distant love because, in contrast to Hank and so many other men, Ben was always there when I needed him. In some ways, my relationship with him was one of the best I've ever had. Sad but true.

"You know Ben's wife is pregnant," Pamela tells me after we've said our hellos and how-are-yous. "She's due in February, I think."

"How nice for him," I say, and force a smile. My smile is forced not because I am not happy for Ben—I really am—but because at the moment it seems like a sick joke. Besides, Pamela must have known what was going on between me and Ben, so this has to be some sort of dig. The information does not bother me nearly as much as Pamela's intent to make me feel lousy. As far as I can tell, Pamela is not a catty woman—if anything, she has always seemed to be a contented, fiftyish lesbian. But to be the other woman, the mistress, is so lowly. It is the one role you can choose where—as hurt as you are all the time—people feel absolutely entitled to bear you contempt, to make you feel worse than you already do. *You knew what you were getting yourself into—what right have you got to be upset about it?* As the other woman, you are everybody's opportunity to vent the meanness they feel toward the whole world on a target that seems so deserving. The other woman is a convenient totem for everyone's grievances.

And I find myself wanting to tell Pamela that I know she barely knows me, but she has no idea what I have been through in the last year, has no idea what I am going through right now. Perhaps for the first time in my life I understand the value of good manners: I understand that you must be polite to all people at all times because you never know what difficulties they might be struggling with at that precise moment, you never know how the slightest wrong thing that you say could be the last little iota it takes to send a person who is just barely holding it together into a complete breakdown. The one little mistake you make, bumping into someone as you walk busily across a crowded sidewalk, shoving a woman aside as you push your way into a crowded subway car, spilling red wine on someone else's white shirt because you weren't paying attention as you made your rounds through a cocktail party—you never know if that misguided gesture might not be the reason some poor lost soul ends up in the loony bin. Anyone can be that delicate. In early sobriety, anyone can feel like a crepe paper parasol being held open to a gusty wind. Everything feels like too much, and no one else ever seems to be soft and gentle enough.

I suddenly realize that this shindig for James Joyce is the first social event I have been to since I put down cocaine just over a month ago.

I will never leave my house again for as long as I live.

When I get home, Hank has called, which is good, because I dare not call him. He does not even sound drunk, which is even better.

When I call back, I find him awake in his cabin outside of Taos, and I probably should at least mention that I am pregnant, but instead I decide to tell him about James Joyce. Once again, I want him to think I am a busy, chipper girl, running around New York and having loads of fun, not sad and exhausted from early recovery at all.

Hank has bought himself several hunting rifles, and has taken to shooting rabbits that run around the mesa that he lives on. He's got all these weird survivalist ideas. He is on this new kick about being completely self-sufficient, growing and foraging and killing all the food he eats by himself, never needing to go to a supermarket ever again. Soon he will tell me he is brewing his own moonshine. He now spends many hours of his days on the Internet, going to chat rooms shared with like-minded people, and writing lengthy right-wing tracts about Northeast liberal freaks who are into gun control and high taxes and all kinds of government interference. He has started sending letters with his views to *The New York Times*, and he is sure that he is right, everyone else is wrong, and somehow I have become part of the enemy camp. After all, I am an overeducated, big-city woman who does not understand the agrarian issues of outdoorsmen like Hank.

Now, if I were normal, if any of this were normal, I would just laugh at him. He sounds like the Unabomber or Timothy McVeigh, and as a Harvard graduate, his pieties are entirely misplaced. But instead of finding him ridiculous, I find him frightening. All he does is pick fights with me. He tells me I don't understand the concerns of real people and does everything to make me feel as though I am not just part of the problem, I am actually part of *his* problem. I frequently want to say to him, *If you find me so hideous, why are you calling?* But I want him to call, so I am in a bit of a binding loop here.

I want him to call because every time he does, I hope he will be Hank again, the one I remember from so many months ago. Instead, I get this right-wing crank whose outrages at everyone and everything seem to go on and on: Once I told him that Karl Marx was one of the greatest thinkers of modern times, a founder of discourse whose analysis of economic systems still holds up today—which is not even a particularly controversial point—and he started yelling at me about how Marxism is responsible for the deaths of millions of people, and he slammed down the phone. And I actually called him back, hoping to placate him, hoping to make him see that I am not talking about what happened in the Soviet Union, I am not talking about how Stalin killed twenty million of his own people, I am only referring to the ideas expressed in *Das Kapital*. And besides, I want to say, you're a scientist, and Einstein's theories are probably responsible—or most certainly will be—for more deaths than any political thoughts ever were, but we don't hold that against that greatest of geniuses. You don't hold Nietzsche accountable for Hitler! You don't hold Led Zeppelin responsible for Def Leppard!

But I never say these things. I never do. I just beg him to stop yelling at me, and I would, but don't dare, beg him to love me again like he once did. I dare not say that I am too tired to fight.

I just keep hoping he will change, that this is all some silly phase. Though I myself am an addict, I somehow fail to understand the totalizing effect that

drugs have on people's personalities, even when they are sober. I don't yet understand that as long as Hank is drinking on a regular basis, he is different even
when he is not drinking. In fact, I like him better when he is drunk, because
he becomes scared and needy. I now understand how codependency occurs;
if you are in love with a drunk, you actually have some interest in keeping that
person inebriated because it is so awful to be around a dry drunk. And it is so
wonderful to be needed the way Hank needs me when he is fucked up. So
much better than being yelled at.

I have this funny feeling that I can't quite articulate that I am turning into a
very sick girl. I am clean, but I am diseased.

And tonight, when I talk to Hank, we discuss James Joyce and William But-
ler Yeats. We discuss great Irish writers. We do not talk about what we need to
talk about because we are actually having a pleasant conversation, and I do
not want to ruin it. We have a bit of an argument about Irish versus Jewish literature. I come out on the side of Mailer, Roth, and Bellow, while he insists
that Yeats is the greatest poet and Joyce is the greatest novelist of the twentieth
century, and these points cannot be disputed. And for once, when he makes
these pronouncements, Hank does not sound as if he thinks I am the enemy.
The conversation is actually fairly academic. What a relief.

But then suddenly, I cannot believe we are having one of those sophomore-
year debates you'd have on the steps of the dormitory the night before an English 10 final. We are arguing about literature, about Jews and Irish men,
about stuff that I certainly do care about, but the elision here is too large: we
are not talking about us. I am pregnant, and I don't dare tell him. I am pregnant, and we are discussing Yeats. And I am doing everything to be agreeable,
conceding points I do not even mean, saying that "For Anne Gregory" is one
of my favorite poems, which it is, but still. I will say anything to get Hank back
on my side.

We used to sit at Gates in New Canaan and argue whether there should be
a minimum national income; we'd discuss the plight of the working poor, of
the resentful middle class; and we'd talk about designing a standardized edu-
cational curriculum. Would you require tenth-graders to read *The Catcher in
the Rye?* Would you need to take trigonometry to graduate from high school—
or would geometry be adequate? How I would love to argue with him. He was
just my favorite person. Nothing was more agreeable than disagreeing with
him. I know that sounds cutesy, like a silly song lyric, but for me that is love,
that is intimacy: you don't think the same things, but there is this huge respect
and delight in the differences.

But now Hank has turned into this insane right-wing dictator. He does not
listen, to me or anyone else. Talking to him is the opposite of fun. And so I sit

on the phone, trying so hard to be pleasing, to say anything that will show that we are on the same side. I know that what he really wants is for me to fight back, for us to have a phone-slamming debate, because when he is drunk he is violent, but I can't do it. I want to cry. I want to say, *Please, please, Hank, I'm pregnant, I'm soft, I'm sad, I'm scared, I need you. Please, come back to my side, or take me to the other side. Please take me there.*

I want to say it, but can't. Or don't. What's the difference? I hate this moment in a relationship, any kind of relationship, when you are just obligated to act cool, to pretend it's normal for love to feel so chilly, to go along with it until the mood passes, and you reconcile again. Years later, you laugh: Remember those few months when you were so mean to me, you called me a Democrat as an accusation? Remember? That was so crazy! That was so hard! Thank God it's over!

You laugh later. Trouble is, I am pregnant now, and I am starting to realize that Hank will not know about it until later, much later, if at all.

"I need to talk to you, in person," I say.

"I'll be in Connecticut for Thanksgiving."

"Are you sure?"

"Promise."

"Okay, because if not, I can come out there and visit you. I need to go to Los Angeles to do a story, so I can stop there on my way, but we really need to talk about something in person."

"That's fine. I'll see you in a couple of weeks."

"Maybe I should come out there anyway. You know, I'm curious about your life out there."

"Maybe New Year's."

"Okay, but why not sooner?"

"Look, Elizabeth, I guess you should know that I'm seeing someone out here."

"What?"

"Look, she's really more of a friend. A skiing buddy, a drinking buddy, you know."

This makes me feel terrible, because I can't ski and I can't drink, which makes me inadequate, which means he had to find someone else to do that with. If only I had just gone out to Taos over the summer, insisted on it when things were still good. We'd be in love and happy, and he would not be drinking. I could have gone there and never left. I could be in his house on the mesa writing, and he would be doing whatever it is that he does, and we would be this adorable couple, like we were meant to be. The sex would be good and sweet and real, not at all how it was when he was here a month ago.

"Well, if she is just a friend, what do you mean when you say you are seeing her?" I try desperately to not sound desperate. "Are you fucking her?"

"Not really, maybe once or twice, but it's pretty much platonic. Actually, I'd have to say that it's platonic in the truest sense of the word. Anyway, it's a Taos thing. It doesn't change anything between us at all. When I come back to New York, it will all be the same."

"So nothing's changed?" I hesitate. "I mean, everything is still the same with us?"

"Nothing's changed."

*P*latonic in the truest sense of the word.

After I get off the phone, I look up *platonic* — Hank is very much the ety-mologist, he is a scientist of language, he is as literal as a mathematician, and he loves the precision of numbers. He chooses his words as carefully as some-one who knows that $2 + 2 = 4$ and believes that everything should be that ab-solute. I search first in *The American Heritage Dictionary*, which says, "Of, relating to, or characteristic of Plato or his philosophy: Platonic dialogues; Pla-tonic ontology. 2. Transcending physical desire and tending toward the purely spiritual or ideal." This leads me to look up *ideal*, and I like definition 4a, which says, "existing only in the mind; imaginary," and 4b, which is "lacking practicality or the possibility of realization." I guess that means that, because it takes place in Taos, the relationship has no real potential. Then I plow through my *New Oxford English Dictionary*, which reports that the term *pla-tonic* was coined in 1631. The first given meaning is the one we all think of: "intimate and affectionate but not sexual." But being an extremely detailed lexicon, the *OED* also includes the definition of *Platonic body*, which is: "one of five regular solids (a tetrahedron, cube, octahedron, dodecahedron, or icosahedron)." So caught up am I in getting an exact denotation that I actually consider looking up all these five figures, because Hank could actually see a relationship in terms of geometry. But I stop myself. This is crazy. Enough al-ready. Basically, he's either involved in a relationship that resembles some solid shape, or he is close with a woman in an essentially nonsexual way, or both.

I figure this means everything is okay.

Twenty-six

HAVE A HAPPY ENDING

God sometimes you just don't come through
Do you need a woman to look after you?

TORI AMOS
"God"

I get into a taxi at six in the morning to go to the abortion clinic. The driver has just begun his shift, and he is very chatty. He keeps asking me questions and being friendly in his terrible Chinese accent, and it just grates on me. I want to kill him. I would like to reach across the open Plexiglas shield and choke him, if that will get him to shut up. I always feel so bad for cab drivers. They work these long hours for no money. They're all immigrants. I think about how awful it must have been for my great-grandparents. But I just don't care right now. I should just ask him to be quiet, but it seems so rude, so uncongenial to this poor schmo who just drives around in traffic with nasty New Yorkers carping at him all day. But what the fuck? I'm having a really bad day, and it's only just begun.

"Please, sir, I'm sorry, but it's really early. I just can't talk. I'm going somewhere difficult." And then, wanting to be conciliatory, I try to be a little funny. "No one is going anywhere happy at this hour."

"I see," he says, and that ends it.

I really don't want to be going to a clinic. All my friends told me to have it done in a doctor's office. But my gynecologist doesn't take my insurance. I spent all of Friday going through the GHI pamphlet to find a listing of one who does, but it was all pretty grim. No Park Avenue offices, and none even in addresses or ZIP codes I recognized. Besides, it seemed hard to go to a doctor for the first time and just announce that I need an abortion. Just not a good way to begin a relationship.

I'm going to this place on Twenty-eight and Park Avenue South that everyone I know who hasn't done it in the doctor's office has ever gone to for an abortion. I picked Daisy up there a few years ago, twice in a two-month period because she thought after you have an abortion, you can't get pregnant again anytime soon. Actually, it's the opposite, you're even more fertile. Daisy wasn't sure who the would-be fathers were, so I went.

I guess Hank should be coming with me, that seems to be the traditional way to do things. It seems horrible, terribly askew, that there is a protocol for abortions, but there is: the guy pays, and the guy accompanies you. It's hard to say what the point of that is. No one else is allowed in the operating room, no one can hold your hand through it, and besides you get completely knocked out. It's total anesthesia. But I guess it would be nice to have someone to sit with in the waiting room, it would be nice to have somebody waiting at the other end, and I guess it would just plain be nice to not feel so all alone, which is how I feel. But I tell myself to buck up. After all, it's nothing, a minor surgical procedure, not really a big deal, I am pro-choice, I've marched twice through Washington, in 1989 and 1991, to make it clear that I believe in abortion. An unwanted fetus is just a tumor to be removed, right? It's that simple. I'm going to treat it like the simple matter that it is.

But still. One of the reasons I am going to the Parkmed clinic is a lack of funds. I have not worked at all since my book came out; I've been using full-time or in recovery full-time. Silver Hill put me out about sixty thousand dollars, therapy three times a week is a costly matter, and I just don't have the money to get an abortion done privately. If I had told Hank, he would have at least kicked in for the fee, but it's too late now. And who can say if he would have been helpful? Who can say if he would have come up from New Mexico and, for lack of a better phrase, done the right thing? I have no idea how he would have reacted. He is scary and unreliable in his responses to me or probably anything these days.

The truth, I admit to myself on the ride to the clinic, is that I did not tell Hank because I did not want to give him the chance to disappoint me. For all my spiel about being an independent woman, being able to handle this on my own, the honest truth is I was just scared that telling him would only give me a chance to hurt even more. And I can't hurt anymore. I can't do it. It's going to be hard to get through this day without Hank, but it would be even worse to have to go through it knowing that he said no, that he refused to be here, that he left me when I needed him most. So far, his being in New Mexico has been about him, about what he needs to do; if he didn't show up for this, it would be about me, about not caring about me. And I am too scared to find out right now what I already know deep down inside: If Hank ever did love me, he doesn't anymore. He's gone for real.

But I just deny it to myself. I deny it over and over again. And I ask Daisy to pick me up.

Outside the office building that houses the clinic, a young woman in a long white robe with a babushka on her head sits Indian-style on the sidewalk, counting her rosary beads and praying for dead babies. The thing I love about New York is that antiabortion protesters here don't look much different from homeless people, so it's hard to be bothered by their presence. When I get inside and up to the eighth floor, I sign in at the receptionist's window. She checks me off on the list, and I am impressed — as I was when I went to Planned Parenthood for birth control when I was a teenager — by how she is personable and friendly, wants me to feel comfortable, smiles like it's going to be all right.

And then I get to the waiting room, and it is definitely not all right. It is an obviously low-income, inner-city crowd. Everyone here is black or Hispanic and very young except me. There is no demographic diversity at all: I am the only person here who is like me; I am the only woman in her thirties who is here and who should know better.

With one exception, there are no men in the room. All of us are here alone. On the television set, which is suspended from the ceiling, Jerry Springer is doing his thing, and I am moved by how appropriate this seems. One girl wants to put on *Guiding Light* — who knew soap operas aired in the morning? — and an altercation ensues. *Altercation*, which is the word cops use when they write crime scene reports, is actually a good description of what is happening here. There is nothing sisterly about this dispute.

I fill out papers and am called in by different counselors who ask me questions about nothing much — my medical history, my statistical information, nothing emotional — and after each encounter, I go into a yet smaller waiting room, as if I am applying for admission to some elite college, and after each interview, the pool of candidates has shrunk. I keep nearing the pinnacle of the abortion pyramid.

After I've changed into a smock, I'm shown to my last stop before I go into the operating room. In the plastic chair next to me is a young woman who is six months pregnant, getting a double procedure. This is her second day of surgery, when the abortion will be complete. She is visibly pregnant, she has probably been showing for at least a month. I ask why she did not do this sooner. She shrugs her shoulders. Things were going well with the prospective baby's father; then things were not going so well with him.

And I want to say, *You idiot.*

But here I am sitting next to her. I am older, I am wiser, and still here I am. I am hanging on to a relationship that barely exists, I am living in a dream world, and yet this twenty-year-old's stupidity is making me feel superior. Or maybe it's making me disgusted with myself. I can't distinguish. We are all pots and kettles, we are all children of God, we are all sinners.

Finally I go into the OR. First the nurse does a sonogram to make sure that I am really pregnant. On the screen she shows me an image of the developing embryo, which is supposed to make me feel confident about what I am doing, but it seems kind of insensitive. Then I realize that the picture looks a lot like the images of comets in outer space that I used to see on those Carl Sagan series on Channel 13. And then I think about all those people who believed that the first moon walk was actually staged somewhere in New Mexico, and I think about all the silly things I and everybody else think, and before I've had time to let my mind wander any further, it is time for the abortion. I get full anesthesia, which I am told is for my own good, but I later realize it is because that allows the doctor to work quicker, to perform more abortions in less time. In private practice, you almost always get a local anesthetic, partly because it is safer, and mostly because doctors don't like to knock anyone out unnecessarily. It is traumatic to go completely under; it means you will wake up disoriented and depressed. But as the anesthesiologist fits the suction mask on my face that releases the ether into my system, I am grateful.

I don't want to know.

I come to on a cot in a darkened room. What time is it? How long have I been here? I have no idea.

I am lying in a fetal position, with terrible cramps in my lower back and abdomen, a thick pad in my panties to absorb the blood. I am woozy, my contact lenses are dry, but I begin to focus on what's around me. All I see is girls. Two rows of cots, at least twenty along each side of the room, all with girls in blue smocks, curled into fetal position, wrapped in baby blue blankets on white pillowcases and white sheets. In an aerial photograph, we would all look the same. We would look like rows of pastries coming out of the oven on a baker's tray. The only variation is that some of us are coiled to the right, and some to the left, but we are all in the same position.

Some of us are here because we didn't bother with birth control, some because we were sloppy, maybe the diaphragm failed—but we are all here because somewhere along the way, we did something stupid.

We are all here for the same reason: we are women, and we are stupid.

I go home with an antibiotic prescription to prevent infection, and a bottle of Motrin for pain. Daisy has lunch with me, but she has to go back to work, so she puts me in a cab to go back to my apartment.

And I want to beg her to take the rest of the day off, to sit with me at home while I lie in bed, but I know I can't ask. After all, this is my own damn fault. I am so drugged at the moment, the lingering anesthesia and the painkillers kicking in, that I don't feel that awful, but I feel very apprehensive. Apprehensive, as in: a bad moon is rising. As in: I am about to crash. All the energy it has taken to be cool with Hank, to make plans for this abortion, to get through it, is slipping away, and I can tell I am going to be so depressed, and I cannot be alone. I feel that terrible, itchy feeling creeping up on me. I've suppressed it this long, but I know I am about to sink.

Before we say good-bye, Daisy tells me not to worry; it isn't so bad. She went to work after she had both her abortions; it's really not that big a deal.

As I stumble into my apartment, my walk weaving a little bit as I go through the door, I know I can't pretend this is just some tooth extraction. I know this is different. So I just keep telling myself that I'll go to sleep, that I won't think about it. What right have I got to bother any of my friends with this? Hank is the one who should be here. It's not their fault that I got pregnant. This is my problem. I'm just going to have to pull through this. It is Wednesday, and Lily and I have our weekly girls' night out this evening, and I've told her if I feel up to it, I'll let her know. If I need anyone, she'll be there.

And then I let myself rest. I have terrible dreams. I wish I could remember them. I wish they were somehow full of fitting images, dead babies, lost heartbeats, that kind of thing. But all I know is that they are horrible, it is a fitful sleep that is more tiring than just staying awake, and then I wake up with a start at ten at night.

I feel horrible, scared and horrible, but still too drugged to cry, to do anything about some terrible pain I feel creeping all over me. This is the worst: pain you can't make sense of, that you just can't express. I've always felt that as long as I could still talk about it, I was always safe. But right now there is nothing to say. I just need someone to hold me, to take care of me, to hug me, to make me a cup of tea. I need Hank.

I think about calling him and just telling him what happened today, coming out with it. I mean, why not? But it's all too humiliating. And once again, what if he disappoints me? What if his new girlfriend is there with him? What if I can't find him? What if this makes me seem like an annoying nag and he decides I am too much to deal with and he cuts me out of his life? I can't take a chance on calling Hank.

In meetings they teach you to ask for help, to always say what you need, not to expect people to figure it out on their own. The logic for this suggestion is that often addicts use drugs because the world disappoints them, and often the world disappoints them because they have not been clear about what they expect from it. So I decide this would be a good time to ask for help.

I call Lily and ask her to please come over. Whatever else she is doing, she needs to just come see me. This is a physical and emotional emergency.

By this time it's after eleven o'clock, and she needs to get up early to go to work.

"Lizzie!" she exclaims. "Why didn't you call me earlier? I would have come over hours ago, but it's late now. I can't leave my apartment! I'm in my pajamas. I'm ready to go to sleep."

"Please don't make me beg." I feel myself about to cry. At last I have a specific grievance to define my misery: my best friend will not pull herself together to come over to my house and check up on me on the day I've had an abortion. This seems like a terrible betrayal. Lily had surgery a few years back, and I stayed at her apartment for a couple of days to make sure she was okay. I'm not always the best or most reliable friend, but I am a great clutch player: When someone is in definite trouble, I will usually drop everything and run to see her, to talk her through the crisis, to make sure everything is okay. And now, for once, I have a good reason to be calling for help, and if I understand correctly, Lily is actually saying no to me. And this makes me cry.

"Lily, how can you do this?" I am definitely crying. "Lily, I am so scared and so lonely. Please come here. Please forget about everything else. I am really desperate."

"Look, baby," she says. "What you need to do is get in a cab and come over here. I'll fix you something to eat. You can lie in my bed and watch TV, or we can still rent a movie. I'll make you some tea. I even have lemon and honey here for you. If you can't be alone, you need to come over here. But I just can't go out right now. It's too late."

"Damn it, Lily." What do I say? "Please don't do this to me. I'm all bloody and I'm exhausted. I can barely move. I shouldn't be leaving the house. Please just come here."

"Look, Lizzie, I mean it," she says calmly. "I am really happy to do anything you want, I'll do anything at all, but you just need to get here. If you want, I'll even meet your taxi downstairs, so you won't even need to walk into the building alone. But I won't come over there. It's too late."

"Oh Lily," I cry. I cry and cry and cry, the kind of heavy bawling that I should be used to by now, but it still feels just as bad every time it happens.

I think about how just a month before, when I really needed someone to come through for me, God guided me to Stone O'Malley, and he sat with me the whole night through on my last coke run. And I keep wishing that God would send someone to come through for me right now, because I really need it. And then I remember that I have not been much of a friend to much of anybody for a while. After Lily had her accident on the way to my thirtieth birthday party, I did not even bother to call her at the hospital, or even once she got home. What right do I have to expect her to even be talking to me still? And yet, all my friends have pretty much stood by me, visited me at Silver Hill, come to my AA qualifications—they've all done a pretty good job of sticking around when I do not deserve it at all. So I guess it's fair enough for Lily not to want to leave the house right now.

I get out of bed, pull on some sweatpants, stumble out into the street, and get inside a cab.

You can have all kinds of good, solid beliefs, but in practice, it all goes out the window. They say there's no such thing as an atheist in a foxhole. But that doesn't mean you really believe in God when the enemy shoots your head off. At this point, I am almost antiabortion, not in a legal or even a moral sense— it's just that I cannot imagine why anyone would put herself through it. I can't imagine why anyone would put herself through an unwanted pregnancy or an unwanted child either—I'm sure that's much worse—but I'm left with a feeling that no one should have an abortion. At any rate, I will never have one again.

But my whole life has fallen through the divide between theory and practice. I never quite live up to what I'm supposed to be. I'm one of those women whom people call a dynamo, a powerhouse, that kind of thing. I practically raised myself; I've been working since I was in high school, supporting myself since college; I'm tough, I'm scrappy, I've got my own money; I don't need nothing or no one. So whenever I get involved with some guy, he's shocked to find out that I'm so human. I have such needs, a welter of needs—I'm like everyone else, only more so. I've been waiting for a break from holding it together for so long that sometimes I just fall apart. And I always fall in love with these men who seem so sweet and angelic, gentle guys with softness and love. And then I'm shocked to find out that they, too, are human. They can be harsh, they can be mean, and

sometimes I see them start to hate me for being such a sad girl, after all. We're all
hurt and disgusted by the bait-and-switch, like I never asked for this, where did
that other person go?

And here's what it comes down to: Most people would expect that my financial, artistic, and intellectual independence would be matched with an equal
degree of emotional independence. But that's not how it is at all. All my good,
solid ideals, all my feminist principles, all my hardy beliefs—and in the end, I
just go to mush.

That's why I do drugs: they fill the lacuna between who I am and who I want
to be; between what I think and what I feel.

Hank never makes it to New York for Thanksgiving. I try to call him the
Monday before to make plans, but there's no answer. I leave messages. I leave
a whole bunch of them. I no longer care if that makes me seem needy and
crazed, because I finally realize that I *am* needy and crazed and I can't pretend otherwise.

When I don't hear from him, I figure he is probably drunk and wandering
around somewhere. For all I know he's been killed in some highway wreck. I
finally decide to call a friend of his in Taos to find out if he is okay.

"He left town earlier for Thanksgiving," his friend says, like I should know.
"I drove him to the airport a couple of hours ago."

"Oh good." I am relieved. He'll be here later tonight. "So he's on his way to
New York."

"Oh, no, he didn't say anything about going there. He went to Saint Louis."

"Saint Louis?" *What?*

"Yeah. To his friend Rachel's house. He didn't tell you?"

He certainly did not.

"Who's Rachel?" I ask.

"His friend," he says, like I'm supposed to know.

"Is this his new girlfriend? Because he told me about that," I say, not wanting to completely embarrass myself. "But he was supposed to come here
today. He said it wasn't anything serious."

"Look, I don't want to get involved," he says, wisely. "You should talk to him
about this, not me."

"I guess I should."

Hank calls me drunk the day after Thanksgiving. He says he's in a blues bar
somewhere. He says he decided to just skip Thanksgiving and wander around
the country and get wasted. He's staying at a motel somewhere. He doesn't say

anything about Rachel, and I don't say anything about her either. I just feel relieved. He's drunk and lost, as always. He's not in love with anybody else, nothing's changed. His friend must have made a mistake.

Hank gives me the number of the place he's staying. When I call it a couple of hours later, it turns out to be a pay phone in a laundromat. Then I look at my caller ID, and dial that number. I get an answering machine. "This is Rachel. I'm not home right now. Please leave a message."

What a fool I am. I just can't seem to get it right with anybody.

I want so badly to be in one relationship that works. Just one. That's all. I start talking to God all the time. Mostly I just say, God, if You're out there, please show me the way. *Or I'll try,* Please help me to get through this; please help me to stay clean. *I've stopped asking for specific things, because it is so clear to me that I have no idea what's good for me. All I can do is hope that there is some kind of guiding force out there that can carry me through this, that can help me to get over Hank, that can help me stop doing bad things to myself. In the program, people always say,* Just do the next right thing. *It's good advice, except that they don't tell you what to do if you don't know what the next right thing is.* God, I beg, *please take away all my destructive impulses. Please teach me to love and live a good life. Please do for me what I cannot do for myself.*

Most drug addicts who stay clean will tell you that they did all the things they were supposed to, they went to meetings, they took care of themselves, but in the end, it really was some higher power that pulled them through. In the end, it was grace. I've been told over and over again that only one in thirty-five addicts gets clean and stays that way, and I know I have to be one of them.

So I keep begging God for a state of grace. And I thank Him. I thank Him for never giving up on me, even though there were plenty of times I would have been happy to give up on myself. I thank Him and promise to try.

REDEMPTION

Twenty-seven

THE LORD IS MY SHEPHERD

For the ones who have a notion
A notion deep inside
That it ain't no sin to be glad you're alive

BRUCE SPRINGSTEEN
"Badlands"

There is nothing left for me to do but go through recovery. I get some late-night drunk phone calls from Hank, but it's obvious that this relationship is over. It has been for a while; he's just forgotten to tell me. So now that he's gone, there's just me, and I can't hide anymore.

I go to meetings all the time. I'm not sure I do anything besides sleep and go to meetings. No matter how early I get into bed, I can't seem to get up and out before sunset. Five o'clock, six o'clock—that's not unusual for me at all. I lie with the covers intricately wrapped around me like a sari, folded between my legs and behind my knees and in the crooks of my arms. I shiver underneath them, wet with cold sweat in my overheated apartment. Even after lying there for sixteen hours, I do not feel refreshed—I feel more tired, ill. Sleeping only makes me sleepier. I have to force myself to get out of bed at all. I realize that I am plain old depressed. Take away the drugs, take away the nonworking relationship to obsess about, and I am left with my depression. Does nothing ever change?

But I am going to deal with it. Dr. Singer puts me on a new antidepressant, an old-fashioned tricyclic called nortriptyline, which does not make me tired the way Prozac and the other drugs in its family do. And after a week of this fresh regimen, I am actually able to stay awake more. I get one of those full-spectrum lamps, a light box that is supposed to mimic sunshine during the dark months of the year. I sit in front of it for at least fifteen minutes every day, to help counteract the seasonal affective disorder that I seem to come down with whenever winter approaches and the clocks get reset. I'm kind of dubious about the idea that light therapy can actually make a difference, but I give it a try. At this point, I'll do anything that might help.

I pray all the time. I get on my knees and beg God to just get me through this. I am inarticulate, without poetry, without words even: mostly I just kneel on the floor in front of my bed, my palms open on top of it, and no matter what I am trying to say, I usually just end up crying with my face in my hands until I can't cry anymore. God is a clever guy; I think He gets the idea.

At every meeting I go to, I talk about getting pregnant, I talk about Hank, I talk about my abortion, I talk about how desperate I feel, and this actually helps. I also listen very carefully. I listen to everything everybody says. I no longer differentiate between good meetings and bad ones—they are all just meetings, and they are all somehow helping me to stay clean. And in some strange way, they are also helping me, very slowly, to feel less depressed. I don't know why it works, no one really knows why it works—if it were just about being with fellow sufferers, group therapy would have the same effect—but somehow, I feel better. Maybe it's knowing that I am trying so hard to stay clean, to get healthy. Maybe it's just having a place to go whenever I need it. Maybe it's making me feel like less of a burden to my friends. At any rate, I stick with it. It's not that I made a commitment in my mind to devote myself to this program; it's more that I don't know what else to do, and I'll do just about anything.

I find a sponsor. I meet her at a meeting at Midnite, a place on Houston Street where, in typical AA fashion, there isn't actually a meeting at midnight. But there's one at 12:15 and another at 2 A.M., which is later than they are anywhere else. I go there whenever I have not managed to get to a civilized meeting at an earlier hour. I prefer Perry Street and Tribeca, and I attend some NA meetings in the East Village, where people are arty and intellectual, where everyone's response to their personal poverty is to read Marx and refuse to go to business school. But the scene at Midnite has its advantages. Midnite after midnight is a hard-luck, hard-case hangout, full of preoperation transsexuals and bikers who live in Rockland County and factory workers on their way to the graveyard shift across the tunnel, in New Jersey. No one here is even sort of like me—no one here is even sort of like anyone else here, even the transvestites bicker and bitch about whether they should identify as male or female before the surgery is complete—but instead of using this as a way to distance myself, I make it a reason to believe: here we are, all of us, all so different, but we all need help, we're all here looking for it, we're all trying. At this point, trying is more important than succeeding. But the two do seem to go together: at any meetings I attend, when the chairman asks if anyone who is counting days wants to give their number, I always do—and the days are accumulating; they are well into double digits. I am staying clean.

Isabel goes to late meetings at Midnite because she is the lighting director at a Broadway show, so she's not out of work until late. Isabel is from some hellish part of Appalachia in Kentucky. She started drinking when she was nine years old. She was addicted to heroin by the time she was twelve. She was married and divorced at seventeen, and she got clean right after that. Isabel's mother is a junkie, and of course—could a story like this *not* include incest?— Isabel was molested by a series of stepfathers and their surrogates. So much for anyone who believes that life in the hinterlands is purer and sweeter than it is in the big city. Isabel is now thirty-five, she somehow managed to graduate from Vassar College and move to New York, and she lives with her lesbian lover and two longhaired cats in the Fort Greene section of Brooklyn. After I've shared at the Midnite meeting—spoken about having just had an abortion, talked about how I still haven't told Hank about it because he's drunk, discussed how my work life and my personal life both seem to be completely over and I don't know why I am even persisting at all—Isabel walks over to me as I am bundling on my shearling coat.

"Do you have a sponsor?" Isabel asks, as we walk down the stairs and out into the street where she can light up an American Spirit.

"No," I answer.

"Well, then, I'm going to be your sponsor," she says as she exhales into the freezing air. It is cold and dark and too late to be outside. "If it doesn't work out, that's fine. You can find someone else. But you need someone looking after you right now."

"Okay," I say, and maybe even smile. Isabel is tall and thin, with a tangle of blond hair and too many pimples. I would love to give her some skin care tips. But sobriety, not dermatology, is the point, and I am so sleepy and spent that I don't even have the energy to be funny or friendly or anything besides grateful that someone is trying to reach out to me. "That's very kind of you."

"No, not at all," she says, working on her second cigarette. "You would be helping me by letting me help you."

"Look, please, not this again," I say. "I know all the program stuff about how you have to give it away to keep it, and how working with newcomers and doing service helps you keep your sobriety green, but that doesn't mean that you're not being kind to offer."

"Okay, that's fine," she says, and I am relieved that she does not argue. We go to the Grey Dog, a coffee place on Carmine Street opposite my old apartment, and have pecan pie and café au lait, and talk for a couple of hours. I promise Isabel that I will call her once a day—she has just bought a cell phone, so she should not be hard to reach, even at the theater—and we agree to meet again the same time the following week. By then I will have written out my first step, which simply involves making a list of what it means to me to be "powerless" and how I know that my life has become "unmanageable."

"That's pretty easy," I say to Isabel about this assignment as I walk her to the subway on Sixth Avenue. "It's obvious to me that I am completely powerless over drugs and pretty much everything in my life, and it's really obvious that things are completely unmanageable, or I would not have gotten pregnant, I would not have started using after four months in rehab—I mean, I could probably tell you everything you need to know in five minutes."

"That's good," she says. "Then it won't take you very long to write it all down."

It is part of the Twelve Step ritual to put a list of your past misdeeds—everything that made you an addict and brought you to the miserable place that you are now, which is to say, going to meetings—down on paper, where it's clear. It's not enough to just talk it through in therapy, or share it at meetings, or chat with friends over coffee about all the dumb things you did. In AA, the belief is that you must have it before you in plain ink, so that it's *there*, it's tangible, it is a thing you can hold in your hands and refer to. The idea is to keep the nature of addiction from becoming this huge amorphous mass that follows you everywhere in the ether, that infiltrates everything like sawdust. Because, in fact, that is precisely what an active addiction is like. But a recovered addiction, one that is in remission, should have parameters, it should have a place in your life that is clear and simple and obvious. It should be as flat and real and finite and unthreatening as a piece of paper; it should assume two dimensions. So every step needs to be written out, starting with the first one, which is my task for the week.

Isabel gives me a hug as she descends toward the turnstile. "Okay, sweetie," she says. Everyone in the program seems to use this diminutive pet name. "Get some sleep and call me when you wake up. You realize that you're a living miracle, and you are going to make a great sober person."

"Sure," I say, because there really is no good answer for a remark like that. And I remind myself to *act as if.*

*J*udaism is a problem for recovery. Not because of the Twelve Steps, which are simply Judeo-Christian morality laid out. Not because of the God thing, because, of course, we believe in God. We do not believe in praying on our knees, a basic tenet of AA—in fact, I think that is pretty much a no-no for those of us whose Bible ends with the Old Testament. But that's okay. I like to fall before my bed, to "hit my knees" as they say in meetings.

The problem is that in Judaism we lack iconography, we do not pray before a cross, we do not believe in intermediaries, we scowl at the patheticness of idolatry. All the troubles that befell the Jews in prehistory had to do with getting rid of those pesky idols that the Greeks and Romans and Amalekites, that whichever enemies, placed in our holy Temple. If you wanted to hurt the Jews, or at least make them good and mad, you stuck statues in their tabernacles.

Every Jew has a direct line to God, and that is that. Which you would think would be kind of nice, a relief. But the idea of human intervention, of some mortal flesh who cares for us, who offers absolution, who will die for our sins and absorb any of the new ones, is an even greater assuagement, a pleasure. Confession must be a thrill, with the collared man behind the curtain or scrim taking an inventory of your ills. How fun to fondle rosary beads. Hail Mary, full of grace! Ave Maria!

Jews only get to confess once a year, and we go straight to the Man, to God Himself. Before Yom Kippur, during the ten days of penitence, we throw our sins into a body of water, and let them go. And believe me, when you are a recovering addict, you feel like the worst kind of sinner. Forget all the bad things you have done to other people: The real evil is how you have sinned against yourself, how you have violated your precious soul, made in the image of God.

I want so badly to believe in God. Like most Americans who answer those annual polls saying that they are religious, I think I am typical: instinctively I will tell you that of course I believe in Him. I even capitalize His name, even as a pronoun, because I accord Him that kind of respect. But I know I want to believe more than I actually do. I hope He is out there looking after me, and the evidence is in favor of it: I am alive, after all; I have a good life. But I just cannot go all the way with it. If I could, I would never have had a drug problem, because all those things I feared and that made me use, I'd have believed He was taking care of it all. This is why Step Two is so important to recovery: We came to believe that a power greater than ourselves could restore us to sanity. And, of course, Step Three: We made a decision to turn our will and our lives over to the care of God.

I always go back to the Psalms written by King David with all their imploring desperation and prostrate questing: "Though I walk through the valley of the shadow of death, I will not fear, for You are with me." Now, I know David was a man in serious doubt at that moment: his child with his beloved Bathsheba was stillborn, his son Amnon had raped his daughter Tamar, his son Absalom was leading a revolt against him, his household was in disarray. Like many a great man before and after him, King David had retreated to the desert to beg for God's forgiveness and aid. He spoke these strong words because he wanted to believe, more than because he did. And he had a rapport with the Almighty already. They chatted. And still, David was not quite sure that God was really on his side, was really there at all.

Every day since I have been clean, I have longed for the kind of faith that would allow me to walk through those painful knolls and dells and believe I was safe. I have prayed for it. In AA they say that if you don't believe, then pray for belief. Pray for willingness. So I do.

And then I think of the Velvet Underground's doleful song "Jesus," from their third and least renowned or appreciated album. It is my favorite. "Jesus / Help me find my proper place / Help me in my weakness / 'Cause I'm falling out of grace." The only words in the song, repeated repeatedly, composed by Lou Reed, a Jew. You see, in the hour of darkness, it is easier to turn to the Son of God than to God Himself, for some reason. I'm not sure why.

So maybe I am not supposed to accept Jesus Christ as my savior, but that trembling stir of awe would be good enough for me. It would do the trick. It really would. If I cannot pray with it, I can at least beg for it. That faith will save my life.

Twenty-eight

THE POSSIBILITY OF HOME

Sometimes I heard voices muttering in my head, and a lot of the time the world seemed to smolder around its edges. But I was in a little better physical shape every day. I was getting my looks back, and my spirits were rising, and this was all in all a happy time for me. All these weirdos, and me getting a little better every day in the midst of them. I had never known, never even imagined for a heartbeat, that there might be a place for people like us.

DENIS JOHNSON
Jesus' Son

I speak to Mary, my counselor at Smithers. Technically, she should kick me out because I am always at least a half hour late to session, which violates the rules, and it's supposed to be three strikes and you're out. I've probably amassed three outs by now. She's going to recommend to Dr. Singer and to the Smithers administration that I be moved to the day program, five days a week, four hours a day. She won't let me stay in her evening group, so it's go all the way, or get expelled from Smithers altogether. I think about the line in the Big Book: *Half measures availed us nothing.*

"I already spent four months at Silver Hill," I say to Mary. "Why should I go through a full-time program again? I'm staying clean. I'm going to meetings. What am I doing wrong? Besides I guess, being too disorganized to be prompt."

"Instead of seeing this as a punishment, why don't you think of it as an opportunity?" Mary suggests. "You have the luxury of arranging your own time, your insurance will pay for it, and you can take advantage of some very good treatment. You can get completely better. Why don't you accept help when it's being offered? You've been through a lot. Just try it."

"Okay, I guess." I hate the idea. "It's just that I liked everything about Silver Hill *except* going to group therapy. So why would I want to enroll in a program that is *only* group therapy, that does not have the advantage of being a beautiful place in the rolling nutmeg hills of Connecticut? Why would I want that?"

"Because it's a very good thing. The counselors are excellent. It's tough. It's what you need." She pauses. "Smithers is nothing like Silver Hill. The clientele is extremely bright and diverse. It will challenge you. Think about it."

But actually, I realize as we're talking, I really don't want to think about it. I need some sort of plan. I don't have a lot to do with myself right now. My employment life is in tatters. I can probably take a few months off before I need to plan my next work project. I've got another check due to me from Doubleday when the paperback of *Bitch* is released. Since everything I do seems to turn out wrong, I might as well take a mandated time-out and think about my next move—maybe I'll even try to get some low-stress sobriety job. I can always waitress or fold T-shirts at the Gap. I could obviously use some rigorous treatment in the meanwhile.

"All right," I say.

Here we go again. When will I be a normal girl? When will I be out of recovery? And while this question nags at me, I also feel great relief about committing myself to going to Smithers full-time after the first of the year. I am surrendering, waving the white flag, holding my hands up in a gesture of peace—mainly with myself. Before I've even made it to my first day at the outpatient program, I have already changed. I've made it through the first step: I've admitted that I am powerless, that my life is unmanageable, and that I ought to get every bit of help I can.

It takes me a couple of weeks after my intake interview to finally show up for my first day at Smithers. The idea of being somewhere every day at nine in the morning is not appealing. I know that's what most people do, but the thing they have to show up for is called a job, and at the end of the week they get paid for their trouble. I cannot imagine what's in this for me.

The first thing I notice about the patients at Smithers is that everyone is very smart and very damaged. Even more than people here are smart, they are clever. Since most of the addicts at Smithers are not rich, they have had to be pretty crafty to get their dope. They've been prostitutes and hustlers, they've stolen and embezzled, they've worked at restaurants and taken money out of the till, they've found sugar daddies, they've robbed pharmacies. They've burgled their grandmothers' Social Security checks, and they've been dealers themselves.

It is a depressing atmosphere, partly because of the scenery. Roosevelt Hospital is an ugly place, the high-gloss mauve paint on the walls desperately needing a new coat, the furniture all gray and collapsing, the mesh on the cushions full of holes that need to be rewoven, everything indicating that this is not a place you come to for healing or convalescence — it feels more like a hospice, a place to await death. And the rooms where groups gather at Smithers are joyless. Every morning I feel like I'm going to a wake — and not the kind you have for a grandmother who's died peacefully in her sleep in Boca Raton. It's more like one for a five-year-old victim of leukemia, where everyone can't stop crying. Partly, this is simply because it's so early in the day, and drug addicts are not morning people. There's a somnambulism to the grief. But mostly it's just that very few people have more than a few days or weeks clean, and everyone is indeed in mourning for their substance of choice. This place is not cushy and relaxing like Silver Hill. If you're here, you have to do the work, or you are asked to leave.

Even relapsing is not a particular crime at Smithers. But failing to participate, to examine the mess that is your life, is cause for dismissal. Nobody here gets to cheat on the therapeutic process. In theory, the relapse rule is three strikes and you're out, but in fact, if you come back to group and make a conscientious attempt to face up to it and "process" it, first in small group and then in front of everybody in large group, you're allowed to stay. The main thing that I have learned about treatment programs is that the rules are pretty slippery, and not because drug counselors are pushovers. It's just that the process of recovery is so complicated, and relapse is part of it. Had I not relapsed after Silver Hill, I never would have found out just how sick I was, and that my problem was not my addiction — it's that I myself am an addict. In fairness, people who keep falling off and using in the day program are usually sent to Smithers inpatient facility to detox for several days. The mansion, as it is known, used to be the Smithers family's regal home on Fifth Avenue. The house itself is still pretty grand, but the accommodations for junkies are quite tawdry — there are bunk beds and eight to a room, and by all accounts it is extremely unpleasant. I have trouble imagining a baseball star like Daryl Strawberry confined to such a place, but the closest he has come to staying clean happened while he was there, so maybe it works. At any rate, the thought of going there is enough to scare most people straight. People in real trouble are advised to go to long-term rehabs out of town, but many of them simply drop out of the program and go back to using. The prospects are pretty bleak.

There are four small groups, and we meet for an hour and a half first thing every day, followed by two sessions with the whole Smithers community, which adds up to about forty people. Apparently, there is a long waiting list that I bypassed because I came from the evening program, but at least one effect of the demand to get in is that everybody wants to be here pretty badly. Perhaps that's another reason for the dolorous aura of the place: these are desperate people, completely exposed in their desperation. I often feel that instead of skin, we all have clear plastic wrap coating our bodies, and it seems always on the verge of tearing. Not a day goes by when at least three people don't start crying in small group, and at least five of us bawl our way through large meetings. Each of the big groups has a theme, like vocational problems, time management, family-of-origin issues, and twice a week there are men's group and women's group. On Thursdays we have a community meeting, in which we discuss whatever we want to without the counselors present, and mostly it just involves complaining that no one is bothering to fill the coffee urns in the morning and stuff like that. We try to get these meetings over with quickly, so we can all leave. We also have an in-house AA meeting once a week. And on Fridays, the last session is weekend planning, to ensure that everyone will be busy with something that does not involve drugs. We're all quite generous about including each other in whatever we're doing—mostly going to movies and meetings. No one ever seems to want to go to parties, partly because the temptation to drink or use is too much, but mostly because we're all tired and sick of it all. Everyone's favorite leisure activity is sleep.

Every morning we have to be in small group by nine o'clock, but Kiku, our group counselor, tends to grant us a ten-minute grace period. If you're not on time, you can't come in, which I usually find a relief. But again, if it happens more than three times, you get kicked out of the program, which I don't really want, so I somehow manage to get there. There's a direct subway line from Chambers Street, where I live, to Columbus Circle, the stop for Roosevelt Hospital, but after a while I start to indulge in taxis taken up the West Side Highway so I can nap on the way.

Kiku is small and Indonesian and stereotypically so. She has a heavy accent, she often can't locate the correct word, but this is all a decoy, a deception so that you underestimate her; she sees all.

First thing in the day, we all check in, and then Kiku asks if anyone needs to "rent space" in group today, does anyone have a particular issue to discuss? Has anybody relapsed? If you do have something you need to "process," you better be prepared to go all the way with it. Kiku will push until you get to the bottom of it. Drug counselors are dealing with life and death, so they do not have time to let anyone get away with anything; they call you on your bullshit immediately. Their impatience is glorious. Their style is confrontational. At Twelve Step meetings, there is no cross talk; people listen quietly while other people share. At Smithers, everyone comments on every little thing.

Kiku may push pretty hard, but no one else will let you get away with any-thing either.

For instance, after my first week at Smithers, Hank shows up in New York City and calls me very late, after midnight, and I am already asleep. He is here for a job interview, some Wall Street thing he is considering. By this time I have long since given up on him, but when he calls me from the Liquor Store Bar, which is only a few blocks from my house, I can't help myself. I pick him up after he's been eighty-sixed by the bartender for being so drunk, and I sweetly and tenderly bring him back to my house. As if. As if he deserves that kind of treatment from me. I even spend the night with him, and as a conse-quence, I am too tired the next morning to go in for program.

When I show up at Smithers the day after that, there is no one in my small group who is not angry at me. Everyone keeps telling me that as a member of the community, I am obligated to be here and participate, we all have to trust each other to see one another through, and calling in absent because of some drunk creep I am dating is not acceptable.

At first I find the whole thing ridiculous: after all, if I want to see Hank, that's my stupid problem. As everyone yells at me and tells me I am being irre-sponsible to my own and everybody else's recovery, it feels like one of those stupidly imposed constructs, like Gestalt therapy; I might as well be an empty chair that people are yelling at as a proxy for their abusive father. They barely know me, and the notion that I matter to them is spurious. The idea that any single individual matters to anyone else's recovery is silly.

But over the next few weeks I learn that it is the group process and absolute devotion to it that makes the whole thing work. If your fuck-ups matter to everyone else, maybe they will eventually start to matter to you too.

So the day I come in after being with Hank, I am bombarded with ques-tions: Why would you want to see this asshole? Yes, we all know that love is blind—and deaf and dumb as well—but c'mon already. What more does he have to do to make you realize he doesn't care about you at all? Sure, you're at-tached to him, but why? It's a sickness. You need a guy like him like you need another abortion. You know that. What is so bad about you that you are so bad to yourself?

And I stammer and say something about how when I met Hank at Silver Hill, when he was sober, he was the most wonderful person on earth. He was an A+. I was going to marry him. Now he is drunk and awful, but that does not mean that I cannot remember the person he once was. It does not mean that I don't hope that person will return someday. He will, won't he?

And it is this question from me that brings home the whole point of recov-ery: When you're getting clean, all you have is today. In fact, it could be argued that in all of life, all any of us has is today. What was true about Hank yesterday, the possibility of how he might be tomorrow—well, that just doesn't matter. There is simply no time to hang on to what was and what may be. You're an addict; your life is messy enough without regretting the past or worrying about the future. That is the big lesson of Smithers: there is no time but the present; *now* is a desperate enough place to be without bringing in the rest of life, before and after.

It is exhausting. Four hours a day of emotional boot camp.

Every day I get back to my apartment at whatever time it is—maybe two or three, I usually grab a bite before I get on the subway—and immediately go to sleep. I mean to wake up for the 8:30 meeting at Perry Street, or I mean to get up for dinner with a friend or to see a movie, but I just can't. I am too spent. I go see *Shakespeare in Love* one night, and fall asleep in my seat in the theater, and wake up to find that my pocketbook has been stolen. I am afraid I've become narcoleptic.

One day I go to Kathlyn's house to feed her cats after Smithers, she is away on a business trip. I get under the thick down covers in her bed, I am so cold and exhausted, and set her alarm clock for eight. She lives right near Perry Street, so I figure I'll just nap until the meeting. The alarm clock buzzes at 8 P.M. I open my eyes for a minute, then crinkle them into a squint. The reading light is on, and the cats are arrayed on the bed elegantly, the black one at my feet, the tabby in the crook of my arm. The hell with it. I reach over and flick the lever to stop the alarm, turn off the light switch and fall back off to sleep. I don't wake up until seven in the morning, time to get together to go up to Smithers again.

I am supposed to stay in the program for ten weeks. I cannot imagine that I will be able to make it beyond a month, if that.

I get fat. Sometime between December and February, I gain thirty-five pounds, my Levi's jeans size goes from a 27 waist to a 34, and as a consolation prize, my boobs grow to a sexy C. When I get on the scale at Lily's house on a chilly winter day, I am 165 pounds, which seems like a normal weight for a six-foot man, but not a woman who is five foot six. I have no idea what is happening to me or what to do.

I figure it's a metabolism change. After a few years of a steady diet of speed, cocaine, and little else, maybe just eating normally, with nothing to quicken the burn, makes my body absorb calories too quickly, like someone who has quit smoking. If that's all it is, it's bound to pass if I exercise more and eat less. Trouble is, I *do* exercise, and I'm not much of an eater. I try Pilates because I am embarrassed to be seen at a normal gym, but it is so expensive—$70 a lesson—that I have to quit. I get an exercise bicycle that I set up near the window of my bedroom. I take boxing lessons with a guy I know from Perry Street, who was a prison boxing champion during his seven years in Attica. But I do not lose weight, and I tire so quickly, like a fat person, which I am. I'm thirty-one now, and maybe it's an age thing. Maybe the body change that people say occurs when you are over thirty is happening to me. Maybe this is the residue of my pregnancy.

Whatever it is, it is scary. I have never had an eating disorder or a distorted image of my own body. I've always had serious hips, Mediterranean curves, and I've never tried to be skinny. In fact, I am the only woman I know who likes how she looks exactly as is. I think I'm gorgeous. I don't care if anyone disagrees. I think I am ten times prettier than I actually am. That probably sounds arrogant, and obviously it is, but in a world where it's not even a malady—it is in fact a female norm—to despise your own body, I like to think I have cultivated a healthy self-regard. I am so self-loathing in so many ways that it is actually good to feel good about some aspect of myself. My parents did not necessarily get everything right with me, but they always made me feel cute as a kid, and I think it has stuck.

For the first time in my life, I identify with anorexics and bulimics. I start to understand how most women walk around feeling all the time. I am used to a friend showing me a new outfit she just bought and asking if it makes her look fat, and I always think it is a ridiculous question. What a stupid thing to worry about, especially since all my friends are thin. If any of them were models or actresses, there might be some point to this concern, but for us normal human beings, this is just silly. We are not static images, our vitality is part of our beauty, and so long as you're not obese, I cannot imagine why anyone would worry.

But now I understand. I understand what it's like to never feel quite pretty enough, to always feel concerned with how you look. Because for once, that's how I feel all the time. Maybe this is karma, punishment for my lack of empathy when it comes to dysmorphic body image. Whatever it is, it is unbearable. I start to do things I have never done before, like purchase diet books: *The Zone* and *Dr. Atkins' Diet Revolution*. I read them with horror: I cannot imagine thinking about food enough to actually follow the regimens. It's not that they are so harsh—the Zone is basically a balanced diet of protein and fat and carbohydrates—but I hate the idea of being this concerned about what I eat. On the Atkins diet, you can eat bacon and cheese omelettes and other fatty foods, but no bread products, which is very hard if you live on sandwiches, which I do. I have never thought about such things in my life! I have always eaten what I wanted when I wanted, which has amounted to not all that much food, because when you satisfy your desires, they turn out to be surprisingly slight, or at least reasonable. It's deprivation that creates hunger. My only understanding of this idea when it comes to nutrition is in relation to my own feelings about love: if some man gave me precisely what I needed, it would probably not be all that much, but the famine of feelings makes me needy and desperate. It is amazing for me to understand for the first time that many, if not most people, have the same feelings about food that I have about love. What a nightmare. I can't live like this!

But something's got to give. I feel unattractive, unsexy, probably for the first time ever.

I consider the possibility that it's psychosomatic. I'm not supposed to be dating right now, so maybe I'm padding myself with a layer of fat to keep the men away. Apparently, incest victims often get fat because they are frightened of sexual attention. After Hank, after the pregnancy and abortion, it would make sense if, at least for the moment, I never want to have sexual contact with anyone ever again.

Unfortunately, I seem to be getting my wish, and it is not very pleasant. I hate not being in a relationship. Of course, I never actually am in one, but for as long as I can remember, I have been in pursuit of romance. The chase never leads me to anything good—I get into these miserable situations that only last a month or two and leave me obsessed and full of longing—but I always hope against hope. In AA, one of the *suggestions*—there are no rules in the program, only suggestions—is that you stay out of relationships for your first year of sobriety. One of the jokes is that nobody knows if that recommendation works, since no one has ever tried it. The theory behind this wise bit of counsel is that addicts will replace their desperate need for drugs with an obsession with a person, and then they will never truly recover; they will always be at the mercy of something or someone. That is, of course, precisely what happened with me and Hank: we started out in this lovely love, we were going to go to meetings together and stay clean together, but all those good intentions soon went by the wayside. We did nothing to stay sober, we never once went to AA or NA together, and soon I relied on *him* to keep me sane and happy. There was no other mooring in my life besides Hank. I thought our healthy love, which was predicated on the friendship and caring we developed—completely asexually—at Silver Hill would be a beautiful and salubrious thing.

The sensible thing for me to do with this upsetting information would be to take a break from the whole business of romance, of mad love, but instead my failure makes me want to try even harder, just to prove I can do it. I have absolutely no desire or plans to stay away from men, because it would only demonstrate that men prefer to stay away from me.

Meanwhile, with or without a love life, my body is driving me to distraction. I'm used to my mind being out of control, but not my body. So I go see a plastic surgeon that Lily sometimes works for. She's been writing the text for his Web site, and she thinks he's extremely competent, one of the best. I go for a consultation, I strip down and show him my hips and thighs and my bulging stomach, and I explain that I have never been fat like this in my life, I don't know what's wrong with me. He says that sometimes people come to him to just get their love handles or their butts suctioned off, and then the sudden surgical weight loss inspires them to get thin all over, to start exercising and eating sensibly.

"So I don't need to lose weight first?" I ask. "I remember reading somewhere that you need to get as thin as possible before you get this kind of surgery."

"Oh no," he says. "That was years ago. With the new technology, we can suction out much more fat at one time. We just vacuum it all off."

As he says this, I feel myself creeping with horror. This is not the kind of person I am or ever want to be. I want to be the girl who doesn't worry about this stuff. As awful as it feels to be fat, it feels even ickier to be in a plastic surgeon's examination room, with all his lovely Japanese and Chinese assistants to help him communicate with his many Asian clients. Plastic surgery just isn't me. This office on Park Avenue is, well, gnarly. The way the doctor talks to me, as if it is perfectly normal to have flesh vacuumed off your body, as if this is not the extreme thing that it obviously is, makes me feel dirty. And still, I'm ready to try anything.

I go into the surgeon's tidy office after I dress and leave the examination room, and we discuss the options. I explain that I am on all kinds of psychotropic medication, and I am not sure how well that will work with ether. I give him Dr. Singer's phone number, and he says he'll have the anesthesiologist call her. I tell him that if I decide to go through with the liposuction surgery, it will probably be in the next month. He explains that there will be swelling at first, and for several days after the operation, I will be lying in bed with saline and blood leaking out of the scars. As he says this to me, I start to feel nauseated. This is what it's like to be fat. When you're fat, you are willing to soak in your own blood and fluids for several days, because it seems a small price to pay for thinness.

This is not me! This is someone else! I am living in another person's body.

I get up to leave his office, and I walk into the rest room and vomit. Then I cry.

The next day I have an appointment with Dr. Singer after Smithers, and it seems that I ought to discuss this with her. But the decision has already been made for me, because the anesthesiologist has already called her that morning. When she tells me this, I am once again nauseated: I have not even committed to surgery, and already the doctor has gotten in touch with her; he has not even given me a chance to talk to her first. I can't decide if this is professional efficiency or vile overeagerness, but either way, I don't like it.

"I thought he must have been calling from the emergency room," Dr. Singer says, sounding more alarmed that I have ever heard her. "I was afraid you'd had an accident or that you were in some kind of trouble. I interrupted a session to pick up the phone. The answering machine happened to be turned up—it was a mistake—and I got so scared I ran and picked it up."

"I'm sorry," I say. "That was not supposed to happen."

"So what's this about?"

"I'm thinking of having liposuction."

"I see," she says, like she really doesn't.

"I just—I'm so tired of being fat."

"Look, I understand how you feel, but I am sure that this is a big mistake," she says. "Your weight gain, I'm sure, is temporary, and even if it's an office procedure, don't let that make you think that this isn't major surgery with real risks."

"What makes you so sure it's temporary?"

"I'm not *so* sure, but I'm *pretty* sure, and my feeling is that you should at least wait six months and see what happens," she says. "If you still feel fat after that, we can talk about it then."

"*Feel* fat?" I yell. "Did you say *feel*? I don't *feel* anything. I *am* fat. And I hate it. I can't stand it. Six months? I can't go on like this for six months!"

"The thing is," Dr. Singer continues, "as I told the anesthesiologist, you would have to stop taking Lamictal for at least a few weeks before you could go under." Lamictal is a mood stabilizer that Dr. Singer put me on several months ago as a replacement for lithium, and it seems to be working very well. I may be fat, but at least I'm not depressed or moody. "I don't think it's a good idea to risk that right now. You're doing so well, and that's so precarious. I'm willing to bet the fat will go away on its own somehow, but getting you emotionally stable is not a small accomplishment, and I don't know why you would be willing to take a chance on that."

"Because my body is making me depressed."

"No, it's not," she says. "It's making you *unhappy*. That's different from depressed, and you know it."

I sigh. I'm not comfortable with the idea of plastic surgery, and Dr. Singer's lack of support is not helping. Besides, the whole procedure will probably cost ten thousand dollars, all told, which I don't really have to spare, especially since I'm not working. In fact, I am sometimes afraid I may never work again. I suppose I'd rather be unemployed with thin thighs than with fat ones, but that's beside the point.

"All right," I say, as our session is coming to an end. "I'll give it some thought. I won't do anything for a while. You win."

"Trust me," she says. "*You* win."

In the meanwhile, Monica Lewinsky is about to do her televised interview with Barbara Walters, her book is about to be published, and I am suddenly getting requests to appear on various television shows. I am on *Rivera Live!* two weeks in a row, and Kathlyn tapes the shows so that we can watch them later. I sit in her living room to see the shows with her, and I am astonished by how chubby I look on TV. My face is round, my arms sausage out of my short-sleeved shirt. Kathlyn can no longer pretend that this is normal.

"Maybe we should go to a spa for a week," she suggests, after we've watched both episodes. "If you don't have the money, I'll put it on my AmEx, and you can pay me back later." She must truly think that this is a desperate matter.

"Is it really that bad?" I ask.

"Yes," she says. What are best friends for, if not brutal honesty? "When I watched this with Toby when it first aired, we both agreed that you look, um, plump."

All of my friends have their own ideas about what has happened to my body, and they are surprisingly blunt. Lydia suggests that this might just be the price I pay for happiness. She tries to convince me that I look zaftig and hot. I try to convince myself of the same. I'm not buying it.

Then one fine day, I happen to be flipping through Peter Davison's book *The Fading Smile: Poets in Boston 1955–1960, from Robert Frost to Robert Lowell to Sylvia Plath*. I'd read it once, years before, but the opening line of the chapter on Anne Sexton—"I don't recall ever having been with Anne Sexton when she did not require someone to take care of her"—amuses me sufficiently that I peruse the section again. Davison mentions that her antidepressants made her fat and bloated, and that it was heartbreaking to see this beautiful blue-eyed creature, whose dramatic public readings were so enhanced by her breathtaking presence, look flabby and sad. Just as that article about Roman Polanski in *Vanity Fair* first alerted me to the possibility that I might be addicted to Ritalin, this essay about Anne Sexton makes me, rather suddenly, think the problem might be medication. After all, I am taking nortriptyline, a tricyclic antidepressant that would have been available when Sexton was alive—unlike Prozac and the SSRIs, which have only been around since the eighties. Perhaps the problem is the nortryptaline.

I think about it and realize that my weight gain has been coterminous with my new drug regimen. Holy shit! The next day I go to an NA meeting and talk about my insecurities with being overweight, and another woman tells me that when she was on nortryptaline, she felt as if she was retaining water for an entire island.

After that, I tell Dr. Singer that I think that my getting fat is all her fault. Didn't she know that nortryptaline could do this to me? She insists that it's a very rare side effect, but all the same, I switch to Wellbutrin, which is supposed to be helpful for addiction anyway.

Within a month I've lost the entire thirty-five pounds I gained. Within two I've lost another ten pounds. I've not exercised or changed my diet at all. The weight just goes away. Just like that.

Thank God.

Meanwhile, Smithers is testing me, trying me. It is emotional boot camp.

To begin with, I was the only person here with ninety days clean, which means that I get to use my treatment to do the work of staying clean, instead of just getting there in the first place. Sometimes I wish I'd come back here over the summer so I could have used it to "process" my relapses, but the fact that I am using it to get down to the bone instead is an advantage. I am really learning.

At Silver Hill, Dr. Geller did a pretty good job with me, but I obviously was not ready to get sober, or I would not have done cocaine as soon as I checked out. All her observations about my resistance to my own feelings, about the way I get overwrought over nothing because it's better than having real emotional experiences—I never forgot any of it. I never disagreed with her. But I lost it. I just did. You don't use it, you lose it, as a French professor of mine used to say about foreign languages. And, I guess, the language of the human heart is a foreign one for me. But Kiku helps me to acquire it.

I've started to think of her as a magician, because whenever anyone finally admits to a hard truth in group, Kiku does some variation on hypnosis on her. In my case, Kiku's main goal is to get me, as she puts it, "out of the Riviera." That's her word for how I respond to any emotional experience: I check out, my mind heads to the south of France or any place more pleasant than here, and when I return to New York City or wherever I actually am, I just make it all into an amusing story, I denigrate the pain. One morning, as we discuss this, Kiku performs her strange magic.

"How do you feel about everyone in this room?" she asks.

"Believe it or not," I say, without hesitation, "I've really come to love everyone here. I feel lucky to be in treatment with such smart, thoughtful, wise people."

"If that's how you feel, why do you qualify it with 'believe it or not'?" Kiku asks.

"Because it's a verbal tic."

"Stop that!" she yells. "My English is not as good as yours, and you make everything complicated by saying that it's just the way you speak, as if the way you speak is all an accident. You say 'believe it or not' because you don't want to be caught saying that you actually care."

"Look," I say, because I don't think it's quite that simple, "trust me that when I told Hank that I loved him, I did not say 'believe it or not,' so it's not like I'm always unexpressive or stilted."

"Hank," Kiku says, "is an idiot! It's easy to say how you feel when you're wasting your time—the hard part is when it actually matters."

I'm not going to argue with her about whether or not Hank is an idiot, because when all is said and done, that would seem to be the case. And I'm not going to argue with her about the way I hem and haw when I speak, because I'm not sure how much it matters, but I'm willing to buy her overall point.

"So now," Kiku says. "Just sit here. Get out of critical mind, which we all know is good for your writing, and get into feeling mind, which is the only thing that is going to help you get through life. If you had been in feeling mind during that whole time you were involved with Hank, you'd have let yourself feel as bad as you could, and the whole thing would have been so unbearable that you would have gotten rid of him long ago."

"But it *was* unbearable!" I say, because it's true.

"Yes, but your critical mind talked you out of feeling that way. It kept telling you to persist, and that is stupid," Kiku says. "So why don't you close your eyes and sit here for a few minutes in your feeling mind, and you'll see that it's okay."

So I sit there with my eyes closed. Part of me thinks that this is silly, but most of me thinks that this works in its corny, recovery way.

"Okay, now just stay with it," Kiku says after a few minutes. "And remember it. Store it away. And the next time something happens that you know is bad, that you feel is bad, do you think you can access this feeling? Do you think you can access the part of you that knows that something feels wrong and just believe it, trust it?"

"Yes," I say. I mean to say, *I guess* or *I think,* but I know that's not what Kiku wants to hear and, come to think of it, it's not what I want to hear myself say either. *Yes.* Yes, yes, yes. From now on, yes is the answer.

Kiku teaches me a good lesson. She says that if you already know what your response will be before you've heard what the other person has said, you are not listening. And that's me. Evidently that is many addicts, or she would not have said it. It all comes down to this: I am not a participant in life—I am an observer, or else I need attention, in which case I am a performer. Either way, I am removed from what is happening, and I am sad because of that. I don't give people a chance to get attached to me or vice versa, because I am too busy observing or performing. I am lonely, as a result. I only date men if they attract me on impact. That didn't happen with Hank because I had a chance to get to know him by living with him. But most men I will meet on dates, I will get to know them slowly, and I will have to give them time to appeal to me. I can't write them off right away if I don't feel that big huge love immediately. I have to give everyone a chance, or I will never get close to any man, or anybody at all probably, for real.

As I am trying to absorb this information, which really should not be news even if it is, I decide that, far from wanting to get the hell out of Smithers as soon as possible, I now don't want to leave. In fact, I *refuse* to leave. After three months, Kiku thinks I should start phasing out of the program, only coming three times a week, and after that twice a week, and then graduation shortly thereafter. She says that the managed care person at my insurance company has insisted that my visits be cut down. So I tell Kiku to fuck GHI, that I will pay out of pocket. Smithers, which is supported by a foundation, happens to be one of the great recovery bargains: it will only cost me thirty dollars a day to come to sessions, because I am technically unemployed—and frankly, I am really and truly not working, I'm not sure why I am comforting myself with this linguistic distinction—so I am at the bottom of the sliding scale.

"Look," I say to Kiku one day when we meet in her office, "to begin with, you couldn't get me to show up here. Now that I've started to get something out of this, you are not going to get rid of me."

"The thing is, in terms of sobriety you are so far ahead of everyone else here," she explains. "How long has it been?"

"Six months," I say. *Six months? Is that possible?*

"This program is for early sobriety," Kiku says. "Back before managed care, people could be here for a year or two, but now it's meant to be shorter, and at this point you should be moving into an evening group, or something that meets a couple of times a week."

"So you're going to penalize me for not relapsing?" I ask. "Does that make any sense?"

"Not really."

"Well then, I'm not leaving." I smile. "You're stuck with me, you insane Indonesian nightmare. I could not stand you at first. Now I'm staying."

Now she is smiling too. "Okay, we'll work it out."

And so it is that my whole life is devoted to recovery. When I don't go home and pass out, I go to a meeting at Perry Street at 8:30 and then coffee or dinner afterward with other AA people. On Saturday nights I watch boxing or go to the movies with other people from there or from Smithers. This is all there is for me now. For the first time in my life, I am taking something seriously. And for the first time ever, I am good at something besides writing.

One night I walk into Perry Street, and see Oona sitting on the dais. I haven't seen her in nearly three years, since our heroin binge in the fall of 1996. She lives in Washington, D.C., now, at her parents' house, but she has come back to Perry Street to qualify for her two-year anniversary. She had ended up a homeless crack whore before finally going into a long-term residential treatment program outside San Diego in early 1997, after waking up on a bench in Tompkins Square Park and deciding enough was enough. She spent a year there. And seeing her now, both of us clean, it feels like coming home.

After Oona talks, I go up and give her a hug, and we both start to cry. She tells me she has sent me several letters in the last couple of years, and I explain that I've had a backlog of mail dating back to 1995, that I haven't opened any of it. She thought I hated her, that I was avoiding her.

"I would never avoid you," I say. "I've missed you so much."

She is slim and her hair doesn't have obvious dark roots like it used to. She is blond and lovely, her eyes are clear, her skin is translucent—Oona is beautiful. She tells me that she has some great job working for a senator, but she's moving back to New York in a month, to settle in before she goes back to Barnard to finish up.

"You're an advertisement for sobriety," I say as we walk outside for the break. "You look gorgeous. You've turned into the person you were always meant to be. I can't believe it."

"You too," she says.

"I'm so glad you're back," I say.

"You too," she says, and we both stand outside and cry and smile.

I am committed. Dare I say that I am gung ho? I have never been gung ho about anything in my life. What is happening to me?

Everybody is supposed to do some kind of service at Smithers. At one point I take the job of finding speakers to come in for our AA meeting. I get a couple of people I know from Perry Street to tell their stories, and Isabel does it one time, and pretty much blows everyone away because, well, it's amazing how she got from there to here.

After that, I become the treasurer, and my main job is to collect money in the basket for the community fund, which is used to buy presents for people when they graduate, and to get MetroCards for people who cannot afford to take the subway to Smithers. During my tenure, the cash fund increases greatly because I begin every collection by saying, "If you cannot afford to give anything, please don't and don't feel ashamed. But if you can afford to give a dollar, you can afford to give two or three, so please be generous." It seems I have the Jewish knack for fund-raising after all. One week, there is almost a hundred dollars in the till.

My other responsibility is to actually buy the presents for the people who graduate. This is the perfect task for me, since I don't know anyone who likes shopping more than I do. I love doing this, and I love picking out things that are appropriate to the person. I had always hated it that people would get these silly things that they'd never use or want—you know, novelty items purchased at the last minute, or paperweights with a piece of green felt slapped on the bottom. But it's easier to buy nice things under my aegis, because the treasury fund is so much richer. One girl is studying design at the School of Visual Arts, and she wants to work in the music business, so I get her the *Rolling Stone* collection of the best album covers ever. One of the guys who is always losing his gloves gets a very nice pair from Banana Republic, along with a caveat from me that if he loses them, I will kill him. A tennis player gets a sterling silver key ring with a racquet charm from Tiffany. One of the guys who never knows what time it is gets a Swiss Army watch. A couple of people get *Traveling Mercies* by Anne Lamott, a collection of essays about recovery and faith. Some of the girls get earrings from artsy ethnic shops on Bleecker Street. I get some old collectors' Spiderman comic books for a guy who is obsessed with superheroes. The gifts are supposed to be fairly frugal and unfussy, but I figure, fuck it. I know it's the thought that counts, but some thoughts are better than others.

I get lots of people to come to meetings with me at Perry Street. Sometimes we go to another meeting called Fireside, at the YMCA on Sixty-third Street and Central Park West, which is a lunchtime meeting right near Smithers. But mostly I can't stand it. We are right near the ABC studios, and Fireside is loaded with very annoying soap opera actors—although there are also a couple of aging punk rockers who got clean and moved from the Lower East Side to the Upper West Side to escape the insanity.

When the heat gets turned off in her building in Williamsburg, I have Nicole stay at my house with me for a few days, which means I have to share my bed with her, which I absolutely hate, but it seems like the right thing to do. I accompany Veronica to meet an agent at Innovative Artists and to dinner with her family. She's like my kid sister. There is a woman at Smithers who is a computer programmer at the Federal Reserve, and one day I go to work with her and she shows me the gold bullion that is kept on display in the building to guarantee the U.S. Mint. I go with a couple of the older ladies, a Columbia professor and a single mother who lives in New Jersey, to see a French movie called *The Dinner Party* at the Paris Theatre. Luke and I sit through almost an entire Truffaut festival at the Film Forum. I go to Nicole's art opening. I go to Veronica's play. I go to Susannah's performance art thing at a miserable little theater in the East Village. This is the kind of thing you could never have paid me to do. I almost never see my own friends.

Once the weather warms up, in April, I organize outings to Central Park after program. We buy sandwiches at a place called Hadleigh's, and Luke, who is pretty useless about most things, always remembers to bring a blanket. We all lie in the sun and chat for a few hours.

And then *The New York Times* calls to ask me to write an op-ed piece. A kid died at MIT as a result of alcohol poisoning during a fraternity hazing incident, and several universities are planning to invoke their rights in loco parentis to protect students from harming themselves with drugs and drinking. So one of the editors asks if I'd write a little essay about it. A couple of days after my op-ed runs, Howell Raines, who oversees the editorial page, writes me a note complimenting me on my work. Perhaps more strangely, I get a letter from Helen Gurley Brown saying she really enjoyed it. Apparently, I can still write after all. I'd thought there was nothing left of me or my career, but it turns out that it might just be okay. I'm in no condition to take on any big projects, but maybe I can do a few small things here and there, get started on working again, figure out what's next. I start to think that, maybe, God is doing for me what I cannot do for myself.

That transformation that I have been waiting for all my life, that moment when I would be me, really me, true to myself and feel all right—it has finally arrived. For the first time ever, when people ask me how I am, I say that I am happy.

Happy.

Finally, at the end of July, a little more than a week before my thirty-second birthday, it is time for me to leave Smithers.

MORE, NOW (AGAIN)

But I was so much older then
I'm younger than that now

BOB DYLAN
"My Back Pages"

Here's how the story begins.

I was born on July 31, 1967, in New York City. The number one song in America was "Light My Fire," and the number one song in England was "All You Need Is Love." That is how I know that on that day the world was good. For a long time I thought I was born under a bad sign, that I was born cursed, but that's just wrong. I came out of my mother's womb smiling, and the only thing wrong with me was that my tear ducts didn't work quite right; they needed stimulus; I needed drops in my eyes to make me cry. I was born without tears. And I was a happy baby after that, I didn't cry a lot and did not need a lot of attention. I was contented in my crib. My parents needed me more than I needed them.

There is a picture of me from when I was four years old, sitting on the floor in my mother's office, in a little red-checkered dress, giggling like crazy. I look at that photograph now, I have it propped up on my bookshelf, to remind me that I was joyous as a little kid, and I chased squirrels in Central Park and fed them peanuts and acorns in shells, and I played with Lincoln Logs and LEGO. There was not a single thing wrong with me. I was born with everything I needed.

And then something went terribly wrong. When I was eleven or twelve, all that joy just went away. I don't know where it went, and I don't know why. I could sit here and blame it on bad parents, on divorce, on my father's drugs, on growing up in a crazy time. I could say it was a bad thing to be a child in New York City during the Beame administration, when the municipality nearly went bankrupt, when the country was in the midst of the Vietnam War, when we invaded Cambodia, when all day long all that was on the news were the Watergate hearings and bad things. I could say that my chemistry got twisted, that depression took over my body and soul like a sickening plague of the cells, like the terrible disease it is. I could tell you that I cut up my legs and arms with a razor blade and a knife on my key ring for hours every day, and for several years, because the pain was a relief from pain, other kinds of pain. I could try to give you so many reasons why, but none of them matter, and even worse, none of them is true. I look back now, and I know there are no reasons. It's just that somewhere along the way, I lost that huge capacity for joy. I just let it go. I stopped caring. I did not even know I had it in me.

In the end, in some way it was up to me. I turned off the switch. I forgot, or did not even want to know, how to find all that joy.

For most of my life I just thought I was bad, that it did not matter how many bad things I did to myself and, in turn, to everyone around me: If it's all bad, nothing can make it worse. But then I found out when I took away everything that was awful, when I pushed all the dark away, I was just good. Underneath I was good.

I would be lying if I told you that I wish I had not just stayed that little girl, that I did not wish I had never lost all the joy I had. But still, this is the way it is, this is what happened to me, and all I have left inside is gratitude. All I can ever feel anymore, even when I'm in my worst moods and on days when everything goes wrong, is gratitude. And some days, especially in the summer, are so phosphorescent and buoyant. The sky opens, the people are glowing, the sidewalk is gold flecked, and it is impossible to hate life or anything about it. And I remember I was born in a good time, and I was in love with the whole wide world, everything was possible, I was propped upon my future arms.

In the book of Exodus, in a tract known as the Prayer of Mercy, we are promised that "God visits the sins of the fathers upon the sons, and the third generation, and the fourth generation." I have no idea why this is given as evidence of God's benevolence. All I know is that my great-grandfather was a drunk, my grandfather was a drunk, my father is a drug addict, and I am the fourth generation of sinners.

Enough is enough of this sad family, with all its grief and depression and sorrow that get passed on and on, this miserable birthright, this ugly heirloom. The legacy stops here with me. Anything that happened before is gone. This is my world. This is my home.

Here's how the story begins:

Acknowledgments

The acknowledgments for my previous books were so elaborate—in the case of the first one, they were actually reprinted in the Book-of-the-Month Club calendar—that I now feel like I am competing with myself to come up with increasingly grand words of praise. Instead, I am going to try to keep it simple and hope I've made it plain, in person and in private, to all concerned how much I love and appreciate them in all their forbearance and wisdom. Well, I'll try.

Betsy Lerner, first my editor and now my agent, thought this was a good idea for a book when I was still stuck in the catacombs of Silver Hill Hospital. While she never actually said, *Take notes*, Betsy has always recognized a book in progress before it's even started, and she was once again correct. Thank you, as ever, for everything—editorial advice, all the patience it took to figure out how to make a bunch of crazy experiences into a presentable book, and then an astute sense of who ought to publish it, which house would be, well, *safe*. Betsy is one of the great editors, and she is now one of the great agents. She is also as dear to me as family. My cup runneth over.

How lucky I was when Marysue Rucci became my editor. She is astonishingly, acutely smart, and turned a bloated mess of text into a sleeker, smoother model. Every time I have read through the manuscript I am stunned by how much of Marysue is in there, and what a difference all her notes and suggestions and guidance and ideas have made; Marysue is part of every word. I cannot imagine that any editor has been this central and crucial to a book. And I am eternally in debt for every time my obsessions and confusions made this process more complicated than it needed to be. Thank you, and once again, the extent of my gratitude goes beyond anything I can say here.

David Rosenthal took a chance on me when, by my own admission, I was a mess and not necessarily the best gamble. But David just seems like one of those people who says it will happen, and it just kind of does. *God said, let there be light, and . . .* All right, maybe David is not quite *that* creative, but as soon as he told me that I just had to write my book and they'd take care of everything else, I knew I was in the right place. David's faith in me has been infectious.

Erin Hosier is the secret weapon at the Gernert Company. I bless the day that I found her in the *Ms.* magazine intern pool. Thank you for being a great first reader, a great friend, and just plain old great. And thank you for keeping me up on what the kids are up to. I think the good people of the state of Ohio broke the mold after you were born; if not, the world needs more than one of you. All I can ask is that you remember my name once you have conquered the world. Tara Parsons—my heart goes out to you. I think you got the brunt of the brunt of this project, and I am so grateful that you somehow made it seem like everyone else there did not want to kill me; that is a talent. At any rate, we have had a few fun moments with some Marlboro Lights, and I can only hope that somehow made messenger messes, unreadable text, overdue pages, and everything else worth it.

I guess this plan for streamlined acknowledgments is not working out.

Thank you always, with love and sorrow, to Lydia Wills, for so much and for so long.

The poor beleaguered people in the Simon & Schuster production depart- ment should know I appreciate all they put up with, and I am awestruck by the way they somehow pulled this off. You all deserved better than me. Thank you most especially to Martha Schwartz. Frank Veronsky made me look just like me but better in the jacket photo, and Jackie Seow came up with elegant, un- expected renderings for the cover. Thank you to Aileen Boyle, Rachel Nagler and, of course, Victoria Meyer for a publicity campaign that seems to have started even before Simon & Schuster signed up this book.

Thank you to Galt Niederhoffer, Paul Miller, Erik Skjoldbjaerg and all in- volved in the production of *Prozac Nation*, the movie. And thank you to Christina Ricci for getting it perfect.

Well, Mom, what can I say? After all these years, we still seem to be in the thick of it. So thank you for always opening your home to me, even when you wanted to kill me, and thank you for always tolerating what you could not un- derstand. You're the best. I must also thank all the members of the Fort Lau- derdale Habad. And thanks to Sam and Toby Hecht, and all at the Chai Society of Yale University, for giving me space to work and welcoming me into your community.

Thank you to Aunt Zena, Uncle Bill, Lewis, Wandy, Meredith and Saman-

About the author

ELIZABETH WURTZEL is the author of the best-selling books *Prozac Nation* and *Bitch*. She graduated from Harvard College, where she received the 1986 Rolling Stone College Journalism Award for essay writing. She was the popular-music critic for *The New Yorker* and *New York* magazine. Her articles have appeared in numerous magazines. She lives in New York City.

tha Druss—my Florida relatives. Elian Gonzalez should have been so lucky. Thank you Laura Breuer, my Florida pal and friend forever.

It is ridiculous to thank Jim Crimmins and ridiculous not to, so there you go. I've met some people who are very dear to me along the way: Brenda Abbandandolo, Kelly Cole, Brian Mertes, Cynthia Wang, Daniel McIver, Brandon Marto, Maryanne Sculley, and Casey Cook—I wish you all long life. Thank you, Zoë Glassman, for all we've been through together and then some. Thank you, Chris, for so many reasons. Thank you, Stephen Jenkins, for visiting me at Silver Hill. Thank you, Mary T. Browne for solid, sensible counsel; and thank you, Sheila Browne for reading me the riot act when someone really needed to.

Thank you, Doctor Paula Eagle for therapy and treatment through the years. And thank you to Doctor Ellyn Shander and all the staff at Silver Hill Hospital, which did me more good than I ever knew at the time. Thank you to Susie Vicencio and all the extraordinary counselors at Smithers.

And, of course, thank you to all the people in Alcoholics Anonymous and Narcotics Anonymous who, over the last several years, have shared their experience, strength, and hope with me. Everything else helps, but nothing else works.

Most important, I have been blessed with many friends who never gave up on me, never ever. Some were closer to the mess than others, some were more involved than others, but they were all there, the big miracle. Whenever anyone asks how I have managed to stay clean, the first thing I say—before I mention meetings or hospitals—is my great good fortune in having such a solid, loyal group of friends who made me feel like my life was worth more than all this. This book was written for them, with all my love. Each of these people has had my unique gratitude expressed to them privately and specifically. For the purpose of acknowledgment, I must name each of them in alphabetical— not preferential—order: Jason Bagdade, Kera Bolonik, Roberta Feldman Brzezinski, Tom Campbell, Heather Chase, Christine Fasano, Jody Friedman, Elizabeth Ackerman Kaiden, Mark McGurl, Sharon Meers, Peter Robles, and David Samuels. David Lipsky shared his home and his love—or something like that—with me while I wrote this book. Thank you for this extraordinary kindness.

And thank you to everyone else, especially some people—you know who you are.